Epistemology, Context, and Formalism

SYNTHESE LIBRARY

STUDIES IN EPISTEMOLOGY, LOGIC, METHODOLOGY, AND PHILOSOPHY OF SCIENCE

VOLUME 369

For further volumes:
http://www.springer.com/series/6607

Franck Lihoreau • Manuel Rebuschi
Editors

Epistemology, Context, and Formalism

Springer

Editors
Franck Lihoreau
Institute for the Philosophy of Language
New University of Lisbon
Lisbon, Portugal

Manuel Rebuschi
Henri Poincaré Archives
University of Lorraine
Nancy, France

ISBN 978-3-319-02942-9 ISBN 978-3-319-02943-6 (eBook)
DOI 10.1007/978-3-319-02943-6
Springer Cham Heidelberg New York Dordrecht London

Library of Congress Control Number: 2013957714

Printed on acid-free paper

Springer is part of Springer Science+Business Media (www.springer.com)

In memory of Paul Gochet.

Contents

Contributors

Maria Aloni ILLC/Department of Philosophy, University of Amsterdam, Amsterdam, The Netherlands

Peter Baumann Department of Philosophy, Swarthmore College, Swarthmore, PA, USA

Yves Bouchard Department of Philosophy and Applied Ethics, University of Sherbrooke, Sherbrooke, QC, Canada

Jan Broersen Department of Information and Computing Sciences, Utrecht University, Utrecht, The Netherlands

Paul Égré Institut Jean-Nicod (CNRS, ENS, EHESS), École Normale Supérieure, Département d'Études Cognitives, Paris, France

Sven Ove Hansson Division of Philosophy, Royal Institute of Technology (KTH), Stockholm, Sweden

Andreas Herzig University of Toulouse, IRIT-CNRS, Toulouse, France
Université Paul Sabatier, IRIT-LILaC, Toulouse Cedex 9, France

Jaakko Hintikka Department of Philosophy, Boston University, Boston, MA, USA

Bruno Jacinto Arché – Philosophical Research Centre for Logic, Language, Metaphysics and Epistemology, The University of St Andrews, St Andrews, Scotland, UK

Franck Lihoreau Faculdade de Ciências Sociais e Humanas, Instituto de Filosofia da Linguagem, Universidade Nova de Lisboa, Lisboa, Portugal

Emiliano Lorini University of Toulouse, IRIT-CNRS, Toulouse, France
Université Paul Sabatier, IRIT-LILaC, Toulouse Cedex 9, France

John-Jules Charles Meyer Department of Information and Computing Sciences, Utrecht University, Utrecht, The Netherlands

Martin Montminy Department of Philosophy, University of Oklahoma, Norman, OK, USA

Erich Rast Faculdade de Ciências Sociais e Humanas, Instituto de Filosofia da Linguagem, Universidade Nova de Lisboa, Lisboa, Portugal

Manuel Rebuschi LHSP – Archives H. Poincaré (UMR 7117)/MSH Lorraine (USR 3261), Université de Lorraine, Nancy, France

Richmond H. Thomason Department of Philosophy, University of Michigan, Ann Arbor, MI, USA

Robert van Rooij Institute for Logic, Language and Computation (ILLC), University of Amsterdam, Amsterdam, The Netherlands

Gregory Wheeler CENTRIA, Universidade Nova de Lisboa, Lisbon, Portugal
Department of Philosophy, Carnegie Mellon University, Pittsburgh, PA, USA

Chapter 1
Introduction

Franck Lihoreau and Manuel Rebuschi

The modeling of knowledge and the modeling of context proceed, historically speaking, from two relatively independent enterprises. In an effort to bridge the gap between the two, the 13 essays collected in this book are all concerned with the notions of knowledge and context, the connections between them, and the ways in which they can be modeled, and in particular formalized. The question is of prime importance to such diverse disciplines as philosophy, linguistics, computer science and artificial intelligence, and cognitive science. The purpose of the book is to advance our understanding on that question by focusing on some of the most pressing issues that it raises in and across those disciplines:

- **Context and Epistemology.** In the last decades, mainstream epistemology has seen a major "linguistic turn", through the increased reliance on syntactic, semantic and pragmatic "evidence" about ordinary uses of linguistic constructions in terms of "know". An ever-increasing emphasis is put on the possibly crucial epistemological role of various notions of context (of inquiry, of utterance, of assessment, etc.) in knowledge and talk about knowledge, most notably as a result of the florishing discussions between "invariantists", "contextualists", "relativists", etc., of all sorts. But despite a (very small) number of attempts, the formal modeling of these positions, notions and distinctions has not yet been pursued.
- **Epistemology and Formalism.** In addition to its "linguistic turn", epistemology has also seen a very sensible "logical turn". This is witnessed by the

F. Lihoreau (✉)
Faculdade de Ciências Sociais e Humanas, Instituto de Filosofia da Linguagem, Universidade Nova de Lisboa, Av. de Berna, 26-4° piso, 1069-061 Lisboa, Portugal
e-mail: franck.lihoreau@fcsh.unl.pt

M. Rebuschi
LHSP – Archives Henri Poincaré (UMR 7117)/MSH Lorraine (USR 3261), Université de Lorraine, 91, avenue de la Libération, BP 454, 54001 Nancy, France
e-mail: manuel.rebuschi@univ-lorraine.fr

F. Lihoreau and M. Rebuschi (eds.), *Epistemology, Context, and Formalism*, Synthese Library 369, DOI 10.1007/978-3-319-02943-6_1,

recently revived and rising conviction, forcefully promoted by Hendricks and van Benthem among others, that traditional epistemological discussions (about skepticism and the definitions of various epistemic notions) may benefit from the use of the formal methods of epistemic modal logic, Formal Learning Theory, Belief Revision, and so on. However, one might feel that to this day formal epistemology has remained relatively little explicit about context and how exactly it enters the epistemic world. But there are exceptions, and the situation has recently been evolving.
- **Formalism and Context.** Well-known formal approaches to context can be found in natural language semantics – most notably in the treatment of indexicality – and in formal pragmatics – e.g. in the treatment of presupposition and implicature, or illocutionary logic. "Logics of context" can also be found in theoretical computer science, like those proposed by McCarthy and Buvač, or by Giunchiglia and Serafini. In both fields, however, the main formal approaches owe nothing to epistemology. Although here too the number of exceptions has recently been growing, one might have the impression that no general attempts have yet been made to pull together the formal modeling of context and the formal treatment of knowledge.

Bringing together original articles written by world-leading experts and emerging researchers in epistemology, logic, philosophy of language, linguistics, and theoretical computer science, the book presents a sample of the best research work currently carried out at those intersections.

In the opening chapter of this volume, Chap. 2, **Erich Rast** is concerned with issues that the notion of context raises in what might be thought to be its most natural setting, viz. the analysis of natural language meaning and the multifaceted problem of the semantics-pragmatics interface. After giving a valuable overview of the role of the notion of context in philosophical linguistics and beyond, Rast goes on to spell out a number of linguistic distinctions and adequacy requirements against which candidate models for a certain class of context-dependent expressions, "contextuals" like "ready", "tall", etc., are to be evaluated. With these criteria in mind the author sketches a proposal on how to represent those expressions in a formal truth-conditional setting. Rast addresses *en passant* several points of interest to the linguist as well as to the philosopher, like the relationships between context-dependence, contextuality, and indexicality, or the idea that "know" might be an indexical, an expression with contextually constant character but contextually variable content.

This latter idea is commonly associated with *epistemic contextualism*, a view famously championed by Stewart Cohen, Keith DeRose, and David Lewis. Contextualism stems from the necessity to account for an observation already made by Wittgenstein and Austin about our linguistic practice of attributing and denying knowledge to ourselves and to other people, viz. the observation that a knowledge claim may be perfectly acceptable as made in one context but totally inacceptable as made in another context. The most straightforward explanation for this contextually variable acceptability of knowledge claims is semantic: it is the *truth value* of such claims that varies with the context in which they are made. What the contextualist adds is that this is so because the *truth-conditions* of those claims vary from one such context to another. The next three essays – by Baumann, Montminy, and Bouchard – are all concerned with defending some form or other of contextualism about knowledge(*-that*) ascriptions.

Some have objected to contextualism that it is incompatible with the fact that ordinary speakers often take themselves to disagree with other users of "know" located in contexts where different epistemic standards are in place. On the same grounds it has also been argued that we had better opt for *epistemic relativism*, the view that knowledge ascriptions depend for their truth not on the context in which they are made by a speaker, but on the context in which they are assessed for truth or falsity by a judge. In his essay, Chap. 3, **Martin Montminy** sets out to defend contextualism against this objection "from disagreement". He defends that ordinary speakers often make the mistake of thinking that they are disagreeing with speakers in contexts with different epistemic standards. Based on a careful analysis of this mistake and how it can be overcome, Montminy insists that when figuring out whether there is disagreement between speakers, the "perspectives" by which they stand towards a proposition play a crucial role which no version of relativism can accurately render. Montminy concludes that when it comes to accounting for the intuition of disagreement, relativism does not fare any better than contextualism after all.

In Chap. 4, **Peter Baumann** focuses on another important objection to contextualism due to Crispin Wright, the "Factivity Objection". The objection consists in deriving a contradiction from the truth of contextualism, the principle of factivity – i.e. that knowledge requires truth – and the principle of epistemic closure – i.e. that knowledge is closed under known entailment. Baumann acknowledges that this objection is a serious threat to contextualism in its most common form, the view that "know" behaves like an indexical. But he insists that the threat can be removed provided that we opt for an alternative, *relationalist* form of contextualism on which "know" denotes a ternary relation between a subject, a proposition, and an epistemic standard. The subsequent, unorthodox reformulation of epistemic closure makes it possible to account for cross-context knowledge attributions and enables us to explain away the factivity objection as equivocating on subtle contextual differences.

In his contribution, Chap. 5, **Yves Bouchard** too considers that the context-sensitivity of "know" is best understood in terms of a ternary relation between a subject, a proposition and an epistemic standard. His account is based on a "logic of context" originally developed by McCarthy and Buvač in Artificial Intelligence to represent ordinary knowledge and how it enters inferential processes operating on knowledge bases. Bouchard proposes to associate with each epistemic context c_ε a unique epistemic standard ε, identified with a subset of the axioms in the knowledge base associated with c_ε. These axioms specify the introduction rule for the knowledge operator in c_ε, and further axioms specify a number of "transposition rules" governing the relations of the standard of the context to other epistemic contexts. This, Bouchard contends, allows a precise formal modelling of how "know" contributes context-sensitivity by having part of its content fixed by epistemic standards. It also provides a viable explanation of how exactly the alleged shifts in epistemic standards are regulated in a way that does not make epistemic standards shift with any fluctuation of conversational contexts whatsoever. Finally, Bouchard's proposal yields interesting solutions to well-known skeptical puzzles.

The next three chapters – by Aloni and Jacinto, by van Rooij, and by Hansson – are still concerned with contextualism, but focus on largely neglected, albeit highly important aspects, dimensions, and forms of the context-dependency of knowledge claims.

In Chap. 6, **Maria Aloni** and **Bruno Jacinto** shift attention from the context-sensitivity of "knowing-that" ascriptions to that of "knowing-*wh*" ascriptions – sentence-like constructions in terms of "know which" and "know who" to be precise. They insist on a particular form of context-sensitivity that the latter exhibit and that cannot be traced back to the context-sensitivity of "know" but to the *perspective sensitivity* of the embedded wh-questions. Wh-clauses are indeed interpreted relative to a *conceptual perspective*, that is, to one of the different ways to look at the domain of objects under consideration or "conceptual covers". Building on previous work by Aloni, they formalize this idea by means of a language of first-order predicate logic enriched with a question operator. The language is akin to the one used in Groenendijk and Stokhof's semantics of questions but augmented so as to make it possible to talk about conceptual covers and to capture the perspective-sensitive nature of questions. Aloni and Jacinto then engage in a tight discussion of which of contextualism, relativism, and two forms of invariantism can best account for that sensitivity. They are eventually led to endorse what they call an "explicit contextualist existential closure" view on the matter.

The context-sensitivity of knowledge-wh ascriptions is also thoroughly acknowledged by **Robert van Rooij** in his Chap. 7. He argues that just like the interpretation of standard answers to questions, whose conventional meaning is underspecified and whose exact meaning is determined by a contextually relevant decision problem, the context-dependence of knowledge constructions with embedded questions involves decision problems as well as conversational relevance. Van Rooij implements this idea in the formal game-theoretic framework of Optimal Assertions, originally developed in joint work with Benz to capture the notion of an optimal answer and here extended to the interpretation of embedded questions. He makes a further step and indicates how the framework of optimal assertions can be used to understand the context-dependence of knowledge-that ascriptions, and examines how the resulting analysis relates to standard contextualist accounts like David Lewis's. The paper thereby offers a good example of how formalism can help handling together knowledge-related problems and context-related issues in a philosophically rigorous manner.

In his essay Chap. 8, **Sven Ove Hansson** too examines knowledge claims in contexts of decision problems, but this time the relevant kind of knowledge is scientific knowledge. Hansson first discusses two models of science, one on which science aims exclusively at knowledge for its own sake, the other on which science is primarily a system of pure knowledge which gets secondarily adjusted when exposed to contexts of practical applications with evidential requirements possibly differing from those of knowledge *per se*. Hansson argues for an alternative model according to which scientific knowledge continuously develops from the start under the combined, sometimes conflicting requirements of knowledge *per se* and knowledge *ad applicandum*. He draws the picture of a dynamic process alternating "epistemic" and "decisional" adjustments, in such a way that the influence of demands of practical applications on the acceptability of knowledge claims in science is never to the detriment of the reliability of scientific knowledge. Hansson also gives an indication of how the model he proposes can be formalized.

An aspect of knowledge strongly emphasized by Hansson and by van Rooij in their essays is that it is intimately related to action and choice. This tight connection is also the starting point of **Jan Broersen** and **John-Jules Meyer**'s contribution, "A STIT Logical Study into Choice, Failure and Free Will Action". The authors propose to formally investigate and develop a number of conceptual distinctions to do with the philosophical issue of freedom and cognate notions, like free will, free choice, and free action. They do so through means of a STIT-logical framework with epistemic operators, whose purpose is to logically represent action failure as having a mistaken belief about the choice one makes. This has interesting consequences for the definition of free will choice and Broersen and Meyer explore how they can be brought to bear on such questions as determinism, compatibilism, and moral responsibility.

What picture of belief can most appropriately capture its "practical dimension", its crucial links to action and intention in practical deliberative reasoning, is also the main purpose of **Richmond H. Thomason's** essay, Chap. 10. Thomason considers the Belief-Desire-Intention (BDI) framework a fruitful theoretical framework to engage deliberation about what goals to pursue, how to pursue them, and the relation of goals and plans to what to do on a given occasion. He describes and defends a *modular* approach to *practical belief*, which understands belief not as a single modality or belief attitude, but as an open-ended family of loosely related modalities or belief-like attitudes emerging from the need to act on particular practical occasions. *Ad hoc* attitudes of this sort that are appropriate for one particular occasion need not be consistent with other such attitudes appropriate for another, and the resulting conception of belief and related attitudes is more flexible and realistic for agents with human-like cognitive abilities and limitations. Doxastic attitudes come with contextual sensitivities of various kinds, including for instance sensitivity to time and social pressure, but also *stake-sensitivity*, the tendency of a belief to appear or disappear in response to such pragmatic factors as the sense of risk and the significance of what is at stake.

Although he acknowledges that belief depends on the subject's practical interests, **Gregory Wheeler** places a caveat on stake-relative views of belief in his essay Chap. 11, where he addresses the connections between qualitative and quantitative belief. While one might propose equating qualitative or "full belief" with "high level of confidence", this "Lockean" proposal has been criticized by orthodox probabilists like Jeffrey because it licenses ruling out perfectly good information. In the course of defending Lockeanism against this objection, Scott Sturgeon has advanced a normative principle to the effect that the character of a belief should match the character of the evidence on which it is based. This principle of *character matching* is the target of Wheeler's essay, who sets out to turn it inside out by means of a counterexample. Interpreted in the light of a risk-reward theory of full belief inspired by Kyburg, the counterexample shows that although full belief depends on a subject's practical context, it does not depend on the total magnitude of the stake put at risk.

Belief is the topic of **Andreas Herzig** and **Emiliano Lorini**'s Chap. 12 too, but approached from the angle of its logical relationships with perception. They describe a number of variants of a "logic of perceptual belief" whose semantics is not based on possible worlds models, but on models consisting simply in valuations of atomic formulas having consistent data, where a datum is a special construction describing what an agent has perceived to be true (or false) and corresponding to Fred Dretske's "perceptual recognition" or "meaningful perception". The resulting framework makes it possible to represent and reason about the connections between an agent beliefs and the information she obtains by his senses. In the basic version of the logic, perception is construed as a private action: one's meaningful perception that ϕ directly determines one's belief that ϕ, even though one does not thereby learn that one perceives that ϕ. Herzig and Lorini consider extending the base logic by adding introspection principles, by turning from perceptual belief to perceptual knowledge, and by adding events in the style of dynamic epistemic logic.

Paul Egré's paper Chap. 13 also deals with an important logico-doxastic issue, namely the phenomenon of hyperintensionality of belief reports in natural language, and proposes to account for it in terms of context-dependence. His proposal, elaborating on the analysis of hyperintensionality by Cresswell and von Stechow, rests on the idea that belief sentences can be given a generalized *de re* logical form, even in situations where opacity would standardly be treated *de dicto* as in Hintikka's modal framework: a subject's opaque belief can be analyzed as a *de re* belief about the same thing but under different contextually determined counterpart relations. To capture this idea, Egré extends Gerbrandy's counterpart semantics for first-order epistemic logic to a second-order epistemic logic which enables handling cases of hyperintensionality involving expressions of distinct syntactic categories (coreferential proper names, cointensional predicates, and logically equivalent sentences), thereby allowing for a uniform treatment of these cases on a par with other classical cases of opacity. The merits and limits of his proposal are discussed in respect of issues like pragmatic enrichment, iterated belief reports, logical consequence, conjunction and identity.

In the closing chapter of the volume, Chap. 14, the founder of contemporary epistemic logic half a century ago, **Jaakko Hintikka**, takes up the ongoing epistemological debate over the proper analysis of knowledge. Hintikka proposes to depart from the definition, famously inherited from Plato, of knowledge as justified true belief. First disconnecting knowledge from belief in favor of the more flexible notion of "information", Hintikka adds a non-standard justification clause whose effect is that knowledge of propositions is no longer to be thought of as knowledge that these propositions can be verified, but *how* they can be verified, that is to say, knowledge of corresponding Skolem functions whose very existence attests to the truth of those propositions. Elaborating on this idea, Hintikka shows how it finds a natural setting in the frameworks of game-theoretical semantics and independence-friendly logic, and points to subtle relationships of utmost philosophical significance between knowledge, justifiability, and truth. In this respect, Hintikka's contribution serves as the best illustration of a Wittgensteinian dictum that he himself pertinently reminds us of, that "one can distill a great deal of epistemology into a drop of logic".

Acknowledgements Five out of the 13 contributions to this volume originate from papers which were presented at the international workshop on "Epistemology, Context, Formalism" held at the MSH-Lorraine in Nancy, France, on November the 12th–14th, 2009. The workshop was organized under the auspices of the LHSP – Archives H. Poincaré (UMR 7117 CNRS), the Université Nancy 2, and the *Dialogue, Rationality, Formalism* Project (MSH-Lorraine, USR 3261). The rest of the authors were contacted after the workshop had taken place. They all accepted straight away to contribute a paper to our volume, and we thank them a lot for that, as well as for their great competence and patience.

We are grateful to the editors-in-chief of the *Synthese Library* series, Vincent F. Hendricks and John Symons, for their interest in publishing this book, and to the anonymous reviewer for his/her useful comments. Sandrine Avril has been a precious and reliable ally and we would like to thank her warmly for her invaluable help and efficiency in the technical work on the chapters.

Franck Lihoreau's work on the book project was carried out at the Instituto de Filosofia da Linguagem, Universidade Nova de Lisboa, in part within the "Context and Communication" project (PTDC/FIL/68643/2006), and in part within the "Argumentation, Context, and Communication" project (PTDC/FIL-FIL 110117/2009), both supported by the Portuguese Foundation for Science and Technology. Manuel Rebuschi's work on the project was carried out at the LHSP – Archives H. Poincaré, within the DiaRaFor project of the MSH-Lorraine (2008–2011).

Chapter 2
Context as Assumptions

Erich Rast

2.1 Introduction

In this article some phenomena of linguistic context-dependence are investigated from the perspective of regarding context as being constituted by the assumptions of individual discourse participants. In Sect. 2.2, a general overview of linguistic context-dependence is given and a distinction between indexicals and contextuals is introduced. After this exposition some adequacy criteria, or at least reasonable rules of thumb, for modeling the linguistic context-dependence of typical contextuals in a truth-conditional setting are laid out (Sect. 2.3). Finally, in Sect. 2.4 the modeling of contextuals will be addressed in some more detail. Simple type theory is used for giving examples. The central idea of that section is that interpretation is based on broadly-conceived abductive reasoning, an idea first investigated by Hobbs et al. (1993).

The distinction between indexicals and contextuals made in this paper has evolved from a recent philosophical debate about the nature of semantic content and the amount as to which pragmatic factors play a role in its computation. The main positions in this debate are currently semantic minimalism, see Cappelen and Lepore (2004, 2006) and Borg (2004, 2010, 2012b) and in a special form by Bach (2005, 2006, 2007a,c), moderate contextualism defended by indexicalists such as Stanley and Szabó (2000) and Stanley (2000, 2002), radical contextualism defended by Récanati (2004) and in another form by relevance theorists such as Sperber and Wilson (1986, 2006), occasionalism of Travis (2008), and assessment-relativism like in MacFarlane (2005b, 2007a,b, 2008, 2009) and Lasersohn (2005, 2008). However, it is not the purpose of this article to lay out all of these positions in

E. Rast (✉)
Faculdade de Ciências Sociais e Humanas, Instituto de Filosofia da Linguagem,
Universidade Nova de Lisboa, Av. de Berna, 26-4° piso, 1069-061 Lisboa, Portugal
e-mail: erich@snafu.de

F. Lihoreau and M. Rebuschi (eds.), *Epistemology, Context, and Formalism*,
Synthese Library 369, DOI 10.1007/978-3-319-02943-6_2,

detail.[1] Instead, we assume in what follows a moderate contextualist position as in Rast (2009). Many of the theses about context that will be defended below are neutral with respect to or compatible with other broadly-conceived contextualist positions, but they are more or less incompatible with occasionalism and Cappelen and Lepore's version of minimalism. These positions will be criticized indirectly, but presenting detailed arguments against them is beyond the scope of this paper and has been done elsewhere.[2]

2.2 Forms of Linguistic Context-Dependence

2.2.1 Context: A Brief Overview

Contexts are theory-dependent entities similar to propositions or electrons, and for this reason there is no such thing as *the* context. What a context is depends on the purpose and the intricacies of a specific theory of context. In the linguistic domain, broadly-conceived two traditions have evolved. First, based on work by Frege (1986), Reichenbach (1947), Russell (1966), and Bar-Hillel (1954) a view on linguistic contexts has become popular according to which contexts either represent these features of an utterance situation that are needed in order to determine the semantic value of indexical expressions or particular linguistic signs (tokens) of indexicals are represented explicitly. Originally having been motivated by the foundational question whether indexical context-dependence is in principle reducible or not, this tradition has shifted to a more descriptive perspective and in a sense culminated in the work of Kaplan (1988), whose type-based two-dimensional semantic approach has been very influential. In these accounts based on double-index modal logics the meaning of indexicals is represented by a function from context parameters to intensions ('semantic content') that are in turn functions from indices to extensions (see Fig. 2.1). The idea of parameterizing context-dependences is also exploited by relativists like MacFarlane and Lasersohn mentioned above, where in contrast to the classical contextualist position in their view certain contextual variations have to be located in the modal index instead of the context

Linguistic Meaning	+ Context	$\Rightarrow$	Content
Content	+ Index	$\Rightarrow$	Extension

Fig. 2.1 Two-dimensional semantics following Kaplan (1988)

[1] See Stojanovic (2008) and Borg (2007) for overviews.

[2] See for example Bach (2007a,b,c) for a critique of Cappelen and Lepore (2004) and Borg (2012a) for a critique on Travis.

parameter of a double-index modal logic, thereby allowing contextual variation of the same semantic content and the modeling of different evaluations or judgments thereof.

According to an alternative view that has been popularized by Perry in a vast number of publications, see for instance Perry (1977, 1979, 1997, 1998, 2005), the dependence of indexicals on features of the utterance situation is expressed by explicitly quantifying over reified utterances. Broadly-conceived token-based approaches like Perry's go back to Burks (1949) and Reichenbach (1947).[3]

A quite different view on linguistic context can already be found in work by linguists like Jespersen (1922), Bühler (1934), and Fillmore (1972), where context is investigated from a more general linguistic and cognitive perspective. Formal theories of cognitive contexts have been developed much later based on ideas by Stalnaker (1978) and their subsequent implementations in dynamic semantic frameworks such as Kamp and Reyle (1993), Heim (1983), and Stokhof and Groenendijk (1991) and, more generally, the influential Amsterdam tradition of dynamic epistemic modal logics such as van Benthem (2006) and van Benthem et al. (2006). Roughly speaking, context is in this tradition constituted by certain doxastic or epistemic states of discourse participants and these are updated when an agent obtains new information, accepts an utterance, or silently accommodates a presupposition. While Stalnaker (1978) was primarily interested in modeling the common ground between discourse participants, i.e., the communicative assumptions that they mutually share at a given time, in a more general approach assumptions, beliefs, or knowledge of individual discourse participants may be modeled explicitly in order to be able to faithfully represent cases of communication success *and* failure. In dynamic models context can also be considered in a more abstract fashion as a representation of content that is updated by context-change potential of linguistic expressions.

A third tradition of dealing with contexts has started in Computer Science with McCarthy (1993). In Artificial Intelligence research, contexts are often reified and made available within the object language, making it possible to reason explicitly about contexts within the object language and formulate so-called bridge rules for transitions between them. Work by Giunchiglia (1993), Serafini and Bouquet (2004), Buvač et al. (1995), Buvač (1995, 1996), and Thomason (2003) exemplifies this tradition. The way context is treated in these languages is similar to the way it is treated in descendants of Kaplan's Logic of Demonstratives insofar as contexts act as reference points, but since it is possible to explicitly formulate rules between contexts by using the full power of first- or even higher-order quantification the languages used in these accounts are generally more expressive than mere double-index modal logics.

[3]Token-reflexive analyses can also be found in earlier work by Peirce and Russell but not with the same amount of systematicity as that of Reichenbach (1947). Although Perry speaks about token-reflexive meaning, his account is strictly speaking utterance- and not token-based (see Perry 2003).

2.2.2 Linguistic Distinctions

It is fair to say that the toolbox available to the average philosopher or linguist has increased tremendously during the past few decades and in light of the sheer number of options for dealing with context formally in a truth-conditional setting some independent criteria are needed for determining which sorts of context-dependence are at play in a given linguistic example. First and foremost, linguistic context-dependence has to be detected. According to simple *context shifting arguments* (CSAs) a sentence ϕ is semantically context-dependent if an utterance of it is true and another utterance of it is false. Practically all sentences of any language are context-dependent in this way, because almost all languages have tenses.[4] A second question to ask is whether the expression in question semantically depends on the deictic center, i.e., the speaker, his location, body alignment, his pointing gesture (if there is one), and the time at which the utterance is made. These features comprise the narrow context Perry (1998) and an expression that semantically depends on these features is indexical. Whether or not an expression is indexical in this sense is implicitly known by a competent speaker and can be made explicit by the semanticist when he is informed by competent speakers. There are also a number of tests that can be used as a rule of thumb to detect indexicality in a sentence, although they do not work reliably in each and every case. For example, in order to report (1) *Alice: I am hungry* in indirect speech *I* needs to be replaced by *he*, whereas (2) *Bob: Alice says that I am hungry* obviously doesn't report (1). In contrast to this, (3) *Alice: John is tall* can be adequately reported as (4) *Alice has said that John is tall* in indirect speech without any need for additional transformations. This shows that *I* is indexical and *tall* is not, although both expressions are semantically context-dependent.[5]

To fix some terminology, let a context that represents features of the deictic center needed for the saturation of indexicals be an *utterance context* and one that represents doxastic or epistemic states of discourse participants be a *doxastic context*. Expressions that semantically depend on the utterance context will from now on be called indexicals. To these belong for example *I*, *you*, *here*, a special

[4]Cappelen and Lepore (2004) have terminologically introduced CSAs merely to criticize them, but we agree with Bach (2007a,c) that their arguments have remained inconclusive. Notice that according to Comrie (1985) there are some languages in which tenses are not grammatically realized (e.g., Burmese) or in which not all of them need to be grammatically realized (e.g., Mandarin Chinese). Nevertheless, suitable temporal relations between the reported event or situation and the time of utterance are still required from a semantical point of view.

[5]The test was devised by Cappelen and Lepore (2004) for checking whether an expression is context-dependent in general, but it obviously only separates expressions that semantically depend on the deictic center from others. Contrary to what Cappelen and Lepore (2005) have claimed, it is the semanticists job to determine whether or not *tall* is relational. Just like *and* cannot be regarded as a unary junctor—even in fully curried languages like $T\tilde{y}$ of the Appendix *and* must be considered as the composition of two other functions—no sensible non-relational account of tallness can be given.

and relatively rare use of *actually*, all absolute tenses, and also demonstratives such as *this* or *over there* uttered with an accompanying pointing gesture. Other cases of context-dependence cannot be explained by a dependence on features of the utterance situation and, as will be laid out further below, are subject to being interpreted on the basis of the doxastic context of an agent. These expressions will from now on be called *contextuals*. Most indexicals are also contextuals. For example, the boundaries of the time interval denoted by *now* are not determinable from the time of utterance or any other objective feature of the utterance situation and the same holds for the boundaries of spatial indexicals like *here*.[6]

Although many indexicals are also contextuals in the sense that a certain relevant feature of the deictic center is needed for but does not suffice for fixing their semantic value, indexicals, demonstratives, and anaphora form in many respects well-distinguishable and special classes of expressions that can be subcategorized according to further criteria like the respective dimension (temporal, spatial, grammatical person, modality) or the distinction between endophoric and exophoric context.[7] In contrast to this, contextuals do not form a homogeneous class and are merely defined ex negativo. Some of them such as *tall* require a semantic ingredient when they occur in a syntactically complete sentence, whereas others such as *to have breakfast* seem to only suggest certain default interpretations like *having breakfast on the day of utterance* while their use in a tensed sentence also expresses some literal meaning, for instance (5) *John had breakfast* expresses *there is a time before the time of utterance at which John had breakfast*. One may speak of primary context-dependence in the first case and secondary context-dependence in the latter.

2.3 Adequacy Requirements

In this section, a number of desiderata for the adequate modeling of linguistic context-dependence will be laid out. Not all cases of linguistic context-dependence will be considered, though, and for example anaphora will be excepted because their linguistic behavior has been studied in detail by semanticists in dynamic settings like DRT or DPL and their explicit dependence on the endophoric context makes them rather peculiar in contrast to other contextuals. Likewise special and not considered in what follows are uses of indexicals in narrative contexts, i.e., when a story is told, and text-deictic expressions like *former* and *latter*.[8]

---

[6]See Bach (2004, 2005), Perry (2005), Mount (2008), and Rast (2009) on the underdetermination of indexicals.

[7]See Rast (2007, Chap. 5).

[8]In contrast to ordinary contextuals like *tall* or *enough*, anaphora and genuine text-deictics seem to depend to a large extent on the grammatical, rhetorical, and informational structure of the previous discourse in addition to how it has been interpreted so far.

2.3.1 Utterance Contexts Cannot Be Reduced to Doxastic Contexts and Vice Versa

Utterance contexts cannot be reduced to doxastic contexts and vice versa if semantic and pragmatic adequacy is desired. It is fairly trivial to show that the first direction of this thesis holds. Suppose, for example, that Alice believes it is 2 pm whereas it is in fact 1 pm, and utters (6) *Alice: It is now 2 o'clock*. With respect to the meaning of *now* the utterance content is underdetermined in the sense that it does not specify explicitly by linguistic means whether 2 am or 2 pm is meant and the boundaries of the time interval denoted by Alice's use of *now* are vague and not further specified by any linguistic meaning rule. There are also interpretations of *now* according to which the boundaries are fairly large, for example in (7) *Carla earns much more now than she used to 10 years ago*. However, a reasonable interpretation of (6) is constrained by general world-knowledge according to which the boundaries of the indexical in (6) are much smaller. Suppose that on the basis of their background knowledge all discourse participants agree that (6) is true in the given situation if the time of utterance was 14:00 h $\pm$ 2 min.[9] Then (6) is clearly false and Alice is mistaken about the denotation of her use of *now*. Neither her epistemic state nor her referential intentions determine that denotation. Features of the deictic center are given independently of the epistemic states of discourse participants.

The other direction of the thesis is more complicated, as there are seemingly many ways to 'objectify' aspects of doxastic context. First, one might attempt to simply store a relevant aspect in context parameters of a double-index modal logic. From a purely logical point of view, almost anything can be stored in a parameter according to which truth is relativized and for some technical purposes enriching parameters might make sense. However, the way in which relevant features of epistemic states are encoded formally should properly reflect the role they play in the resolution of context-dependence. Beliefs and assumptions of agents don't generally *determine* missing ingredients of contextuals, because the (deep) interpretation of contextuals is optional in case of secondary context-dependence, and, moreover, beliefs and assumptions are individual. For example, particularly when uttered with verum-focus, a speaker might intend (8) *John <u>had</u> breakfast* to be interpreted according to its literal meaning rather than its usual default interpretation (see Sect. 2.3.3). In this case nothing is missing that could be stored

[9]For the sake of the current argument, the potential 'higher-order' vagueness of the $\pm$ margins or cases when discourse participants assume different standards of precision can be ignored. It is assumed in the above example that all discourse participants agree on the margins and that they are much smaller than 1 h. From a more philosophical angle one could also claim that expressions like *now* or *2pm* denote instants in time rather than time intervals and the above interpretations are only adequate when Alice is considered as speaking loosely. As interesting as it may be from a philosophical perspective about time, this view is not helpful for doing natural language semantics. People do not have such rigid standards in ordinary conversations.

in a context parameter.[10] Even in the case of primary context-dependence an agent might refrain from deep interpretation and instead only existentially quantify over missing argument places.

It is also crucial to notice that referential intentions of speakers are not part of the context and generally are not adequate for determining the truth-conditional contribution of indexical contextuals.[11] If for example Bob points to the K2 while intending to refer to the Mount Everest (9) *Bob: This is the highest mountain on earth* is false, just like in example (6), since the pointing gesture picks out the K2 instead of the Mount Everest.

Although the above considerations speak against it, they do not constitute a principal 'knockdown' counter-argument against parameter-based contextualism according to which contextual variation of a contextual is expressed by using different, suitably enriched parameters of a double-index modal logic that may vary from agent to agent to reflect his or her interpretation. For example, relativists like Lasersohn (2005, 2008) have suggested to put a judge into the index parameter, thereby allowing for two people to disagree about the same semantic content of an utterance containing a predicate of personal taste without one of them being at fault.[12] The general usefulness of these kind of theories is questionable, though. Contextual variation is in these theories merely expressed formally without explaining how an agent arrives at a particular interpretation, and when the interpretation of contextuals is modeled by resorting to parameters, context or index parameters are multiplied respectively: one parameter is needed for the deictic center and other parameters for representing different interpretations and what the speaker has in mind. As a result, the connection between communicative assumptions and beliefs of discourse participants and their preferred interpretation of an utterance at a given time is left unexplained. As long as one is only interested in expressing or encoding contextual variabilities in a logical language this might be acceptable, but in the long run it is not satisfying. A good theory of contextuals needs to say something about how rational agents arrive at interpretations based on what they believe and assume.

2.3.2 *Knowledge Is Not Indexical*

Both contextualism and relativism about knowledge or knowledge ascriptions have been defended recently.[13] While a general critique of these positions is beyond the

[10] Cf. Bach (2004, 2005).

[11] See (ibid.), Bach (2009).

[12] Note that a relativism like that of MacFarlane (2008) is quite a different story; here, a metaphysical claim about the truth or falsity of utterance content at different evaluation times is made and whether this view is adequate hinges on metaphysical arguments.

[13] See for example Cohen (1990) and DeRose (1996, 2009) for contextualist and Richard (2004), and MacFarlane (2005a) for relativist positions.

scope of this article, there is a strong argument against a crude form of indexicalism of factive knowledge. Let there be a weak epistemic context c_w and a strong one c_s, let Kp stand for 'it is knowable that p', and $M, c \models \phi$ express the fact that ϕ is true with respect to context c in a model M. Now assume that p is itself not sensitive to epistemic contexts. Given all that, according to the indexicalist premise it can be the case that (i) $M, c_w \models Kp$ and (ii) $M, c_s \models \neg Kp$. But from (i) it follows by factivity of knowledge that $M, c_w \models p$. Since p is by assumption not sensitive to epistemic contexts, it is also the case that $M, c_s \models p$. Given all that, the last and crucial step of the argument is as follows: The fact that p holds in the strong context and the fact that this fact in turn can be derived on the basis of uncontroversial logical principles, the factivity of knowledge, and the indexicalist premise taken together should suffice as a justification for the claim that it is also knowable in c_s that p, i.e., for establishing $M, c_s \models Kp$, in any particular case. This contradicts the contextualist assumption (ii).

Some epistemologists don't seem to like this argument. They tend to attack it either by resorting to an alternative notion of contexts or by attacking the last inference step. Regarding the first counter-argument, notice that the original argument is independent of the actual formal modeling of the contexts in question and so it does, for instance, not help to consider contexts as sets of possible worlds instead of simple reference points.[14] The argument does not rest upon any assumptions about the structure of contexts at all; it applies to any sort of *determinative* context, i.e., to any sort of context that partly determines the truth or falsity of a knowledge attribution such that (i) and (ii) may hold at the same time and within the same model. Second, it is hard to see how the very fact that some claim can be derived by logical principles from acceptable assumptions cannot be a valid justification. Conversely, the justificational value of such a fact should be stronger than any empirical claim. It is easy for an agent to ascertain in any particular case that the embedded proposition is true in the strong context when it is already known in a weak context. Hence, the agent certainly has good reasons to believe that it holds in the strong context and, since the embedded proposition is true and the justification is correct, according to the justified true belief view the agent also knows that the proposition holds. The only thing that would keep an agent from knowing the embedded proposition would be a lack of awareness about the logical principles that govern strong knowledge or a lack of inferential skills in general. After all, a heavily resource-bound agent might not even be able to recognize simple instances of modus ponens as correct inferences. However, it is not easy to see how switching to resource-bound agents could salvage epistemic contextualism, since the resulting kind of contextualism would be fairly trivial. In this view, the agent would simply fail to recognize that it follows from the fact that he knew the embedded proposition in the weak context that the embedded proposition is also true in the strong one, yet it would still be knowable in the strong context that the embedded proposition holds. We should be able to convince such an agent of the fact that the embedded

[14] Many thanks to Manuel Rebuschi for fruitful discussion of this issue.

proposition is true as easily (or hard) as it might be to convince someone of the fact that modus ponens is a valid inference scheme.

What lesson should be drawn from this argument? One might be tempted to consider the verb *to know* a contextual as laid out above. If *to know* indeed worked exactly in parallel to expressions like *tall*, then stronger or weaker readings of it would be obtained by interpreting the respective knowledge ascription, and a statement of the form *A knows that p* would be semantically underdetermined in a sense that will be laid out in more detail in the next sections. No such readings seem to be available, though, and so invariantism is a better response. Strong knowledge might have its place in epistemology only as a limit to which justified beliefs converge ideally.

2.3.3 Deep Interpretation Is Sometimes Optional and Sometimes Mandatory

Bach (2004, 2005) has argued that the recipient does not always need to find a missing ingredient of a contextual. As mentioned earlier, in (5) *John had breakfast* a default interpretation is indicated according to which John had breakfast on the day of utterance, but the literal meaning of the sentence can be prevalent in a given conversational situation. For example, when previously someone has mentioned that John has never had breakfast in his life, Alice may reply with (5) and add that she has seen John having breakfast last week, although it was a quite hasty one. Another example is (10) *Alice bought a car.* From the point of view of lexical semantics buying something involves a legally binding transfer of a property between a buyer and a seller at a certain price, since otherwise the act of buying cannot be distinguished from similar acts like borrowing or stealing. But many times when (10) is uttered, the recipient does not need to determine a *specific* seller or price in order to understand what (10) says or what the sender intended to say by uttering (10). Finding a specific contextual ingredient is optional in such a case, but by virtue of semantic competence a recipient must still know implicitly that buying something involves a purchased object, a buyer, a seller, and a price. When a specific ingredient is determined by the recipient, this is called *deep interpretation.* In contrast to this, the existential completion that for the above example may be paraphrased as *There is a seller and there is a price at which Alice bought a car at some time in the past* is the result of *partial interpretation.* If Bach (2007b) is right, partial interpretation by existentially quantifying over open argument places is optional as well, because sometimes other than existential quantifiers might yield the desired interpretation. It is, however, presently unclear under what circumstances contextual sentences can be interpreted using another than the existential quantifier. For example, it seems that (11) *John ate* cannot be interpreted as (12) *John ate most of the cookies* and (11) cannot be uttered felicitously to convey this interpretation.

Sometimes deep interpretation seems to be mandatory. For example, assuming some place of arrival for (13) *Alice arrived last week* seems to be required by the conventional meaning of *to arrive*.[15] In other words, there is a sense in which someone who interprets (13) as (14) *Alice has arrived at some place during the week before the utterance of (13)* has not fully understood (13) in the given conversational situation, although he has grasped its linguistic meaning, whereas the same cannot be said about the existential completion of (10). The fact that *to arrive* has an indexical and a nonindexical reading similar to *left* and *right* might account for this difference. While certain contextuals are not indexical in the narrow sense of semantically depending on the deictic center, they still semantically depend on features of another center in the same way as indexicals.

2.3.4 Doxastic Contexts Are Constituted by Assumptions

Doxastic contexts are in a sense given by the belief states of discourse participants, but as plenty of research on presuppositions has shown: not directly. Stalnaker (1978, 2002) and many others have argued that in order to account for the silent accommodation of presuppositions doxastic contexts are comprised of mutual assumptions of discourse participants, i.e., their common ground. Consider the following example due to von Fintel: (15) *I am sorry that I am late. I had to take my daughter to the doctor.* Among the presuppositions of these sentences is the existential presupposition that the speaker of (15) has a daughter. It is fairly obvious and a common phenomenon that a hearer doesn't need to know that the speaker has a daughter in order to fully understand (15), because he can simply add this presupposition to his belief base on the fly, thereby maintaining the common ground.

However, mutual assumptions alone do in a trivial sense not suffice for modeling discourse in general, if the model is supposed to reflect not only what happens during successful, but also what happens during unsuccessful communication. What happens if the hearer doesn't accommodate the presupposition? Clearly, the assumptions of discourse participants have to be modeled on an individual basis as well, and from these epistemic states the common ground can be computed at any time. Moreover, although mutuality plays a crucial role in explaining certain cases of Gricean interdependent reasoning processes by means of which an agent arrives at an interpretation, its role for everyday communication has been exaggerated in the past. Often a hearer just maintains a model of what the speaker appears to believe and on the basis of that model interprets his utterances and accommodates presuppositions accordingly. It should also be remarked that assumptions, as opposed to beliefs, play a less important role for the interpretation of contextuals than for dealing with presuppositions. In case of primary context-dependence the fact that a contextual misses an argument can be inferred from the

[15] Many thanks to Richmond Thomason for having brought this to my attention.

lexicon, but usually the speaker does not presuppose or implicate any particular instance of the missing ingredient. For example, when someone interprets (3) *John is tall* he cannot accommodate the missing comparison class, because it is not indicated by the utterance at all—it is neither expressed explicitly nor does it have to be implicated or presupposed. In this case, the agent might arrive at a comparison class by taking into account the *question under discussion* (QUD) and might not need to resort to Gricean reasoning at all. Is the utterance about playing basketball and John plays basketball? Then the members of his team might be a preferred comparison class.

In a simplified view of assumptions without iterated mutuality (what I assume that you assume that I assume…), a doxastic basis for interpreting utterance can be generated from what the recipient believes about what the message sender believes. Ideally, these beliefs should be compartmentalized in dependence of the QUD. How agents compartmentalize beliefs on the basis of what has been said so far and how this dependence may be modeled in a logical setting under ideal rationality assumptions is currently still an open question, though.

2.4 Some Remarks on the Modeling of Contextuals

In the remainder of this article the question of how to represent contextuals in a formal, truth-conditional setting shall be addressed. Most of what follows is merely meant as a suggestion to explicate some of the points made previously in a more rigorous fashion. To provide a link to general semantics in the Montague tradition mechanisms from epistemic modal logic are directly encoded in higher-order logic. The reader is asked not to pay too much attention to the particular implementation, which serves no more than as a proof of concept, and to consider the general ideas underlying it.

2.4.1 *Using Free Variables*

We take a closer look at the semantic content of some contextuals in a simple type theory called $T\tilde{y}$ (see Appendix), whose only difference to standard type theory is that a special notation is used to give functions a second extension. In case of a function A from entities of some type to truth-values $\{1,0\}$, $\sim A$ is interpreted as inner negation. This means, for example, that for an ordinary, non-intensional predicate $P_{(et)}$, $\neg P(a) \wedge \neg \sim P(a)$ may be true in a model, thereby representing the fact that P is not applicable to a. Consequently, semantic objects of type s can be regarded as situations as opposed to worlds, because from the fact that $\neg P_{(st)}(s_0)$ it does not follow that $\sim P_{(st)}(s_0)$, whereas the opposite direction holds, and the inner negation must be considered the 'genuine' negation. In general, this makes the logic very similar to a partial logic that corresponds to a 3-valued Kleene system, but without giving up bivalence or having to introduce additional junctors.[16]

Two-dimensional semantics can be implemented in this framework by combining terms of type $(s(sT))$ for various types T. The type $(s(st))$ for sentences is abbreviated τ and the type $(s(se))$ for intensional objects is abbreviated ϵ. In what follows, the variable u is used for the utterance situation and s for what may be called the topic situation, i.e., it stands for the situation that is implicitly described by the utterance. To give an example, let (16) $\lambda u \lambda s.speaker(u)$ be an expression of type ϵ for the English first-person pronoun, (17) $\lambda P_\tau \lambda u \lambda s.PRES(u, s) \wedge P(u)(s)$ for the present tense, where $PRES(s_1, s_2)$ is true if s_2 overlaps s_1 from the right and does not end significantly later than s_1, and (18) $\lambda x_\epsilon \lambda u.\lambda s.wait(s, x(u, s))$ is a lexicon entry for the verb *to wait*. The sentence *I wait* is then analyzed as (19) $\lambda P_\tau \lambda u \lambda s.PRES(u, s) \wedge P(u, s)[\lambda u \lambda s.speaker(u) \lambda x_\epsilon \lambda u.\lambda s.wait(s, x(u, s))]$, which reduces to (20) $\lambda u \lambda s.\ PRES(u, s) \wedge wait(s, speaker(u))$.[17]

If what has been said so far is correct, the context-dependence of *tall* in (3) *John is tall* cannot be adequately expressed in the same manner in terms of a function of the utterance situation like in (21) $\lambda u \lambda s.PRES(u, s) \wedge Tall(s, j, f(u))$, where f is a function from a situation-type variable to a comparison class (viz. corresponding predicate). This representation would not be adequate because the missing comparison class of *tall* is not actually provided by a shared context. For this reason it is better to represent the missing comparison class as a free variable, like in (22) $\lambda u \lambda s.PRES(u, s) \wedge Tall(s, j, C)$.[18]

For the present purpose of investigating interpretations of utterances, a free variable must at some point be bound by an existential quantifier in contrast to the usual practise in mathematical logic of assuming implicit universal quantification. Formula (24) $\lambda u \lambda s.\exists C\,[PRES(u, s) \wedge Tall(s, j, C)]$ represents the *existential completion* of (22). Existential completion plays a crucial role in keeping interpretation conventional from a logical perspective, because it allows one to avoid explicit

[16]This view goes back to non-traditional predication theory of Sinowjew (1970), Sinowjew and Wessel (1975), and Wessel (1989). Some philosophers and logicians don't like it, because it cannot be readily extended to deal with quantified statements and moreover one or both of $\neg$ and $\sim$ might no longer satisfy ones favorite criteria for negation. Non-traditional predication theory is nevertheless useful for expressing some form of situations without making the underlying logic partial. See Muskens (1995) for a genuine partial type theory.

[17]Details of the tense logic and underlying interval relations cannot be addressed here; the reader is referred to Allen (1983), Ladkin (1987), and van Benthem (1991). Notice that 'not significantly later' is a condition for the English present tense as opposed to, say, the German present tense which may extend significantly into the future. For simplicity the fact that the tenses like most other indexicals are also contextuals is ignored and we focus on nonindexical contextuals in what follows.

[18]In contrast to this, the present tense predicate *PRES* is indexical and therefore does depend on u. A crude definition for *tall* could be given as (23) $Tall := \lambda u \lambda s \lambda x \lambda C.\ most\ y(C(s, y))(height(s, y) < height(s, x))$, where the quantifier and function names are self-explanatory. These details don't matter in what follows.

representations of incomplete content such as structured propositions with all of the problems that come along with such approaches.[19]

Admittedly, not all missing ingredients of contextuals *have* to be represented as a free variable. First, it would, of course, also be possible to bind the variable by a λ-operator and delay the evaluation until the end of semantic composition. This would significantly complicate syntactic and semantic construction, though. Secondly, dependences on the utterance situation can be modeled to some extent by introducing an accessibility relation for a new modality and quantifying over situations reachable by this relation in a suitable way just like it is done in case of the modal index. When quantifiers are properly relativized to these situations, for example by a domain predicate of type $(e(st))$, even quantifier domain restriction, nominal restrictions, and other implicit domain dependences like that of spatiotemporal indexicals can be dealt with. However, generally open variables are preferable over implicit dependences on the underlying semantic objects because they allow for a more controlled modeling of deep interpretation.

2.4.2 Belief and Assumptions

Instead of a normal modal logic account of belief, such as assuming the familiar modal logic KD45, strong belief will be modeled as the minimum of a total preorder relation over states.[20] The reasons for this choice will become apparent further below. For generality the preorder may be implemented as a relation that additionally depends on an agent and a base state. Let R of type $essst$ represent this relation and $C_{x,u}(s,t)$ be a shortcut for $C(x,u,s,t)$; the subscripts are left out if they are arbitrary. The following constraints are needed:

$$C(s,s) \tag{REF}$$

$$[C(s,t) \wedge C(t,u)] \rightarrow C(s,u) \tag{TR}$$

$$\forall P.\exists v P(v) \rightarrow \exists s(P(s) \wedge \neg\exists t[P(t) \wedge C(t,s)]). \tag{WO}$$

The well-ordering principle WO is only needed for infinite domains, because in such a domain there could be an infinite descending chain $s_{i-n} \leq \cdots \leq s_{i-2} \leq s_{i-1} \leq s_i$.

[19]Kent Bach is one of the primary advocates of 'propositional skeletons', see Bach (2005). However, this position leads to a number of logical problems. Specifying the logical consequences of incomplete content and attitudes towards such content in particular is far from trivial. Apart from that, structured propositions also tend to lure philosophers of language into metaphysically dangerous parlance, as if there was an ethereal 'third realm' of meanings.

[20]For belief such a preference relation is also used by Baltag and Smets (2006, 2011) and Lang and van der Torre (2007). The following implementation is based on Rast (2010, 2011) with changes made to account for the use of non-traditional predication theory.

The condition prohibits the existence of such chains for any non-empty intension P of type st. We stipulate that these conditions also hold for $\sim C$.

To obtain strong belief first the minimum has to be obtained by making use of

$$\lambda xuCP\lambda s.P(s) \land \neg\exists t[P(t) \land C(x,u,t,s) \land \neg C(x,u,s,t)], \qquad \text{(MIN)}$$

where C is of type $essst$ and P, Q are of type st. An agent x's unconditional belief set at u can be expressed as (25) $MIN(x, u, R, \top)$, where $\top$ is a Verum-intension of type st like, for example, $\lambda s.p \lor \neg p$ for arbitrary p of type t. We write $\mathcal{B}^{C}_{x,u}(P)$ for $\forall s.MIN(x, u, C, \top)(s) \rightarrow P(s)$ and leave out x, u, C when they can be inferred from the context.

In an account with truth-functional negation only, beliefs can be updated in light of new evidence that P by making all P-worlds minimal for the respective agent at a given time. This method is known as lexicographic update and can be used with only slight alterations in the present setting, too.[21] Additional care needs to be taken that the update methods deals adequately with the respective anti-extensions $\sim P$ of a given P.

Let *if* p_t *then* q_t *else* r_t abbreviate $(p \rightarrow q) \land (\neg p \rightarrow r)$. The lexicographic update of an ordering C of type $essst$ to C' of the same type by P of type st with respect to an agent x's belief in a base situation u_o is computed by the following function[22]:

$$\begin{aligned}&\lambda xu_0CP\lambda C'.\forall u_1, y, s, t[\mathit{if}\ x = y \land u_1 = u_0 \land P(s) \qquad \text{(LUP)}\\ &\land \neg P(t) \land C(y, u_1, t, s)\ \mathit{then}\ C'(y, u_1, s, t)\\ &\mathit{else}\ C'(y, u_1, s, t) \equiv C(y, u_1, s, t)].\end{aligned}$$

This is ordinary belief update. We also need a way to generate assumptions from a hearer's beliefs about what the speaker believes, where only definite beliefs of the hearer about what the speaker believes are taken into account when generating the assumptions. Let $\mathcal{B}_{(a*b)}P$ stand for the belief obtained from updating a's beliefs entirely by those of b. (Iterated belief is represented as a separate belief in this setting.) Let $\overline{A}$ be $\sim P$ if A is of the form P and P if A is of the form $\sim P$. Then the desired belief update must satisfy the condition that (26) for any non-empty P of type st, be it in positive or negative form, if $\mathcal{B}_b P$ then $\mathcal{B}_{(a*b)}P$; otherwise $\mathcal{B}_{(a*b)}P$ iff. $\mathcal{B}_a P$.

[21] See Baltag and Smets (2011) for a detailed investigation of lexicographic update and similar update method for qualitative graded belief based on prior work by van Benthem and Liu (2005) and Liu (2008).

[22] Cf. Rast (2010, p. 394).

Spelled out as a conditionalization dependent on two agents x_0, y_0 and a base situation u_0 this revision operation is very similar to the above simple revision:

$$\lambda x_0 y_0 u_0 C \lambda C' \forall P.\exists s P(s) \rightarrow \forall s, t, u_1 \forall x_1, y_1 [\mathit{if}\ u_1 = u_0 \quad \text{(REV)}$$
$$\wedge\, x_1 = x_0 \wedge y_1 = y_0 \wedge P(s) \wedge C(y_1, u_1, s, t)\ \mathit{then}\ C'(x_1, u_1, s, t)$$
$$\mathit{else}\ C'(x_1, u_1, s, t) \equiv C(x_1, u_1, s, t)].$$

We write $\leq_{a*b,u}$ for $REV(a, b, u, \leq)$ and leave out arguments when they are not relevant for the discussion. This revision is clearly based on lexicographic update, but notice that if $\mathcal{B}_{x,u} P$ then $\neg\mathcal{B}_{x,u}\overline{P}$. The same holds for revised belief, which follows from the definition of $B_{x,u} P$ as $\forall s.MIN(x, u, \leq_{x,u}, \top)(s) \rightarrow P(s)$ and the inner negation constraint from the Appendix. Second, the revision has the property that if $\mathcal{B}_b ?P$ and $\mathcal{B}_a P$ then $\mathcal{B}_{a*b} P$, where $?P$ abbreviates $\lambda s.\neg P \wedge \neg \sim P$. The antecedent condition of (REV) cannot shift any P- or $\sim P$-situation into the new minimum; by the *else* clause all situations in the new minimum will thus be P-situations. Finally, it is also the case that if $\neg\mathcal{B}_b P$ and $\neg\mathcal{B}_b \sim P$ but $\mathcal{B}_a P$, then $\mathcal{B}_{a*b} P$. The first two assumptions say that there are one or more situations s in the minimum of b such that $\neg P(s)$ (viz., $\neg \sim P(s)$). But for any such situations the *else* clause will apply and so by the third assumption a P-situation will be preferred over these. On the other hand, if $\mathcal{B}_b P$ then $\mathcal{B}_{a*b} P$ by the *then* clause of (REV), and likewise for the $\sim P$ case. So the update operation really just takes over the definite beliefs from the second beliefs which in the present case represent the hearers iterated beliefs about the speaker's beliefs.

To give a rationale for this kind of updating consider an utterance of the sentence (27) *John is ready*. Suppose that in a given interpretation situation the hearer believes that the speaker believes that the conversation so far has been about John's pending advancement (P). The hearer needs to take this belief into account when interpreting the utterance even if he disagrees with it. Suppose further that the hearer believes that the speaker does not believe that P or that he is undecided in the sense that he believes that $?P$.[23] In this case the hearer will have to resort to his own non-iterated beliefs when interpreting the utterance. In other words, when interpreting an utterance involving contextuals the hearer *may* take into account a model of what the speaker believes but the model might only be partial; what is not specified clearly by the model is completed by the hearer on the basis of his ordinary beliefs.

[23] We have chosen one particular way to interpret $?P$ that is not the only one. In another context it could also be argued that an agent decidedly believes that $?P$ if $\mathcal{B}?P$ is true. Under this interpretation the above update operation would need to be adjusted to also revise by $?P$.

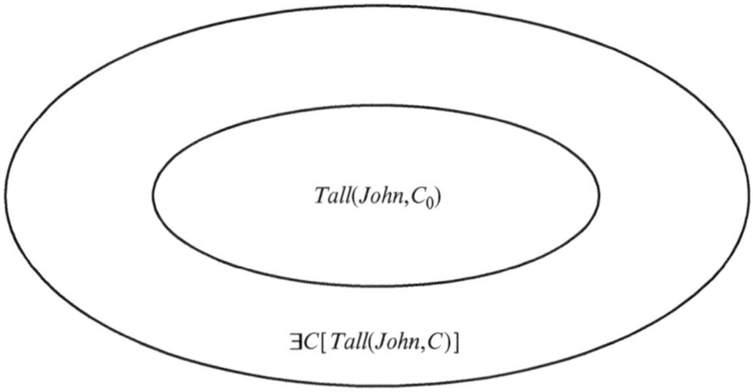

Fig. 2.2 Relation between an interpretation and an existential completion, where C_0 is a constant

2.4.3 Towards Interpretation

In the previous section it was suggested to represent the meaning of contextuals by open variables of an appropriate type. Subsequently, these have to be bound by existential quantifiers. The semantic content representing this existential completion is then narrowed down—or, from a syntactic point of view, enriched—to some more specific content that implies the existential completion. This step is essentially an abductive inference; it involves finding the interpretation of the literal meaning that the hearer finds most plausible at a given time. Subsequently the hearer might check this interpretation against his own beliefs to see whether he finds some perhaps even more restricted interpretation compatible with what he believes in the given situation. This last step, involving a checking, is a form of non-prioritized belief revision, which is problematic from a philosophical point of view. On the one hand, if the checking step never succeeds the hearer will never learn anything new from another person. On the other hand, if the checking always succeeds like in ordinary belief revision or the above lexicographic update the hearer will come to believe anything he is told. Obviously, some middle ground seems to be desirable. The checking issue is left open in what follows.[24]

Figure 2.2 illustrates the relation between an interpretation and its existential completion. The process of arriving at an interpretation is an instance of free enrichment, see Récanati (2004, 2010), and seems to be the usual, albeit not

[24]The checking problem might be the main reason for switching to quantitative accounts, where for example belief update by Jeffrey Conditioning is available and well-understood. For it is quite obvious that a checking step only makes sense if the hearer is able to learn something from the speaker not with apodictic certainty but only to some degree. In any case, these issues are fairly complicated both from a philosophical and a technical perspective and there is no room in this article to further delve into them.

mandatory way of interpreting contextuals. Although we do not assume this here, interpretation by narrowing down semantic content could be taken as a criterion for separating contextuals from other phenomenas of linguistic context-dependence such as semantic transfer in cases of metaphor, metonymy, and deferred ostension.

The idea of regarding deep interpretation as a form of abductive inference has first been explored in a formal setting by Hobbs et al. (1993).[25] However, Hobbs et al. use a purely syntactical, cost-based account. They assign numerical preference values to formulas of a first-order language and their parts, whose 'cost' is then minimized, but they do not provide a way to update these valuations in light of new evidence. In the present setting where qualitative graded belief (viz., assumptions) is available, a semantic account is more natural and also mandatory for the simple fact that higher-order logic with standard models is not compact and therefore does not fare well with syntactic symbol manipulation.

Before laying out a fairly simple 'proof of concept' some general words of caution are advisable. As is argued in more detail in Rast (2011), *merely* assuming abduction will not do. A reasonable account of interpretation as abduction based on preferences needs to be accompanied by a theory of how these preferences are updated in the light of new evidence since otherwise the formal model will amount to no more than an unnecessarily complicated way of expressing the trivial fact that discourse participants consider some interpretations more plausible than others. The question is not whether they do that but *how*, and a fruitful answer to this question in a logical setting must presume additional ideal rationality criteria. The limits of the representation of graded belief and its update method—in this case belief as a set of situations and a variant of lexicographic update—also determine the limits of the respective account of abductive interpretation.

With that caveat in mind, we now briefly take a look at interpretation. Two-dimensional semantic representations slightly complicate the matter because the context variable is not always treated on a par with the one representing the modal index. At one occasion the hearer might take into account his beliefs about the utterance context directly whereas on another occasion he might have reasons to take into account his beliefs about what the speaker believes about the utterance situation.[26] This issue is ignored for simplicity and only the interpretation of intensions of type st obtained from intensions of type sst $(=\tau)$ by applying the actual context u_0 is considered in what follows. (In reality hearers also interpret indexicals, of course.)

According to what has been said so far, first the hearer's iterated beliefs about what in his opinion the speaker believes are updated by the literal meaning of the utterance provided that the hearer also believes that the speaker is honest and sincere. It is assumed that a stands for the hearer and b is an index for a's beliefs about what the speaker believes. Given some existential completion P, in an interpretation situation u the first step is then represented by $LUP(b, u, \leq, P)$.

---

[25] Cf. also Stone and Thomason (2002).

[26] See Rast (2010) for more on this topic.

Subsequently, the revision of a's beliefs by b is computed. The final step is then to 'abduce' the most plausible states that imply P on the basis of this revised ordering relation. For generality, we assume that there is an abduction relation R of type sst between situations that is similar to an accessibility relation in modal logic. The following function then characterizes a hearer a's interpretation of an existential completion P uttered by b in a given situation u: (28) $MIN(a, u, REV(a, b, u, LUP(b, u, \leq, P)), \lambda s.\forall t[R(s,t) \rightarrow P(s)])$. Relation $R(s,t)$ could for example be interpreted as *s causes t*, *s is a reason for t*, or just as the identity relation. Different readings of the abduction relation give rise to different sorts of abductive inference. In the present case, all of them are limited to being based on a point-wise comparison of states. Both for the ordering and for the abduction relation it might be fruitful to explore the possibilities of relaxing this requirement and consider set-wise comparisons.

Primitive as it may be, this form of abduction should convey the general idea. The hearer infers from the assumption what he considers the most plausible interpretation in the given situation. As mentioned before, a way to revise the plausibility ordering in light of new evidence is crucial in any such model, since otherwise the modeling would be vacuous and ad hoc.

From the discussion in the previous section it is, however, clear that many cases of secondary context-dependence require additional machinery to obtain a convincing picture of how a rational agent arrives at an interpretation. In particular, some adequate representation of common sense knowledge that includes default rules or inferences based on typicality seems to be needed for even seemingly simple examples. Consider for instance the case of *having breakfast* + tense again. One typically has breakfast in the morning after having woken up. Moreover, when someone talks about a past event in the afternoon that describes a daily activity that typically takes place in the morning, it is likely that this past event took place in the morning of the day of utterance unless there is additional information that suggests another past reference time frame. (Such additional information may for example be introduced explicitly as the origin of a sequence of narrated events.) In the meantime, exceptional inferences like the one from (5) *John had breakfast* to (29) *John didn't have breakfast in the morning of the day of the time of utterance of (5)* must not be prohibited. So in this example, defeasible reasoning and a rich background common sense belief basis is needed to make the underlying inference chain explicit. Likewise, in order to arrive at preferred interpretations of (6) and (7) one has to resort to the QUD and a lot of common sense assumptions about the typical precision of talking about the time of the day, the periods during which salaries remain constant, how average salaries are typically measured, and so on. For these reasons the modeling of genuine contextuals can become a rather complex task. At least in the foreseeable future such models will only be able to approximate certain aspects of human interpretation for the very simple reason that humans regularly (though not always) make use of their intelligence when they interpret utterances—and only certain aspects of this intelligent behavior can be captured by formal tools under strong rationality postulates.

2.5 Summary and Conclusions

It has been argued that indexicality needs to be carefully distinguished from other forms of linguistic context-dependence. Contextuals such as *ready* and *tall* are semantically incomplete or—as in the case of expressions like *having breakfast*, tenses and the boundaries of spatiotemporal indexicals—their apparent semantic completeness is an artifact of the underlying possible world, event, or situation ontology and they commonly require additional interpretation. They may be indexical or not. Some adequacy criteria for dealing with contextuals in a truth-conditional setting have been laid out and it has been argued that modeling the context-dependence of contextuals like indexicality is generally inadequate. It has been suggested to compute existential completions first and consider how an agent arrives at an interpretation on the basis of that content by free enrichment instead. An example has been given how to achieve this in a qualitative setting by ordering the intensional base states by a preference relation and 'abduce' the most plausible subset of states satisfying a certain intension.

A crucial problem for modeling deep interpretation in this way is, however, how to obtain and explain the preference relation in the first place which yields an agent's preferred interpretation. In an ideally rational approach this relation has to be connected to ways in which an agent deals with evidence obtained from sources of varying reliability. The account needs to be linked up with existing results in Formal Epistemology such as theories of graded belief based on probabilities, Dempster-Shafer belief, and possibility theory. It is likely that in the context of modeling natural language interpretation more mechanisms than graded belief and some form of abductive inference are needed. In particular, the role played by the QUD has to be investigated in more detail and richer ontologies with default reasoning are needed.

Appendix: Language $T\tilde{y}$

Types. Base types are e for entities in D_e, s for situations in D_s, and t for truth-values. If α, β are types, then $(\alpha\beta)$ is a type. Nothing else is a type. $D_t = \{1, 0\}$. For better readability, parentheses around types are sometimes left out; for example, sst may abbreviate $(s(st))$.

Terms. We assume a fixed vocabulary of expressions, using x, y, z for variables of type D_e and s, u and indexed variants for variables of type s. An expression of base type α is a term of type α. If A is of type $(\beta\alpha)$ and B is of type β, then (AB) and (BA) are of type α. If x is a variable of type β and A is an expression of type α, then $(\lambda x.A)$ is a term of type $(\beta\alpha)$. For each pair of terms A, B of type α, $(A = B)$ is a term of type t. Familiar infix notation may be used for the standard logical connectives $\vee, \wedge, \equiv, \rightarrow$. The binder notation will be used for standard quantifiers, i.e., $\forall x A$ is written instead of $(\forall(\lambda x.A))$, and a dot may be used to indicate a left parenthesis whose implicit closing right parenthesis has maximal scope. Traditional operator syntax will also be used in many places, types and parentheses are sometimes omitted, and implicit β-conversions are allowed for better readability. This means that for instance $Hungry(s, Alice)$ may be written instead of $(((\lambda s_s(\lambda x_e.Hungry_{(s(et))}))\, s_s)\, Alice_e)$. A term of the form $\sim A$ is the inner negation form of A and there is no inner negation form of an inner negation form.

Semantics. A standard $T\tilde{y}$ frame consists of a set containing sets D_α for each base type α and domains $D_{(\alpha\beta)} = D_\beta^{D_\alpha}$ for all compound types $(\alpha\beta)$. We write g for an assignment and $g[x/a]$ for the assignment that is the same as g except that $g(x) = a$. A standard model $\mathcal{M}$ for $T\tilde{y}$ is a tuple $\langle \mathcal{F}, [\![.]\!] \rangle$ consisting of a standard frame $\mathcal{F}$ and an interpretation function $[\![.]\!]$ that in dependence of a variable assignment g maps terms to their denotation according to their type as follows:

1. $[\![x_\alpha]\!]^{\mathcal{M},g} = g(x)$ if x is a variable, where $g(x) \in D_\alpha$.
2. $\left[\!\left[(A_t \wedge_{(t(tt))} B_t)\right]\!\right]^{\mathcal{M},g} = 1$ if $[\![A]\!]^{\mathcal{M},g} = 1$ and $[\![B]\!]^{\mathcal{M},g} = 1$; 0 otherwise.
3. $[\![\neg A]\!]^{\mathcal{M},g} = 1$ if $[\![A]\!]^{\mathcal{M},g} = 0$; 0 otherwise.
4. $\left[\!\left[(A_{(\beta\alpha)} B_\beta)\right]\!\right]^{\mathcal{M},g} = [\![A]\!]^{\mathcal{M},g}\,([\![B]\!]^{\mathcal{M},g})$, where $[\![A]\!]^{\mathcal{M},g} \in D_{(\beta\alpha)}$; likewise for terms of the form $(B_\beta A_{(\beta\alpha)})$.
5. $\left[\!\left[(\lambda x_\beta . A_\alpha)\right]\!\right]^{\mathcal{M},g}$ is that function f in $D_{(\beta\alpha)}$ such that for any a in D_β, $f(a) = [\![A]\!]^{\mathcal{M},g[x/a]}$.
6. $[\![(\forall(\lambda x_\alpha.A))]\!]^{\mathcal{M},g} = 1$ if $[\![A]\!]^{M,g[x/a]} = 1$ for any $a \in D_\alpha$; 0 otherwise.

Inner Negation Constraint. $[\![A]\!]^{M,g} \cap [\![\sim A]\!]^{M,g} = \emptyset$ for any expression A, i.e., a positive term A and its inner negation form $\sim A$ have distinct extensions.

References

Allen, J. F. (1983). Maintaining knowledge about temporal intervals. *Communications of the ACM, 26*(11), 832–843.

Bach, K. (2004). Minding the gap. In C. Bianchi (Ed.), *The semantics/pragmatics distinction* (pp. 27–43). Stanford: CSLI Publications.

Bach, K. (2005). Context ex machina. In Z. G. Szabó (Ed.), *Semantics versus pragmatics* (pp. 16–44). Oxford: Oxford University Press.

Bach, K. (2006). The excluded middle: Semantic minimalism without minimal propositions. *Philosophy and Phenomenological Research, 73*, 435–442.

Bach, K. (2007a). From the strange to the bizarre: Another reply to Cappelen and Lepore. Department of Philosophy, University of San Fransisco. Retrieved in may 2008 from http://userwww.sfsu.edu/~kbach/.

Bach, K. (2007b). Minimal semantics. *Philosophical Review, 116*, 303–306.

Bach, K. (2007c). Minimalism for Dummies: Reply to Cappelen and Lepore. Department of Philosophy, University of San Francisco. Retrieved in may 2008 from http://userwww.sfsu.edu/~kbach/.

Bach, K. (2009). Why speaker intentions aren't part of context. Technical report, San Francisco State University. Compilation of arguments from earlier papers, published online at http://userwww.sfsu.edu/~kbach/Bach.Intentions&Context.pdf.

Baltag, A., & Smets, S. (2006). Conditional doxastic models: A qualitative approach to dynamic belief revision. *Electronic Notes in Theoretical Computer Science, 165*, 5–21.

Baltag, A., & Smets, S. (2011). Keep changing your beliefs and aiming for the truth. *Erkenntnis, 75*(2), 255–270.

Bar-Hillel, Y. (1954). Indexical expressions. *MIND, 63*, 359–376.

Borg, E. (2004). *Minimal semantics*. Oxford/New York: Oxford University Press.

Borg, E. (2007). Minimalism versus contextualism in semantics. In G. Preyer & G. Peter (Eds.), *Context sensitivity and semantic minimalism: Essays on semantics and pragmatics* (pp. 546–571). Oxford: Oxford University Press.

Borg, E. (2010). Minimalism and the content of the lexicon. In L. Baptista & E. H. Rast (Eds.), *Meaning and context* (pp. 51–78). Bern/New York: Peter Lang.

Borg, E. (2012a). *Pursuing meaning*. Oxford: Oxford University Press.

Borg, E. (2012b). Semantics without pragmatics (chap. 25). In K. Allen & K. M. Jaszczolt (Eds.), *The Cambridge handbook of pragmatics* (pp. 513–528). Cambridge: Cambridge University Press.

Bühler, K. (1934). *Sprachtheorie*. Stuttgart/Jena: Fischer.

Burks, A. (1949). Icon, index and symbol. *Philosophical and Phenomenological Research, 9*(4), 673–689.

Buvač, S. (1995). Formalizing context. Technical report FS-95-02, AAAI.

Buvač, S. (1996). Quantificational logic of context. In *Proceedings of the thirteenth national conference on artificial intelligence*, Portland.

Buvač, S., Buvač, V., & Mason, I. A. (1995). Metamathematics of contexts. *Fundamenta Informaticae, 23*(3), 263–301.

Cappelen, H., & Lepore, E. (2004). *Insensitive semantics*. Oxford: Blackwell.

Cappelen, H., & Lepore, E. (2005). A tall tale: In defence of semantic minimalism and speech act pluralism. In G. Preyer & G. Peter (Eds.), *Contextualism in philosophy: Knowledge, meaning, and truth* (pp. 197–220). New York: Oxford University Press.

Cappelen, H., & Lepore, E. (2006). Shared content. In E. Lepore & B. Smith (Eds.), *Oxford handbook of philosophy of language* (pp. 1020–1055). Oxford/New York: Oxford University Press.

Cohen, S. (1990). Skepticism and everyday knowledge attributions. In M. D. Roth & G. Ross (Eds.), *Doubting* (pp. 161–169). Dordrecht: Kluwer.

Comrie, B. (1985). *Tense*. Cambridge: Cambridge University Press.

DeRose, K. (1996). Relevant alternatives and the content of knowledge attributions. *Philosophy and Phenomenological Research, 56*, 193–197.

DeRose, K. (2009). *The case for contextualism: Knowledge, skepticism and context* (Vol. 1). Oxford: Oxford University Press.

Fillmore, Ch. J. (1972). Ansätze zu einer Theorie der Deixis. In F. Kiefer (Ed.), *Semantik und generative Grammatik I* (pp. 147–174). Frankfurt a.M.: Athenäum.

Frege, G. (1986). Der Gedanke. In G. Patzig (Ed.), *Logische Untersuchungen* (pp. 30–53). Göttingen: Vandenhoeck. First published in: *Beiträge zur Philosophie des deutschen Idealismus 2*, 58–77 (1918).

Giunchiglia, F. (1993). Contextual reasoning. *Epistemologia, XVI*, 345–364.

Heim, I. (1983). File change semantics and the familiarity theory of definiteness. In R. Bäuerle, C. Schwarze, & A. von Stechow (Eds.), *Meaning, use, and interpretation of language* (pp. 164–189). Berlin/New York: De Gruyter.

Hobbs, J. R., Stickel, M., Appelt, D., & Martin, P. (1993). Interpretation as abduction. *Artificial Intelligence, 63*(1–2), 69–142.

Jespersen, O. (1922). *Language: Its nature, development and origin*. London: Allen and Unwin.

Kamp, H., & Reyle, U. (1993). *From discourse to logic*. Dordrecht: Kluwer.

Kaplan, D. (1988). On the logic of demonstratives. In N. Salmon & S. Soames (Eds.), *Propositions and attitudes* (pp. 66–82). Oxford/New York: Oxford University Press.
Ladkin, P. B. (1987). *The logic of time representation*. PhD thesis, University of California, Berkeley. Reference http://wwwlib.umi.com/dissertations/fullcit/8813947.
Lang, J., & van der Torre, L. (2007). From belief change to preference change. In G. Bonanno, J. Delgrande, J. Lang, & H. Rott (Eds.), *Formal models of belief change in rational agents: Number 07351 in Dagstuhl seminar proceedings*, Internationales Begegnungs- und Forschungszentrum für Informatik (IBFI), Schloss Dagstuhl.
Lasersohn, P. (2005). Context dependence, disagreement, and predicates of personal taste. *Linguistics and Philosophy, 28*(6), 643–686.
Lasersohn, P. (2008). Quantification and perspective in relativist semantics. *Philosophical Perspectives, 22*(1), 305–337.
Liu, F. (2008). *Changing for the better*. Number DS-2008-02 in ILLC dissertation series. Institute for Logic, Language, and Computation, Amsterdam.
MacFarlane, J. (2005a). The assessment sensitivity of knowledge attributions. In T. S. Gendler & J. Hawthorne (Eds.), *Oxford studies in epistemology* (Vol. 1, pp. 197–233). Oxford: Oxford University Press.
MacFarlane, J. (2005b). Making sense of relative truth. *Proceedings of the Aristotelian Society, 105*, 321–339.
MacFarlane, J. (2007a). Nonindexical contextualism. *Synthese, 166*(2), 231–250.
MacFarlane, J. (2007b). Relativism and disagreement. *Philosophical Studies, 132*(1), 17–31.
MacFarlane, J. (2008). Truth in the garden of forking paths. In M. Carcía-Carpintero & M. Kölbel (Eds.), *Relative truth* (pp. 81–102). Oxford: Oxford University Press.
MacFarlane, J. (2009). Nonindexical contextualism. *Synthese, 166*, 231–250.
McCarthy, J. (1993). Notes on formalizing context. In R. Bajcsy (Ed.), *Proceedings of IJCAI*, Chambéry (Number 13, pp. 555–562). Morgan Kaufmann.
Mount, A. (2008). The impurity of "pure" indexicals. *Philosophical Studies, 138*, 193–209.
Muskens, R. (1995). *Meaning and partiality*. Stanford: CSLI Publications.
Perry, J. (1977). Frege on demonstratives. *Philosophical Review, 86*, 474–497.
Perry, J. (1979). The problem of the essential indexical. *Noûs, 13*, 3–21.
Perry, J. (1997). Indexicals and demonstratives. In R. Hale & C. Wright (Eds.), *Companion to the philosophy of language*. Oxford: Basil Blackwell.
Perry, J. (1998). Indexicals, contexts and unarticulated constituents. In *Proceedings of the 1995 CSLI Amsterdam logic, language and computation conference*. Stanford, CA: CSLI Publications, 1–16.
Perry, J. (2003). Predelli's threatening note: Contexts, utterances, and tokens in the philosophy of language. *Journal of Pragmatics, 35*, 373–387.
Perry, J. (2005). Using indexicals. In M. Devitt (Ed.), *Blackwell guide to the philosophy of language* (pp. 314–334). Oxford: Blackwell.
Rast, E. H. (2007). *Reference and indexicality*. Berlin: Logos Verlag.
Rast, E. H. (2009). Context and interpretation. In J. M. Larrazabal & L. Zubeldia (Eds.), *Meaning, content, and argument. Proceedings of the ILCLI international workshop on semantics, pragmatics, and rhetoric* (pp. 515–534). San Sebastian: University of the Basque Country Press.
Rast, E. H. (2010). Plausibility revision in higher-order logic with an application in two-dimensional semantics. In X. Arrazola & M. Ponte (Eds.), *Proceedings of the logKCA-10 – proceedings of the second ILCLI international workshop on logic and philosophy of knowledge, communication and action*, Donostia/San Sebastián (pp. 387–403). ILCLI/University of the Basque Country Press.
Rast, E. H. (2011). Non-indexical context dependence and the interpretation as abduction approach. *Lodz Papers in Pragmatics, 7*(2), 259–279.
Récanati, F. (2004). *Literal meaning*. Cambridge: Cambridge University Press.
Récanati, F. (2010). *Truth-conditional pragmatics*. Oxford: Oxford University Press.
Reichenbach, H. (1947). *Elements of symbolic logic*. New York: Macmillian.

Richard, M. (2004). Contextualism and relativism. *Philosophical Studies, 119*, 215–242.
Russell, B. (1966). *An inquiry into meaning and truth*. London: George Allen and Unwin LTD.
Serafini, L., & Bouquet, P. (2004). Comparing formal theories of context in AI. *Artifical Intelligence Journal, 155*(1), 41–67. ITC-IRST technical report 0201-02.
Sinowjew, A. A. (1970). *Komplexe logik*. Berlin/Braunschweig: VEB Deutscher Verlag der Wissenschaften/Vieweg Verlag/C. F. Winter'sche Verlagshandlung Berlin.
Sinowjew, A. A., & Wessel, H. (1975). *Logische Sprachregeln*. Berlin/Braunschweig/Basel: Deutscher Verlag der Wissenschaften.
Sperber, D., & Wilson, D. (1986). *Relevance: Communication and cognition*. Oxford: Blackwell.
Sperber, D., & Wilson, D. (2006). Relevance theory (chap. 27). In L. R. Horn & G. Ward (Eds.), *Handbook of pragmatics*. Oxford: Blackwell.
Stalnaker, R. (1978). Assertion. In P. Cole (Ed.), *Pragmatics: Vol. 9. Syntax and semantics* (pp. 315–332). New York: Academic.
Stalnaker, R. (2002). Common ground. *Linguistics and Philosophy, 25*(5–6), 701–721.
Stanley, J. (2000). Context and logical form. *Linguistics and Philosophy, 23*(4), 391–434.
Stanley, J. (2002). Nominal restriction (chap. 12). In G. Preyer & G. Peter (Eds.), *Logical form and language* (pp. 365–388). Oxford: Oxford University Press.
Stanley, J., & Szabó, Z. G. (2000). On quantifier domain restriction. *Mind & Language, 15*(2–3), 219–261.
Stojanovic, I. (2008). The scope and the subtleties of the contextualism/literalism/relativism debate. *Language and Linguistics Compass, 2*, 1171–1188.
Stokhof, M., & Groenendijk, J. (1991). Dynamic predicate logic. *Linguistics and Philosophy, 14*(1), 39–100.
Stone, M., & Thomason, R. H. (2002). Context in abductive interpretation. In *EDILOG 2002: Proceedings of the sixth workshop on the semantics and pragmatics of dialogue*, Edinburgh (pp. 169–176).
Thomason, R. H. (2003). Dynamic contextual intensional logic: Logical foundations and an application. In P. Blackburn, C. Ghidini, R. M. Turner, & F. Giunchiglia (Eds.), *Modeling and using context: Fourth international and interdisciplinary conference CONTEXT 2003*, Stanford (pp. 328–341). Springer.
Travis, C. (2008). *Occasion-sensitivity*. Oxford/New York: Oxford University Press.
van Benthem, J. (1991). *The logic of time* (2nd ed.). Dordrecht/Boston: Kluwer. (first ed. publ. 1983).
van Benthem, J. (2006). Dynamic logic of belief revision. ILLC tech report, Institute for Logic, Language and Computation, University of Amsterdam.
van Benthem, J., & Liu, F. (2005). Dynamic logic of preference upgrade. ILLC tech report PP-2005-29, Institute for Logic, Language & Computation, University of Amsterdam.
van Benthem, J., van Eijck, J., & Kooi, B. (2006). Logics of communication and change. *Information and Computation, 204*(11), 1620–1662.
Wessel, H. (1989). *Logik*. Berlin: Logos Verlag.

Chapter 3
Knowledge and Disagreement

Martin Montminy

3.1 Introduction

Epistemic contextualism holds that the content of a knowledge sentence of the form 'S knows that P' is context sensitive. This view respects the context sensitivity of ordinary speakers' use of knowledge sentences. But this context sensitivity can be accommodated equally well by relativism, which holds that the content of a knowledge sentence is the same in every context, but the truth-value of this content depends on context-sensitive epistemic standards. Relativists argue that their view should be preferred to contextualism, because it respects what we may call the *intuition of disagreement*: ordinary speakers take themselves to be disagreeing with speakers in contexts where different epistemic standards prevail. I will distinguish between two forms of relativism, and show that neither can provide a better account of disagreement than contextualism. The intuition of disagreement thus does not favor the relativist's revisionist semantics over contextualism. I will explain briefly how contextualism can account for the intuition of disagreement.

3.2 Contextualism

Epistemic contextualism holds that different utterances of the same knowledge sentence of the form 'S knows that P' express different propositions in different contexts – even when 'S' and 'P' do not contain any indexical or context-sensitive expression. To support their view, contextualists invoke data about the context sensitivity of ordinary speakers' use of knowledge sentences. What proposition an

M. Montminy (✉)
Department of Philosophy, University of Oklahoma, 455 West Lindsey Street,
Norman, OK 73019-2006, USA
e-mail: montminy@ou.edu

F. Lihoreau and M. Rebuschi (eds.), *Epistemology, Context, and Formalism*,
Synthese Library 369, DOI 10.1007/978-3-319-02943-6_3,

utterance of 'S knows that P' expresses depends on the epistemic standards in place in the context of utterance. In ordinary, everyday contexts, the epistemic standards are low. So when a speaker located in such a context says, 'I know that birds are dinosaurs,' he is asserting that he knows that birds are dinosaurs relative to low epistemic standards. And when a skeptic in a "high-standards" context says, 'We don't know that birds are dinosaurs,' she is asserting that we do not know that birds are dinosaurs relative to high epistemic standards.[1]

Contextualism, it is often argued, fails to respect what we may call our *intuition of disagreement*: we have the impression that the skeptic, who denies that we 'know' anything, disagrees with ordinary speakers, who take themselves to 'know' many things. Consider the following exchange:

Judge: Did you know on December 10 that your car was in your driveway?
Sam: Yes, your honor. I knew this.
Judge: Were you in a position to rule out the possibility that your car had been stolen?
Sam: No, I wasn't.
Judge: So you didn't know that your car was in the driveway, did you?
Sam: No, I suppose I didn't, your honor (MacFarlane 2005, p. 210).

Judge takes herself to be disagreeing with Sam (at least until he retracts his initial knowledge claim). And it is also our impression, as external observers, that there is a disagreement between them. But, the objection goes, contextualism holds that the content of Sam's initial knowledge claim is that he knew that his car was in the driveway relative to low epistemic standards, whereas the content of Judge's knowledge denial is that Sam did not know that his car was in the driveway relative to high epistemic standards: these two contents are perfectly compatible. It thus seems that contextualism fails to respect the perceived disagreement between Sam and Judge.

Contextualism, the objection continues, also fails to explain Sam's retraction. As MacFarlane points out, it would be odd for Sam to say, "My claim was that on December 10. I knew, by the standards for knowledge that were in play before you mentioned car thieves, that my car was in my driveway. That was true, your honor, so I did not speak falsely." (ibid.) But this is the kind of response contextualism would predict. Hence, this view cannot explain Sam's concession that his initial knowledge claim was false.

Before I go on to explain why relativism is thought to avoid these problems, I want to say a few words about MacFarlane's case. It is far from clear that such a case poses a problem for contextualism. This view does not hold that

[1] I will remain neutral about what *epistemic standards* consist in. Contextual variations in epistemic standards may be identified with variations in the alternatives the subject must rule out, or with the set of possible worlds in which the subject must track the truth, or with some other epistemic requirement. Furthermore, I will remain neutral between the following two contextualist accounts: an indexicalist view that holds that the predicate 'know' is context sensitive and designates a binary relation (between a person and a proposition) corresponding to different epistemic standards in different contexts; and an account according to which 'know' designates a ternary relation between a subject, a proposition and (context-sensitive) epistemic standards.

every speaker's retraction of a prior knowledge attribution is tied to a shift in epistemic standards. Perhaps no such shift occurred during Sam's conversation with Judge. Contextualists could legitimately complain that MacFarlane's story is under-described: since we are not told enough about Sam's practical interests, such as his presuppositions, purposes, intentions, etc., it is unclear whether the epistemic standards associated with his knowledge attribution are the same as those associated with his knowledge denial. Indeed, it is plausible to hold that they have remained the same throughout the whole conversation. First, Sam's initial knowledge claim is made in the courtroom, where, we can presume, default epistemic standards are high. In a courtroom, the stakes are high, since mistakes can have serious practical consequences, and this tends to put in place relatively high epistemic standards. The fact that high standards prevailed right from the start is also suggested by Sam's disposition to concede that he did not know, *immediately* after having heard the error possibility introduced by Judge. There is thus a plausible story contextualists can tell as to why we have the impression that Judge and Sam disagree: in giving his initial answer to Judge, Sam *wrongly* neglected to consider error possibilities such as the one mentioned by Judge, for according to the high standards Sam was already associating with his knowledge claim, he should have been in a position to rule out such error possibilities in order to count as 'knowing.'

Furthermore, contextualists can hold what Keith DeRose (2004) calls a *single scoreboard view*, according to which there is only one set of epistemic standards in place in a given conversational contexts. On a single scoreboard view, two speakers who are engaged in a debate about whether a certain subject 'knows' that P are in disagreement, for the knowledge attribution and the knowledge denial are made according to the same epistemic standards. This means that to be at least prima facie problematic for contextualism, a case should involve two conversational contexts in which different epistemic standards are in place.[2]

Furthermore, the case should be *properly constructed*, to borrow DeRose (2005) phrase; that is, speakers in both contexts should be informed about the all the relevant features of the other context, such as the purposes, presuppositions, interests, intentions and raised error possibilities. The problem is that the intuition of disagreement is much less strong where properly constructed cases are concerned.[3] Consider for example a case involving a speaker currently in a low-standards context who is considering her own prior knowledge denial made in a high-standards context. Yasmine asks her friend Leila if she knows what the capital of Qatar is. 'I know,' replies Leila, 'it's Doha.' Aisha, who overhears the exchange, reminds Leila that yesterday, during the epistemology seminar, she denied she 'knew' anything.

[2]However, as I argue in my Montminy (2013), there are good reasons to reject the single scoreboard view. See also DeRose (2009, pp. 148–152), for a proposal about how to deal with cases in which a speaker says, 'S knows that P,' and another speaker in a later context disputes the first speaker's claim. Although I do not have the room to discuss this proposal here, I should mention that many of my objections against the single scoreboard view also apply to it.

[3]DeRose (2005) makes the same point.

Would Leila think that she is disagreeing with her prior self? Or, to put the question differently, would she consider that she was wrong yesterday to say that she ‘doesn’t know’ anything, or that she was wrong just now to hold that she ‘knows’ that Doha is the capital of Qatar? These questions, it seems to me, do not have *obvious* answers, and I doubt that speakers in Leila’s situation would have a clear sense of how to answer them. They would likely experience some tension between their uses of ‘know’ on the two occasions, but it is far from clear that this tension should be explained by the fact that what they said on one occasion contradicts what they said on the other.[4]

At any rate, for the sake of the argument, let us assume that Judge and Sam are located in two different contexts: Sam is (at least initially) in a low-standards context and Judge is in a high-standards context. Let us also assume that Sam and Judge are each informed about all the relevant features of the other speaker’s context, and that both have the impression that they disagree with each other. In the next few sections, I will examine how relativism proposes to account for this disagreement.

3.3 Relativism

Like contextualism, relativism holds that knowledge claims have context-sensitive truth values; however, unlike contextualism, it denies that the *content* of a knowledge claim is context sensitive. According to relativism, Judge rejects the very same proposition that Sam accepts. Relativists can achieve this result by positing “non-classical” propositions.

Propositions are generally thought to have truth values relative to *circumstances of evaluation*. These are typically regarded as possible worlds. However, according to *temporalists*, circumstances of evaluation also include times. On this view, the proposition that Napoleon is frowning is *temporally neutral*, that is, it does not contain a specification of time. That same proposition may be true at one time and false at another time. Two utterances of ‘Napoleon is frowning’ made at two different times t_1 and t_2 express the same (temporally neutral) proposition, namely that Napoleon is frowning. And an utterance of ‘Napoleon is frowning’ is true just in case the proposition it expresses is true at the time and world of the context of utterance. By contrast, eternalism holds that propositions have their truth-values eternally: their truth-values are relative to worlds, but not to times. On this view, an utterance of ‘Napoleon is frowning’ made at time t_1 expresses the eternal proposition that Napoleon is frowning at t_1, while an utterance of ‘Napoleon is frowning’ made at time t_2 expresses the proposition that Napoleon is frowning at t_2.

Relativism about knowledge claims holds that the proposition that S knows that P is *epistemic-standard-neutral*. This means that pace the contextualist, rather than belonging to the propositional content of an utterance of ‘S knows that P,’ epistemic

[4] I will say more about how contextualists can deal with this issue in Sect. 3.7.

standards are elements of the circumstances of evaluation. Like contextualism, relativism respects our use of simple knowledge claims of the form 'S knows that P': the standard-neutral proposition that Sam knew his car was in the driveway is true relative to Sam's low epistemic standards, and false relative to Judge's high epistemic standards. Furthermore, relativism claims to respect the intuition of disagreement, since Sam accepts the same proposition that Judge rejects.

But this issue deserves more scrutiny. First, we need to distinguish between two forms of relativism that differ as to how knowledge claims (or assertions, or beliefs) should be assessed. MacFarlane (2007) uses the term 'acceptance' to apply to both assertion and belief. When convenient, I will follow this usage.[5] According to *moderate* relativism, a knowledge claim (or acceptance) is true just in case the standard-neutral proposition expressed by that claim is true relative to the standards in place in the context of utterance.[6] Hence, Sam's knowledge claim is true just in case the proposition that he knew his car was in the driveway is true relative to low standards. According to moderate relativism, a given knowledge claim has the same truth-value, regardless of the context in which it is assessed. Again, this is because epistemic standards relevant to assessing a knowledge claim are fixed by the context of utterance.

According to *radical* relativism, the standards that are relevant to evaluating a knowledge claim (or acceptance) are those in place in the context of assessment. Hence, the same knowledge claim may be assigned different truth-values in different contexts of assessment. Although Sam's claim 'I knew my car was in the driveway' is true relative to low standards, it is false relative to high standards. The revisionist semantics proposed by radical relativism thus involves two major departures from traditional accounts: first, instead of being included in the propositional content of a knowledge claim, epistemic standards belong to the circumstances of evaluation of that claim; second, unlike other parameters of the circumstances of evaluation such as world and time, which are fixed by the context of utterance, epistemic standards are fixed by the context of assessment.

3.4 The Moderate Relativist's Account of Disagreement

How does relativism account for disagreement? Let us start with moderate relativism. On this view, disagreement results from the fact that Judge rejects the same proposition Sam accepts, namely that Sam knew his car was in the driveway. Unfortunately, this is not sufficient for disagreement. Consider again temporalism, which is a form of moderate relativism. On this view, an utterance of 'Napoleon is frowning' is true just in case the temporally neutral proposition it expresses, namely

---

[5] However, unlike MacFarlane, I will talk of the *truth* of an acceptance rather than its *accuracy*. This terminological difference will not affect the points made here.

[6] Moderate relativism is the view that MacFarlane (2009) calls *nonindexical contextualism*.

that Napoleon is frowning, is true relative to the context of utterance. Suppose that at 2 pm, Joséphine says, 'Napoleon is frowning,' whereas at 3 pm, Marie Louise says, 'Napoleon is not frowning.' Suppose further that Napoleon was frowning at 2 pm, and was not frowning at 3 pm. According to temporalism, both Joséphine's and Marie Louise's utterances are true. Furthermore, according to temporalism, Marie Louise rejects the very same proposition that Joséphine accepts, namely, the temporally neutral proposition that Napoleon is frowning. But obviously, there is no disagreement between Joséphine and Marie Louise. This shows that the moderate relativist's account of disagreement is unsatisfactory. On this view, disagreement cannot simply amount to the fact that one speaker rejects the proposition that another speaker accepts.[7]

The same point holds regarding the view according to which there are *locationally neutral propositions*, expressed by utterances such as 'It's raining.'[8] We would not regard Joe, who says, 'It's raining,' in Seattle, and Sally, who utters, 'It's not raining,' in Las Vegas, as disagreeing, even though, on this view, Sally denies the same locationally neutral proposition that Joe accepts. The same point applies to views advocating *centered propositions*, expressed by such utterances as 'I am in New York.'[9] On such views, disagreement does not occur whenever a speaker rejects the same centered proposition another speaker accepts.[10]

To be clear, this does not mean that we should reject the simple account of disagreement, according to which two speakers disagree if one rejects a proposition that the other accepts.[11] The eternalist, for example, can accept the simple account without being committed to holding that Joséphine disagrees with Marie Louise, for the (eternal) proposition rejected by the latter (i.e., that Napoleon was frowning at 2 pm) is not the same as the eternal proposition accepted by former (i.e., that Napoleon was frowning at 3 pm). The moral is rather that a view such as temporalism, which invokes temporally neutral propositions, cannot endorse the

[7] MacFarlane (2007, p. 22) makes the same point.

[8] On this view, the propositional content expressed by an utterance of 'It's raining' does not contain a location: the location is rather included in the circumstances of evaluation.

[9] Roughly, centered propositions have truth-values relative to a world and a center, that is, an agent and time. So the centered proposition that I am in New York is true at a world/time/agent triple $< w, t, i >$ just in case i is in New York at t in w.

[10] Or consider agents in two different worlds (or the same agent in actual and counterfactual situations) respectively believing that P and believing that not-P. It seems that these agents are not in disagreement, since their beliefs concern different worlds. See MacFarlane (2007, p. 23) for the same point. However, Cappelen and Hawthorne (2009, pp. 63–66) dispute this intuition.

[11] Note that disagreement can also occur between two speakers if they do not give the same credence to a certain proposition, say, if one is extremely confident that P and the other merely thinks that it is likely that P.

simple account of disagreement. On this view, the fact that a speaker rejects the proposition accepted by another speaker does not entail that the two speakers are in disagreement.

This shows that moderate relativists cannot hold that the disagreement between Judge and Sam amounts to the fact that Judge rejects the same (standard-neutral) proposition Sam accepts. Moderate relativism cannot endorse the simple account of disagreement, according to which two speakers disagree if one rejects a proposition that the other accepts. Hence, the alleged advantage of moderate relativism over contextualism does not withstand scrutiny.

The account of disagreement proposed by Max Kölbel (2004) faces the same problem.[12] Kölbel writes, "every thinker *possesses* a perspective, and moreover everyone ought not to believe contents that are not true in relation to their own perspective" (p. 307). Kölbel uses this constraint on belief to account for disagreement. On his view, two speakers disagree if they could not rationally believe the (perspective-neutral) proposition asserted by the other without changing their minds. Judge's perspective involves high epistemic standards. Given that she ought not to believe something that is not true relative to these high standards, she could not come to believe what Sam said without changing her mind.

But as we just saw, this account of disagreement cannot work. To see why, let us apply the account to the case of Marie Louise and Joséphine. Joséphine's perspective includes the time 2 pm. Given that she ought not to believe something that is not true relative to this time, she could not come to believe what Marie Louise said without changing her mind. But clearly, there is no disagreement between Marie Louise and Joséphine. To repeat, the fact that there is a proposition a speaker rejects relative to a perspective and that another speaker accepts relative to a different perspective does not entail that the two speakers disagree.

The moderate relativist's proposed account of disagreement thus fails. An important lesson of this discussion is that the perspectives by which speakers accept or reject a proposition should be taken into consideration when figuring out whether these speakers disagree. My objection to the radical relativist's account of disagreement will draw from this lesson.

3.5 The Radical Relativist's Account of Disagreement

Let us now look at the radical relativist's account of disagreement. According to radical relativism, Sam's knowledge claim, as assessed by Judge, is false, since the proposition it expresses, namely that Sam knew his car was in the driveway, is false relative to high standards. The radical relativist can thus account for disagreement as follows: Judge takes herself to be disagreeing with Sam, because she rejects his knowledge claim.

---

[12]Kölbel's view is a form of moderate relativism.

But this is not quite the way MacFarlane (2007) proposes to account for disagreement. On his view, two speakers disagree (as assessed from context C) if (a) there is a proposition that one speaker accepts and the other rejects, and (b) the acceptance and the rejection cannot both be true (as assessed from C). The problem with this account is that it does not tell us what it is that the speakers disagree about. Or to put the point slightly differently, it does not tell us the location of the disagreement. An account of disagreement, it seems, should explain that; in other words it should specify what the *target* of disagreement is.

To appreciate this point, consider the following response contextualists could give to the objection that their view fails to account for disagreement. According to contextualism, the response goes, two speakers disagree if (a) there is a (context-sensitive) sentence that one speaker accepts in context C_1 and the other rejects in context C_2, and (b) there is no single context in which the context-sensitive sentence can be truthfully accepted and rejected.[13] On this account, Judge and Sam disagree, since (a) there is a knowledge sentence (namely, 'Sam knew his car was in the driveway') that Sam accepts in his low-standards context and Judge rejects in her high-standards context, and (b) that sentence cannot be truthfully accepted and rejected in the same context.

Such an account of disagreement is unsatisfactory, because it is silent about what Sam and Judge disagree about. True, the sentence 'Sam knew his car was in the driveway' can be truthfully accepted in a low-standards context but not in a high-standards context. But why should this entail that Judge disagrees with Sam, given that Sam accepted the knowledge sentence, not in a high-standards context, but only in a low-standards context? Contextualists need to explain just what it is that Judge takes herself to be disagreeing with. And they cannot hold that the target of disagreement is Sam's acceptance of the knowledge sentence, without attributing an error to Judge. If contextualism is correct, Judge should assess Sam's acceptance of the knowledge sentence according to low standards; and if she did so, she would have no grounds for disagreement.

This point can be made more simply with the following example. The sentence 'Today is Monday' is context-sensitive, and there is no single context in which it can be truthfully accepted and rejected. However, we should not hold that there is any disagreement between two speakers on the basis of the fact that one accepts this sentence on Monday and the other rejects it on Tuesday.

In this respect, radical relativism seems to be at an advantage, for it can hold that Judge takes herself to be disagreeing with Sam, because she rejects his acceptance of the proposition that he knew his car was in the driveway. And she can do so without making an error, for according to radical relativism, she should assess Sam's acceptance relative to high standards. So radical relativism can hold that Judge's disagreement with Sam does have a target: it is Sam's acceptance of the proposition that he knew his car was in the driveway.

[13] Beebe (2010, p. 706) for a similar account. Note that this account talks about the acceptance (rejection) of sentences rather than propositions.

Unfortunately, this account does not explain disagreement. What is the mental attitude Sam expresses in uttering 'I knew my car was in the driveway'? Saying that it is the belief that Sam knew his car was in the driveway, does not completely capture Sam's state of mind. On the radical relativist's account, one cannot believe a standard-neutral proposition without employing some epistemic standards. Hence, the standard by which Sam accepts the proposition should be made explicit if one wants to fully specify his state of mind. This point applies to any view according to which the truth of a proposition is relative to a perspective. The temporalist, for example, should hold that in uttering 'Napoleon is frowning' at 2 pm, Joséphine expresses her belief that Napoleon is frowning, relative to 2 pm. Similarly, fully specified, Sam's attitude is the belief that he knew his car was in the driveway, relative to low standards. But Judge does not disagree with that: she would grant that, relative to low epistemic standards, it is true that Sam knew his car was in the driveway. What Judge rejects is the proposition that Sam knew his car was in the driveway. She also rejects Sam's knowledge acceptance of that proposition. But Judge should not find anything wrong with Sam, since his acceptance is relative to low standards, whereas her rejection is relative to high standards.[14]

It is important to be clear about what radical relativists can explain and what they cannot explain. They can explain why a speaker in a high-standards context may say, 'No, that's not true,' regarding a knowledge attribution made by a speaker in a low-standards context. This is because the speaker in the high-standards context employs high standards to assess the knowledge attribution. But they cannot explain the disagreement between the two speakers, for the knowledge attribution is made relative to low standards, whereas its assessment is made relative to high standards.

Of course, Judge might mistakenly believe that Sam employs high standards. This would explain why she takes herself to be disagreeing with him, but it would provide no comfort to the radical relativist. An adequate theory cannot rely on the judgment of an assessor who is mistaken about another speaker's perspective. If she mistakenly assumes that Joséphine uttered 'Napoleon is frowning' at the same time as she uttered 'Napoleon isn't frowning,' Marie Louise will form the impression she disagrees with Joséphine. But this does not count as an admissible datum that a theory should explain. Similarly, we should be concerned only with assessors who are informed about the perspectives by which the claims they evaluate are made. This, it seems to me, raises doubts about the kind of cases invoked by relativists against contextualism. If it were made clear to Judge that Sam made his assertion relative to low standards, would she be inclined to disagree with him? As I indicated at the end of Sect. 3.2, I doubt that Judge would have a clear inclination. In Sect. 3.7, I will examine this question further. But first, I must consider some possible responses to my criticism of the radical relativist's account of disagreement.

[14]Perhaps Judge thinks Sam is wrong to employ low standards, and this is where their disagreement is located. This suggestion, which strikes me as plausible, will be discussed further in Sect. 3.7.

3.6 Possible Responses

It may be thought that my criticism is based on a misconstrual of radical relativism. According to this view, the standards by which one ought to assess a knowledge claim (and the proposition it expresses) are the ones in place in one's own context. This is why, on the radical relativist account, the standards by which Judge should evaluate Sam's knowledge claim are the high standards of her context. Hence, it is perfectly acceptable for Judge to ignore the standards by which Sam makes his knowledge claim, and conclude that they disagree, for his claim is false relative to her standards.

Let us assume that the radical relativist's story about how knowledge claims are to be assessed is correct: Judge ought to employ her own standards in assessing Sam's knowledge claim. This still does not yield an account of disagreement between Judge and Sam. Judge will reject Sam's acceptance of the proposition that he knew his car was in the driveway; but this is just because she assesses Sam's acceptance relative to her high standards, rather than relative to the standards Sam employs. Hence, the radical relativist's story explains why Judge rejects Sam's knowledge claim, but it does not entail any disagreement between Judge and Sam, for Sam's knowledge claim is made relative to low standards, while Judge's assessment is made relative to high standards.

The radical relativist could respond that what Judge objects to is not Sam's acceptance of the proposition that he knew his car was in the driveway, relative to his low standards; what she objects to is Sam's acceptance of that proposition *simpliciter*. Since this acceptance is incorrect, relative to Judge's high standards, Sam and Judge disagree.

Once again, the fact that Judge objects to Sam's acceptance of the proposition that he knew his car was in the driveway does not entail that she disagrees with him. It is also the case that Sam accepts the proposition that he knew his car was in the driveway, relative to his low standards. Relativists cannot reject the latter description of Sam's acceptance. But the accuracy of such a description should dispel the impression that Judge and Sam disagree.

Perhaps radical relativists could invoke the fact that according to their view, a speaker possesses a particular perspective, and cannot but evaluate a claim or a belief from that perspective. In other words, an assessor can occupy only one context of assessment. Following Kent Bach (2011), call this *perspectival solipsism*. If Judge can entertain the proposition that Sam knew his car was in the driveway only relative to high standards, and this proposition is false relative to high standards, then she is bound to disapprove of all who accept that proposition, regardless of the standards they employ. Therefore, once she learns that Sam accepts the proposition that he knew his car was in the driveway, Judge takes herself to be disagreeing with him, because she cannot but consider that proposition relative to high standards.

The problem with this response is that the fact that Judge cannot but evaluate Sam's acceptance relative to high standards does not negate the fact that Sam's acceptance is formed relative to low standards. Perhaps Judge cannot but entertain the proposition that Sam knew his car was in the driveway relative to high standards. However, it remains the case that Sam accepts that proposition relative to low standards. And because of that, Judge and Sam cannot be said to disagree.

It may be thought that perspectival solipsism is inconsistent with relativism, for grasping the relativist thesis seems to require the ability to consider the same perspective-neutral proposition from different perspectives. Relativism holds that the standard-neutral proposition that S knows that P may be true relative to low epistemic standards, and false relative to high epistemic standards. Grasping this thesis seems to require that we be able to entertain the same proposition, namely, that S knows that P, relative to low standards and relative to high standards. But this is not the case, for we need not assume that relativism ought to be expressed in terms of standard-neutral propositions. Relativism can be articulated in terms of classical, standard-involving propositions such as the proposition *that S knows that P is true relative to low standards and the proposition that S does not know that P is true relative to high standards*. Hence, a relativist who is, say, in a high-standards context, will accept, relative to high standards, the standard-neutral proposition that S does not know that P; but the relativist can also accept the standard-involving proposition that S knows that P relative to low standards. Furthermore, our relativist can consider the standard-involving proposition that a given speaker accepts, relative to low standards, that S knows that P. The relativist can consider a perspective-neutral proposition only from her current perspective; however, nothing prevents her from considering perspective-involving propositions that involve perspectives other than her own.

But this highlights the inadequacy of the radical relativist's account of disagreement. If radical relativism is right, Sam accepts the standard-neutral proposition that he knew his car was in the driveway, relative to low standards. And when Judge assesses Sam's acceptance, she does so relative to high standards. But this does not prevent her from entertaining standard-involving propositions when she is considering Sam's state of mind. So, for instance, she can come to believe the standard-involving proposition that Sam accepts that he knew his car was in the driveway relative to low standards. And it seems that this is what Judge *should* do, if she wants to figure out whether she disagrees with Sam. But clearly, if Judge does that, it will not seem to her that she is disagreeing with Sam. Hence, the fact that Judge rejects the standard-neutral proposition that Sam accepts, as well as Sam's acceptance of that proposition, does not indicate any disagreement between Judge and Sam.

3.7 Disagreeing About Standards

Radical relativists may propose an alternative account of disagreement. They could hold that disagreement boils down to a dispute about the perspective one should take concerning a certain perspective-neutral proposition. On this view, Judge's disagreement with Sam concerns not Sam's acceptance of the (standard-neutral) proposition that he knew his car was in the driveway, but the standards Sam employs. In other words, while Judge thinks that high standards should be associated with knowledge claims, Sam is content to employ low standards. Some of MacFarlane's remarks are in this spirit. He writes, "If you say 'skiing is fun' and I contradict you, it is not because I think that the proposition you asserted is false as assessed by you in your current situation, with the affective attitudes you now have, but because I hope to change these attitudes. Perhaps, then, the point of using controversy inducing assessment-sensitive vocabulary is to foster coordination of contexts" (MacFarlane 2007, p. 30).[15]

I find this account of disagreement promising. Unfortunately for the relativist, such an account is also available to the contextualist. The contextualist can characterize the disagreement between Judge and Sam in a very similar way: Judge thinks the low standards employed by Sam are inadequate, and that high standards should be associated with knowledge claims. Judge disagrees with Sam, not because she rejects the content expressed by Sam's claim, but because she rejects the low standards he associates with that claim.

This account of disagreement attributes an error to Judge, but, such an error is understandable.[16] Let me begin by a comment made by Richard Lewontin in a recent piece he wrote for the *New York Review of Books*. Lewontin criticizes the tendency, among certain evolutionary biologists, to hold that the evidence that natural selection is the driving force of evolution is just as strong as the evidence that evolution has occurred. He writes, "There are different modes of 'knowing,' and we 'know' that evolution has, in fact, occurred in a stronger sense than we 'know' that some sequence of evolutionary change has been the result of natural selection" (Lewontin 2009, p. 21). Lewontin recognizes that 'know' has different uses, and proposes what we may call a 'proto-contextualist' account of that phenomenon.

The thesis that our use of 'know' is context sensitive is of course an empirical one, but despite some alleged evidence to the contrary,[17] I take this thesis to be well established. Many invariantists concede this thesis.[18] However, assuming that he is not acquainted with the literature on contextualism, Lewontin's remarks are quite perceptive. I would think that the context sensitivity in our use of 'know' is not

[15]It should be clear from this passage that MacFarlane defends a radical relativist account of judgments of taste such as 'Skiing is fun.'

[16]For more on this issue, see my Montminy (2009, 2013).

[17]See, for instance Buckwalter (2010) and May et al. (2010).

[18]Consider, for example, invariantists who favor what DeRose calls a *warranted assertability maneuver*. On this view, speakers often do not use 'S knows that P' literally. According to WAMs, what a speaker means in uttering 'S knows that P' may differ from what 'S knows that P' conventionally means. In some contexts, one may use 'know' to convey stronger (or weaker) epistemic standards than what 'know' conventionally requires. Hence, on this view, there is a possibility that you and I are not in disagreement if I say, 'We know that natural selection is the driving force of evolution' and you say, 'We don't know that natural selection is the driving force of evolution,' for one of us may not be speaking literally.

generally recognized by ordinary speakers. For this reason, many will tend to judge a speaker who says,

(1) We know that natural selection is the driving force of evolution,

in one context, as disagreeing with another speaker who says,

(2) We don't know that natural selection is the driving force of evolution,

in another context. So why isn't Lewontin's take on such cases more widespread?

There are two obstacles to reaching the conclusion that the two speakers are not in disagreement, and overcoming each obstacle requires complex and controversial reasoning. Because of that, it should not be surprising that ordinary speakers are inclined to regard the speakers as disagreeing.

The first obstacle is that it is far from clear that the speakers respectively uttering (1) and (2) are associating different epistemic standards with 'know.' Perhaps they do employ the same standards, but do not have access to the same evidence adduced in favor of natural selection, or do not assign the same credibility to alternative accounts of evolution, etc. In such cases, even contextualists would hold that one speaker is denying the same proposition accepted by the other. However, according to contextualism, there are cases in which the two speakers are associating different standards with 'know,' and their respective utterances of (1) and (2) do not express disagreement. Now the difficulty in recognizing such cases is that they are often very difficult to distinguish from cases of the first type in which there is no disagreement, even by the contextualist's lights.[19] Ordinary speakers should thus not be faulted for believing that the speakers who respectively utter (1) and (2) are disagreeing.

The second obstacle to judging that the speakers who respectively utter (1) and (2) are not disagreeing is also difficult to overcome. One may recognize that the two speakers are associating different epistemic standards with 'know' and still think that they are disagreeing. This would occur if one believes that the conventional meaning of 'know' entails invariant standards. And this is (probably) a popular belief. To be sure, ordinary speakers would be more likely to express this belief in the object language ('There are fixed requirements for knowledge') rather than meta-linguistically ('There are invariant standards associated with the conventional meaning of "know"'). If they hold this belief, our speakers will be inclined to think that they disagree with each other, not because they think that the content of the other's claim is false, but because they think that the other is using 'know' incorrectly, or more simply, because they think that the other is wrong about what knowledge requires.

Contextualists, it seems to me, should not be troubled by the fact that ordinary speakers tend to subscribe to the thesis that the standards for knowledge are

[19] What epistemic standards is G.E. Moore invoking when he claims to 'know' that he has hands? He is typically assumed to adopt low epistemic standards, but BonJour (2010, p. 78) holds that Moore claims to meet the skeptic's high standards. This interpretive issue is, it seems to me, far from easy to resolve.

invariant. Unlike sentences containing obvious indexicals such as 'here' and 'now,' knowledge sentences do not wear their context sensitivity on their sleeves. Figuring out that sentences of the form 'S knows that P' lack context-independent truth conditions (or that there is no such a thing as *knowing that P, simpliciter*), requires complex theoretical considerations, and ordinary speakers can hardly be faulted for failing to effortlessly reach the correct view on this matter. In other words, it should not trouble contextualists that unlike Lewontin, ordinary folks are not inclined to conclude that there is no unique sense of 'know.'[20]

There are, we have seen, two obstacles to judging that the speakers respectively uttering (1) and (2) are not disagreeing. First, it is no simple task to figure out that different standards are employed by these speakers. Cases in which different standards are employed by different speakers can be quite difficult to distinguish from cases in which speakers employ the same standards but disagree about whether the putative knower satisfies these standards. Hence, the failure to recognize that the speakers associate different standards with 'know' is an understandable mistake. The second obstacle concerns the question whether the correct and literal use of 'know' is governed by invariant epistemic standards. The fact that ordinary speakers tend to think that it is should not be held against contextualism, for this is a theoretical question about which we should not expect a convergence of opinion among ordinary people, and even specialists.

It should be clear that a relativist account that holds that the disagreement between the speakers who respectively utter (1) and (2) boils down to a disagreement about epistemic standards entails the same kind of error. If the person uttering (2) were a relativist, she would have to grant that 'know' can be associated with different standards in different contexts, and that no standards can be regarded as privileged. Perhaps she would hold that certain epistemic standards are most appropriate, given her own presuppositions, interests, purposes, etc. But she would not hold that all knowledge claims ought to be associated with such standards. Hence, she would not take herself to be disagreeing with the speaker uttering (1). In other words, from the relativist's perspective, it is a mistake for the speaker of (2) to see herself as disagreeing with the speaker of (1).

3.8 Conclusion

Contextualism entails that ordinary speakers often mistakenly take themselves to be disagreeing with speakers located in contexts in which different epistemic standards are in place. I have shown that this mistake is understandable, since overcoming it

[20]To be accurate, contextualism does not hold that 'know' has multiple senses. According to the indexicalist view (see Footnote 1), 'know' has an invariant character, but a context-sensitive content. And on an alternative contextualist account, 'know' designates the same relation in every context; however, this relation involves context-sensitive epistemic standards.

requires sophisticated and controversial reasoning. But the main point of my paper is that relativism fares no better than contextualism regarding this mistake. Data about disagreement thus provide no reason to espouse the revisionist relativistic semantics.[21]

References

Bach, K. (2011). Perspectives on possibilities. In A. Egan & B. Weatherson (Eds.), *Epistemic modality* (pp. 19–59). Oxford: Oxford University Press.

Beebe, J. (2010). Moral relativism in context. *Noûs, 44*, 691–724.

BonJour, L. (2010). The myth of knowledge. *Philosophical Perspectives, 24*(1), 57–83.

Buckwalter, W. (2010). Knowledge isn't closed on saturdays. *Review of Philosophy and Psychology, 1*, 395–406.

Cappelen, H., & Hawthorne, J. (2009). *Relativism and monadic truth*. Oxford: Oxford University Press.

DeRose, K. (2004). Single scoreboard semantics. *Philosophical Studies, 119*, 1–21.

DeRose, K. (2005). The ordinary language basis for contextualism and the new invariantism. *Philosophical Quarterly, 55*, 172–198.

DeRose, K. (2009). *The case for contextualism, vol. 1: knowledge, skepticism, and context*. Oxford: Clarendon.

Kölbel, M. (2004). Indexical relativism versus genuine relativism. *International Journal of Philosophical Studies, 12*, 297–313.

Lewontin, R. (2009, May 28). Why Darwin? *New York Review of Books, 61*, 19–22.

MacFarlane, J. (2005). The assessment sensitivity of knowledge attributions. In T. Szabó Gendler & J. Hawthorne (Eds.), *Oxford studies in epistemology* (Vol. 1, pp. 197–233). Oxford: Oxford University Press.

MacFarlane, J. (2007). Relativism and disagreement. *Philosophical Studies, 132*, 17–31.

MacFarlane, J. (2009). Nonindexical contextualism. *Synthese, 166*, 231–250.

May, J., Sinnott-Armstrong, W., Hull, J. G., & Zimmerman, A. (2010). Practical interests, relevant alternatives, and knowledge attributions: an empirical study. *Review of Philosophy and Psychology, 1*, 265–273.

Montminy, M. (2009). Contextualism, invariantism and semantic blindness. *Australasian Journal of Philosophy, 87*, 639–657.

Montminy, M. (2013). The role of context in contextualism. *Synthese*, 190, 2341–2366.

[21] I am grateful to Sherri Irvin for useful comments on an earlier version of this article.

Chapter 4
A Contradiction for Contextualism?

Peter Baumann

Epistemic contextualism concerning knowledge says that the truth conditions of knowledge attributions (including denials of knowledge) vary with the context of the attributor (cf. Cohen 1987; Lewis 1996; DeRose 1999). There have been recently quite a number of objections to contextualism (cf., e.g., Rysiew 2009). One objection, however, has not been discussed much at all even though it might be the most serious one so far: the so-called "Factivity Objection" according to which contextualism is inconsistent at its core. This objection has been developed mainly by Brendel (2003, 2005) and Wright (2005); see also, from a different perspective, Lihoreau and Rebuschi (2009) (cf. also short passages in Luper (2003, pp. 196–7), Veber (2004, pp. 268–269), Brueckner (2004), Engel (2005, pp. 58, 63), Kompa (2005, pp. 18–19, 25–26), Kallestrup (2005), Steup (2005, Sect. 1–2, 6), and Montminy (2008)). In my Baumann (2008) I defended the idea that there is a problem (cf. Brueckner and Buford 2009; Baumann 2010; Brueckner and Buford 2010 for an exchange on this) but also proposed a solution, namely a relationalist version of contextualism. In this paper I will first present the problem and then discuss some proposed solutions (some of them denying that there is a problem in the first place) before I move on to my own proposal of a solution.

4.1 The Problem

Consider two knowledge attributors, Ordi and Spec. Ordi finds herself in an ordinary and not so demanding context while Spec finds herself in a much more demanding (but not skeptical) context S. According to contextualists, the epistemic standards

P. Baumann (✉)
Department of Philosophy, Swarthmore College, 500 College Avenue,
Swarthmore, PA 19081, USA
e-mail: pbauman1@swarthmore.edu

F. Lihoreau and M. Rebuschi (eds.), *Epistemology, Context, and Formalism*,
Synthese Library 369, DOI 10.1007/978-3-319-02943-6_4,

for the correct attribution of knowledge vary with the context of the attributor. A given knowledge sentence can be true as uttered in one context but false as uttered in another context; it can be true (false) in one context while its negation can also be true (false) in another context. So, let us assume that the following is true:

(1) Ordi's utterance of "Spec knows that Spec has hands" in O is true,

and

(2) Spec's utterance of "Spec knows that Spec has hands" in S is not true.

Suppose now that Spec is a contextualist about knowledge. Since Spec does not find herself in a dramatic skeptical context, she can still correctly claim knowledge of some propositions. For instance, she can correctly claim to know (1). Why should this not be possible for Spec (see below)? Thus, we get

(3) Spec's utterance of "Spec knows that (1)" in S is true.

Furthermore, a plausible general disquotation principle tells us that

$$\text{“}p\text{” is true} \rightarrow p$$

while the principle of factivity of knowledge tells us that

$$(\text{S knows that } p) \rightarrow p.$$

Both combined and adjusted for contextualism (I won't go into the details here) we get

(DF) "S knows that p" (as uttered in some context) is true $\rightarrow p$.

And (DF) applied to (1) gives us

(4) Ordi's utterance of "Spec knows that Spec has hands" in O is true $\rightarrow$ Spec has hands.

There is certainly no problem for Spec to correctly claim knowledge of (4). Hence, we get

(5) Spec's utterance of "Spec knows that (4)" in S is true.

Finally, we should assume a closure principle which is adapted to the needs of the contextualist:

(Closure) For all contexts C, speakers S and propositions p, q: ["S knows that p" (as uttered in C) is true and "S knows that $(p \rightarrow q)$" (as uttered in C) is true] $\rightarrow$ "S knows that q" (as uttered in C) is true.

A more adequate closure principle would look a bit more complicated (see Baumann 2011) but for our purposes here we can stick with this simple version.

The important point here is that from (3) and (5) plus (Closure) it follows that

(6) Spec's utterance of "Spec knows that Spec has hands" in S is true.

And (6) contradicts (2). This is the threat of inconsistency contextualism faces.

What can the contextualist do about this? Something must be given up. (1)–(3) express what a contextualist seems committed to in our example. Principles of disquotation, factivity and closure should not be given up (certainly not just in order to save some epistemological theory). (5) is unproblematic. But (3), (5) and (Closure) entail (6) which contradicts (2). Should we therefore give up the weakest link, namely contextualism?

4.2 Ways Out?

Interestingly, many people deny that there is a problem for contextualism in the first place and argue that (3) is false. One way to do this is to point out that if Spec finds herself in a skeptical context, then she could not correctly claim any knowledge in that context. However, a demanding context like S need not be a skeptical one (see above). It also won't help much to argue that (3) must be false because it leads, 3 together with the unproblematic (5) and (Closure) to a contradiction for contextualism. This would be a case of begging the question against the view that there is a contradiction here. Similarly implausible is the idea that since (2) is true, (6) must be false; since (6) follows from (3), (5) and (Closure) and since (5) and Closure are non-negotiable, (3) must be false. Again, this kind of move begs the question against the inconsistency objection.

More interesting is another way to argue against (3) (for all this see also Brueckner and Buford 2009, 2010). Roughly, one could say that in order for A to know that B knows that *p*, A needs to know that *p* herself:

(A knows that B knows that *p*) → A knows that *p*.

Applied to our case concerning contextualism we get:

(3) → (6).

And since (6) is false, according to contextualism, (3) must be false, too, so the argument goes.

If this is not just the question begging point above again – (6) is false because (2) is true –, then there must be something else behind this argument against (3). The most promising move I can think of is based on a principle of epistemic priority according to which (in its more straightforward non-contextualist version)

(EP) (A knows that B knows that *p*) → A knows (independently from and prior to the knowledge that B knows that *p*) that *p*.

A contextualist version of such a principle of epistemic priority would look a bit more complicated; I won't go into this here because the basic point does not depend on such variations.

The problem is simply that (EP) is not true. Consider this example. I know, four having read a reliable newspaper, that Andrew Wiles found out, proved and came to know that Fermat's conjecture is true. I myself thus came to know that Fermat's conjecture is true. However, I was able to come to know that Wiles knows that Fermat was right without independently – and prior to reading the papers – knowing that Fermat was right (for the contextualist, all this will be a bit more complicated to express; see below for some aspects). (EP) is false and the argument against (3) relying on it does not go through.

But can it really be correct to say in a demanding context that "S knows that B knows that *p*" – when it is not correct to say in that demanding context that "S knows that *p*"? Yes, that S meets the demanding standards for "knowledge" of B's epistemic situation concerning *p* does not entail that S also meets the demanding standards for "knowledge" concerning *p*. Even if (i) *B knows that p* entails (ii) *p*, it does not follow that meeting the epistemic standards relevant in a certain context for (i) entails meeting the epistemic standards relevant in that context for (ii) (for more on this, cf. Baumann 2008).

But doesn't all this neglect an important temporal aspect (cf. Brueckner and Buford 2010)? Sure, at an earlier time t_1 (2) might be true. But then, at t_2, Spec learns that (1) is the case and engages in some reasoning, arriving at a later time t_3 at a relevant conclusion concerning herself having hands such that (6) is true. At t_3 (but not at t_1) (6) will be true and (2) will be false – while at t_1 (2) is true and (6) is false. Hence, the contradiction evaporates. However, our problem does not depend on such an equivocation. (2) as well as (3) can easily be true at the same time t_1: (2) is true because Spec does not meet the relevant standards while (3) could be true on the basis of testimony (see above). (5) can also easily be true at the same time. Given (Closure) which is also true (not just at t_1), (6) just follows and must thus be true at t_1, too. Nothing changes if one replaces the non-dynamic (Closure) by some dynamic principle of closure with some temporal dimension (some transmission principle, for instance cf. Baumann 2011).

However, there is a kernel of truth in this kind of objection which will be brought out in the solution proposed below. Before I go into that, I should stress that denying (3) comes with serious costs. Under certain quite common conditions one subject cannot be correctly said to "know" another subject's epistemic situation:

(Restrict) For all subjects A and B, for all propositions *p*, and for all pairs of contexts O and S such that "A knows that *p*" is true in O but not true (false) in S: "S knows that 'A knows that *p*' is true in O" is not true in S.

This restriction (cf. Baumann 2008, p. 583) is very severe. Not only does it limit the statability of contextualism in non-trivial ways. It also seems like a truism that subjects can in principle and under non-extreme circumstances come to know about other subjects' epistemic situation without there being farreaching and systematic restrictions to this kind of knowledge. Giving up such a principle requires very good independent reasons. It is not enough to want to save some pet epistemic theory.

Adhering to something like (Restrict) or denying (3) also seems to commit the epistemologist to accepting utterances of abominable conjunctions (cf. DeRose 1995, pp. 27–29) by an epistemic subject in a demanding context, like Spec:

> I don't know whether Ordi knows I have hands but if my standards were less strict I might well know that!

4.3 A Relationist Solution

Here is a different thought which helps us dissolve the above paradox of contextualism. For independent reasons it is plausible to analyze the knowledge-relation not as a binary relation between a subject and a proposition ("S knows that *p*") but rather as a ternary relation between a subject, a proposition and an epistemic standard ("S knows – with respect to standard S – that *p*"; cf. Schaffer 2005 or Steup 2005, Sects. 2, 6). Let us, for the sake of simplicity, use the terms "knowledge-relative-to-low-standards" or "knowledge-low" on the one hand and "knowledge-relative-to-high-standards" or "knowledge-high" on the other hand (cf. Sosa 2004, pp. 43–44; Bach 2005, pp. 58–59; Cohen 2005, pp. 201–204). We can thus reformulate (1) and (2) above in the following way:

(1*) Spec knows-low that Spec has hands

and

(2*) Spec does not know-high that Spec has hands.

(1*) and (2*) do not themselves have context-sensitive truth conditions but that's fine and compatible with contextualism taken as a view about the truth conditions of our ordinary sentences and utterances.

(3) can be replaced by

(3*) Spec knows-high that (1*).

Or, spelled out in more detail: Spec knows-high that Spec knows-low that Spec has hands. This makes more specific sense of the more general remarks above that there can be different standards for knowing that "S knows that *p*" is true and for knowing that "*p*" is true.

(DF) as well as (4) and (5) also need slight modifications:

(DF*) (S knows-relative-to-some-standard that $p) \rightarrow p$,
(4*) (Spec knows-low that Spec has hands) $\rightarrow$ Spec has hands,
(5*) Spec knows-high that (4*).

Now, the crucial question here concerns the adequate closure principle. Given that a subject might meet high epistemic standards concerning "*p*" as well as concerning

"$p \rightarrow q$" but only low epistemic standards concerning "q", we have to modify (Closure) along the following lines (I won't give the non-relativized version here and will restrict myself to the case of two kinds of knowledge only):

(Closure*) For all subjects S, knowledge relations knows-low and know-high, and for all propositions p and q:
If (i) S knows-high that p and if (ii) S knows-high that ($p \rightarrow q$), then (iii) S knows-low that q.

Here is the application to our case of knowledge that someone knows:

(Closure**) For all subjects O and S, knowledge relations knows-low and know-high, and for all propositions p:
If (i) S knows-high that O knows-low that p and if (ii) S knows-high that [(O knows-low that p) $\rightarrow p$], then (iii) S knows-low that p.

(Closure**) seems plausible as soon as one accepts contextualism; hence, the contextualist should be allowed to help himself to such a modification of (Closure).

(Closure**), (3*) and (5*) entail that

(6**) Spec knows-low that Spec has hands.

However, (Closure**), (3*) and (5*) do not entail

(6) Spec's utterance of "Spec knows that Spec has hands" in S is true

or, in other words,

(6*) Spec knows-high that Spec has hands.

So, since we can only infer (6**) but not (6*) we do not get a contradition. (6**) is, in contrast to (6*), perfectly compatible with

(2*) Spec does not know-high that Spec has hands.

A relational version of contextualism thus avoids our contradiction; it shows how the argument for the contradiction between *(6) and (2)* equivocates on subtle context differences. This is a major advantage of relationalist contextualism over other versions of contextualism (e.g., purely indexical versions according to which "know" functions more or less like an essentially indexical expression). Relationalism can thus account for cross-context attributions – something that poses a serious difficulty for other versions of contextualism. It also explains in what sense subjects "lose" their knowledge when the attributor moves into a more demanding context and in what sense they "keep" it: Even if the subject may not know-high that p they might still know-low that p. Focusing exclusively on knowledge-high, the attributor might forget that there is still knowledge-low left. But contexts are not completely closed: Even if the context determines high standards one can still acknowledge, within that context, that the subject's epistemic position still satisfies less demanding standards.

Someone might doubt the generality of our solution and argue that we're still facing a problem. Assume again that Spec, the contextualist, finds herself in a demanding context. She accepts (see above)

(1) Ordi's utterance of "Spec knows that Spec has hands" in O is true

from which she can infer, using

(DF) "S knows that *p*" (as uttered in some context) is true $\rightarrow p$

that (given her knowledge that she is Spec)

(7) I have hands.

At the same time, given (2) Spec also accepts that (in her words)

(8) I don't know that I have hands.

This also commits Spec, in so far as she is rational, to the conjunction of (7) and (8), namely

(9) I have hands but I don't know that.

This, however, is clearly Moore-paradoxical and not acceptable (though not inconsistent) (cf. for this kind of objection, Williamson (2001, pp. 26–27) and Kallestrup (2005, pp. 249–50), as well as Hans Kamp in conversation).

However, given what I said above, the solution of this problem is straightforward. Spec, the contextualist in a demanding context, is not committed to (8) but only to

(8*) I don't know-high that I have hands.

No utterance of

(10) I have hands but I don't know-high that

is Moore-paradoxical or problematic in any way.

Similar things can be said about the problems arising with the change of context over time, especially when the attributor moves from a less demanding to a more demanding context. Doesn't it sound incoherent to say something of the form "Yesterday, in the pub, I knew that I have hands but now, in conversation with a skeptic, I don't know it any more!" (cf. DeRose 2009, Chap. 6)? No, and if one were more precise and less misleading one would rather say something along the lines of "Yesterday, in the pub, I knew by low standards that I have hands but now, talking to the skeptic, I realize that I don't know-high that".

4.4 Conclusion

In its most common form contextualism faces a serious objection: that it is simply inconsistent. I have tried to show that this objection needs to be taken seriously and that there is a way out for the contextualist if he opts for a particular version of contextualism: relationalist contextualism. This view can account for cross-context attributions of knowledge – something which creates problems for other versions of contextualism.

Acknowledgements I am grateful to Joachim Aufderheide, Anthony Bruecker, Christopher T. Buford, Nick Fenn, Carrie Jenkins, Darrell Rowbottom, Martin Montminy, Joe Salerno, Timothy Williamson, Crispin Wright, anonymous referees, and audiences at a conference on contextualism at the University of Stirling (March 20–21, 2004), at the Joint Session at the University of Manchester (July 8–11, 2005), a discussion group at the Aberdeen Philosophy Department, and at a workshop on Epistemology, Context, Formalism at the Université Nancy 2 (November 12–14, 2009).

References

Bach, K. (2005). The emperor's new "knows". In G. Preyer & G. Peter (Eds.), *Contextualism in philosophy: Knowledge, meaning, and truth*. Oxford: Clarendon.

Baumann, P. (2008). Contextualism and the factivity problem. *Philosophy and Phenomenological Research, 76*, 580–602.

Baumann, P. (2010). Factivity and contextualism. *Analysis, 70*(1), 82–89.

Baumann, P. (2011). Epistemic closure. In S. Bernecker & D. Pritchard (Eds.), *The Routledge companion to epistemology* (pp. 597–608). London: Routledge.

Brendel, E. (2003). Was Kontextualisten nicht wissen. *Deutsche Zeitschrift für Philosophie, 51*, 1015–1032.

Brendel, E. (2005). Why contextualists cannot know they are right: Self-refuting implications of contextualism. *Acta Analytica, 20-2*(35), 38–55.

Brueckner, A. (2004). The elusive virtues of contextualism. *Philosophical Studies, 118*, 401–405.

Brueckner, A., & Buford, C.T. (2009). Contextualism, ssi, and the factivity problem. *Analysis, 69*, 431–438.

Brueckner, A., & Buford, C.T. (2010). Reply to Baumann on factivity and contextualism. *Analysis, 70*(3), 486–489.

Cohen, S. (1987). Knowledge, context, and social standards. *Synthese, 73*, 3–26.

Cohen, S. (2005). Knowledge, speaker and subject. *Philosophical Quarterly, 55*, 199–212.

DeRose, K. (1995). Solving the skeptical problem. *The Philosophical Review, 104*, 1–52.

DeRose, K. (1999). Contextualism: An explanation and defense. In J. Greco & E. Sosa (Eds.), *The Blackwell guide to epistemology*. Oxford: Blackwell.

DeRose, K. (2009). *The case for contextualism, vol. 1: Knowledge, skepticism, and context*. Oxford: Clarendon.

Engel, M. (2005). A noncontextualist account of contextualist linguistic data. *Acta Analytica, 20-2*(35), 57–79.

Kallestrup, J. (2005). Contextualism between scepticism and common-sense. *Grazer Philosophische Studien, 69*(1), 247–253.

Kompa, N. (2005). The semantics of knowledge attributions. *Acta Analytica, 20-1*(34), 16–28.

Lewis, D. (1996). Elusive knowledge. *Australasian Journal of Philosophy, 74*, 549–567.

Lihoreau, F., & Rebuschi, M. (2009). Contextualism and the factivity of knowledge. In D. Łukasiewicz & R. Pouivet (Eds.), *Scientific knowledge and common knowledge*. Bydgoszcz: Publishing House Epigram and University of Kazimierz Wielki Press.

Luper, S. (2003). Indiscernibility skepticism. In S. Luper (Ed.), *The skeptics: Contemporary essays*. Aldershot: Ashgate.

Montminy, M. (2008). Can contextualists maintain neutrality? *Philosophers' Imprint, 8*, 1–13.

Rysiew, P. (2009). Epistemic contextualism. In E.N. Zalta (Ed.), *The stanford encyclopedia of philosophy*. Stanford: Stanford University.

Schaffer, J. (2005). Contrastive knowledge. In T.S. Gendler & J. Hawthorne (Eds.), *Oxford studies in epistemology*, vol. 1, (pp. 235–271). Oxford: Clarendon.

Sosa, E. (2004). Relevant alternatives, contextualism included. *Philosophical Studies, 119*, 35–65.

Steup, M. (2005). Contextualism and conceptual disambiguation. *Acta Analytica, 20-1*(34), 3–15.

Veber, M. (2004). Contextualism and semantic ascent. *The Southern Journal of Philosophy, 42*, 261–272.

Williamson, T. (2001). Comments on Michael Williams' "Contextualism, Externalism and Epistemic Standards". *Philosophical Studies, 103*, 25–33.

Wright, C. (2005). Contextualism and scepticism: Even-handedness, factivity and surreptitiously raising standards. *Philosophical Quarterly, 55*, 236–262.

Chapter 5
Epistemic Contexts and Indexicality

Yves Bouchard

5.1 Contextualism and Indexicalism

5.1.1 The Problem of Indexicality

One of the major challenges that contextualism is facing pertains to the clarification of the mechanisms at play in the indexical interpretation of the knowledge operator. This difficulty is not exclusive to contextualism, but it belongs to indexicality as a semantic theory and to the interpretation of any linguistic item of indexical nature.[1] The knowledge operator, as an indexical predicate, should behave linguistically in the very manner as other indexical predicates do. This idea is the basis of an argument developed by Davis (2004) to confront indexical contextualism. Davis contrasts the behavior of other indexical expressions with the behavior of knowledge claims interpreted indexically in order to show that, contrary to other indexical items, knowledge claims generate skeptical paradoxes. So, according to him, resorting to an indexical interpretation of knowledge claims does not provide any

[1]A high degree of generalization of contextual dependence may give rise to fine-grained distinctions. For example, Bianchi (1999) distinguishes several forms of contextual dependence, following Perry and Searle, among which indexicality is only one case. Besides, Bianchi and Vassallo (2007) even defend the idea that epistemological contextualism might help in clarifying the semantic thesis, if the theory of meaning includes a notion of justification.

Y. Bouchard (✉)
Department of Philosophy and Applied Ethics, Université de Sherbrooke,
2500, boul. de l'Université, Sherbrooke, QC J1K 2Rl, Canada
e-mail: yves.bouchard@usherbrooke.ca

F. Lihoreau and M. Rebuschi (eds.), *Epistemology, Context, and Formalism*, Synthese Library 369, DOI 10.1007/978-3-319-02943-6_5,

solution to the problems raised by the skeptical argument.[2] Even though I do not share every point of Davis' analysis, I definitely agree with him on the idea that if the indexical interpretation of knowledge claims is to be correct, then the knowledge operator should behave (generally) like any other indexical expression. The problem of indexicality for contextualism consists in showing in the case of the knowledge operator, as in the case of any indexical expression, how its reference is contextually fixed with precision and how it is possible to disambiguate its meaning by means of its indexical content. All of this contributes to dissolving the skeptical paradoxes.

5.1.2 The Problem of Context Shifting

Epistemological contextualism faces also an important related problem, essential to its methodological relevance. How are epistemic contextual shifts regulated? If contextualism is to be contributive to epistemology, it must explain the dynamics within which our epistemic transactions are taking place. For instance, Lewis (1979, 1996) considers that shifts from one epistemic context to another are governed by accommodation rules that determine a conversational score for each state in a conversational context. Lewis' rules tend to favor the development of a conversational game by accommodating (i.e., presupposing the truth of) each conversational move as much as possible. This kinematics however conceals a significant drawback. Contextual accommodations are *automatically* operated, i.e., when a new alternative (say a skeptical one) has been called into play, as far-fetched this alternative might be, the epistemic standard is at once raised to accommodate this alternative, consequently knowledge is harder to achieve.[3] Lewis' perspective does not account for the autonomy of epistemic contexts with respect to epistemic agents, and this autonomy is one important issue for the representation of what is going on when a context shift takes place. If epistemic standards are entirely enslaved to characteristic fluctuations of conversational contexts, then there is no possibility of representing the properties of epistemic contexts other than provisionally fixing alternatives (or counterfactual situations) that are relevant to the conversational context *hic et nunc*. In the proposed perspective, an epistemic context should be robust enough to allow any relevant hypothesis, even those that compromise the current or given epistemic framework, to be subjected to the *very same epistemic standard*, and this presupposes that the mere mention of a remote alternative, for

[2]Blaauw (2005) has developed another line of attack against the indexical interpretation of knowledge attributions by conceiving K either as a scalar predicate (like *tall*) or as a pointer predicate (like *here*). In Sect. 5.2, I will take the knowledge operator as a success term.

[3]This is why knowledge tends to be elusive, according to Lewis (1996). The more an epistemic context prompts uneliminated (or uneliminable) possibilities of error, the less there is knowledge. So, the process of context shifting has for limit nothing less than impossible knowledge.

instance, does not entail a context shift (from a strictly epistemological point of view, at least). Suffice it to say for the moment that the clarification of the constraints governing epistemic context shifts is of tantamount importance for the contextualist response to the problem of qualifying epistemic normativity.

5.2 Conceptual Framework

Contextualists like Lewis (1996), Cohen (1987, 2000), and DeRose (1995, 2009) have put forward their epistemological options in the guise of a response to some skeptical argument, and this has not favored the elaboration of a notion of epistemic context that is explicit and well defined. Instead of being analyzed in the conceptual foreground, this notion has been kept in a more or less intuitive form and instrumentalized for the higher goal of a counteroffensive to skepticism. The proposed analysis here will follow a different direction and the notion of epistemic context will be given priority and will be at the center of the epistemological investigation. The notion of epistemic context that will be developed in Sect. 5.2.2 is inspired by several elements already present in the literature, especially in the field of artificial intelligence (Brézillon 1999). By means of an explicit characterization of this notion of epistemic context, it will be possible to formulate an adequate response to both the problem of indexicality and the problem of context shifting.

In a preliminary fashion, let us say that an epistemic context can be defined broadly as a context whose vocabulary is determined by an epistemic operator like *Know*(ϕ), *Believe*(ϕ), *Doubt*(ϕ), *Prove*(ϕ), *Confirm*(ϕ), and so on. According to contextualism, the knowledge operator must be analyzed as a triadic relation $K(x, \phi, \varepsilon)$, where x is an agent variable, ϕ a propositional variable and ε a variable that refers to an epistemic standard. The indexical content of the knowledge operator is precisely given by ε. The invariable part of the meaning of K (or its character) makes it a success term (Williams 2001; DeRose 2009). has satisfied some standard, some epistemic demands. But the content of this standard is only given by the variable part of the meaning of K, which is ε. In a game of chess, for instance, the predicate $Win(x, y, z)$ must be interpreted indexically, i.e., *Win(William, Yves, chess)* means that William has satisfied the conditions for a winning position against Yves, but the content of these conditions, the rules of chess themselves, is only given by the context of the game. Likewise, in a given epistemic context, the content of the standard in use is always inhibited, or tacit as a presupposition, while remaining accessible.

5.2.1 Contextual Logic of McCarthy and Buvač

The notion of context and the contextual logic originally developed by John McCarthy in the field of artificial intelligence aim at providing a solution to the problem of generality, i.e., the problem of representing ordinary knowledge and its integration into inferential processes operating on knowledge bases. The contextual logic of McCarthy and Buvač (CL_{MCB}) can be defined generally as *FOL* $\cup$ $\{ist(c, \phi)\}$, where *FOL* is classical first-order logic and $ist(c, \phi)$, is an operator meaning that the formula ϕ is true in context c. The operator *ist* expresses a relation between a formula and a set of first-order true formulas which is reified as a formal object, a context. In CL_{MCB}, the completeness of *FOL* is preserved (Buvač and Mason 1993; Buvač et al. 1995), and even though this contextual logic is not strictly speaking an epistemic logic, comparable for instance to Lemmon and Henderson (1959) or Hintikka (1962, 1975), it can be nonetheless represented in a standard multimodal logic (Buvač et al. 1995).

The key advantage offered by CL_{MCB} for epistemological contextualism consists in the fact that it allows for a complete expression of the knowledge operator as a triadic relation, since the epistemic standard, which defines uniquely an epistemic context as we shall see, can be kept explicit throughout all the operations on epistemic items. It then becomes possible to set explicitly the properties of each epistemic context and to study the variety of intracontextual and intercontextual relations among epistemic contexts.

Buvač (1996) defines the syntax of CL_{MCB} by means of the following axioms and rules[4]:

(PL) $\vdash_k \phi$, where ϕ is an instance of a propositional tautology

(UI) $\vdash_k (\forall x)\phi(x) \supset \phi(a)$

(MP) $$\frac{\vdash_k \phi \quad \vdash_k \phi \supset \psi}{\vdash_k \psi}$$

(UG) $$\frac{\vdash_k \phi \supset \psi(x)}{\vdash_k \phi \supset (\forall y)\psi(y)}$$, where x is not free in ϕ

(K) $\vdash_k ist(k', \phi \supset \psi) \supset (ist(k', \phi) \supset ist(k', \psi))$

(D) $\vdash_k ist(k_1, ist(k_2, \phi) \vee \psi) \supset ist(k_1, ist(k_2, \phi)) \vee ist(k_1, \psi)$[5]

(Flat) $\vdash_k ist(k_2, ist(k_1, \phi)) \supset ist(k_1, \phi)$

(Enter) $$\frac{\vdash_{k'} ist(k, \phi)}{\vdash_k \phi}$$

(Exit) $$\frac{\vdash_k \phi}{\vdash_{k'} ist(k, \phi)}$$

(BF) $\vdash_k (\forall v) ist(k', \phi) \supset ist(k', (\forall v)\phi)$

The first group (*PL, UI, MP, UG*) comprises axioms and typical rules of *FOL*. In the second group (*K, D, Flat, Enter, Exit*), the axioms and rules express propositional properties of contexts; axiom *K* is a principle of deductive closure (an analogue of

---

[4]Instead of $\vdash k : \phi$, I simply use $\vdash_k \phi$ to mean that a formula ϕ is provable (or assertable) in the context k.

[5]Buvač used Δ instead of D to refer to this propositional property of contexts. I shall use D in order to avoid confusion with the usual symbol for knowledge bases, Δ.

the axiom K in modal logic), axiom D (which Buvač called *contextual omniscience*) permits the qualification of any information accessible from any given context, axiom *Unif* is a principle of information preservation through contexts, and the rules *Enter* and *Exit* permit to access or to leave a context. Finally, in the group of quantificational properties of contexts, there is one axiom (*BF*) analog to the Barcan formula specifying the relation between the *ist* operator and the universal quantifier.

5.2.1.1 Classes of Contexts

Buvač (1996) makes a distinction between two classes of contexts, the *knowledge base* contexts (c_{kb}) and the *discourse* contexts (c_d). Whereas in c_{kb} predicates are univocal, in c_d predicates may be ambiguous. A c_{kb} is a set of true propositions, or facts, in a given knowledge base. A c_d is characterized by two components, a set of *epistemic states* and a set of *semantic states*. In an epistemic state, one finds typical elements of a knowledge base, i.e., facts. A semantic state sets the interpretation of a predicate by means of a relation to another predicate in a knowledge base. It is by virtue of such a relation that an ambiguous predicate in a c_d can be disambiguated.

The main motivation behind CL_{MCB} consists precisely in providing a formal framework for eliminating ambiguity.[6] This is where CL_{MCB} presents a special interest for epistemology. Since the knowledge operator has to be interpreted as an indexical term, according to epistemological contextualism, it is an operator that requires disambiguation in function of its context of utterance, and by the same token, an epistemic context has to be conceived as a c_d. In this view, CL_{MCB} can shed light on the dynamics at play between the interpretation of the knowledge operator and the epistemic contexts of utterance.

5.2.2 *Epistemic Contexts*

In order to take advantage of CL_{MCB}, I will need to load the notion of c_d with some epistemological content. The notion of epistemic context (c_ε) that I will be using rests on the idea that *an epistemic context c is a context defined by an epistemic standard ε that is an introduction rule for the knowledge operator in c*. In CL_{MCB} terms, the standard ε is a subset of the axioms of the knowledge base of c (Δ_c), and to each epistemic context c_ε is associated one and only one epistemic standard. Since it is the epistemic context that determines the meaning of the knowledge operator, then an epistemic context can be envisioned as a c_d, i.e., $\varepsilon \subseteq \Delta_{c_d}$ and more specifically $\varepsilon \subseteq SemanticStates(\Delta_{c_d})$ because ε provides the *indexical*

[6] It can also be extended to other types of contexts (Guha and McCarthy 2003).

content (variable part) of the meaning of the knowledge operator. In accordance with CL_{MCB}, the complete characterization of an epistemic context depends on a twofold characterization: a characterization of its *epistemic standard* (ε) and (if any) a characterization of its *transposition rules* (τ), which are the rules that govern its relations with other c_ε.

These conceptual choices center the investigation on the conditions for context shifting and, by way of consequence, on the conditions for epistemic standard shifting. This is in line with the contextualist goal of accounting on the one hand for the dynamics observable in our epistemic exchanges, that express the variability of the epistemic standards in use, and on the other hand, for the legitimacy of these variations (i.e., they are not epistemic faults).[7] These variations in the use of epistemic standards show clearly our capacity as epistemic agents to regiment our epistemic practices according to a plurality of norms in function of our epistemic needs. That knowledge has been for a long time, too long a time, conceived as one and indivisible, in other words as completely transcontextual, proceeds more from a kind of philosophical tribalism than from a close analysis of our epistemic practices.[8]

One immediate consequence of the above definition of c_ε is that it entails a relativization of all contexts, including logical contexts, that is to say logical contexts are local epistemic contexts like any other epistemic contexts. This creates a difficulty of representation in CL_{MCB} since CL_{MCB} has been devised with the explicit goal of making available logical reasoning in local contexts (via *lifting*) by means of a grammar incorporating *FOL*. The rules *PL*, *UI*, *MP* and *UG* render accessible the resources of *FOL* in every local context. However, this structure cannot account entirely for contextualism, because from the contextualist point of view *FOL* is only one epistemic context among others, and one can imagine that in some rich and complex epistemic situations many logics, stronger or weaker than *FOL*, may be called upon. Consequently, CL_{MCB} has to be amended in order to reify *FOL* so as to become an object of the language, which in turn requires the conversion of the rules *PL*, *UI*, *MP*, *UG*, *K*, and *D* into properties of epistemic contexts defined by logical standards.

Before considering some examples of epistemic contexts, it is worth to underline that the whole idea here is to give some insight into this notion of epistemic context through a (very) programmatic approach, and the proposed formalism will depart slightly from CL_{MCB} in that it make an explicit distinction among axioms between epistemic standards and transposition rules. By definition, an epistemic context will require one and only one epistemic standard, and most of CL_{MCB}'s grammatical rules (*PL*, *UI*, *MP*, *UG*, *K*, *D*) will be directly incorporated into contextual transposition rules. As a toy example of a set of epistemic contexts, consider the following three

[7]Contrary to what Schiffer (1996) suggested, contextualism does not need an error theory to accommodate an indexical interpretation of knowledge attributions.

[8]In that regard, the renewal of interest for a conception of knowledge in terms of a factive mental state (Williamson 2000) seems to be an echo of a static and monolithic framework.

partial and plausible definitions of some ordinary (and common) epistemic contexts, $c_{logical}$, $c_{empirical}$ and $c_{perceptual}$:

Axioms of $c_{logical}$ (c_{log})

($\varepsilon_{log}.1$) $(\forall x)(\phi \supset K(x, \phi))$, where ϕ is an instance of a propositional tautology or of a first-order valid formula

($\tau_{log}.1$) $ist(c_{log}, \phi \supset \psi(x)) \supset ist(c_{log}, \phi \supset \forall y \phi(y))$, where x is not free in ϕ

($\tau_{log}.2$) $(\forall x)((ist(c_{log}, ist(c, K(x, \phi))) \wedge ist(c_{log}, ist(c, K(x, \phi \supset \psi)))) \supset (ist(c_{log}, ist(c, K(x, \psi)))))$

($\tau_{log}.3$) $(\forall x)(ist(c_{log}, ist(c, K(x, \phi \supset \psi))) \supset (ist(c_{log}, ist(c, K(x, \phi))) \supset ist(c_{log}, ist(c, K(x, \psi)))))$

($\tau_{log}.4$) $(\forall x)(ist(c_{log}, ist(c, K(x, \phi) \supset K(x, \psi))) \supset (ist(c_{log}, ist(c, \neg K(x, \psi))) \supset ist(c_{log}, ist(c, \neg K(x, \phi)))))$

c_{log} corresponds to the classical system of *FOL*. The axiom $\varepsilon_{log}.1$ is the epistemic standard defining c_{log} and it means that any instance of a propositional tautology or of a valid formula of *FOL* is sufficient for knowledge.[9] $\tau_{log}.1$, $\tau_{log}.2$, and $\tau_{log}.3$ are respectively the syntactic rules UG, MP, and K of CL_{MCB} expressed in terms of rules of transposition. It is worth noting that $\tau_{log}.2$ guarantees reasoning by *modus ponens* within the scope of the knowledge operator in a given and fixed context, in the very same manner $\tau_{log}.3$ preserves deductive closure in a logical context.[10] According to the formulation of $\tau_{log}.3$, the epistemic context c of the antecedent and of the consequent remain fixed. Even though the problem of deductive closure escapes the limits of this paper, it should be observed nonetheless that failures of deductive closure take their origin in a confusion between distinct epistemic contexts, something for which the present proposal can account. Finally, $\tau_{log}.4$ is a rule of contraposition, which is introduced here for the sake of an analysis in Sect. 5.3.1. One can easily see that any valid pattern of inference can be expressed in the form of a rule of transposition and the set of these rules could be ultimately reduced to a single axiom schema.

Axiom of $c_{empirical}$ (c_{emp})

($\varepsilon_{emp}.1$) $(\forall x)(EmpiricalControl(x, \phi) \supset K(x, \phi))$

$\varepsilon_{emp}.1$ stipulates that the condition to satisfy in order to introduce the knowledge operator in this context is some sort of empirical control made by an agent x towards the state of affairs described by a proposition ϕ. The notion of empirical control in $\varepsilon_{emp}.1$ consists only in a set of procedures providing a sufficient level of discrimination between a state of affairs described by a proposition ϕ and a state

[9] One will recognize in $\varepsilon_{log}.1$ an analogue to the rule of necessitation in modal logic.

[10] $\tau_{log}.3$ is comparable to a kind of principle of scope alteration that switches the scope of K (superior level) with the one of $\supset$ (inferior level). Such a permutation is tolerable solely in a logical order.

of affairs described by a proposition (or several propositions) incompatible with ϕ. In the present illustration, no transposition rule enables one to export empirical knowledge into another c_{ε}.

Axiom of $c_{perceptual}$ (c_{per})

(ε_{per}.1) $(\forall xv)((See(x, v) \vee Hear(x, v) \vee Taste(x, v) \vee Smell(x, v) \vee Touch(x, v)) \supset K(x, \phi))$, where ϕ is immediately linked to v

As regards the perceptual standard, things are different since v is not a propositional content but rather a perceptual content. The knowledge operator is introduced only in virtue of a perceptual state (or a percept). The knowledge operator is in this way dependent on our physiological mechanisms and their respective limitations (think of the various perceptual biases identified by cognitive psychology for instance). No transposition rule is available in c_{per}.

The fact that neither c_{emp} nor c_{per} contain a transposition rule is determined exclusively by the definitions of the epistemic standards. A transposition rule makes possible the propagation of knowledge either within a given context or between different contexts. As opposed to the grammatical rules *Enter* and *Exit* which are only rules of access to information, the transposition rules act as qualification rules in much the same manner epistemic standards themselves do. The transposition rules of c_{log} (τ_{log}.1, τ_{log}.2, τ_{log}.3, and τ_{log}.4) are intracontextual rules of transposition. For reasons of simplicity, no such rule has been defined in c_{emp} and c_{per}. Furthermore, there is no intercontextual rule of transposition for $\{c_{log}, c_{emp}, c_{per}\}$. In c_{per}, for instance, the assertability conditions are evidently too weak to satisfy the assertability conditions of c_{log} and c_{emp}. There is no intercontextual rule of transposition between c_{per} and c_{emp}, because the satisfaction of ε_{per} does not imply the satisfaction of ε_{emp} (ε_{per} is simply too weak), and conversely, the satisfaction of ε_{emp} does not entail the satisfaction of ε_{per} (a property, for example, may be tested empirically while not being itself an object of direct perception). This shows clearly the primitive character of the notion of epistemic standard, which dictates the possibility or the non-possibility of transposition rules. As for the question whether a transposition rule can be valid a priori, i.e., independently of any epistemic standard, one can easily see its irrelevance within the proposed contextualist framework.

Another noticeable aspect of the previous definitions is that no intracontextual rule of transposition specifies the conditions of transmission of a knowledge item from one epistemic agent to another. One could think, for instance, that if an agent a has run an empirical control with respect to ϕ and $K(a, \phi)$, then an agent b, who knows that a has performed a test, would know by some testimonial relation that ϕ. More formally: if $\vdash_{c_{emp}} K(a, \phi)$ and $\vdash_{c_{emp}} K(b, K(a, \phi))$, then $\vdash_{c_{emp}} K(b, \phi)$. The main difficulty in the formulation $\vdash_{c_{emp}} K(b, K(a, \phi))$ can be straightforwardly isolated. If b knows that $K(a, \phi)$, then it is surely not in virtue of ε_{emp} since b is not the one who has run the test, but in virtue of another epistemic standard, namely $\varepsilon_{testimony}$. The specification of all the transposition rules for testimonial knowledge constitutes a major issue from an epistemological point of view. These rules require a fine-grained analysis that is beyond the limits of the present paper. Given that the proposed treatment aims only at presenting a workable notion of epistemic context, it is preferable on this occasion to avoid the problem of the transmission of knowledge from one agent to another.

5.2.2.1 Epistemological Theory

It seems that in our ordinary epistemic situations, the perceptual standard, the empirical standard, and the logical standard (all defined above) are representative of the epistemic resources at our disposal as epistemic agents. But the chief interest in the toy example lies elsewhere. In defining epistemic contexts by means of explicit epistemic standards, one not only gives the knowledge operator its various meanings, but one also describes a structure into which epistemic normativity is spelled out in different terms. Such a conception of epistemic normativity allows for multiple configurations of epistemic contexts, which in turn can be captured by the idea that *an epistemological theory is as a set of* c_{ε}. The epistemological theory presented above, say Θ, is defined as $\Theta = \{c_{log}, c_{emp}, c_{per}\}$. An epistemological theory is consequently defined by a specific set of epistemic contexts (or knowledge bases), that is to say a specific set of epistemic standards and transposition rules. The epistemological structure of the theory is given by the transposition rules that govern the inter and intracontextual relations between contexts. This definition provides a new perspective on major debates in contemporary epistemology. Foundationalism, coherentism, reliabilism, and other options based on the JTB model, may be construed as exemplifying different epistemological structures designed to meet different epistemic demands. None of them is the ultimate epistemological theory simply because all of them are instances of particular structural configurations.

The specific structure of an epistemological theory shows the relations between the different assertability conditions of the knowledge operator proper to each context. It could seem that such a treatment of epistemic normativity is eluding the crucial problem of the truth conditions of the knowledge operator. Of course, this difficulty has to do with the debate between a realist and an antirealist interpretation of the knowledge operator. One merit of the proposed view is its clear response: the truth conditions of K in a given epistemic context are provided by the assertability conditions of K in the given context, so that truth-conduciveness from one context to another follows assertability from one context to another. The purpose of a transposition rule is to authorize the dissemination of assertions in multiple contexts on the basis of one given context. The function of transposition rules though is to be sharply distinguished form the function of the ist operator, because the formula in the argument position of the operator is in mention not in use. The $Exit$ rule makes explicit the genealogy, so to speak, of the truth of a formula from another context, whereas the *Enter* rule does the inverse, i.e., it encapsulates the truth into the assertability conditions of a context. For a realist, this isomorphic relation between truth conditions and assertability conditions boils down to the elimination of the truth conditions, conceived as contextually independent. Some realists, e.g., Williamson (1996, 2000), go as far in the opposite direction as making knowledge the norm of assertion. Such a reversal in the assertability conditions does not do justice to the observable variability of epistemic standards in our epistemic practices.

These considerations lead naturally to another important difficulty that a contextualist perspective is facing. Can contextualism account for the implication between knowledge and truth, as the factivity (or veridicality) condition requires it, i.e., $K\phi \supset \phi$? This time the debate takes place between a fallibilist and an infallibilist conception of knowledge.[11] The factivity condition springs from an analysis centered on the necessary conditions for knowledge (analysis *in consequentia*). The framework developed here makes explicit only the sufficient conditions for knowledge (analysis *in antecedentia*); the epistemic standards are nothing else than introduction rules for the knowledge operator, and the antecedent of the epistemic standard may not even contain any epistemic terms, depending on the context. Here lies the main interest of contextualism as it constitutes a general epistemological framework within which epistemic normativity can be analyzed primarily in terms of its function rather than its content. So, in order to make explicit the characterization of some K by means of necessary conditions, the general contextualist framework has to be singularized and that process amounts to the specification of an epistemological theory, as previously defined.

According to the proposed framework, and in conformity with McCarthy and Buvač (1994), the epistemic contexts are conceived independently from the epistemic agents. This only means that the epistemic perspective of a given agent does not alter in any way the facts, or the epistemic states of Δ_{c_ε}. This property of *flatness* makes it easier to isolate the contextual variations at the level of the contexts, in other words at the level of their respective transposition rules. This reification of an epistemic context brings autonomy to the context with respect to the epistemic agents, and this accounts for the constraint that within one given epistemic context all of the epistemic agents are regimented by the very same epistemic standard and submitted to the very same epistemic demands. Certainly one could define an epistemic context with a parameter in relation to the propositional attitudes of the epistemic agents so that a context would vary as a function of the agents. But such a change would represent more than a change of epistemological theory, it would be a more radical change of logic (or grammar) since one would have to give up the $Unif$ axiom of CL_{MCB} in order to render possible alterations of the epistemic states of one context by means of another context. No doubt the rejection of $Unif$ would be relevant in some particular epistemological investigations, but within the limits of the proposed approach that would have the undesirable effect of concealing (at least partially) the dynamics between the epistemic standards.

[11]It is instructive to notice that Lewis' contextualism is grounded on an infallibilist conception of knowledge (Lewis 1996). In the epistemological theory Θ presented above, ε_{per} shows a high level of fallibility, compared to ε_{emp} which is moderated, and to ε_{log} which is null.

5.3 Skeptical Argument Revisited

The framework provided by CL_{MCB} and the notion of epistemic context characterized above prove useful in the investigation of the source of epistemic normativity in allowing for a precise identification of the resources at play in epistemic contexts. In this regard, it constitutes a valuable contribution to some debates in contemporary epistemology. One way to appreciate the extent of this contribution is to test the virtues of CL_{MCB} against some of the crucial and current epistemological disputes. The skeptical challenge constitutes such a crucial dispute and the usual skeptical arguments one finds in the literature typically appeal to several epistemic standards. The notion of epistemic context, once it is embedded in CL_{MCB}, can shed light on this issue by clarifying the basis of the skeptical challenge—which rests on a confusion, namely a confusion between epistemic standards (and consequently between epistemic contexts). The treatment of the skeptical argument will show not only the importance of an indexical interpretation of the knowledge operator but also the mechanics behind epistemic context shifts, thus substantiating a response to the two problems presented in Sect. 5.1.

5.3.1 Skeptical Argument à la Dretske

One of the most exemplary skeptical arguments is the one analyzed by Dretske (1970). The argument presents a visitor at the zoo. The aim of the skeptic is to show that the visitor, who presumably knows that the animals in the pen marked "Zebras" are zebras, cannot know that these animals are really zebras since she does not know whether these animals are cleverly disguised mules. In other words, the visitor cannot eliminate a possibility of error that jeopardizes her knowledge. In order to rebut the visitor's knowledge (or *alleged* knowledge, as the skeptic would say), the skeptic logically derives a contradiction out of the visitor's knowledge, using an epistemic closure principle (knowledge under entailment). Several distinct epistemic contexts are at play in this argument and the sketch of an epistemological theory characterized in Sect. 5.2.2, Θ, can serve to make them explicit.

This skeptical argument articulates three epistemic facts: (1) the visitor knows (or presumably knows) that the animals in the pen are zebras, (2) the visitor knows that if an animal is a zebras then this animal is not a cleverly disguised mule, but (3) the visitor does not know whether the animals in the pen are cleverly disguised mules. The primary difficulty here is ambiguity. The epistemic contexts that determine the meaning of the knowledge operator are entirely concealed, which suggests (wrongly) that the meaning of K remains constant in each knowledge attribution. A correct analysis of this problem demands first a disambiguation of the meaning of K by means of its indexical content, i.e., the epistemic standard used to qualify knowledge in a given epistemic context. Let's say that p stands for *the animals in the pen are zebras*, q for *the animals in the pen are cleverly disguised mules*, and

$\vdash_k \phi$ for ϕ *is assertable (or asserted) in context k*, then one can express in Θ the epistemic facts in the following manner:

(1) $\vdash_{c_{per}} K(a, p)$
(2) $\vdash_{c_{emp}} K(a, p \supset \neg q)$
(3) $\vdash_{c_{emp}} \neg K(a, \neg q)$

The assertion 1 means that the visitor (a) knows that p in virtue of ε_{per}. It could not be otherwise, because in the situation of an ordinary visit at the zoo a is not in a position to satisfy ε_{emp} of Θ. The formula 2 asserts that a knows empirically, i.e., according to ε_{emp}, that $p \supset \neg q$. It is rather clear that a could not know perceptually that $p \supset \neg q$, since ε_{per} does not allow for (perceptual) discrimination between p and q.[12] The third epistemic fact 3 expresses the empirical ignorance of a with respect to $\neg q$, given that a has not performed any empirical test in the situation.[13] Up to this point, there is nothing controversial in this Θ–representation of the epistemic facts proper to the argument *à la Dretske*.

The contradiction the skeptic wants to obtain can be derived either in the perceptual context or in the empirical context. In the first case, the skeptic will need $\vdash_{c_{per}} \neg K(a, p)$ (strategy 1), which would contradict 1, and in the second case, the skeptic will need $\vdash_{c_{emp}} K(a, \neg q)$ (strategy 2), which would contradict 3. In order to represent the logical reasoning of the skeptic on the information available in c_{per} and c_{emp}, we first need to export the epistemic facts 1–3 into the logical context, c_{log}:

(4) $\vdash_{c_{log}} ist(c_{per}, K(a, p)) \quad Exit, 1$
(5) $\vdash_{c_{log}} ist(c_{emp}, K(a, p \supset \neg q)) \quad Exit, 2$
(6) $\vdash_{c_{log}} ist(c_{emp}, \neg K(a, \neg q)) \quad Exit, 3$

Now, the desired contradiction may be obtained, according to strategy 1, by using closure (τ_{log}.3) and contraposition (τ_{log}.4):

(7) $\vdash_{c_{log}} ist(c_{emp}, K(a, p)) \supset ist(c_{emp}, K(a, \neg q)) \quad \tau_{log}.3, 5$
(8) $\vdash_{c_{log}} ist(c_{emp}, \neg K(a, \neg q)) \supset ist(c_{emp}, \neg K(a, p)) \quad \tau_{log}.4, 7$
(9) $\vdash_{c_{log}} ist(c_{emp}, \neg K(a, p)) \quad \tau_{log}.2, 6,8$[14]
(10) $\vdash_{c_{emp}} \neg K(a, p) \quad Enter, 9$

[12]This situation is akin to the one evoked by Goldman (1976) concerning fake barn façades.

[13]Of course, in an epistemological theory other than Θ the expression of these same epistemic facts could differ significantly. The point of the argument though does not consist in promoting one particular epistemological theory, but rather to shed light onto the contextualist dynamics present in any epistemological theory.

[14]The skeptic could also reason by *modus tollens*, but that would conceal the resort to the principle of deductive closure since the required rule of transposition would be: $(\forall x)$ $((ist(c_{log}, ist(c, \neg K(x, \psi))) \wedge ist(c_{log}, ist(c, K(x, \phi \supset \psi)))) \supset (ist(c_{log}, ist(c, \neg K(x, \phi)))))$.

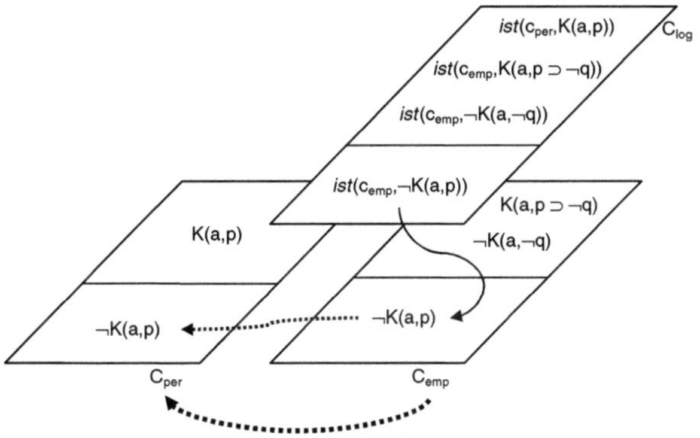

Fig. 5.1 Strategy 1

Steps 7–9 conform with the parameters of the situation, for the visitor cannot know according to ε_{emp} that the animals in the pen are zebras (9) because she has not performed any empirical test. Assertion 10 expresses this logical result in the empirical context. At this stage of the argument, it is important to stress the point that 10 does not prevent the visitor from knowing according to ε_{per} that the animal in the pen are zebras (1). And there is no contradiction (nor incompatibility) between $\vdash_{c_{emp}} \neg K(a, p)$ and $\vdash_{c_{per}} K(a, p)$. The only way the skeptic can produce a contradiction in c_{per} is by transposing 10 into c_{per}:

(11) $\vdash_{c_{per}} \neg K(a, p)$?

Assertion 11 exhibits the critical move, that relies on a transposition from $\vdash_{c_{emp}} \neg K(a, p)$ to $\vdash_{c_{per}} \neg K(a, p)$ (11). With 11, the skeptic would show that Δ_{per} of a is inconsistent on the grounds of $\vdash_{c_{per}} K(a, p)$ and $\vdash_{c_{per}} \neg K(a, p)$. The strategy 1 can be diagrammed as follows (where the dotted lines represent the litigious transpositions) (Fig. 5.1).

The validity of the transposition (11) between c_{emp} and c_{per} (dotted lines) however cannot be presupposed regardless of the given epistemological theory. Yet, in Θ, the relation between the standards ε_{per} and ε_{emp} does not allow for a transposition from c_{emp} to c_{per}, thus the passage from $\vdash_{c_{emp}} \neg K(a, p)$ to $\vdash_{c_{per}} \neg K(a, p)$ is not permitted. So, this strategy of the skeptic rests on a false presupposition with regard to the possibility of a transposition.

One virtue of the framework proposed in Sect. 5.2.2 consists precisely in providing the conceptual precision needed to isolate and to identify the source of the difficulty, namely a confusion between epistemic contexts. Of course, one could envisage the skeptical argument in a different epistemological theory, for instance one that would authorize a transposition from c_{emp} to c_{per} (a transposition rule

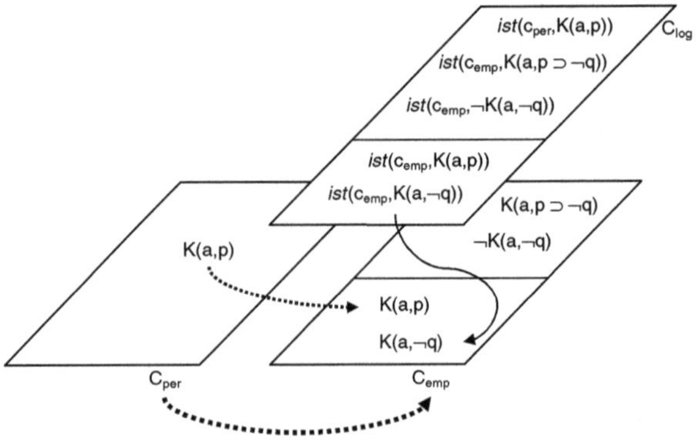

Fig. 5.2 Strategy 2

that would require an epistemological justification), but the point here is that the argument would still remain invalid in Θ, whose plausibility is left untouched.

According to the second strategy, the skeptic wants to construct a contradiction in the empirical context with $\vdash_{c_{emp}} K(a, \neg q)$. This can be achieved by means of an initial transposition from $\vdash_{c_{per}} K(a, p)$ to $\vdash_{c_{emp}} K(a, p)$ and *modus ponens*:

(12) $\vdash_{c_{emp}} K(a, p)$?
(13) $\vdash_{c_{log}} ist(c_{emp}, K(a, p))$ $Exit$, 12
(14) $\vdash_{c_{log}} ist(c_{emp}, K(a, \neg q))$ $\tau_{log}.2$, 13,7
(15) $\vdash_{c_{emp}} K(a, \neg q)$ $Enter$, 14

The strategy 2 can be diagrammed as in Fig. 5.2.

Here again the skeptic presupposes that one can transpose $\vdash_{c_{per}} K(a, p)$ to $\vdash_{c_{emp}} K(a, p)$ and, by logic, one can obtain a contradiction with $\vdash_{c_{emp}} \neg K(a, \neg q)$ (3) and $\vdash_{c_{emp}} K(a, \neg q)$ (15). Yet such a transposition is only possible if the relation between ε_{per} and ε_{emp} permits of it, which is not the case in Θ (as it was for strategy 1). The skeptical argument demands a rule of transposition such as $(\forall x)(ist(c_{per}, K(x, \phi)) \supset ist(c_{emp}, K(x, \phi)))$, with or without its converse.[15] In the absence of such a rule, the skeptical argument is plainly invalid.

The preceding contextualist analysis shows that the explicitation of the properties of epistemic contexts enables one to cope with the skeptical argument in a satisfactory manner. The contextualist model explains not only why the skeptical argument cannot be generalized, but also why deductive closure is not at fault. Within the contextualist framework, transgression of transposition rules between

[15]If the skeptic wants to produce a contradiction also in the perceptual context, with $\vdash_{c_{per}} K(a, \neg q)$, the needed transposition rule must be stronger, namely $(\forall x)(ist(c_{per}, K(x, \phi)) \equiv ist(c_{emp}, K(x, \phi)))$.

epistemic contexts are made entirely explicit. In the particular case of the skeptical argument, a context shift is taking place tacitly.[16] In the proposed model, once an epistemic qualification (or its epistemic genealogy) has been made explicit, it is no longer possible to tacitly shift from one context to another. In a given epistemological theory, all of the transposition rules are defined such as to preserve the designated epistemic property (namely K) through context shifting, whenever it is possible. Furthermore, this notion of a transposition rule dispenses with the usual considerations regarding the notion of *relevant alternative* understood in counterfactual terms,[17] as well as the complications pertaining to the semantics of counterfactuality.

5.3.2 *Skeptical Argument* à la DeRose

Another typical case of a skeptical argument has been treated by DeRose (1995). It proceeds by way of ignorance, that is it propagates the ignorance with respect to a given skeptical alternative to an ordinary proposition. It evidences a different structure compared to the argument *à la Dretske*. Consider a skeptical hypothesis h (*I am a brain in a vat*), an ordinary empirical proposition o (*I have two hands*), and the following *modus ponens*:

(16) $\neg K(a, \neg h)$
(17) $\neg K(a, \neg h) \supset \neg K(a, o)$
(18) $\neg K(a, o)$ $\quad$ *Modus ponens*, 16,17

The reconstruction of 16–18 in Θ in order to render explicit the indexical references of the knowledge operators at play gives rise to two different interpretations. According to the first interpretation, 16–18 is simply an instance of *modus ponens* in the logical context:

(19) $\vdash_{c_{log}} (\neg K(a, \neg h) \wedge (\neg K(a, \neg h) \supset \neg K(a, o))) \supset \neg K(a, o)$

However 19 does not yield any conclusion as to the ignorance of a with regard to o, and there is no possible transposition of this epistemic state into any other context. 19 is only an object of contemplation from the logical point of view, providing no particular insight about the skeptical argument.

According to the second interpretation, the inferential mechanisms unveil a hidden premiss (a presupposition). In 17, the conditional is the main connective and does not fall within the scope of a knowledge operator, thus $\neg K(a, \neg h) \supset \neg K(a, o)$

[16] Cohen's 1988 diagnosis turns out to be totally correct: "The apparent closure failures are illusions that result from inattention to contextual shifts" (111). Hendricks (2006) underlines rightly that the closure principle is valid in a fixed context.

[17] See Dretske (1970), Stine (1976), Nozick (1981), Cohen (1988), and Heller (1999).

cannot be an epistemic state of $\Delta_{c_{emp}}$.[18] One way to arrive at 17 is by using epistemic closure and contraposition:

(20) $\vdash_{c_{emp}} K(a, o \supset \neg h)$
(21) $\vdash_{c_{log}} ist(c_{emp}, K(a, o \supset \neg h)) \quad Exit, 20$
(22) $\vdash_{c_{log}} ist(c_{emp}, K(a, o)) \supset ist(c_{emp}, K(a, \neg h)) \quad \tau_{log}.3, 20$
(23) $\vdash_{c_{log}} ist(c_{emp}, \neg K(a, \neg h)) \supset ist(c_{emp}, \neg K(a, o)) \quad \tau_{log}.4, 21$

The formulation 20–23 makes it clear that assertion 20 is the hidden premiss that, once exported to c_{log} (21), can be used with the principle of epistemic closure (22) to arrive at the contrapositive (23), which is the correlate of 17. DeRose's formulation of the argument does not reflect this information which is nevertheless indispensable to the strength of the argument, for what 23 expresses is nothing else than a logical exploitation of 20. If this analysis is correct, then the argument from ignorance is based on an element of prior knowledge.[19] Now, introducing 16 (DeRose's premiss) in the empirical context, one gets the expected skeptical result (27, or the correlate of 18):

(24) $\vdash_{c_{emp}} \neg K(a, \neg h)$
(25) $\vdash_{c_{log}} ist(c_{emp}, \neg K(a, \neg h)) \quad Exit, 24$
(26) $\vdash_{c_{log}} ist(c_{emp}, \neg K(a, o)) \quad \tau_{log}.2, 23,25$
(27) $\vdash_{c_{emp}} \neg K(a, o) \quad Enter, 26$

This reconstruction (20–27) preserves the validity of the argument while making explicit the assertion 20 according to which a knows empirically that the truth of o implies the falsity of h. The validity of the argument requires that 20, 24 and 27 be qualified in virtue of the very same epistemic standard, namely ε_{emp}, and that the logical resources be deployed within the very same context so that no epistemic property is altered. Here, no transposition is taking place, contrary to the argument *à la Dretzke*.

However, despite the validity of the argument, the skeptic will not grant 20 because ε_{emp} demands a possibility of discrimination between the two states of affairs that are referred to by o and h. Yet, part of the epistemological strength of the skeptical argument comes from the impossibility of discriminating the truth-value of the skeptical hypothesis, which amounts to accepting that the states of affairs in question have to be underdetermined with respect to both the ordinary proposition and the skeptical hypothesis.[20] So, the skeptic cannot accept 20, for the hidden premise short-circuits the skeptical argument. Why not then simply interpret $K(a, o \supset \neg h)$ according to ε_{per} and reconstruct the whole argument in c_{per} so as to retain the possibility of a perceptual underdetermination? Well, in Θ,

[18]Only in a logical context does the knowledge predicate fall under the scope of a logical connective. In any other epistemic context, the opposite is the case.

[19]This situation is not foreign to the classical critique of autorefutation in response to the skeptical argument.

[20]Our analysis is in line with Vogel (2004).

$\nvdash_{c_{per}} K(a, o \supset \neg h)$ since it is false that a can know perceptually that $\neg(o \wedge h)$. The perceptual standard is too weak to allow the knowledge of a conditional relation between o and $\neg h$. In this view, no matter which epistemological theory (other than Θ) one picks, the skeptic will need a premise analogous to 20 in order to reach her conclusion, and any premise analogous to 20 will compromise the underdetermination the skeptical argument rests on. This skeptical underdetermination must be understood in terms of a kind of ignorance *in principle* with regard to the negation of the skeptical hypothesis. For the skeptic, it is not that a does not know that $\neg h$, it is rather that *a cannot possibly know* that $\neg h$, in other words $\neg \Diamond K(a, \neg h)$. This suggests a modal reading of 24, to wit $\vdash_{c_{emp}} \Box\neg K(a, \neg h)$, and its treatment would require a modal extension of CL_{MCB}.[21]

The analysis of these two types of the skeptical argument has shown two important structural aspects of the argument. The first aspect, discernible in the argument *à la Dretske*, consists in a transgression of the transposition rules. The second aspect, discernible in the argument *à la DeRose*, consists in a hidden premise incompatible with the underdetermination required by the skeptical hypothesis. In both cases, the contextualist framework has made manifest those structural defects by means of a precise notion of epistemic context characterized by an epistemic standard and transposition rules.

5.4 Indexicality and Context Shifting

5.4.1 Solution to the Problem of Indexicality

We may now get back to our two initial problems. From the perspective of epistemological contextualism, the main issue consists in accounting for the variations in the meaning of the knowledge operator as a function of the variations of the epistemic contexts while preserving part of the meaning throughout these variations, and all of this can be achieved by means of an indexical interpretation of K. This is precisely what the conceptual framework provided by CL_{MCB} can model and clarify. By defining an epistemic context as a context regimented by a unique epistemic standard, the application of the knowledge operator is thereby oriented by this precise contextual parameter that fixes the indexical content of K. It becomes then possible to disambiguate the various uses of K in virtue of the knowledge bases and the axioms characteristic of the epistemic contexts.

But, as one might object, this structure is by far to idealized to represent all the richness and complexity of our epistemic practices. I do not claim that epistemic agents should behave in the same way knowledge base systems work, and that the

21 Taking into account this reading would require a modal extension of *FOL*, a type $S5$ for instance (if one wants to reduce all iterated modalities), and the whole argument would have to be reinterpreted in modal terms.

former should be reduced or even brought in conformity to the latter. The claim is rather that CL_{MCB} makes explicit what is constitutive of our ordinary and very complicated epistemic practices, namely that we use K in accordance with some contextual determinants and these determinants vary from context to context. An informative way to analyze these determinants is to conceive of them as introduction rules that give K its contextual meaning. It is this process that can be captured and abstracted into a knowledge base system as CL_{MCB}. The main benefit of such an abstraction is the clear view it provides on epistemic normativity, a view that is too easily obscured by a priori philosophical considerations. As an object of inquiry, epistemic normativity emerges from the manifold of epistemic practices. Only once the mechanisms by which a set of epistemic conditions may transform into an epistemic norm have been explicited can one appreciate the density and the fitness of our ordinary epistemic practices. The variations observable at the higher level of abstraction (indexicality) reflect the variations observable at the basic level of the epistemic practices. This is no surprise since we are responsible for our epistemic practices, and even though some of them are very robust and some of them are very weak (depending on the epistemological theory at stake), in any case epistemic agency is what makes them all possible as, ultimately, an adaptative response to our environment.

5.4.2 *Solution to the Problem of Context Shifting*

The problem of context shifting receives a direct solution insofar all contextual changes are regulated by transposition rules that proceed from the epistemic standards defining the contexts. The content of the transposition rules determines explicitly the possible relations between epistemic contexts, so that illicit contextual shifts can be identified with precision. Illicit context shifts are like illegal moves on an epistemic chessboard. They are sometimes very subtle but often well meshed into the fabric of natural language, and the confusion they generate frequently takes the form of a philosophical aporia, as the debates around deductive closure show.[22] In the contextualist framework, deductive closure permits of an epistemic version of a rule of detachment: if $\vdash_{c_\varepsilon} K(\varphi)$ and $\vdash_{c_\varepsilon} K(\varphi \supset \psi)$, then $\vdash_{c_\varepsilon} K(\psi)$. The knowledge operator must be fixed first, i.e., it must have the same meaning in the conclusion and in the premises. The application of the principle of deductive closure requires that the destination-context of the conclusion (via *Enter*) be the same as the source-context in the premises. When a skeptical argument, for instance, exhibits a failure of deductive closure, that indicates clearly that a context shift has taken place tacitly.

[22] In addition to the usual skeptical paradoxes, one can think of the paradox of confirmation, the Gettier problems of type II, the lottery and the preface paradoxes.

In that regard, a failure of deductive closure can even serve as a reliable indicator of a tacit context shift.[23]

The core of an epistemological theory consists in making explicit the rules that govern the use of the knowledge operator, the epistemic standards, and the rules that govern the possible relations between epistemic contexts, the transposition rules. The distinction between epistemic standards and transposition rules confers to the theory more expressivity, and to the epistemic standards, more autonomy. Context shifting involves both aspects of the epistemological theory, the transposition rules and the epistemic standards. And one important virtue of the contextualist framework is that it can contribute to the clarification of the conditions under which this process of context shifting can take place.

5.5 Conclusion

Epistemological contextualism is misrepresented when it is understood as the opposite term to invariantism, to use Unger's 2002 terms. The contextualist thesis is fundamentally a hybrid thesis, incorporating a partial invariantism, inasmuch as it relies on an indexical interpretation of the knowledge operator. For contextualism, the invariable aspect and the variable aspect of the meaning of K are integral in the understanding of epistemic normativity. And the relation between contextualism and indexicality is so tight that the relevance of contextualism as an epistemological framework depends for a large part on the explanation of the dynamics at play in the indexical interpretation of the knowledge operator.

In providing a logical framework capable of representing indexical operators, as well as the required resources to disambiguate them, CL_{MCB} sheds new light on epistemological contextualism. The framework makes possible a distinction between epistemic standards and transposition rules, a distinction that in turn clarifies the relationship between epistemic contexts within an epistemological theory. Besides, CL_{MCB} offers a perspective on epistemic normativity that does not appeal to the notion of epistemic justification. Indeed, the central notion is the notion of satisfaction of an epistemic standard (the Kaplanian character of K). Not that the notion of justification is incompatible with contextualism, but justification is better conceived of as an additional epistemic layer intended to exhibit the different connections between the nodes in a belief network, whose opacity however perturbs the analysis of epistemic normativity *simpliciter*. The notion of justification does not contribute significantly to the analysis of the normative function of epistemic standards since justification is essentially a consequence of the satisfaction of a standard; it does not inform the analysis on the various ways of satisfying and of articulating epistemic standards. This is where epistemological contextualism

[23]This is a view developed in Bouchard (2011). For other views on the failure of deductive closure, see Brueckner (1985), Vogel (1990), Hales (1995), and Warfield (2004).

presents a major conceptual gain: it is a theory about the normative function of epistemic standards. In this respect, epistemological contextualism presents itself as a *general epistemological framework*. It furnishes some kind of grammar for expressing epistemic normativity. Because (total) invariantism confuses the (normative) epistemic *function* with its epistemic *argument*, it cannot envisage contextually oriented normativity other than as a fragmented normativity, shattered by the multiplicity of contexts, weakened by the variety of standards. From the contextualist point of view, epistemic normativity is rather a normative function distributed and realized into a plurality of spaces whose dimensionalities are defined by different epistemic standards.

References

Bianchi, C. (1999). Three forms of contextual dependence. In P. Bouquet (Ed.), *Modeling and using context* (pp. 69–76). Berlin: Springer.

Bianchi, C., & Vassallo, N. (2007). Meaning, contexts and justification. In T. R. Roth-Berghofer, B. Kokinov, D. C. Richardson, & L. Vieu (Eds.), *Modeling and using context* (pp. 69–81). Berlin: Springer.

Blaauw, M. (2005). Challenging contextualism. *Grazer Philosophische Studien, 69*, 127–146.

Bouchard, Y. (2011). Deductive closure and epistemic context. *Logique et Analyse, 54*, 439–452.

Brézillon, P. (1999). Context in problem solving: A survey. *The Knowledge Engineering Review, 14*, 47–80.

Brueckner, A. L. (1985). Skepticism and epistemic closure. *Philosophical Topics, 13*, 89–117.

Buvač, S. (1996). Resolving lexical ambiguity using a formal theory of context. In K. van Deemter & S. Peters (Eds.), *Semantic ambiguity and underspecification* (pp. 101–124). Stanford: CSLI.

Buvač, S., & Mason, I. A. (1993). Propositional logic of context. In American Association for Artificial Intelligence (Ed.), *Proceedings of the eleventh national conference on artificial intelligence*, Menlo Park (pp. 412–419). AAAI Press.

Buvač, S., Buvač, V., & Mason, I. A. (1995). Metamathematics of contexts. *Fundamenta Informaticae, 23*, 263–301.

Cohen, S. (1987). Knowledge, context, and social standards. *Synthese, 73*, 3–26.

Cohen, S. (1988). How to be a fallibilist. *Philosophical Perspectives, 2*, 91–123.

Cohen, S. (2000). Contextualism and skepticism. *Noûs, 10*, 94–107.

Davis, W. A. (2004). Are knowledge claims indexical? *Erkenntnis, 61*, 257–281.

DeRose, K. (1995). Solving the skeptical problem. *The Philosophical Review, 104*, 1–52.

DeRose, K. (2009). *The case for contextualism: Knowledge, skepticism, and context, Vol. 1.* Oxford: Clarendon Press.

Dretske, F. (1970). Epistemic operators. *The Journal of Philosophy, 67*, 1007–1023.

Goldman, A. I. (1976). Discrimination and perceptual knowledge. *The Journal of Philosophy, 73*, 771–791.

Guha, R., & McCarthy, J. (2003). Varieties of contexts. In P. Blackburn, C. Ghidini, R. Turner, & F. Giunchiglia (Eds.), *Modeling and using context: Vol. 2680. Lecture notes in computer science* (pp. 164–177). Berlin: Springer.

Hales, S. D. (1995). Epistemic closure principles. *The Southern Journal of Philosophy, 33*, 185–201.

Heller, M. (1999). Relevant alternatives and closure. *Australasian Journal of Philosophy, 77*, 196–208.

Hendricks, V. F. (2006). *Mainstream and formal epistemology*. Cambridge: Cambridge University Press.

Hintikka, J. (1962). *Knowledge and belief*. Ithaca: Cornell University Press.
Hintikka, J. (1975). Impossible possible worlds vindicated. *Journal of Philosophical Logic, 4*, 475–484.
Lemmon, E. J., & Henderson, G. P. (1959). Is there only one correct system of modal logic? *The Aristotelian Society, 33*, 23–40.
Lewis, D. (1979). Scorekeeping in a language game. *Journal of Philosophical Logic, 8*, 339–359.
Lewis, D. (1996). Elusive knowledge. *Australasian Journal of Philosophy, 74*, 549–567.
McCarthy, J., & Buvač, S. (1994). Formalizing context (expanded notes). In A. Aliseda, R. van Glabbeek, & D. Westerståhl (Eds.), *Computing natural language* (pp. 13–50). Stanford: CSLI.
Nozick, R. (1981). *Philosophical explanations*. Cambridge: Belknap Press.
Schiffer, S. (1996). Contextualist solutions to scepticism. *Proceedings of the Aristotelian Society, 96*, 317–333.
Stine, G. C. (1976). Skepticism, relevant alternatives, and deductive closure. *Philosophical Studies, 29*, 249.
Unger, P. (2002). *Philosophical relativity*. Oxford: Oxford University Press.
Vogel, J. (1990). Are there counterexamples to the closure principle? In M. D. Roth & G. Ross (Eds.), *Doubting: Contemporary perspectives on skepticism* (pp. 13–27). Dordrecht: Kluwer.
Vogel, J. (2004). Skeptical arguments. *Philosophical Issues, 14*, 426–455.
Warfield, T. A. (2004). When epistemic closure does and does not fail: A lesson from the history of epistemology. *Analysis, 64*, 35–41.
Williams, M. (2001). *Problems of knowledge: A critical introduction to epistemology*. Oxford: Oxford University Press.
Williamson, T. (1996). Knowing and asserting. *The Philosophical Review, 105*, 489–523.
Williamson, T. (2000). *Knowledge and its limits*. Oxford: Oxford University Press.

Chapter 6
Knowing Who: How Perspectives and Context Interact

Maria Aloni and Bruno Jacinto

6.1 Introduction

6.1.1 Card Scenario

In front of John lie two cards face down. One is the Ace of Hearts, the other is the Ace of Spades, but John doesn't know which is which. He is playing the following game. He has to choose one card: if he chooses the Ace of Spades, he wins 10 euros, if he chooses the Ace of Hearts, he loses 10 euros. Consider now the following sentence:

(1) John knows which card is the winning card.

Is this sentence true in the situation described, or false instead? The natural reaction seems to be 'it depends ... '

Suppose Mary utters (1) in context α as a reply to Sue's question:

(2) Does John even know the rules of the game?

In such a context, (1) is, *prima facie*, true. But now suppose that Mary utters (1) in context β as a reply to Sue's question:

(3) Do you think John will win?

M. Aloni (✉)
ILLC/Department of Philosophy, University of Amsterdam, P.O. Box 94242, 1090 GE, Amsterdam, The Netherlands
e-mail: m.d.aloni@uva.nl

B. Jacinto
Arché – Philosophical Research Centre for Logic, Language, Metaphysics and Epistemology, The University of St Andrews, 17–19 College Street, St Andrews, Fife KY16 9AL, Scotland, UK
e-mail: jacinto.bruno@gmail.com

F. Lihoreau and M. Rebuschi (eds.), *Epistemology, Context, and Formalism*, Synthese Library 369, DOI 10.1007/978-3-319-02943-6_6,

In β, contrary to what was the case in α, sentence (2) appears to be false.

Examples like the card scenario can be multiplied, and seem to lead to the conclusion that the truth of sentences where 'knowing which' or 'knowing who' (henceforth 'knowing-wh') constructions occur is context-dependent.[1]

Consider again contexts α and β. It is appealing to adopt the view that one of the roles that these contexts are playing in the determination of the truth of (1) is that of triggering different ways to 'look' at the objects in the domain (i.e. the cards). Context α demands that one looks at the cards by 'their suit/figure' (that is, as being, respectively, *the Ace of Spades* and *the Ace of Hearts*), in which case (1) is true, since John knows that the Ace of Spades is the winning card. As to context β, it demands that one looks at the cards by their relative position (that is, as being, respectively, *the card on the left* and *the card on the right*), in which case (1) is false, since it is neither the case that John knows that *the card on the left* is the winning card nor that he knows that *the card on the right* is the winning card.

Let us refer to each of these different ways of looking at the cards (and, in general, to the domain of discourse) through the expression 'conceptual cover'. The difference in truth-value can thus be traced to a difference on the conceptual cover at play in contexts α and β. Consider now sentence

(4) John doesn't know which card is which.

where (4) is uttered by Mary in a context δ as a reply to Sue's utterance

(5) Do you think John will win?

In (4) there seems to be an interplay of contextual covers. That is, what Mary is stating is that John doesn't know that the objects of the domain looked at in a certain way, correspond to the objects in the domain looked at in a different way (since she appears to be stating that John doesn't know that the Ace of Spades is the card on the left and that the Ace of Hearts is the card on the right).

However, if (4) was uttered in context η, as a reply to Sue's utterance

(6) Do you think John can play this game?

what Mary appears to be stating is that John doesn't know that the Ace of Spades is the winning card (nor that the Ace of Hearts is the losing card).

Thus, the truth of (4) also seems to be context-dependent in a way similar to the truth of sentence (1). However, with respect to sentence (4), what appears to be

[1]Even if we assume that the epistemic standards are the same in context α and β, (1) will, *prima facie*, have different truth-values with respect to α and β. Thus, this shift in truth-value from α to β cannot be traced back to the fact that in each context there is a different epistemic standard at play and the meaning and/or the semantic value of 'know' is sensitive to that difference in context. What cases like the card scenario therefore seem to show is a kind of context sensitivity which is characteristic of 'knowing-wh' constructions, in the sense that it cannot be explained by the putative context-sensitivity of 'know'.

playing a crucial role is not only a specific conceptual cover at play in context, but a *conceptual perspective*[2]; that is, several different ways to look at the domain.

In this article we will investigate how conceptual perspectives and context interact in the determination of the truth of sentences in which 'knowing-wh' constructions occur.

6.2 A Perspective-Sensitive Semantics for Questions

6.2.1 'Who' and 'Knowing Who'

We have pointed out that the context sensitivity of 'knowing-wh' constructions in which we are interested cannot be traced back to the context sensitivity of 'know'. However, it can, arguably, be traced back to the context sensitivity of 'who' or 'which'. Let us go back to the card scenario. Consider now contexts δ and ϵ. In both these contexts Mary utters the following question:

(7) Which card is the winning card?

In context δ the utterance of (7) is preceded by Mary's utterance of

(8) Sue, I want to know what the rules of that game that John is playing are.

while in ϵ the utterance of (7) is preceded by Mary's utterance of

(9) I wonder whether John will win the game if he chooses the card on the left.

If in context δ Sue replies to Mary by saying that the Ace of Spades is the winning card, Mary will feel completely satisfied with Sue's answer. However, if Sue answers that the winning card is the card on the left, Mary will not take the answers as a satisfactory one, something which she might signal in this context by uttering:

(10) Come on Sue, that's not what I'm asking. What I want to know is this: is the winning card the Ace of Spades or the Ace of Hearts?

As to context ϵ, if Sue answers that the Ace of Spades is the winning card, Mary again won't feel satisfied. She might signal this by saying that:

(11) Come on Sue, that's not what I'm asking. What I want to know is this: Is the winning card the card on the left or the card on the right?

Hence, question (7) apparently demands different answers in contexts δ and ϵ. Furthermore, just as happened with respect to (1), this seems to be so because the

[2]The notions of a conceptual cover and conceptual perspective will be defined later on.

question in context δ is posed with respect to a conceptual cover different than the one with respect to which the question is posed in context ϵ. Thus, the view that the context sensitivity of 'knowing-wh' constructions with which we are concerned is traceable to a context sensitivity of the wh-pronoun is vindicated.

In the rest of this section we will present Aloni's (2001) semantics for wh-clauses. This is a modification of the classical Groenendijk and Stokhof's (1984) analysis, especially geared at capturing the perspective-sensitive nature of questions. The idea is to give the reader a hold on what such a semantics would look like, in order to later on introduce the discussion on the interaction between perspectives and context in our evaluation of 'knowing-wh' constructions.

6.2.2 *Conceptual Covers*

Consider again the card situation discussed at the beginning of the article. In front of you lie two cards face down. One is the Ace of Spades, the other is the Ace of Hearts. You don't know which is which. There are two different ways of identifying the two cards in this scenario: by their position on the table (the card on the left, the card on the right) and by their suit (the Ace of Spades, the Ace of Hearts). Aloni (2001) proposes to formalize such methods of identification in terms of *conceptual covers*. A conceptual cover is a set of individual concepts which exclusively and exhaustively covers the domain of individuals: each individual is identified by exactly one concept in each world. More formally:

Definition 6.2.1 (Conceptual covers). Given a set of possible worlds W and a domain of individuals D, a *conceptual cover* CC based on (W, D) is a set of functions $W \to D$ such that:

$$\forall w \in W : \forall d \in D : \exists! c \in CC : c(w) = d$$

6.2.2.1 Illustration

To formalize the card situation discussed above we need a model with two worlds, w_1 and w_2, and a domain consisting of two individuals, $\heartsuit$ and $\spadesuit$. As illustrated in the diagram below, either $\heartsuit$ is the card on the left (in w_1) or it is the card on the right (in w_2).

$$w_1 \mapsto \heartsuit\ \spadesuit$$
$$w_2 \mapsto \spadesuit\ \heartsuit$$

There are only two possible conceptual covers definable over such a model, namely the set A which identifies the cards by their position on the table and the set B which identifies the cards by their suit:

A = {the card on the left, the card on the right}
B = {the Ace of Spades, the Ace of Hearts}

C below is an example of a set of concepts which does *not* constitute a conceptual cover:

C = {the card on the left, the Ace of Hearts}

For C to be a conceptual cover, every individual should be identified by exactly one concept in every world. But this is not the case. In w_1 for example,♡ is identified by two concepts, while ♠ is not identified by any concept at all.

6.2.3 Question Under a Perspective

Aloni (2001) considers a language of first order predicate logic enriched with a question operator?. A special index $n \in N$ is added to the variables in the language. These indices range over conceptual covers. A *model* for this language is a quadruple (W, D, I, C) where W is a set of possible worlds, D is a set of individuals, I is a world dependent interpretation function and C is a set of conceptual covers based on (W, D). A *conceptual perspective* $\wp$ in M is a function from N to C.

Questions are analyzed in terms of their possible exhaustive answers, as in Groenendijk and Stokhof (1984). The evaluation of a question, however, involves quantification over the elements of a $\wp$-selected conceptual cover rather than over individuals. In the case of multi-constituent questions, different variables can be assigned different conceptualizations. (By **x** we denote the sequence $x_{1_{n_1}}, \ldots, x_{k_{n_k}}$. By $\wp(\mathbf{n})$ we denote the product $\prod_{i \in k}(\wp(n_i))$. And by $\mathbf{c}(w)$ we denote the sequence $c_1(w), \ldots, c_k(w)$.)

Definition 6.2.2 (Questions under Cover).

$$[\![?\mathbf{x}\phi]\!]^{\wp}_{M,w,g} = \{v \in W \mid \forall \mathbf{c} \in \wp(\mathbf{n}) : [\![\phi]\!]^{\wp}_{M,w,g[\mathbf{x}/\mathbf{c}(w)]} = [\![\phi]\!]^{\wp}_{M,v,g[\mathbf{x}/\mathbf{c}(v)]}\}$$

To express knowledge-wh, the language is extended with a knowledge operator K_a selecting questions as complements. A sentence like "a knows whether ϕ" is translated as $K_a(?\mathbf{x}\phi)$. A model for the extended language is a quintuple (W, D, F, I, C), where W, D, I and C are as above and F is a function mapping individual-world pairs (a, w) into subsets of W. Intuitively, $F(a, w)$ represents the epistemic state of a in w. The semantics of the knowledge operator K_a is defined as follows:

Definition 6.2.3 (Knowledge-wh).

$$[\![K_a(?\mathbf{x}\phi)]\!]^{\wp}_{M,w,g} = 1 \text{ iff } F(a, w) \subseteq [\![?\mathbf{x}\phi]\!]^{\wp}_{M,w,g}$$

$K_a(?\mathbf{x}\phi)$ is true in w wrt $\wp$ iff a's epistemic state is contained in the denotation of $?\mathbf{x}\phi$ under $\wp$ in w. Since the denotation of a question in a world corresponds to the question's true exhaustive answer in that world, $K_a Q$ is true in w iff a's epistemic state entails the true exhaustive answer to Q in w.

6.2.3.1 Illustration

Consider again the card situation described above. Furthermore, assume that one of the cards is the winning card, but you don't know which one. We can model this situation as follows (the dot indicates the winning card):

$$\begin{array}{l} w_1 \mapsto \heartsuit \;\; \spadesuit^{\bullet} \\ w_2 \mapsto \spadesuit \;\; \heartsuit^{\bullet} \\ w_3 \mapsto \heartsuit^{\bullet} \; \spadesuit \\ w_4 \mapsto \spadesuit^{\bullet} \; \heartsuit \end{array}$$

Consider the following interrogative sentence:

(12) a. Which card is the winning card?
b. $?x_n.\ x_n = \iota y_n P y_n$

The evaluation of this sentence depends on the perspective that is taken. There are two possible perspectives. Under one ($\wp$), the cards are identified by their position, while under the other ($\wp'$), the cards are identified by their suit:

(13) a. $\wp(n) = \{$the card on the left, the card on the right$\}$;
b. $\wp'(n) = \{$the Ace of Spades, the Ace of Hearts$\}$.

The question in (12) partitions the set of worlds in two different ways depending on which perspective is assumed:

$$\text{under } \wp : \quad \begin{array}{|c|} \hline w_1 \\ w_2 \\ \hline w_3 \\ w_4 \\ \hline \end{array} \qquad\qquad \text{under } \wp' : \quad \begin{array}{|c|} \hline w_1 \\ w_4 \\ \hline w_2 \\ w_3 \\ \hline \end{array}$$

Under $\wp$, (12) disconnects those worlds in which the winning card occupies a different position. Under $\wp'$, it groups together those possibilities in which the winning card is of the same suit. In other words, in the first case, the relevant distinction is whether the left card or the right card is the winning card; in the second case the question expressed is whether Spades is the winning card, or Hearts. Since different partitions are determined under different perspectives, we can account for the fact that different answers are required in different circumstances. For instance, (14) counts as an answer to (12) only under $\wp'$:

(14) The Ace of Spades is the winning card.

Suppose now Anne knows that the Ace of Spades is the winning card, but she doesn't know whether it is the card on the left or the one on the right. In this situation Ann's epistemic state corresponds to the set: $\{w_1, w_4\}$. Sentence (15) is then correctly predicted to be true under $\wp'$, but false under $\wp$.

(15) a. Ann knows which card is the winning card.
b. $K_a(?x_n.\, x_n = \iota y_n P y_n)$

At last consider the following examples of a multi-constituent question:

(16) a. Which card is which?
b. $?x_n y_m.\, x_n = y_m$

(17) a. Ann does not know which card is which.
b. $\neg K_a ?x_n y_m.\, x_n = y_m$

As is easy to see, in Groenendijk and Stokhof's theory, (16) and (17) are wrongly predicted to be vacuous and to entail that Ann's epistemic state is inconsistent, respectively. On this account, in contrast, since different wh-phrases in a multi-constituent question can range over different sets of concepts, (16) and (17) receive a correct interpretation. To see this, assume $\wp$ assigns different covers to n and m, for example:

(18) a. $\wp(n) = \{$the card on the left, the card on the right$\}$;
b. $\wp(m) = \{$the Ace of Spades, the Ace of Hearts$\}$.

If interpreted under such perspective, (16) groups together those worlds that supply the same mapping from one cover to the other, and is not vacuous in our model. The partition determined is depicted in the following diagram:

under $\wp$:

w_1 w_3
w_2 w_4

The question divides the set of worlds in two blocks: $\{w_1, w_3\}$ and $\{w_2, w_4\}$. The first alternative corresponds to the possible answer (19), the second to the possible answer (20):

(19) The Ace of Hearts is the card on the left and the Ace of Spades is the card on the right.

(20) The Ace of Hearts is the card on the right and the Ace of Spades is the card on the left.

If Ann's epistemic state is specified as above, i.e. as $\{w_1, w_4\}$, then (17) would be true in w_1 without entailing inconsistency.

Aloni (2001) takes the meaning of a wh-clause, and therefore of a 'knowledge-wh' ascription to be sensitive to a contextually determined conceptual perspective. There are various positions one can adopt on the notion of a context and its role in interpretation, though. The next section reviews these positions and formulates the different analyses for 'knowledge-wh' ascriptions they would determine, if adopted.

6.3 Three Positions on the Role of Contexts

Contexts of use are typically understood as playing two roles in the determination of the truth of a sentence (Kaplan 1989a,b):

1. They help determine the proposition expressed by a sentence;
2. They help determine the circumstance of evaluation of the proposition expressed by a sentence (and thus its truth or falsity at that context).

That is, the typical understanding of the two roles of the context of use is that a sentence X is true at a context of use α if and only if the proposition expressed by X at α is true at the circumstance of evaluation determined by α.

In order to illustrate the first kind of role, consider the following sentence:

(21) I am intelligent.

Suppose (21) is uttered in context α by Barack Obama. In that case, the proposition expressed by (21) in α is the same proposition as the one expressed by (22) in every context:

(22) Barack Obama is intelligent.

However, if (21) is uttered in context β by George W. Bush, the proposition it expresses is the same as the proposition that (23) expresses in every context:

(23) George W. Bush is intelligent.

Sentence (21) expresses different propositions in the different contexts α and β. Due to this fact, even though the extension of the predicate 'is intelligent' might be the same in both α and β, the sentence can be true with respect to α (β) but false with respect to β (α), for the proposition expressed in α (β) might be true in α (β) while the proposition expressed in β (α) might be false in β (α).

This shows that the proposition expressed by (21) will vary with the context in which the sentence is used. Furthermore, the sensitivity to the context of use displayed by (21) can be traced back to the sensitivity to context displayed by 'I'. This expression, in Kaplan's words, has a content which varies from context to context, in each context its content being a constant function from possible worlds to the speaker of the context.

A paradigmatic case of the second kind of context dependence is contingency. Sentence (24) is true, but could have been false,

(24) Kaplan is a philosopher.

That (24) is actually true is due to the fact that the context of use determines that the world of the circumstance of evaluation of the sentence is the actual world. Had the context of use of the sentence been in a possible world where Kaplan was a blacksmith, then the sentence would have been false.

If one assumes that circumstances of evaluation also possess a time parameter, then this parameter will also be determined by the context of use, as can be seen by considering the following sentence:

(25) Barack Obama is the president of the United States.

Even if John's use of the sentence in 2010 is assessed for truth by Sue in 2030, the sentence as used by John in 2010 will still be true. The context sensitivity of (25) can be traced back to the context sensitivity of the expression 'is the president of the United States'. This expression will have different extensions at different times. By determining the time parameter of the circumstance of evaluation the context of use determines the extension of the expression that will be relevant for the determination of the truth of the sentence.

Recently, McFarlane introduced a whole new dependence: dependence on the context of assessment (e.g., MacFarlane 2005a,b). MacFarlane argues that it is not only the context of use that plays a role in determining the circumstance of evaluation of a sentence. His position is that a sentence X is true at contexts of use U and assessment A if and only if the proposition expressed by X at U is true at the circumstance of evaluation determined by both U and A.[3]

MacFarlane argues that one kind of sentence with respect to which one can see that the context of assessment plays such a role is one in which 'know' occurs. The claim is that circumstances of evaluation contain an epistemic standard parameter, and that the context of assessment determines the value of this parameter. He sees this option as a natural way to account for the following data concerning knowledge ascriptions:

1. Our use of 'know' seems to indicate a variability on the standards according to which someone is taken as knowing something: several times we assert that we know something, but after asserting it we are drawn to assert that we do not know that same thing, when we have learned nothing new nor are correcting a mistake. For instance, John might assert 'I know that Bill is at home', but after Mary mentions the possibility that there might be long queues on the highway, John will afterwards assert 'I don't know that Bill is at home'. One way to explain these phenomena is by saying that after Mary mentions the possibility that there might be long queues on the highway the standards according to which John counts as knowing that Bill is at home have changed.

[3]MacFarlane rejects the hypothesis that the context of assessment of a sentence plays a role similar to the first role played by the context of use. That is, he rejects that there is a context of assessment A of the use of a sentence X in context U such that A is different from U and A helps determine the proposition expressed by X as used in U.

2. The same epistemic standard appears to be in place when 'know' occurs embedded in temporal or modal operators, even though these operators shift the circumstances of evaluation of sentences.
3. After standards have been raised, retraction will take place. For instance, John will say that his previous assertion that he knew that Bill was at home is false.

Suppose John utters (26) in context α:

(26) I know that Susan's computer is in her bedroom.

Assuming John was cooperative, the sentence in the context α of its utterance is, *prima facie*, true. Mary replies to John in the following way:

(27) How do you know that her brother didn't take it to the living room?

Mary's reply forces John to retract, saying:

(28) You're right, what I said before was false. I don't know that Susan's computer is in her bedroom.

What is argued by MacFarlane is that the sentence uttered by John in α is true with respect to α taken also as the context of assessment, but that it is false taken with respect to the context of assessment resulting from Mary's utterance, since her utterance had the effect of raising the epistemic standards.

This shows how relativising truth to the context of assessment can explain the first and third points mentioned above. It can also explain the behavior of 'know' when embedded under modal or temporal operators. The effect of these operators is to shift the world and time parameters of the circumstance of evaluation. For instance, the sentence

(29) Necessarily John knows that Susan's computer is in her bedroom.

is true in contexts of use α and assessment β if and only if the sentence 'John knows that Susan's computer is in her bedroom' is true in all circumstances of evaluation that are just like the one determined by α and β, except perhaps for the world parameter. One can thus see that this operator does not affect the epistemic standard parameter. The same will be the case with respect to temporal operators: they will affect only the time parameter of the circumstance of evaluation. Hence, by assuming that truth is relative both to contexts of use and of assessment, one can explain the three facts about knowledge ascriptions.

As before, the context sensitivity of sentences such as (26) can, in part, be traced back to the context sensitivity of 'know'. Even if world and time parameters are fixed, this expression will have different extensions depending on the value of the epistemic standard parameter at play. And, as argued by MacFarlane, this parameter is determined by the context of assessment.

Three notions were discussed in the previous paragraphs: context of use, circumstances of evaluation and context of assessment. Adopting a taxonomy from MacFarlane (2005a) we will distinguish three positions with respect to the context sensitivity of 'knowledge-wh' ascriptions. Taking for granted that wh-clauses are interpreted relative to a conceptual perspective:

1. **Contextualism** takes the relevant perspective to be that at play in the context of use;
2. **Sensitive Invariantism** takes the relevant perspective to be that at play at the circumstances of evaluation;
3. **Relativism** takes the relevant perspective to be that determined by the context of assessment.[4]

To see the difference between these positions we need to vary one dimension while keeping the others constant. In what follows, we will consider two examples. In the first example, the circumstances of evaluation are kept fixed while varying, separately, the context of use and the context of assessment. In the second example, the circumstances of evaluation will be shifted while keeping the contexts of use and assessment fixed.

6.3.1 The Bombing

Our story begins on Wednesday at a cocktail party. Sue tells Mary that she needs to meet a certain Jack Compton. Mary, who knows that her husband Albert has just been introduced to Jack Compton by a friend, utters (30):

(30) Albert knows who Jack Compton is.

One day later a police investigation is taking place. The police is looking for the accomplice of Jack Compton, who has placed a bomb in the United States's embassy in Bolivia. Mary is being interrogated by the police on Thursday, and the police are interested in finding out whether Albert knew on Wednesday that Jack Compton was the man behind the bombing of the embassy. Assume that Albert's friend who introduced him to Jack Compton at the party, told him nothing concerning the

[4]More precisely: **Contextualism** takes the proposition expressed in a context of use by a sentence containing a wh-clause to be dependent on the perspective that is at play in that context; **Sensitive Invariantism** takes the truth, in a context of use (and of assessment), of sentences containing wh-clauses to be dependent on the perspective at play under the circumstances of evaluation of the sentence (where circumstances of evaluation do not include any perspective parameter, just as sentences such as 'Jupiter is as far apart to Nepture as the Earth is from the Sun' depend for their truth at a given circumstance of evaluation on the distance between the Earth and the Sun at that circumstance, even though the circumstance has no 'distance between the Earth and the Sun' parameter); and **Relativism** takes the truth, in a context of use and of assessment, of sentences containing wh-clauses to be dependent on a perspective parameter under the circumstances of evaluation, whose value is given by the perspective at play in the context of assessment. Aloni (2001), presented in the previous section, is an example of a contextualist analysis. As far as we know, nobody has explicitly defended a sensitive invariantist or a relativist analysis of 'knowledge-wh' in the linguistic or philosophical literature.

connection of Jack Compton to the bombing (and thus Albert remained ignorant of this fact). Consider now Mary's utterance of (31), when being interrogated by the police.

(31) Albert didn't know on Wednesday who Jack Compton was.

In their respective contexts, (30) and (31) are both true. Such data seems to provide a strong argument against sensitive invariantism. If sensitive invariantism was right, the relevant perspective for (30) and (31) would be the one at play at the circumstances of evaluation, i.e. at the party on Wednesday. The perspective at play there was one that assigns identification by ostension. If interpreted with respect to ostension, (31) would be false, contrary to intuition. This suggests that the relevant perspective for the interpretation of 'knowing-wh' constructions does not vary with the circumstances of evaluation.

Intuitively, sentence (31) uttered by Mary at the police station is true. But was Mary's earlier assertion of (30) at the party, if assessed later, false? If Mary were to assess her earlier claim now, would she retract it? We believe she wouldn't. If challenged, Mary could say: 'When I said 'Albert knows who Jack Compton is' on Wednesday I asserted something true, because Albert, who had just been introduced to this man, would have been able to point him out to Sue, who wanted to meet him. When I said today, at the police department, 'Albert didn't know on Wednesday who Jack Compton was', again, I asserted something true, because Albert on Wednesday didn't know that Jack Compton was the man responsible for the bombing of the U.S. embassy in Bolivia'. So, as it seems, shifting the context of assessment does not change our evaluation of earlier utterances. This suggests that the relevant perspective for the interpretation of 'knowing-wh' constructions does not vary with the context of assessment.

We have considered three cases (let c stand for the context of use, e for the circumstances of evaluation, and a for the context of assessment):

1. Sentence (30) used and assessed by Mary on Wednesday at the party $\mapsto$ $c, e, a = \text{wed}$
2. Sentence (30), its context of use and assessment being on Thursday at the police station, and its circumstance of evaluation being on Wednesday $\mapsto$ $e = \text{wed}$; $c, a = \text{thu}$[5]
3. Sentence (30) used by Mary on Wednesday but assessed on Thursday, with the circumstances of evaluation having its parameters determined by the context of use, and of assessment $\mapsto$ $c, e = \text{wed}$; $a = \text{thu}$

In case 1, e, c and a are all the same, and our knowledge ascription is true. In case 2, we have shifted both the context of use and the context of assessment, with dramatic consequences for our evaluation of the knowledge ascription, its negation now is judged as true. This, we argued, shows that the relevant perspective is not the one at play at the circumstance of evaluation. In case 3 we shifted the context

[5]We assume here that circumstances of evaluation do not include any perspective parameter.

of assessment with respect to case 1[6] without consequences for our evaluation of the earlier claim. This, we argued, shows that it was the shift in the context of use that had an impact on our evaluation in case 2, and not the shift in the context of assessment. Therefore, it seems that 'knowing-wh' constructions are sensitive to the perspective at play in the context of use, as contextualism holds, and not to the perspective at play at the context of assessment or at the circumstance of evaluation.

In the bombing example we have varied the contexts of use and of assessment while keeping the circumstances of evaluation fixed. What happens if we vary the circumstances of evaluation while keeping the contexts fixed? Consider the following situation.

6.3.2 The Exam

On Monday, during an exam on European politics, John correctly answered the question 'Who is the president of Italy?'. Some days later, during a party with many European politicians, Mary wants to meet the president of Italy, and asks John whether he knows who he is. John, who has no idea what the president of Italy looks like, utters (32).

(32) I don't know who the president of Italy is, but on Monday I knew who the president of Italy was.

John's utterance is odd (unless one considers the possibility that between Monday and the day of the party there were presidential elections in Italy) but acceptable, if you know all the relevant facts. The relevant methods of identification here seem to vary with the circumstances of evaluation. On Monday, at the exam, identification by name was the most prominent method of identification, and since John knew the name of the president, he knew who the president of Italy was. In the context of use, at the party, identification by ostension is at play, and since John doesn't know what the president looks like, he doesn't know who the president is. Sensitive invariantism seems to get it right here. Does contextualism get it wrong? No, contextualism has a ready explanation of this case in the following terms. Our sentence contains two wh-pronouns. For each of them context has to determine the conceptual cover that constitutes its domain of quantification. Typically, cover indices are resolved to the most salient cover (in this case identification by ostension). But deviation is possible. John wants to appeal to both conceptual covers in the same context, for that's the way he has to convey what he wishes to convey. And thus, the two pronouns will have different conceptual covers as their domain of quantification (the first corresponding to identification by ostension, the second by name). This will strike Mary as odd, for she was considering that the context set was one in which

[6] And, accordingly, added a perspective parameter to the circumstances of evaluation, whose value is given by the perspective at play in the context of assessment.

the perspective at play had as its only conceptual cover the one in which objects are identified by ostension. Nonetheless, if Mary assumes that John wants to conform to the rule according to which a proposition asserted is always true in some but not all of the possible worlds in the context set (a rule that, by default, speakers are assumed to be conforming to), she will have to conclude that John's context set is different than what she took it to be, or otherwise he would be uttering a contradiction, thus violating the rule. This might lead her to immediately conclude that the perspective at play is one also containing the conceptual cover corresponding to identification by name, or this might lead her to ask for further clarification from John, since she is not able to get at what John's context set is. In any case, contextualism can explain away this and similar cases. Contextualism seems to be on the right footing.

Adopting a taxonomy from MacFarlane, we have distinguished between a contextualist, a sensitive invariantist and a relativist position with respect to the role of conceptual perspectives in the interpretation of 'knowing-wh' constructions. There is still one other possibility to consider:

4. **Strict Invariantism** takes the truth of sentences containing wh-clauses to be, in general, independent of the conceptual perspective at play in a given context.

Contextualism and Strict Invariantism will be compared in the following section.

6.4 Contextualism vs Strict Invariantism

A strict invariantist has at least two options with respect to providing an account of the semantic content of 'knowing-wh' constructions. According to one of them, the denotation of the embedded wh-clause is always made with respect to one and the same conceptual perspective. This position gets it wrong. Consider again the card scenario presented at the beginning of the paper. None of the two conceptual perspectives seem to have primacy with respect to the other. It seems that such examples, where there's no reason to consider one conceptual perspective as being privileged, can be multiplied. Hence, if strict invariantism gets it right, it cannot be through the adoption of this first option.

The other option available for the strict invariantist leads to a different semantic analysis of 'know'. The idea is that an agent a knows Q if and only if *there is* a conceptual perspective $\wp$ such that a's epistemic state is contained in the denotation of Q under $\wp$.

The second option seems to be more promising, and related views have already been proposed in the literature. One such view is the one argued for by Braun (2006). Three general arguments for strict invariantism and against contextualism can be extracted from that text.

6.4.1 Arguments in Favor of Strict Invariantism

The first of these arguments is a direct argument for strict invariantism, and consists in claiming that, given a natural analysis of 'knowing-wh' constructions, the strict invariantist position is the one that fits naturally (and the contextualist position doesn't).

Braun proposes the following analysis for 'knowing-wh' constructions:

Knowing Q If Q is the content of a question, then X knows Q if and only if X knows a proposition that answers Q

IP Analysis A proposition answers a question if and only if it provides information about the question's subject matter

where the question's subject matter is taken by Braun to be its queried relation (furthermore, on his analysis, it seems that a proposition that 'is about' the queried relation can fail to provide information about that relation only if it is logically true).

One can now see that the strict invariantist position does seem to fit the analysis provided by Braun (and that, *prima facie*, the contextualist analysis doesn't). For if there is a conceptual perspective such that X knows the answer to the question determined by that conceptual perspective, then, arguably, X knows a proposition that provides information about the question's subject matter. Thus, *prima facie*, if the analysis is right, then the contextualist position is wrong.

However, if more attention is paid to the analysis provided, it can be concluded that it doesn't involve, at all, discarding the contextualist position. For, according to a contextualist, a proposition also answers a question if and only if it provides information about the question's subject matter. The difference between a contextualist and a strict invariantist is that the question's subject matter varies with context. Thus, a contextualist can also embrace the analysis of 'knowing Q' provided. The contextualist's point is that, given the semantic analysis of questions endorsed by him, the class of propositions that constitute an answer to the content of a question is more restricted than it is for a strict invariantist. Therefore, the direct argument for strict invariantism doesn't seem to be enough to vindicate it, for contextualism, a distinct position, is not inconsistent with the analysis of 'knowing Q' provided.

The second and third arguments are indirect, in the sense that they consist in arguments against the contextualist position.

The second argument is as follows: (I) Assume, for *reductio*, that the contextualist thesis is true. Consider a sentence of the form 'X knows who φ' uttered by Y in context α. Since contextualism is correct, it follows that (II) the proposition expressed by that sentence is dependent on the conceptual perspective at play in context α. But then, a sentence of the form 'Y said that X knows who φ' uttered by Z in a context β might be false, even if no context-sensitive expressions occur in φ, since the conceptual perspective at play in context β might be different than the conceptual perspective at play in α, and thus the proposition expressed by 'X knows who φ' when occurring embedded in the latter sentence might be different from the proposition expressed by that same sentence in context α, which would make the sentence 'Y said that X knows who φ' false in β. But, (III) when no context-sensitive expressions occur in φ, 'Y said that X knows who φ' never fails to be true in any context β, provided that in α Y in fact uttered the sentence 'X knows who φ'. Contradiction. Thus, (IV) contextualism is false. *A fortiori*, strict invariantism is the correct position with respect to the way conceptual perspectives are relevant for the determination of the truth of the sentences (it is easy to see that strict invariantism does not fall prey to the same objection, for it predicts no shift on the proposition expressed by 'X knows who φ' in one or another context).

Let us illustrate what the argument boils down to. Consider the following sentences:

(33) I am the president of the United States

uttered by Barack Obama in 2010, and

(34) Barack Obama said that I am the president of the United States

uttered by Vladimir Putin in 2010. Sentence (34) is false (even though the embedded sentence in (34) echoes sentence (33)). This phenomenon is due to the context sensitivity of 'I'. This expression always picks out the speaker of the context. For this reason, the meaning of the embedded 'I am the president of the United States' in (34) is the same as that of sentence (35):

(35) Vladimir Putin is the president of the United States,

and thus not the same as the meaning of (36)

(36) Barack Obama is the president of the United States

which is the meaning of (33). Hence, it is not true that what Barack Obama said is that which Vladimir Putin reports, for the embedded sentence expresses a different proposition than the one that it echoes. The contextualist argues that, just as 'I', 'knows who' is context-sensitive. Consider now the following sentence:

(37) John knows who the president of Namibia is,

uttered by Ann to Agnes, John's teacher, in a context where John is examined by Agnes with respect to the names of the presidents of different countries; suppose that Julie was also present during the conversation, and furthermore that some time afterwards she will be working for the U.N. in a general meeting of the organization. While working there, Julie and other colleagues are trying to track down where some of the presidents of the different countries are sitting exactly. In such context, Julie utters

(38) Ann said that John knows who the president of Namibia is

By uttering (38) Julie is not being cooperative, one would probably say. Nevertheless, Ann doesn't seem to be uttering anything false. If she was uttering something false, then sentence

(39) Ann did not say that John knows who the president of Namibia is

would be true. Suppose Jack, one of the colleagues of Julie was also present at the moment of Ann's utterance. Jack would reject Julie's utterance of (39). And, it seems, rightly so, because in this case Julie would be uttering something false. However, contextualism predicts that (38) is false and (39) is true, for, a contextualist would say, the sentence uttered by Ann did not express the proposition expressed by the embedded sentence 'John knows who the president of Namibia is' as it occurs in (39), and thus contextualism must be rejected.

This last argument can, however, also be rejected. The crucial premise is premise (II). Its strength comes from taking the context-sensitivity of 'knows who' as being of precisely the same type as the context-sensitivity of expressions like indexicals (expressions like 'I', 'here', 'now'). These expressions are sensitive solely to the context of utterance. However, as Partee (1989) has shown, some expressions are sensitive to other contexts: the context of discourse and the internal linguistic context. A known example of an expression that exhibits the three kinds of context-sensitivity is 'local'. Consider the three following sentences:

(40) A local bar is having an 'happy hour' at 19:00.

(41) Agnes was going for a stride in Buenos Aires when she noticed that a local bar was having an 'happy hour' and stopped for a drink.

(42) Every football fan is watching the World Cup match in a local bar.

In sentence (40) 'local' is sensitive to the context of utterance; in (41) the expression is sensitive to the context of discourse, and thus the bar mentioned is local with respect to the city introduced previously in the discourse; and in (42) 'local' is sensitive to the internal linguistic context, and thus each bar is local to the location of each of the football fans. Thus, premise (II) can be rejected. What the argument shows, a contextualist would argue, is not that contextualism is wrong, but that 'knows who' is sensitive not only to the context of utterance, but also to the context of discourse. This is the reason why sentence (37) can be *echoed* (disquoted) in sentence (38) without this last sentence turning out to be false, for the expression 'said that' introduces as the context of discourse the one where the embedded sentence was uttered. One can realize that this is so by considering the following sentences:

(43) I am at a local bar

uttered by John in a telephone call to Ann, and

(44) John said that he is at a local bar

uttered by Mary just after talking with John on the telephone. Even though 'local' in (43) refers to the location of the context of utterance, in (44) 'local' refers to the location of the context of discourse introduced by 'John said that', the location of the context of John's utterance, not to the location of Mary's utterance. Therefore, the second of the strict invariantist's arguments can be dismissed by the contextualist.[7]

The last argument consists in a dilemma for the contextualist. What is claimed is that a contextualist either: (i) is committed to an unintuitive relation between knowing who φ and knowing an answer to the content of 'who φ', it being possible for X to know a proposition that stands in the answering relation to the content of 'who φ' without X knowing who φ; or (ii) is committed to the context-sensitivity of 'answer'.

The argument runs as follows: if 'knowing who' is context-sensitive, then it is possible to know an answer to a question of the form 'who φ', without knowing who φ (due precisely to the context sensitivity of 'knowing who'). But this, it is claimed, is absurd.[8] Thus, it is argued, in order to avoid this consequence, the only alternative available to the contextualist is to regard the answering relation as being itself context-sensitive, the idea being that X knows who φ in a context C if and only if X knows a proposition that stands in the relation that 'answer' expresses in C to the question 'who φ'.

Adopting this solution, one can avoid the absurd conclusion that it is possible to know an answer to a question of the form 'who φ', without knowing who φ. But, Braun argues, the context-sensitivity of 'answer' is equally absurd. Assume otherwise. In this case, reports taking place in a context D stating that X answered Y's question can be false, even though in the context $C \neq D$ where Y posed the question, X answered it.

However, this objection misses its target, for the contextualist isn't committed to it being possible to know an answer to a question expressed by 'who φ' without knowing who φ, even assuming that the answering relation is not context-sensitive. A contextualist can connect the context-sensitivity of 'knowing who φ' to that of the embedded question 'who φ'. Once this position is adopted, he is no longer committed to it being possible to know an answer to a question expressed by 'who φ' without knowing who φ, for what proposition constitutes an answer to 'who φ' will vary with context. Furthermore, it will not vary because 'answer' is context-sensitive, but because 'who φ' is context-sensitive.

Braun states that similar problems arise if context-sensitivity is attributed to other expressions, such as wh-questions. It is not clear to us how Braun would adapt his argument. A plausible way would be as follows: a report taking place in a context D stating that X asked Y can be false, even though in context $C \neq D$, X asked Y. Since this is absurd, for X asked Y, contextualism is wrong.

---

[7]Braun has also recognized that this argument could lose some of its strength because comparative and gradable adjectives would be subject to the same objection as the one he provides, even though these expressions are widely recognized as being context-sensitive.

[8]It is actually possible to know an answer to a question of the form 'who φ', without knowing who φ. For example, 'Mary called' is an answer to the question 'who called?'. But knowing that Mary called is not enough to know who called. Suppose Mary and John called, but you believe that only Mary called. Then you know that Mary called, but you don't know who called. But we will disregard these issues here (see Groenendijk and Stokhof 1984, for further discussion).

An example. Suppose that, in context α, John asks the following question:

(45) Who is the president of the United States?

having in mind a method of identification according to which objects are identified by name.

In context β, a day after α, while discussing where in the U.N. meeting room the presidents of the different countries are seated, Mary reports the following:

(46) John asked yesterday who is the president of the United States.

The idea is that, according to contextualism, sentence (46) is false, for the question that John asked is not the one that Mary reports him as having asked, for the perspectives at play in the two contexts are different. But this, it is claimed, is absurd.

It seems to us that here it is also being assumed that the context-sensitivity exhibited by wh-questions is of the same type as the context-sensitivity exhibited by indexical expressions. But, as we saw earlier, the contextualist can reject such an assumption.

Suppose that Mary and Agnes are going for a stride in Buenos Aires on Wednesday. Mary asks a man on the street:

(47) Does the local bar have good music?

Mary and Agnes are flying back to Amsterdam that same day. One day after, talking about their trip, Agnes says:

(48) (...) and then Mary asked whether the local bar had good music.

Clearly, 'local' here refers to the location of the context of discourse introduced by 'Mary asked', the location of the context of Mary's question, not the location of Agnes utterance.

In the same way, the perspective relevant for interpreting (46) is the one of the context of discourse introduced by 'John asked yesterday', that is, the one that was at play at the time of John's utterance, not the one at play at the time of Mary's report. Hence, the argument does not force us to accept the desired conclusion.

As we have just seen, strict invariantists are unable to provide decisive arguments in favor of their position. Furthermore, they are incapable of dealing not only with the case described by the card scenario, but also with several similar context-shifting arguments that can be produced. The upper hand in the strict invariantism vs. contextualism debate thus seems to lie on the contextualist side. However, there are cases that contextualists cannot account for with the same success.

For instance, suppose Julie is going out today and has just received a phone call. Her father wishes to know with whom she is going out, asking:

(49) Who are you going out with?

To this, Julie's reply is

(50) With the person who has just called me.

Julie is certainly not being cooperative. But, as Braun notes, the reason why such 'smart aleck' replies are annoying seems to be that it is 'incorrect to accuse the respondent of failing to answer the question'. If this is so, then the contextualist must be getting something wrong. For clearly, the conceptual perspective at play in the context where the question is being asked is not one determining a conceptual cover containing the individual concept *the person who called Julie*. Thus, there seem to be cases pulling in either direction. On the one hand, cases like the card scenario seem to provide a reason to adopt the contextualist position; on the other hand, cases like the above seem to provide reason to adopt the strict invariantist position. Let us have a closer look.

6.4.2 Existential Closure or Not

The version of contextualism we have considered so far, based on Aloni (2001), proposes the following representation for 'knowing-wh' constructions containing a free variable n, ranging over conceptual covers, that is supplied with a value by the context of use.

(51) $K_a(?x_n\phi)$ [contextualist – free variable view]

A plausible competitor to the contextualist account of 'knowing-wh' constructions involves the use of a mechanism of existential closure which operates freely on the grammatically determined logical form of the utterance.

(52) $\exists n.K_a(?x_n\phi)$ [strict invariantist – ∃-closure view]

In the previous section we have dismissed a number of arguments presented by Braun against a contextualist approach and in favor of a strict invariantist view, but cases for either positions could be made. In this section we will summarize the empirical and conceptual challenges these two approaches encounter and at the end argue in favor a mixed analysis, a contextualist ∃-closure view which solves these challenges using tools that have been proposed in a parallel debate between contextualist, e.g., Kratzer (1998), and existential closure accounts, e.g., Reinhart (1997) and Winter (1997), of exceptional scope indefinites.

6.4.2.1 Arguments Against the ∃-Closure View

The first problem for the existential closure view is that if we don't somehow restrict the domain of the existential quantification over covers we always get a trivial meaning.

For instance, one knows who Barack Obama is by knowing that he is the man who is called 'Barack Obama', and one knows who the president of the United

States is by knowing that he is the president of the United States. In general, there will always be a cover such that what one knows by knowing who φ under that cover is a proposition which is true in every world.

To solve this problem, one can assume that the existential quantification involved in the analysis of 'knowing who' should be restricted in order to avoid trivial meanings (Braun 2006 makes a similar assumption). This, however, is a stipulation, unless we assume that domain restriction is a contextual process, in which case the required restriction would follow from general principles ruling contextual saturation; but in this case the ∃-closure view would no longer be a representative of strict invariantism.

A second challenge for this view concerns examples like the following used in the card situation:

(53) a. If Ann knows which card is the winning card, then she will win 10 euro.
b. $\exists n . K_a(?x_n\phi) \rightarrow \psi$

It is clear here that the intended meaning is one assuming a specific method of identification, namely identification by position, and not an existentially quantified meaning (even assuming a restriction to a non-trivial resolution). The meaning predicted for 'knowing-wh' constructions by the ∃-closure view is not specific enough for this case.

6.4.2.2 Arguments Against the Free Variable View

The first challenge for the free variable view is of a conceptual nature, and concerns contextualism in general. On the contextualist account what the speaker says involves a determinate way of picking out a method of identification. But the audience is not privy to the way of picking out the conceptual cover which the speaker has in mind. So, what is being proposed is that the speaker can say something which the audience cannot grasp. But even worse is the fact that sometimes the speaker herself seems to say something that she cannot grasp. We agree with Braun's intuition that often we use sentences like (54) to assert that John has a way of identifying Hong Oak Yun, without having a specific method in mind:

(54) John knows who Hong Oak Yun is.

Braun's 'smart aleck' case discussed in the previous section shows the same point. The contextualist, through the free variable view, predicts a meaning which is too specific for these cases.

The contextualist has, however, a pragmatic strategy at his hand. He can claim that, even though the literal meaning of (54) is as predicted on the contextualist account, speakers may intend to convey less specific meanings, which can be derived via diagonalisation (see Breheny 2006 who makes a similar move in the debate on exceptional scope indefinites).

Stalnaker (1978) discusses three principles of rational communication. Only principles 1 and 3 are relevant for our purposes:

1. A proposition asserted is always true in some but not all of the worlds in the context set.
3. The same proposition is expressed relative to each possible world in the context set.

A contextualist could say that cases like (54) involve a deliberate violation (or flouting) of principle 3 (see Grice 1975): the speaker deliberately infringes on principle 3 to thereby convey a different, less specific proposition, namely the diagonal proposition.

6.4.2.3 Illustration

Suppose our context set contains the following context-worlds $\{w_{1n}, w_{1o}, w_{1d}, w_{2n}, w_{2o}, w_{2d}\}$. Assume that in 1-worlds, John knows that Hong Oak Yun is the Head of the Department, but has never met her, and in 2-worlds he has met her at a party but he doesn't know that she is the Head of the Department. Further suppose that in n-contexts, naming is the selected method of identification, in o-contexts ostension is the selected method of identification, and in d-contexts identification via description is selected. So for example in context world $w_{1,n}$ John knows that Hong Oak Yun is the Head of the Department, but has never met her, and the selected method of identification is naming. Suppose we want to update our context set with (54). The relevant part of the propositional concept for (54) is as follows:

	w_{1n}	w_{1o}	w_{1d}	w_{2n}	w_{2o}	w_{2d}
w_{1n}	T	T	T	T	T	T
w_{1o}	F	F	F	T	T	T
w_{1d}	T	T	T	F	F	F
w_{2n}	T	T	T	T	T	T
w_{2o}	F	F	F	T	T	T
w_{2d}	T	T	T	F	F	F

By principle 1, we first eliminate contexts w_{1n} and w_{2n} which would determine a non informative proposition. Here is the propositional concept for the new context set:

	w_{1o}	w_{1d}	w_{2o}	w_{2d}
w_{1o}	F	F	T	T
w_{1d}	T	T	F	F
w_{2o}	F	F	T	T
w_{2d}	T	T	F	F

Although this move narrows down our alternatives, we still cannot figure out whether we are in a d-context or a o-context, and therefore we still don't know which is the intended proposition. The speaker is deliberately violating principle 3. She must have wanted to convey the diagonal proposition.

(55) *The diagonal proposition*

	w_{1o}	w_{1d}	w_{2o}	w_{2d}
w_{1o}	F	T	T	F
w_{1d}	F	T	T	F
w_{2o}	F	T	T	F
w_{2d}	F	T	T	F

We then update with the diagonal proposition. The resulting context set contains now only two possibilities: w_{1d} and w_{2o}.

Although the diagonal proposition in (55) is not equivalent to the existential proposition the ∃-closure view would assign to (54), it does entail it and seems to be 'unspecific' enough to explain the example. It seems fair to conclude that the contextualist, when equipped with a sophisticated pragmatics, can capture cases like (54), and, arguably, in a better way than the strict invariantist, who, without stipulation, would have predicted a trivial meaning for the sentence. Instead, the contextualist, via principle 1, has a principled explanation of why resolutions which determine trivial meanings are discarded.

It is easy to check, however, that by diagonalisation alone, our contextualist cannot capture embedded unspecific readings of 'knowing wh' constructions as in:

(56) If John knows who Hong Oak Yun is, he will tell.

a. $K_a(?x_n\phi) \rightarrow \psi$ [free variable view]
b. $\exists n.K_a(?x_n\phi) \rightarrow \psi$ [∃-closure view]

What it is meant here is: if John has a way of identifying Hong Oak Yun, he will tell. The ∃-closure view (with stipulation) captures this meaning. The contextualist view, even with the help of diagonalisation, doesn't. To see that it doesn't, consider the case where the antecedent is true in 1-worlds, and false in 2-worlds. In such case, the diagonal proposition looks as follows:

(57) *The diagonal proposition for* $K_a(?x_n\phi) \rightarrow \psi$

	w_{1o}	w_{1d}	w_{2o}	w_{2d}
w_{1o}	T	T	F	T
w_{1d}	T	T	F	T
w_{2o}	T	T	F	T
w_{2d}	T	T	F	T

while the proposition expressed by $\exists n.K_a(?x_n\phi) \rightarrow \psi$ is

(58) *The proposition for* $\exists n.K_a(?x_n\phi) \rightarrow \psi$

	w_{1o}	w_{1d}	w_{2o}	w_{2d}
w_{1o}	T	T	F	F
w_{1d}	T	T	F	F
w_{2o}	T	T	F	F
w_{2d}	T	T	F	F

Clearly, the diagonal proposition for $K_a(?x_n\phi) \rightarrow \psi$ is not equivalent nor does it imply the proposition for $\exists n.K_a(?x_n\phi) \rightarrow \psi$. One can see that the problem occurs when we consider context w_{2d}. Even though the antecedent is true if we adopt the existential closure view (for, under ostension, John knows who Hong Oak Yun is, and thus in 2-worlds there is a perspective under which John knows who Hong Oak Yun is), the antecedent that we get by diagonalization is false in context w_{2d} (for, under description, John does not know who Hong Oak Yun is), and thus the implication is true with respect to w_{2d}. The best approximation one can get is: there is a salient n such that if John knows who Hong Oak Yun is under n, he will tell.

To summarize, we have compared a contextualist free variable account with a strict invariantist ∃-closure view. The first view has serious problems of over-specification (the Hong Oak Yun case) which could only partially be solved by diagonalisation. The latter view has unsolved problems of underspecification (the card situation) and relies on a stipulation to predict informative meanings.

6.4.2.4 Two Possible Solutions

One possible way out from our dilemma is to start with the ∃-closure view and obtain an informative and specific meaning via pragmatic enrichment as in Récanati (2002). The card example can be explained along the following lines: in this specific context the truth conditions for (59-a) are not (59-b), the one determined by logical form, but (59-c), obtained by pragmatic enrichment ($n = o$ as unarticulated component):

(59) *Implicit contextualist ∃-closure view*

a. If Ann knows which card is the winning card, then she will win 10 euro.
b. $\exists n.K_a(?x_n\phi) \rightarrow \psi$ [logical form]
c. $(\exists n.K_a(?x_n\phi) \wedge n = o) \rightarrow \psi$ [after pragmatic enrichment]

One characteristic of pragmatic enrichment, however, is that it should be optional, so we cannot rely on it to solve our first problem: the exclusion from the domain of quantification of covers that would cause trivial meaning remains a stipulation.

Furthermore pragmatic enrichment has problems of overgeneration, cf. Stanley (2000, 2005). Not all possible unarticulated constituents should be in fact allowed. However, how to constrain the machinery in order to avoid overgeneration is far from clear.

The solution we prefer (at the moment) also starts with the ∃-closure view, but assumes existential quantification to be explicitly restricted to a contextually determined set of conceptualizations. Like in the previous solution, in this variant the ∃-closure view is no longer a representative of strict invariantism (X stands for a contextually supplied set of conceptual covers):

(60) *Explicit contextualist ∃-closure view*

a. Ann knows which card is the winning card.
b. $\exists n_X . K_a ?x_n \phi$ [logical form]

Contextually restricted sets of conceptualizations will be typically very small, often singleton, sets. Evidence for the adequacy of this account can be provided by the parallel between the types of cases generating smart-aleck replies like the one provided above, and cases involving the usual kind of quantification that also generate this kind of replies:

(61) John: Is everything in your purse?
Mary: No, I haven't put the table in it.

Just as happened with Julie's reply to her father, Mary is giving John a 'smart-aleck' reply by taking the domain of quantification to be larger than what John intended.

Furthermore, in both cases, the options open to the interrogators are the same. Either they accept the answers, thus also accepting a larger domain of quantification, or they refuse to do so.

If Julie's father were to endorse the last of these options, he could utter something in the guise of (62) as a reply:

(62) That was not what I meant, Julie. What I was asking was: who from your class are you going out with?

The same kind of reply is also available to John:

(63) That was not what I meant, Mary. What I was asking was: is everything that you were intending to take with you in your purse?

The similar behavior between the two types of cases seems to indicate that 'smart-aleck' replies are allowed by the quantified form of the questions, and that in such cases the domain of quantification can be enlarged by contextual factors.

Adoption of an explicit contextualist ∃-closure view allows for lack of specificity problems typical of ∃-closure views to be solved by assuming (default) restrictions to singleton domains (see Schwarzschild 2002). Also, being an existential closure approach, the overspecification problems of the free variable view are solved as well. Being a contextualist approach, resolutions which yield trivial meanings can be ruled out without stipulation. And finally, the conceptual problems of contextualism (the audience might still fail to grasp the intended domain of quantification) can be solved by diagonalisation.

6.5 Conclusion

In this paper we addressed the issue of how perspectives and context interact in our evaluation of 'knowing-wh' constructions. We argued for the need of an analysis for wh-clauses that took perspectives into consideration. Afterwards we considered different ways in which perspectives could be context-sensitive. We followed MacFarlane in his taxonomy, and saw that both relativism, and sensitive invariantism were untenable. The options were then reduced to seeing the perspective coming out from the context of use, or there being no context-sensitivity at all. Both options had problems that we tried to address. In the end we found that implicit and explicit contextualist ∃-closure views were the more appropriate in order to explain the data. Both have existential quantification over conceptual covers, the difference being that in the latter case the role played by context in the determination of the domain of covers is constrained by the logical form of the sentence in which 'knowing who' occurs. The explicit contextualist ∃-closure view had our preference for more theoretical reasons, which go back to the Stanley vs. Récanati debate on unarticulated constituents.

References

Aloni, M. (2001). *Quantification under conceptual covers*. PhD thesis, University of Amsterdam.

Braun, D. (2006). Now you know who Hong Oak Yun is. *Philosophical Issues, 16*(1), 24–42.

Breheny, R. (2006). Non-specific specifics and the source of existential closure of exceptional-scope indefinites. *UCLWPiL, 18*, 1–35.

Grice, P. (1975) Logic and conversation. In P. Cole & J. L. Morgan (Eds.), *Syntax and semantics: Speech acts*. New York: Academic.

Groenendijk, J., & Stokhof, M. (1984). *Studies on the semantics of questions and the pragmatics of answers*. PhD thesis, University of Amsterdam.

Kaplan, D. (1989a). Afterthoughts. In J. Almog, J. Perry, & H. Wettstein (Eds.), *Themes from Kaplan*. Oxford: Oxford University Press.

Kaplan, D. (1989b). Demonstratives. In J. Almog, J. Perry, & H. Wettstein (Eds.), *Themes from Kaplan*. Oxford: Oxford University Press.

Kratzer, A. (1998). Scope or pseudo-scope: Are there wide-scope indefinites? In Rothstein, S. (Ed.) *Events in grammar* (pp. 163–196). Dordrecht: Kluwer.

MacFarlane, J. (2005a). The assessment sensitivity of knowledge attributions. In T. S. Gendler & J. Hawthorne (Eds.), *Oxford studies in epistemology* (Vol. 1, pp. 197–233). Oxford: Oxford University Press.

MacFarlane, J. (2005b). Making sense of relative truth. *Proceedings of the Aristotelian Society, 105*, 321–339.

Partee, B. (1989). Binding implicit variables in quantified contexts. In *Papers from CLS 25*. Chicago Linguistic Society.
Récanati, F. (2002). Unarticulated constituents. *Linguistics and Philosophy, 25*, 299–345.
Reinhart, T. (1997). Quantifier-scope: How labor is divided between QR and choice functions. *Linguistics and Philosophy, 20*, 335–397.
Schwarzschild, R. (2002). Singleton indefinites. *Journal of Semantics, 19*(3), 289–314.
Stalnaker, R. (1978). Assertion. In P. Cole (Ed.), *Syntax and semantics: Pragmatics* (Vol. 9). New York: Academic.
Stanley, J. (2000). Context and logical form. *Linguistics and Philosophy, 23*(4), 391–434.
Stanley, J. (2005). Review of François Récanati's Literal Meaning. *Notre Dame Philosophical Reviews, 9*. http://ndpr.nd.edu/news/24857-literal-meaning/.
Winter, Y. (1997). Choice functions and the scopal semantics of indefinites. *Linguistics and Philosophy, 20*, 399–467.

Chapter 7
Knowledge Attributions in Context of Decision Problems

Robert van Rooij

7.1 Introduction

Ever since Dretske (1970) it has been argued that standard knowledge attributions are context dependent. But in this, they are not alone. It is quite clear, for instance, that whether a particular attitude attribution is counted as true or not can vary from context to context. This is true, for instance, of *de re* belief attributions. Consider Quine's (1956) Ralph who, one evening, sees a man with a brown hat whose suspicious behaviour leads Ralph to believe that the man is a spy. This man happens to be Ortcutt. On another occasion, Ralph sees the same man at the beach, but he does not recognize him as the same man; and the thought that the man he sees at the beach is a spy does not even occur to him. Now, does Ralph believe that Ortcutt is a spy or not? That is, is the following sentence true or not?

(1) Ralph believes of Ortcutt that he is a spy.

It is widely assumed (e.g., Stalnaker 1988) that whether (1) is true or not depends crucially on the conversational context. If only the first half of the story is told, and nothing is presupposed, or salient, about Ralph's meeting of Ortcutt at the beach, (1) might intuitively be counted as true. Similarly, if only the second half of the story is told, (1) should be counted as being false. Only if both ways in which Ralph is acquainted with Ortcutt are equally salient in the conversational context, (1) doesn't seem to be (unambiguously) true nor (unambiguously) false. What is important about this example is that (1) can be true in one conversational context and false in another, although Ralph himself believes the same in both contexts.

As a second example, it is also uncontroversial that 'Knowing who' statements are context dependent. Intuitively, one knows who Pele is if one knows an

R. van Rooij (✉)
Institute for Logic, Language and Computation (ILLC), University of Amsterdam, Science Park 107, 1098 XG, Amsterdam, The Netherlands
e-mail: R.a.m.vanRooij@uva.nl

F. Lihoreau and M. Rebuschi (eds.), *Epistemology, Context, and Formalism*, Synthese Library 369, DOI 10.1007/978-3-319-02943-6_7,

appropriate complete answer to the question, *What does Pele refer to?* The answer, *Except for Johan Cruijff and Maradona, the best soccer player of the world* seems clearly an adequate and appropriate answer (at least in one context). So if Mary can answer that question, then she knows who Pele is (at least in that context). But in that context, she may not know who Edison Arantes do Nascimento is, in the sense that she may not know who 'Edison Arantes do Nascimento' refers to, although this is the real name of Pele.

In this paper I will show that knowledge attributions that involve *embedded questions* are context dependent too, and that this context dependence involves *decision problems*, just as the interpretation of standard answers to questions. I will also indicate that *knowledge that* sentences are context dependent in a similar way. As a result, so I will argue, the analysis differs from the standard analyses by not just looking at relevant possible worlds. Instead, on this analysis the notion of fine-grainedness plays an important role. I will use the framework of Optimal Assertions, introduced by Benz (2006) and developed by Benz and van Rooij (2007) to account for optimal interpretations of assertions.

7.2 Optimal Answers

7.2.1 Context Dependence of Questions and Answers

There has been a controversial debate about whether or not strongly exhaustive answers have a prominent status among the set of all possible answers. Groenendijk and Stokhof (1984) are the most prominent defenders of the view that they constitute the basic answer, whereas other types of answers have to be accounted for pragmatically. For a constituent question like '*Who came to the party?*' a complete answer has to tell us for each person whether he or she came to the party or not. This is important for the interpretation of embedded interrogatives: If Peter knows who came to the party, then Peter knows whether John came to the party, and whether Jeff came to the party, and whether Jane came to the party, etc. The set of all possible answers is then the set of all strongly exhaustive answers.[1] On the other hand, there are so-called 'mention-some' questions like 'Where can I buy Italian wine?' the 'complete' answers of which do not seem to imply exhaustivity. Similarly, the sentence 'Peter knows where to buy an Italian wine in Amsterdam' can be true, intuitively, without it being the case that for each x Peter knows whether he can buy

[1]If Ω is a set of possible worlds with the same domain D, and $[\![\phi]\!]^v$ denotes the extension of predicate ϕ in v, then a strongly exhaustive answer to question $?x.\phi(x)$ is a proposition of the form $[v]_\phi := \{w \in \Omega \mid [\![\phi]\!]^w = [\![\phi]\!]^v\}$; i.e. it collects all worlds where predicate ϕ has the same extension. The set of all possible answers is then given by $[\![?x.\phi(x)]\!]^{GS} := \{[v]_\phi \mid v \in \Omega\}$. This poses a problem for mention–some answers as they are not elements of $[\![?x.\phi(x)]\!]^{GS}$, hence not answers at all.

Italian wine at x, where x ranges over all stores in Amsterdam. For reasons like this (van Rooij 2003a,b,c) proposed that the conventional meaning of a question (and its answers) is underspecified, and that the exact meaning is determined by means of context, in particular, by means of the relevant *decision problem*. In Benz and van Rooij (2007) this analysis is embedded in the game-theoretic setting of Optimal Assertions: what is expressed by an interrogative sentence, and what is implied by its answers, depends on the decision problem at stake in the conversation. It was argued that thus the truth value of the whole sentence 'John knows where he can buy an Italian wine' depends on Peter's decision problem as well. In this paper we will argue that the meaning of the embedded question depends not only on Peter's decision problem, but also on what is relevant to the participants of a conversation.

7.2.2 Decision Problems

Let Ω be the set of all possible states of the worlds. For simplicity we restrict our considerations to situations with countably many possibilities, i.e. to countable Ωs. We represent an agent's expectations about the world by a probability distribution over Ω, i.e. a real valued function $P : \Omega \longrightarrow \mathbf{R}$ with the following properties: (1) $P(v) \geq 0$ for all $v \in \Omega$ and (2) the sum of all $P(v)$ equals 1. For sets $A \subseteq \Omega$ we set $P(A) = \sum_{v \in A} P(v)$. Hence $P(\Omega) = 1$. We represent the agent's preferences over outcomes of actions by a real valued utility function over action–world pairs. We collect these elements in the following structure:

Definition 7.2.1. A *decision problem* is a triple $\langle(\Omega, P), \mathcal{A}, U\rangle$ such that (Ω, P) is a countable probability space, $\mathcal{A}$ a finite, non–empty set and $U : \mathcal{A} \times \Omega \longrightarrow \mathbf{R}$ a function. $\mathcal{A}$ is called the *action* set, and its elements *actions*. U is called a *payoff* or *utility* function.

Let us now assume that our agent, Ann, faces a *decision problem*, i.e., she wonders which of the alternative actions in $\mathcal{A}$ she should choose. It is standard to assume that rational agents try to maximise their expected utilities. The *expected utility* of an action a is defined by:

$$EU(a) = \sum_{v \in \Omega} P(v) \times U(a, v). \tag{7.1}$$

Suppose that Ann receives some information, e.g. proposition C. In probability theory the effect of learning a proposition C is modelled by *conditional probabilities*. Let H be any proposition, e.g. the proposition that one sells Italian wine at the station. H collects all possible worlds in Ω where this sentence is true. Let C be some other proposition, e.g. the answer given by Bob. Then, the probability of H *given* C, written $P(H|C)$, is defined by:

$$P(H|C) := P(H \cap C)/P(C). \tag{7.2}$$

This is only well–defined if $P(C) \neq 0$. In terms of this conditional probability function, we can now define the *expected utility of a after learning C* by:

$$EU(a|C) = \sum_{v \in \Omega} P(v|C) \times U(a, v). \tag{7.3}$$

Assuming that Ann is a utility maximizer, it can be expected that after Ann learned C, Ann will choose that action which maximizes the expected utility after learning C, i.e. $max_a EU(a|C)$.

7.2.3 Support Problems and Optimal Assertions

Ann, the hearer, learned C from somebody else, a speaker. Assuming that a speaker is rational as well, he chose to inform Ann of that proposition which he thinks is most useful to give. Instead of hearer and speaker, we will from now on talk about the *decision maker*, D, and the *expert*, E. The decision maker has a decision problem, $\langle(\Omega, P_D), \mathcal{A}, U\rangle$ and we will assume for simplicity that this problem is common knowledge (perhaps after she asked a question). In order to get a model for the questioning and answering situation we have to add a representation for the answering expert's situation. In principle this involves a whole decision problem for the expert. For reasons of simplicity, however, we will assume that the expert's utility function coincides with that of the decision maker, and only add a probability distribution P_E that represents his expectations about the world:

Definition 7.2.2. A *support problem* is a five–tuple $\langle\Omega, P_E, P_D, \mathcal{A}, U\rangle$ such that (Ω, P_E) and (Ω, P_D) are countable probability spaces, and $\langle(\Omega, P_D), \mathcal{A}, U\rangle$ is a decision problem. We call a support problem *well–behaved* if (1) for all $A \subseteq \Omega$: $P_D(A) = 1 \Rightarrow P_E(A) = 1$ and (2) for $x = D, E$ and all $a \in \mathcal{A}$: $\sum_{v \in \Omega} P_x(v) \times U(a, v) < \infty$.

The first condition for well–behavedness is included in order to make sure that E's answers cannot contradict D's beliefs. It implies that for sets $A, B \subseteq \Omega$: $P_E(A) = 1 \Rightarrow P_D(A) > 0$ and $P_D(A|B) = 1$ & $P_E(B) = 1 \Rightarrow P_E(A) = 1$. The second condition in the definition is there in order to keep the mathematics simple.

A support problem represents just the fixed static parameters of the answering situation. We assume that D's decision does not depend on what she believes that E believes. Hence her epistemic state (Ω, P) represents just her expectations about the actual world. E's task is to provide information that is optimally suited to support D in her decision problem. Hence, E faces a decision problem, where his actions are the possible answers. The utilities of the answers depend on the way they influence D's final choice. We look at the dependencies in more detail. We find two successive decision problems:

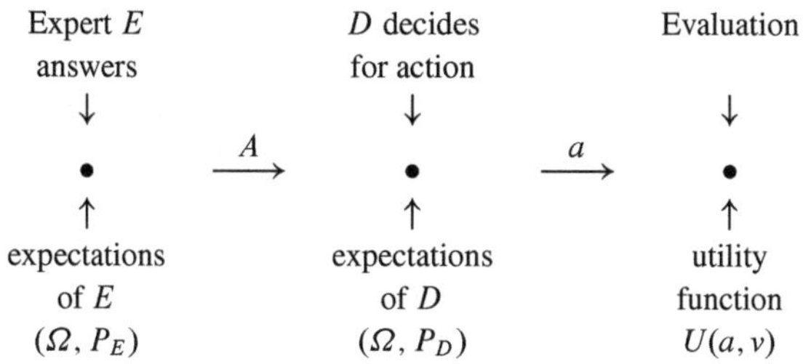

We assume that the answering expert E is fully cooperative and wants to maximise D's final success. Hence, E's payoff is identical with D's (our representation of the *Cooperative Principle*). E has to choose his answer in such a way that it optimally contributes towards D's decision. Due to our assumption that D's information is mutually known, E is able to calculate how D will decide. Hence, we represent the decision process as a sequential two-person game with complete coordination of preferences. We find a solution, i.e. optimal answers and choices of actions by calculating backward from the final outcomes. The following model will be worked out using standard techniques of game and decision theory. We concentrate on *ideal* dialogue.

7.2.4 Calculating Optimal Answers by Backward Induction

7.2.4.1 D's Decision Situation

First we have to consider the final decision problem of D. In the previous section we have determined the *expected utility after learning* A by:

$$EU(a, A) = \sum_{v \in \Omega} P(v|A) \times U(a, v).$$

If the decision maker D tries to maximise expected utilities by her choice, it follows that she will only choose actions that belong to $\{a \in \mathcal{A} | EU_{\langle \Omega, P_D \rangle}(a, A) \textit{ is maximal}\}$. In addition we assume that D has always a preference for one action over the other, or that there is a mutually known rule that tells D which action to choose if this set has more than one element. In this case we can write a_A for this unique element. In short, we assume that the function $A \mapsto a_A$, for $P_D(A) > 0$, is known to E.

7.2.4.2 *E*'s Decision Situation

According to our assumption, questioning and answering is a game of complete coordination (Principle of Cooperation). We have implemented this assumption by taking E's payoff function to be identical with D's payoff function U. In order to maximise his own payoff, E has to choose an answer such that it induces D to take an action that maximises their common payoff. We use definition (1.1) for calculating the expected utility of an answer $A \subseteq \Omega$. With a_A as defined above we get:

$$EU_E(A) := \sum_{v \in \Omega} P_E(v) \times U(a_A, v). \tag{7.4}$$

We add here a further Gricean maxim, the *Maxim of Quality*. We call an answer *admissible* if $P_E(A) = 1$. The Maxim of Quality is represented by the assumption that the expert E does only give admissible answers. This means that he believes them to be *true*. For a support problem $s = \langle \Omega, P_E, P_D, \mathcal{A}, U \rangle$ we set:

$$Adm_s := \{A \subseteq \Omega \mid P_E(A) = 1\}. \tag{7.5}$$

Hence, the set of optimal answers for s is given by:

$$\text{Op}_s = \{A \in Adm_S \mid \forall B \in Adm_s : EU_E(B) \leq EU_E(A)\}. \tag{7.6}$$

Assuming that the expert is making an optimal assertion, the inquirer can conclude from E's assertion that A that she is in a support problem s where it holds that $A \in \text{Op}_s$. Because, by assumption, she knows already E's utility function, D can learn a lot about what kind of worlds E takes to be probable.

We have argued that an informed speaker can and should use backward induction to determine which answer he should give. Notice that by our use of backward induction, the informed speaker assumes that the hearer will perform that act which has the highest expected utility after she has updated her belief by standard Bayesian conditionalization with the *semantic* meaning of the answer. This doesn't mean, however, that the hearer just interprets the answer simply at face value: On the assumption that the speaker is informed of her own decision problem and chooses his answer by making use of backward induction, the hearer can conclude more from the answer than just its standard semantic meaning (cf. Grice 1989).

We saw that an answer must be an element of Op_s for any support problem $s = \langle \Omega, P_E, P_D, \mathcal{A}, U \rangle$. If we assume that E has complete knowledge of all relevant facts, then it follows that for the actual world w it holds that $P_E(w) = 1$. But let's consider only the weaker assumption that E knows which action $a \in \mathcal{A}$ is optimal:

$$\exists a \in \mathcal{A}\, \forall v \in \Omega (P_E(v) > 0 \rightarrow \forall b \in \mathcal{A} : U(a, v) \geq U(b, v)). \tag{7.7}$$

Let's assume that E answered A, then the decision maker D knows that $E's$ answer is optimal, i.e. that $A \in \mathrm{Op}_s$, hence that:

$$P_E(A) = 1 \wedge \forall B : (P_E(B) = 1 \rightarrow EU_E(B) \leq EU_E(A)). \tag{7.8}$$

As $EU_E(B) = \sum_{v \in \Omega} P_E(v) \times U(a_B, v)$, it follows with (7.7) and (7.8) that

$$P_E(\{v \in \Omega \mid \forall b \in \mathcal{A} : U(a_A, v) \geq U(b, v)\}) = 1. \tag{7.9}$$

From this I can infer that:

$$w \in \{v \in \Omega \mid \forall b \in \mathcal{A} : U(a_A, v) \geq U(b, v)\}). \tag{7.10}$$

Interesting about this inference is that although E determines via backward induction what he should assert by making use of naive Bayesian updating on the hearer's side, the speaker in fact realizes that on the basis of this assumption I will update her beliefs via a more sophisticated method than conditionalization.

7.3 Decision Problems and Embedded Questions

7.3.1 Mention-Some Questions

In the last section we showed that the actual interpretation of an answer can be calculated from the fact that this answer is optimal. Before we consider the interpretation of embedded questions, let us first look at what our analysis predicts for standard mention-some questions.

Let us consider the mention-some question in (2) in the natural situation.

(2) I: Where can I buy Italian wine?
E: At the station and at the Bijenkorf but nowhere else. (SE)
E: At the station. (A) / At the Bijenkorf. (B)

The answer (SE) is called *strongly exhaustive*; it tells us for every location whether they sell Italian wine or not. The answers (A) and (B) are called *mention–some* answers.

We denote by a, b the actions of going to the station and going to the Bijenkorf. There may be other actions too. Let $A \subseteq \Omega$ be the set of worlds where one sells Italian wine at the station, and $B \subseteq \Omega$ where one sells Italian wine at the Bijenkorf. We represent the payoffs just as in the previous section: For every possible action $c \in \mathcal{A}$ the utility value is either 1 (success) or 0 (failure); especially we assume that $U(a, v) = 1$ iff $v \in A$, else $U(a, v) = 0$; $U(b, v) = 1$ iff $v \in B$, else $U(b, v) = 0$.

It is easy to see that $EU_D(A) = EU_D(SE)$ and it similarly holds that $EU_D(B) = EU_D(SE)$. This shows that for the inquirer it doesn't matter which information—exhaustive or not—she receives, as long as it is true. Thus, all the answers are equally useful with respect to conveyed information and the inquirer's goals. What we have to show now, however, is that all answers are equally optimal for the answering *expert*. We will show that $EU_E(A) = EU_E(B) = EU_E(SE) = 1$ if A, B and SE are admissible answers, and thus known to be true by the expert.

We start with answer A: If E knows that A, then A is an optimal answer. If learning A induces I to choose action a, i.e. if $a_A = a$, then the proof is very simple:

$$EU_E(A) = \sum_{v \in \Omega} P_E(v) \times U(a_A, v) = \sum_{v \in A} P_E(v) \times U(a, v) = 1.$$

Clearly, no other answer could yield a higher payoff. Obviously, B is also optimal if E knows that B. The same result follows for any stronger answer, including the strongly exhaustive answer SE, $A \wedge B$ or $A \wedge \neg B$. This shows that their expected utilities are all equal as long as they are admissible answers. Hence, all these answers are equally good and E can freely choose between them.

7.3.2 Context-Dependence of Embedded Questions

Let us now see whether our analysis of optimal answers is relevant for the interpretation of embedded questions as well. At first it might seems that this cannot be the case. Consider

(3) a. Peter knows where he can buy Italian wine.
  b. Peter knows where he can *best* buy Italian wine.

As argued for in the previous sections, the first sentence is true if Peter knows any place where he can buy Italian wine. If the set of optimal answers is identical with the meaning of the embedded sentence, however, then we should expect that (3.a) has the same meaning as (3.b). Intuitively, however, this is not the case: if the price of the wine counts as well, although being only of marginal importance, for (3.b) to be true, Peter has to know not only that he can buy Italian wine from a certain store, but also that he can't buy this wine cheaper from any other place.

Still, we will argue that we can account for this distinction by making the meaning of (3.a), but not that of (3.b), depend on what is relevant in the conversational situation. In the following we present a number of examples that strongly suggest that this is the correct way to proceed. If the only relevant property of stores is the fact that they sell Italian wine, then any mention–some answer is an optimal answer, and the only thing that can be inferred from the fact that Peter knows an optimal answer is the fact that he knows some place where it is possible to buy Italian wine. But if there are more relevant properties, we get different interpretations, including interpretations where it is implied that Peter knows where he can best buy Italian wine. The following examples should all be read in the context where Peter, the office assistant, was sent to buy Italian wine for an evening dinner.

(4) In the afternoon Ann tells Bob that Peter went shopping but that he returned without wine. Bob gets very angry about it.

Ann: Maybe, it was not his fault.
Bob: Oh, Peter knows where he can buy Italian wine.

(5) In the afternoon Ann tells Bob that Peter bought some Italian wine but it was obviously completely overpriced. Bob gets very angry about it.

Ann: Maybe, it was not his fault.
Bob: Oh, Peter knows where he can buy Italian wine.

(6) In the afternoon Ann tells Bob that Peter bought some Italian wine but it took a long time because he went to one of the wine shops in the centre and he was caught in the city traffic. Bob gets very angry about it.

Ann: Maybe, it was not his fault.
Bob: Oh, Peter knows where he can buy Italian wine.

In (4) we get the same interpretation as in (3.a). In (5) and (6), however, there are other things that count as well. In (5) "Peter, knows where he can buy Italian wine" must intuitively be interpreted as meaning that he knows a place where he can buy it cheaply, while from (6) we can conclude that Peter knows a place close by where he can avoid the traffic in the city.

7.3.3 Accounting for the Examples

As illustrated with examples (4)–(6), knowledge attributions involving embedded questions depend crucially on context. In particular, it depends on which attributes are relevant in the conversational situation.

If we want to apply the game-theoretic model of optimal answers to the semantics of embedded interrogatives, we have first to decide whose role, i.e. the expert's or the interrogator's, Peter takes in a sentence like: *Peter knows where to buy Italian wine*. The following examples indicate that he takes the expert's role:

(7) a. Ann: Where can I buy Italian wine?
Bob: Ask Peter, he knows where to buy Italian wine.
b. Ann: Does this train stop in Flensburg?
Bob: It is my first time on this train but Peter knows whether the train stops there.

As before we assume here that the answering expert (Peter) knows all relevant facts, i.e. we assume that (7.7) holds. This implies that:

$$\exists a \in \mathcal{A} : P_E(\{v \in \Omega \mid \forall b \in \mathcal{A} : U(a,v) \geq U(b,v)\}) = 1.$$

Let's set $O(a) := \{v \in \Omega \mid \forall b \in \mathcal{A} : U(a,v) \geq U(b,v)\}$, the set of worlds where action a is optimal. Then we say that E knows *what to do* in a given support problem $s = \langle \Omega, P_E, P_D, \mathcal{A}, U \rangle$ if $\exists a \in \mathcal{A} : P_E(O^s(a)) = 1$. Notice that this means that if we look only at the embedded question 'What should John do?', we might give it the following representation: $\{O^s(a) \mid a \in \mathcal{A}\}$. In the case of our example (3) in the situation as described before, for example, it results in $\{\{w_1, w_3\}, \{w_2, w_3\}\}$. In w_1 and w_3, one of the optimal actions is going to the station, while in w_2 and w_3 one of the best actions is going to the Bijenkorf.

In this model of (3.a) we assumed that Peter doesn't care where he should go to (in Amsterdam), as long he goes to a place where he can buy Italian wine at that place. In that case, (3.a) and (3.b) are actually equivalent. But now suppose that in w_3, it is closer to walk to the station than to walk to the Bijenkorf: $U(a, w_3) > U(b, w_3)$. We may then assume our tourist to prefer to walk to the station in w_3. So, in that case, the Bijenkorf is not one of the best places to walk to in w_3, and the question 'What is the best action to do?' is not represented by $\{\{w_1, w_3\}, \{w_2, w_3\}\}$, but rather by $\{\{w_1, w_3\}, \{w_2\}\}$. In this case we know that Peter's actual utility function depends on (i) whether one sells Italian wine at that place, and (ii) how far it is to walk to that place. However, in a particular conversational context, it might be common ground among the conversational partners that only one of those—the first one, for instance—really counts. In such a situation (3.a) can still be counted as true in w_3, although Peter takes w_2 to be a possible alternative. Notice that in this case (3.b) is intuitively counted as false, because by mentioning 'best' the utility function looks at all attributes that Peter considers relevant himself.

If two conversational situations differ in what is considered to be relevant by the interlocutors, then this defines two different support problems. Hence, if we ask whether it is true in a world w that *Peter knows where he can buy Italian wine*, then we have to consider w together with a support problem. Let $s = \langle \Omega, P_E, P_D, \mathcal{A}, U \rangle$ be a given support problem and $w \in \Omega$. We can then say that *E knows where he can buy Italian wine* is true in (w, s) iff $\exists a\ (P_E(O^s(a)) = 1 \wedge P_E(w) > 0)$. But, as we assume that the expert knows all relevant facts, the last condition is always true. The difference between the truth values of (3) and (3) is then due to the difference of the associated support problems. The effect of *best* in *E knows where he can best buy Italian wine* is to accommodate additional attributes which we would not consider if we read *E knows where he can buy Italian wine*.

7.4 Knowledge That

7.4.1 Context Dependence and Decision Problems

Until now we have considered knowledge-where attributions. It seems intuitively clear that knowledge-who, and knowledge-what behave in very much the same way: also here the interpretation seems to depend on what is at stake. More interesting is the question whether our analysis of optimal assertions can account for the context dependence of knowledge-that attributions as well, and in what sense the resulting analysis differs from the standard analyses.

Suppose Peter is at the zoo next to the zebra cage with his son. The zebras are in plain view and when his son asks him what they are, Peter tells him. It make all sense for us to say that Peter *knows* that they are zebras. Still, Peter can't really rule out completely that they are not mules cleverly disguised by the zoo authorities to look like zebras. Dretske (1970) suggests that although Peter can't he still *knows* that the animals he saw were zebras. It is perhaps not true anymore, however, when the possibility that they are cleverly disguised mules is brought up. Thus, the meaning of knowledge-that attributions are context dependent. See also Stalnaker (1993).

But not just any context dependence will do for 'know'. For instance, although there is some similarity with gradable adjectives like 'tall', Stanley (2004) quite clearly showed that there are important disanalogies as well. Whereas 'tall' allows for modifiers (*very*), fits well in comparatives, and is sensitive to comparison classes ('the fly is tall, but the elephant is not'), 'know' does not. This is all just to show that the context dependence won't consist in relating the meaning of the word *with respect to a particular scale*. But that leaves open many other alternatives.

According to the standard context-dependent analysis (e.g., Lewis 1996), Peter knows A is true iff Peter can rule out all (relevant) $\neg A$ worlds. It depends on context what the relevant $\neg A$ worlds are. Thus, $know(p, A)$ is true in w for modal model M iff for all of Peter's epistemically accessible worlds v it holds that, if v is among the (most) relevant worlds, A must be true in v (and M). It depends on the conversational context what are the (most) relevant alternative worlds. The sentence 'Peter knows that he looks at zebras' is true because worlds where he looks at cleverly disguised mules are not considered.

If one determines relevance with respect to decision problems, a slightly different picture arises. Suppose that the relevant decision problem is which action in $\mathcal{A}$ should be chosen. In that case it seems most natural to say that John knows A is true in w (and M) iff this entails that he knows which action in $\mathcal{A}$ he should choose. Thus, just like for knowledge-where attributions, it is natural to assume that in terms of the Optimal Assertion framework, Peter plays the expert role.

Let $s = \langle \Omega, P_E, P_D, \mathcal{A}, U \rangle$ be a given support problem and $w \in \Omega$, where Peter is the expert. The above discussion suggests that $Know(p, A)$ is true in (w, s) iff

$\exists a\ (P_E(O^s(a)) = 1 \wedge P_E(w) > 0)$. But this seems much too weak: the truth of the knowledge attributions seems to be *independent* of (the semantic value of) A. There is an obvious way, however, to make the embedded sentence relevant: it should be the case that A 'corresponds' somehow to the optimal action in the support problem. The natural idea would be to say that Peter knows that he looks at zebras really means (in this context) that Peter knows that he looks at zebras rather than *lions*, because in the relevant support problem two actions are at stake: a and b, and a is best iff it is zebras (or cleverly disguised mules) that he looks at, and b is best iff it is lions. Thus, the actions correspond with alternative sentences, and $Know(p, A)$ is true iff the knowledge attributions with the alternatives are false. In this sense the analysis is close to Schaffer's (2004) contrastive analysis of knowledge attributions.

Notice that context-change might influence the truth of knowledge attributions. If the support problem were more fine-grained, involving also an action c that is better than a in mules-worlds, but worse than a in zebra-worlds, Peter doesn't know anymore that he is looking at zebras, meaning that he wouldn't know anymore which action is preferred in all worlds of the relevant decision problem. Thus, even if nothing changed about Peter's knowledge, the truth of the knowledge attribution might still change. Thus, if the stakes are higher, more actions become relevant, and it is more difficult for the knowledge attribution to be true.

7.4.2 Granularity

In the previous section I suggested that indistinguishability, and thus, coarse-grainedness, plays a role in knowledge attributions. But we haven't been very clear yet about the semantics. If we want to account for knowledge, and knowledge attributions, we have to consider modal models with Peter's epistemic accessibility relation R_p. But some modal models make more fine-grained distinctions than others. In one modal model, M', we don't distinguish situations, or worlds, where the animals Peter sees are zebras or mules cleverly disguised in that way, while in another more fine-grained model, M, we do. Let M' be a model in which we don't distinguish zebra-worlds from mules-worlds. Then we would like to say that Peter knows that he looks at zebras is true with respect to M' iff in all 'worlds' v in M' that are epistemically accessible to Peter it is true that he looks at zebras. But recall that v is now a coarse-grain world, i.e. not really a single world, but stands proxy for a *set* of worlds. How do we determine these coarse-grained worlds, and under what circumstances is a sentence true in such a world?

We will first consider the last question, but ignore for the moment the possible worlds. Rather than looking at when a sentence is true in a coarse-grained world according to a modal model, we will first look at the parallel question when a predicate is true of a coarse-grained 'individual' in a model.

In natural language we conceptualize and describe the world at different levels of granularity. Hobbs (1985) argues that to represent or conceptualize the world at a coarser-grained level, we can just restrict ourselves by looking only at the *relevant* predicates of our original language. Consider a model $M = \langle D, I \rangle$ for the first-order language $\mathcal{L}$, and take $\mathcal{L}'$ to be a sublanguage of $\mathcal{L}$ containing only its 'relevant' predicates. In terms of the monadic predicates of $\mathcal{L}'$ we can now define an equivalence relation '$\sim_{\mathcal{L}'}$' with respect to language $\mathcal{L}'$: $a \sim_{\mathcal{L}'} b$ iff $a, b \in D_M$ and for all monadic predicates P of $\mathcal{L}'$: $M \models P(a) \Leftrightarrow M \models P(b)$.[2] In terms of this equivalence relation, Hobbs (1985) proposed to construct a coarse-grained model M' as follows: (i) the domain $D_{M'}$ is just the set of equivalence classes $D_{M'} = \{\{y \in D : y \sim_{\mathcal{L}'} x\} : x \in D_M\}$, and (ii) the interpretation function is such that for all monadic predicates $P \in \mathcal{L}'$, $M' \models P([a])$ iff $M \models P(a)$, where $[a]$ denotes the equivalence class containing $a \in D_M$.

Hobbs (1985) appealingly suggests to account for *type*-identity as identity at a more coarse-grained level of description. He so explains why we cannot say 'A Ford Falcon was heading south on U.S. 101, went out of control, and crashed into the same car' to mean that it hit another Ford Falcon. The reason is that *type*-level identity is just indistinguishability, but only restricted to distinguishable predicates that are *relevant*. Unfortunately, Lasersohn (2000) showed that the truth definition at the coarse-grained level proposed by Hobbs (1985) does not capture the intuitive motivation. It is clear that (i) 'I own a Ford Falcon. The same car is owned by Enzo.' should be interpreted with respect to a coarse-grained model. According to Hobbs' construction, $M' \leq M$ just in case if for every monadic predicate $P \in \mathcal{L}'$, if $P([a])$ is true in coarse-grained model M', it has to be the case that $P(b)$ is true in fine-grained model M, for *every* $b \in [a]$. However, it is clear that in (i) the predicates 'Owned by me' and 'Owned by Enzo' are relevant, and thus part of $\mathcal{L}'$. Because in M' it is the same car that has both of these properties, Hobbs' construction falsely predicts that every token of this car should have both properties in M as well.

Instead of making use of *universal* quantification as proposed by Hobbs (1985), why not make use of *existential* quantification? We assume a surjective function f from the domain of M, D_M, to the domain of coarser-grained model M', $D_{M'}$,[3] that preserves each relevant predicate P: if $x \in P_M$, then $f(x) \in P_{M'}$. The other direction follows by contraposition: if $x \notin P_{M'}$, then there is no $y \in f^{-1}(x)$ such that $y \in P_M$. To capture the idea of simplification, or coarsening, it is natural to assume that f is *not injective*: it might be that $f(x) = f(y)$, although $x \neq y$. Of course, we want refinements to preserve all the predicates and relations of the restricted language $\mathcal{L}'$, but this preservation is now stated as follows: $M' \leq_{\mathcal{L}'} M$ just in case if $x \in P_{M'}$, then $\exists y \in f^{-1}(x) \in P_M$, for each $P \in \mathcal{L}'$. But is it not problematic that the predicates 'Owned by me' and 'Owned by Enzo' are both relevant, and thus part of $\mathcal{L}'$? Yes, and no! Yes, if one wants the logic of M' to be the same as the logic of the finest-grained M. But no, if one is more flexible here. In particular, if we don't mind that at coarse grained M' for some sentences A it might hold that A is both true *and* false. To account for this feature, I will define two notions of truth simultaneously: a notion of *weak truth* and a notion of *strong*

[2]In general this obviously won't do: one has to look at relations as well. Let us ignore this, however.

[3]A function f from D to D' is surjective iff the range of f is D'.

truth.[4] Intuitively, it is the notion of weak truth that we are after, but it is convenient to state this notion partly in terms of the strong notion. In general, the weak and strong truth conditions of sentences in course-grained model M' are simultaneously defined in terms of their truth conditions in fine-grained model M and function f as follows (where we make use of the substitution analysis for simplicity and where $\underline{a}$ is the unique name of a):

$$\begin{array}{lll} M' \models_w P(\underline{a}) & \text{iff} & \exists d \in f^{-1}(a) : M \models P(\underline{d}) \\ M' \models_w \neg A & \text{iff} & M' \not\models_s A \\ M' \models_w A \wedge B & \text{iff} & M' \models_w A \text{ and } M' \models_w B \\ M' \models_w \forall x A & \text{iff} & \text{for all } d \in I_{M'} : M' \models_w A[\underline{d}/x]. \end{array}$$

$$\begin{array}{lll} M' \models_s P(\underline{a}) & \text{iff} & \forall d \in f^{-1}(a) : M \models P(\underline{d}) \\ M' \models_s \neg A & \text{iff} & M' \not\models_w A \\ M' \models_s A \wedge B & \text{iff} & M' \models_s A \text{ and } M', g \models_s B \\ M' \models_s \forall x A & \text{iff} & \text{for all } d \in I_{M'} : M' \models_s A[\underline{d}/x]. \end{array}$$

In particular, it holds that $M' \models_w \neg P(\underline{a})$ iff $\exists d \in f^{-1}(a) : M \not\models P(\underline{d})$. Notice that for all A it holds that if $M' \models_s A$ it follows that $M' \models_w A^f$ (where A^f is the translation of A corresponding to the surjective function f) but not necessarily the other way around. As it turns out, the weak logic at M' is rather like Priest's (1979) Logic of Paradox.

7.4.3 Knowledge Attributions Again

Back to our modal models. The indistinguishability relation should now be one between worlds. Thus, a modal model consists now of coarse-grained worlds and a sentence is strong or weakly true with respect to such a coarse-grained world (given a more fine-grained modal model and the surjective function f). The parallelism can be highlighted by making use of two-sorted logic: worlds are just seen as arguments of predicates, and we say that atomic proposition q is (weakly) true in coarse-grained world v' in model M', $M' \models_w q(v')$, just in case $\exists v \in f^{-1}(v') : M \models q(v)$.

Now we have to decide how the indistinguishability relation between worlds is determined. The idea is that this indistinguishability relation is determined by the support problem s. We don't distinguish worlds where the utility ordering of actions in $\mathcal{A}_s$ (the actions in s) is the same with respect to U_s (D's utility function in s). Thus, $u \approx_s v$ iff$_{def}$ $\forall a, b \in \mathcal{A}_s : U_s(a,u) \leq U_s(b,u)$ iff $U_s(a,v) \leq U_s(b,v)$. As for the above example, two worlds u and v that are exactly alike except that Peter looks at zebras in v and at cleverly disguised mules in u are considered to be irrelevantly different with respect to $\mathcal{A}$ and U, i.e. $u \approx_s v$, iff the utility orderings of the actions in $\mathcal{A}$ are the same.

[4]These notions are intimately related with the *tolerant* and *strict* notions of truth defined in van Rooij (2012) and Cobreros et al. (2012). For formal developments of these notions see especially the latter paper.

Now we say that $Know(p, A)$ is (weakly) true in v' of coarse-grained modal model M' iff $\forall u' \in R_p(v') : M' \models_w A(u')$. If A is atomic, this, in turn, is true iff $\forall u' \in R_p(v') : \exists u \in f^{-1}(u') : M \models_w A(u)$. This is a very weak notion: if Peter cannot distinguish zebras from mules cleverly disguised to look like zebras, it predicts that Peter also knows that the animals he sees are cleverly disguised mules. But, then, it is not true at coarse-grained world w' that we were after; we wanted to determine when the knowledge attribution is true with respect to our fine-grained world w. The idea is that the truth or falsity of this attribution is determined *via* the truth or falsity of the attribution of the coarse-grained model, but that doesn't mean that it is equated with it. In particular, if in w it is zebras Peter is looking at, we should predict that the attribution that "Peter knows that the animals he sees are cleverly disguised mules" is false. This can be done by assuming not only that the knowledge attribution is true in coarse-grained world w' as seen above, but also that the embedded sentence is true in fine-grained world w (one might call this an implementation of Lewis's (1996) rule of actuality).[5]

In what sense is this different from just restricting the worlds as Lewis proposed? Indeed, it is closely related with it. The Lewisian strategy would be to stay with one pointed modal model $\langle \Omega, w, R, D, I \rangle$ (where $w \in \Omega$ represents the actual world and where R_p is Peter's epistemic accessibility relation), but when interpreting a knowledge claim, one only looks at those epistemically accessible worlds that are most *relevant*. The actual world w is obviously among the relevant worlds, but which other worlds should be in there as well? In terms of our framework, I would like to make the following proposal (which we already argued for implicitly): just as with knowledge-where attributions, also for knowledge-that attributions it is Peter that functions as the expert (at least with respect to the issue at stake). Now look again at our definition of a support problem in Sect. 7.2.2:

Definition 7.4.1. A *support problem* is a five–tuple $\langle \Omega, P_E, P_D, \mathcal{A}, U \rangle$ such that (Ω, P_E) and (Ω, P_D) are countable probability spaces, and $\langle (\Omega, P_D), \mathcal{A}, U \rangle$ is a decision problem. We call a support problem *well–behaved* if (1) for all $A \subseteq \Omega$: $P_D(A) = 1 \Rightarrow P_E(A) = 1$ and (2) for $x = D, E$ and all $a \in \mathcal{A} : \sum_{v \in \Omega} P_x(v) \times U(a, v) < \infty$.

What is important for now is the first constraint for support problems to be well-behaved: for all $A \subseteq \Omega : P_D(A) = 1 \Rightarrow P_E(A) = 1$. By our assumption that E is an expert (with respect to the relevant issue), it seems only natural to say that the expert *knows* A if $P_E(A) = 1$. But this means that if E considers a world epistemically possible, this also holds for D. It follows that the set of epistemically

[5]Bach (2005) argued against context dependent analyses of knowledge attributions, because even with respect to any such model it can still be asked whether Peter *really* knows A, and thus that the sceptical charge is not really met. Peter *really* knows A, if A is true in all (relevant *and irrelevant*) epistemically accessible worlds. I believe that this criticism is unacceptable: the worlds in Ω are just *representations*, and one of them is the representation of the actual world. But representations can be finer and finer grained, and there need not be a *finest grained* representation. It is very natural to relate this impossibility with the power of the sceptic: you will never quite satisfy her.

possible worlds for the expert (at least as far what is relevant for D's decision problem) is a subset of the set of epistemically possible worlds for the decision maker. For knowledge attributions I think it is natural to assume that D's decision problem represents the decision problem of at least one of the participant of the conversation. But this means that all the worlds that D takes to be possible are also worlds that are compatible with what is presupposed by the participants of the conversation. Thus, if E considers a world epistemically possible, this world is also compatible with what is presupposed by the participants of the conversation. It follows that if a world is incompatible with what is presupposed by the participants of the conversation, this world is also not among E's epistemically possible worlds.

Of course, this need not really be the case in general: Peter does not know everything *we* presuppose. But my claim is that this is the case as long as we limit ourselves to what is relevant in the conversational situation. Putting this all together, this comes down to the proposal that in the context of support problem s, the set of relevant possible worlds in a conversational situation is just the set of worlds that are compatible with what we presuppose, which might be thought of as the following set: $\{w \in W : P_D(w) > 0\}$. And this helps: even if Peter cannot distinguish zebras from cleverly disguised mules, if *we* presuppose that the animals Peter looks at are zebras, the knowledge attributions that Peter knows that it is zebras that he looks at is counted as true as well.

What is the relation between Lewis's analysis (with the assumption that world v is taken to be irrelevant iff $P_D(v) = 0$) and ours? Obviously, the two come down to the same iff there is a one to one correspondence between the worlds that have a non-zero probability w.r.t. P_D and the coarse-grained worlds determined by the support problem s. I take this to be the typical case, which means that the two indeed give rise to the same predictions in these case. But perhaps our analysis does something extra: it looks in addition to what the agent (Peter) thinks from his own perspective.

References

Bach, E. (2005). The emperor's new 'knows'. In G. Pryer & G. Peter (Eds.), *Contextualism in philosophy: On epistomology, language and truth* (pp. 51–90). Oxford: Oxford University Press.

Benz, A. (2006). Utility and relevance of answers. In A. Benz, G. Jäger, & v. Rooij (Eds), *Game theory and pragmatics* (pp. 195–219). New York: Palgrave Macmillan.

Benz, A., & van Rooij, R. (2007). Optimal assertions and what they implicate, a uniform game-theoretic approach. *Topoi, 26*, 63–78.

Cobreros, P., Égré, P., Ripley, D., & van Rooij, R. (2012). Tolerant, classical, strict. *Journal of Philosophical Logic, 41*(2), 347–385.

Dretske, F. I. (1970). Epistemic operators. *Journal of Philosophy, 67*(24), 1007–1023.

Grice, P. (1989). *Studies in the way of words*. Cambridge: Harvard University Press.

Groenendijk, J., & Stokhof, M. (1984). *Studies in the semantics of questions and the pragmatics of answers*. PhD thesis, University of Amsterdam.

Hobbs, J. (1985). Granularity. In *Proceedings of the international joint conference on artificial intelligence (IJCAI-85)*.

Lasersohn, P. (2000). *Same*, models and representation. In *Proceedings of the 10th semantics and linguistic theory conference*. Cornell.
Lewis, D. (1996). Elusive knowledge. *Australian Journal of Philosophy, 74*(4), 549–567.
Priest, G. (1979). The logic of paradox. *Journal of Philosophical Logic, 8*, 219–241.
Quine, W.V. (1956). Quantifiers and propositional attitudes. *The Journal of Philosophy, 53*, 117–187.
Schaffer, J. (2004). From contextualism to contrastivism. *Philosophical Studies, 119*, 73–104.
Stalnaker, R. (1988). Belief attribution and context. In R. Grimm & D. Merrill (Eds.), *Contents of thought*. Tuscon: University of Arizona Press.
Stalnaker, R. (1993). Twin earth revisited. In *Proceedings of the Aristotelian society*, (Vol. 93, pp. 297–311). London.
Stanley, J. (2004). On the linguistic basis for contextualism. *Philosophical Studies, 119*(1), 119–146.
van Rooij, R. (2003a). Questioning to resolve decision problems. *Linguistics and Philosophy, 26*, 727–776.
van Rooij, R. (2003b). Utility of mention some questions. *Research on Language and Computation, 2*, 401–416.
van Rooij, R. (2003c). Asserting to resolve decision problems. *Journal of Pragmatics, 35*, 1161–1179.
van Rooij, R. (2012), Vagueness, tolerance and non-transitive entailment. In P. Cintula, C. Fermueller, L. Godo, & P. Hajek (Eds.), *Reasoning under vagueness: Logical, philosophical, and linguistic perspectives* (pp. 205–223). London: College Publications.

Chapter 8
How Context Dependent Is Scientific Knowledge?

Sven Ove Hansson

8.1 Introduction

Knowledge is a complex concept whose internal tensions make a precise and consistent reconstruction difficult. A statement has to be true in order to constitute knowledge. But since we seldom know with full certainty what is true, most knowledge claims are subject to some measure of uncertainty. That which we call knowledge is usually that which we believe that we know, rather than that which we know for sure.

Furthermore, knowledge is supposed to be general, in the sense that it can be acted upon in all contexts. But in practice knowledge arises and is applied in contexts that differ in terms of the epistemic requirements for action. Such differences have given rise to conflicts between demands of (epistemic) universality and (contextual) applicability.

The present contribution has its focus on the context dependence or independence of scientific knowledge. Its starting-point is the traditional view according to which scientific knowledge is completely independent of the context of application. I will attempt to show that this independence claim is untenable, but also that with some modifications, its basic ideals can be saved.

This investigation will be performed on three successively more realistic levels of idealization. On the first and least refined level, to be presented in Sect. 8.2, science is depicted as concerned exclusively with the pursuit of knowledge for its own sake. On the second level (Sect. 8.3) science is still primarily a system of knowledge for its own sake, but it is also applied in a variety of practical contexts, and such applications may necessitate various kinds of adjustments. On the third

S.O. Hansson (✉)
Division of Philosophy, Royal Institute of Technology (KTH), Teknikringen 78, 100 44, Stockholm, Sweden
e-mail: soh@kth.se

F. Lihoreau and M. Rebuschi (eds.), *Epistemology, Context, and Formalism*, Synthese Library 369, DOI 10.1007/978-3-319-02943-6_8,

and final level (Sect. 8.4) science is assumed to be continuously developing under the combined and sometimes conflicting requirements of knowledge per se and knowledge for practical applications. Some final conclusions are offered in Sect. 8.5. An outline of how the proposed model can be formalized is provided in an appendix.

8.2 Science as a System of Knowledge Per Se

In this section we will consider science as a system for acquiring knowledge for its own sake, thus disregarding the influences and demands on science that originate in its practical applications. Even in such a simplified account it has to be recognized that science is a human activity and therefore subject to the limitations of human cognition. This has at least two important consequences for the conduct of science. First, we need scientific discourses on several different complexity levels. This can be seen from the following example: We have good reasons to believe that the chemical reactions that give rise to photosynthesis operate in full accordance with the fundamental laws of physics. Indeed, clarifying models of these reactions can be obtained by solving the Schrödinger equation for the constellations of molecules that are involved in the reactions. (The solutions are approximate and require considerable computing power.) However, there is no way in which humans can understand these reactions directly in terms of quantum mechanics or the Schrödinger equation. Chemists interpreting the outcome of such calculations make use of "intermediate" concepts such as substitution, oxidization, electron transfer, etc. that are not directly definable in terms of fundamental physical laws. The need for such a level of understanding (and similar levels in biology, geology, climatology, etc.) depends on the limitations of human cognition.

8.2.1 The Fixation of Beliefs

The second consequence of our cognitive limitations is even more important in the present context: In order to make our picture of the world cognitively manageable, we must avoid making it too complex. Therefore we cannot keep as much open as an ideal reasoner with unlimited cognitive abilities would presumably have done. In order to simplify our account of the world we treat statements as true or false, although it would be more accurate to assign probabilities other than 1 or 0 to them. It is due to this simplifying strategy that science proceeds by accepting and rejecting statements and hypotheses, rather than by assigning probabilities to them.

Proposals to do otherwise have been made. According to Jeffrey (1956), researchers should never hold empirical statements to be true. Instead, they should assign probabilities to them. These probabilities can be quite close to 0 or 1, but they can never be equal to 0 or 1, since nothing empirical is fully certain. This is an application of the Bayesian ideal of rationality according to which a rational agent should assign (or act as assigning) a definite probability to all contingent statements. Since the probabilities of compound statements are assumed to follow the laws of probability, the resulting belief system will be a complex web of interconnected probability statements.

A chemist who lived according to these Bayesian principles would not take it for granted that gold is an element or, for that matter, that metals consist of atoms. She would regard these as highly probable hypotheses, but she would never say "We know that this is so", only "We hold it highly probable that this is so". This may seem to be an attractive picture of science. But unfortunately, it will never work in practice. It would make science an unmanageably complex net of uncertain but interconnected hypotheses. We humans are not able to keep that much open at the same time.

Instead we "fix" the vast majority of our near-certain beliefs to (provisional) certainty, thus taking as true (false) much of that to which we would otherwise assign a high non-unit (low non-zero) probability. As one example of this, the mother fully believes that the child she rears is the child to which she gave birth, in spite of the slight probability that there was an exchange of babies in the maternity ward. The Bayesian mother would only assign a high non-unit probability to that statement. This process of uncertainty-reduction, or "fixation of belief" (Peirce 1934), helps us to achieve a cognitively manageable representation of the world, thus increasing our competence and efficiency as decision makers.

Such fixations are just as necessary in the collective enterprise of science as they are in individual cognitive processes. In science as well, our cognitive limitations make massive reductions of high probabilities to full belief (provisional certainty) indispensable. As one example of this, since all measurement practices are theory-laden, no reasonably simple account of measurement would be available in a Bayesian approach (McLaughlin 1970).

There is also another important difference between the ideal Bayesian subject and a human being using her (limited) cognitive capacity rationally: The Bayesian subject assigns definite probabilities distinct from 0 to 1 to all contingent factual statements, and thus to an unlimited mass of assertions such as "Gamma Cephei has a planet with 13 moons" and "there exists a hydrocarbon that is more explosive than octanitrocubane". In actual practice, we just consider these statements as unsettled, and assign neither probabilities nor truth-values to them. Thus, whereas an ideal Bayesian scientist would assign probabilities to all statements, a scientist using her limited cognitive abilities rationally will instead (i) fix those with very high or very low probabilities, treating them as (provisionally) known to be true or false, (ii) treat a manageably small set of statements probabilistically, and (iii) treat the vast majority of statements about which nothing or too little is known as uncertain, i.e. assign no probabilities or truth values to them.

It must be emphasized that the fixed empirical beliefs in science are fixed only provisionally. In this they differ from statements assigned the probability 1 in a Bayesian system. According to the standard rules for revision of probabilities, once a statement has been assigned the probability 0 or 1, its probability can never be changed again. In contrast, when we fix a belief, this means only that it is currently undoubted. It need not be undoubtable since in the future new information may lead us to doubt it. Levi (1991) clarified this in terms of the distinction between certainty and incorrigibility. The chemist's opinion that gold is an element is certain knowledge in the sense of being undoubted. But it is nevertheless doubtable and corrigible, since we can (hypothetically) think of empirical evidence that would lead chemists to doubt and correct it.

The distinction between certainty and incorrigibility is particularly important for scientific knowledge, since corrigibility has a central role in science. Science does not claim to have certain knowledge. Instead its claim is to possess both the best (but imperfect) knowledge that is currently available and the best means to improve it. What makes science superior to its rivals is the effectiveness of its mechanisms for uncovering and correcting its own mistakes. Therefore, an account of the fixation of beliefs in science has to be accompanied by an account of the equally important process of revising the fixed beliefs.

8.2.2 The Corpus

The accepted, (provisionally) fixed, scientific statements can be summarized as comprising together the scientific corpus, or mass of scientific knowledge. The corpus consists of those statements about scientific subject matter that are taken as given by the collective of researchers in their continued research, and thus not questioned unless new information gives reason to question them. For practical purposes we can also, roughly, identify the corpus as consisting of those statements that could, at the time being, legitimately be made without reservation in a (sufficiently detailed) textbook (Hansson 1996, 2010).

The corpus consists of generalized statements that describe and explain features of the world we live in, in terms defined by our methods of investigation and the concepts we have developed. Hence, the corpus is not a selection of data but a set of statements of a more general nature. Whereas data refer to what has been observed, statements in the corpus refer to how things are and to what can be observed. Hypotheses are included into the corpus when the data provide sufficient evidence for them, and the same applies to corroborated generalizations that are based on explorative research.

It is important to note that there is only one corpus of science, not different corpora for the different sciences. The different disciplines are connected to each other by numerous ties of shared and interdependent knowledge. This interdependence has increased dramatically in the last half century or so due to the emergence and rapid development of integrative disciplines such as astrophysics, evolutionary biology, biochemistry, ecology, quantum chemistry, the neurosciences, social psychology, and game theory that tie together previously unconnected disciplines. The resulting community of interdependent disciplines includes not only those academic disciplines that are covered by the restrictive English term "science" but also the wider range of disciplines that are covered by the German term "Wissenschaft". This community of knowledge disciplines is characterized by mutual respect; the archaeologist relies on the consensus among physicists in issues of radioisotope dating, the astronomer on that of historians in the interpretation of ancient descriptions of celestial events, etc.

The scientific corpus is a highly complex construction. Due to its sheer size, it cannot be mastered by a single person. Different parts are maintained by different groups of experts. The areas of expertise are overlapping in complex ways, and the division of the corpus into such areas changes over time. Furthermore, the various parts of the corpus, as defined by the areas of expertise, are all constantly in development. Some changes of the corpus concern more than one area of expertise. Consolidations based on contacts and co-operations between interconnected disciplines take place continuously.

In spite of this complexity the corpus is, at each point in time, reasonably well-defined. In most disciplines it is fairly easy to distinguish those statements that are, for the time being, generally accepted by the relevant experts from those that are contested, under investigation, or rejected. Hence, the vague margins of the corpus are fairly narrow.

Since the corpus is intended to consist of statements that are taken (provisionally) to be certain, modifications of the corpus have to be based on strict standards of evidence. These standards are an essential part of the ethos of science. The onus of proof falls to those who want to change the corpus – for instance by acknowledging a previously unproven phenomenon, or introducing a new scientific theory. Another way to express this is to say that the corpus has high entry requirements. Basically, these requirements are determined by a balance between the disadvantages for future research of unnecessarily leaving a question unsettled and the disadvantages of settling it incorrectly. In Carl Hempel's terminology this is a balance between two epistemic values, or epistemic utilities (Feleppa 1981; Hempel 1960).

But whereas epistemic values have an obvious role in determining what we allow into the corpus, according to the traditional view influence from non-epistemic values is programmatically excluded. According to that view, what is included in the corpus should not depend on how we would like things to be but on what we have evidence for. It is indeed part of every scientist's training to leave out non-epistemic values from her scientific deliberations as far as possible. As Ziman (1996) pointed out, although it is often difficult for the individual scientist to avoid such influences, "the essence of the academic ethos is that it defines a culture designed to keep them as far as possible under control".

8.3 The Corpus in Extra-scientific Contexts

The philosophy of science has usually focused on "pure" science that aims at knowledge per se. However, large parts of science are in practice more concerned with finding knowledge for practical uses – for curing diseases, synthesizing chemicals, building computers, curbing inflation, etc. Science provides us with a repository of general-purpose knowledge that we can use for a wide variety of applications. But does the influence go only in one direction, from the scientific corpus to practical implications, or can the practical applications have influence on the entry requirements of the corpus?

8.3.1 *Two Types of Problems*

Due to the high entry requirements, the elements of the corpus typically have the degree of reliability that is needed to use them for most if not all practical purposes. Hence, the theory of acid-base reactions can be used in cheese production, the construction of car batteries, the fertilizer industry, the treatment of life-threatening acidosis, and a multitude of other practical contexts. This is the typical situation. The entry requirements of the corpus have been calibrated to suit the purposes of obtaining reliable knowledge per se, and since the resulting entry requirements are high, the elements of the corpus are reliable enough for the vast majority of practical purposes. This confirms a general property of knowledge (also outside of science) that has been noted by several authors: That which we classify as knowledge can appropriately be relied upon in practical reasoning and action (Brown 2008; Fantl and McGrath 2007). However, although this works in most cases it does not work in all cases. Two major types of discordancies can arise between the entry requirements of the scientific corpus and the requirements of practical action.

First, even though the entry requirements are high, there are cases when they appear not to be high enough. Statements that are considered reliable enough to be counted as scientific knowledge may nevertheless not be reliable enough for some practical application. Suppose that experts in structural mechanics have determined that a particular type of aluminium bar satisfies certain specifications, meaning in practice that it is strong enough to carry a load of 25 kg. The experts consider this to be scientifically valid knowledge. This knowledge is applied in practice, since the bar is used in a common type of dog transport cage. But then an aircraft manufacturer needs a bar with the same dimensions and the same strength to be used as a safety-critical component in the steering mechanism of a large airliner. They consider buying the dog-cage bar that is already under production. In this case it would be unsurprising if the relevant experts called for additional studies of the structural properties of the aluminium bar. Although the information previously available qualified as scientific knowledge, so much is now at stake that additional investigations can be justified. The standard criteria of scientific evidence, i.e., the entry requirements for the corpus, may not be stringent enough, given what is at stake.

Secondly, the high entry requirements of the corpus can also give rise to another type of problem. On some occasions, evidence that was not strong enough for corpus entry may nevertheless be strong enough to have legitimate influence in some practical matter. Suppose that there is significant but yet insufficient scientific evidence that a preservative agent in baby food may have serious negative health effects. Since the evidence is inconclusive, the issue is still open from a scientific point of view. Considering what is at stake, it would nevertheless be perfectly rational to cease the use of the substance. In this case, the standard criteria of scientific evidence, i.e. the entry requirements for the corpus, seem to be too strict for the purposes of practical decision making.

Hence two major types of problems can arise when the scientific corpus is applied in practical contexts: The entry requirements of the corpus (i.e., the evidence criteria of science) can either be too low or too high for the intended practical application. There are also two major ways to solve these problems: epistemic and decisional adjustments. By an epistemic adjustment is meant that the requirements of corpus entry are changed in order to suit practical purposes. By a decisional adjustment is meant that the criteria for decision making are adjusted, rather than those for corpus entry.

8.3.2 Decisional Adjustments

A decisional adjustment can take two forms, depending on the direction of the adjustment. Upward adjustments are justified by a perception that the standard scientific evidence criteria are not strict enough for a particular practical purpose. A decisional adjustment then consists in treating statements as uncertain in a practical decision although they are sufficiently reliable for the corpus. This means that we disregard parts of the corpus. "From a scientific point of view we know that the aluminium bar satisfies the specifications, but in the practical context we will not act upon this knowledge. Instead we act as if we did not have the knowledge in question."

In downward adjustments, the justification is a perception that the standard scientific evidence criteria are too strict for a particular purpose. A decisional adjustment then consists in taking statements to be reliable enough for practical decision making although they are too unreliable to be included in the corpus. "We do not know if the substance is harmful, but in the practical context we will act as if we knew this to be the case."

A decisional adjustment in either direction leaves the corpus unchanged (Hansson 2008). The influence of the practical application is restricted to determining the level of evidence required for particular practical decisions or actions. Decisional adjustments can differ between applications of one and the same scientific information. Hence, we can treat the evidence for the efficiency of an anti-viral drug as sufficient in one clinical context and insufficient in another, depending for instance on how serious the infection is. This we can do without changing our answer to the question whether there is sufficient scientific evidence that the drug is effective.

Downward decisional adjustments are common in many practical contexts. From a decision-theoretical point of view, such adjustments amount to letting decisions be influenced by uncertain information. This is something that we do all the time.

We prevent a child from running into the street even if we do not know that a car is approaching; the mere possibility is enough to justify protective action. We evacuate a building after a bomb threat even though we do not know that the threat is real (which it is only in a small minority of such events). We avoid exposure to chemicals that are suspected of being hazardous even if the evidence is too weak to justify a knowledge claim that the hazard is real, etc. In these and similar cases, the decision-theoretic standpoint is distinguished without much effort from the epistemic issue. "We do not know that this is dangerous, but to be on the safe side ... "

Admittedly, in environmental policies attempts have been made to argue that the limit between "in need of preventive action" and "not in need of preventive action" should be made to coincide with the limit between "scientifically known" and "not scientifically known". According to this view an environmental pollutant should be treated as harmless unless there is sufficient scientific proof of its harmfulness (i.e., unless the statement that it is harmful qualifies for inclusion in the corpus). However if applied consistently this approach would lead to excessive risk impositions. (It was promoted under the name of "sound science" in the early 1990s by tobacco industry lobbyists campaigning against legislation restricting passive smoking. Cf. Mooney (2005)).

Upward decisional adjustments are much more problematic. As mentioned in Sect. 8.3.1, we tend to assume that knowledge can be relied on in practical action. Therefore, when we find ourselves in a situation when we do not rely any more on that which we previously called knowledge, we usually end up not calling it knowledge any more. It would for instance be strange for a physician to say to a patient: "We know for sure that this is not cancer, but to be on the safe side I propose that we take a biopsy." The patient might then ask: "If you think that an additional test is needed, how can you then say that you know it is not cancer?" We would expect the physician to instead say something like the following: "It is very unlikely that this is cancer, but we do not know for sure so therefore I propose that we take a biopsy." As this example shows, our ingrained assumption that knowledge is sufficiently reliable for practical action makes upward decisional adjustments counter-intuitive and difficult to implement.

8.3.3 Epistemic Adjustments

By an epistemic adjustment is meant that the entry requirements of the corpus are adjusted so that its criteria of evidence coincide with (or at least approach) the criteria we wish to apply in practical decisions. Just like decisional adjustments, epistemic adjustments can be directed either upwards or downwards. An upward epistemic adjustment consists in raising the evidence criteria for corpus entry; a downward adjustment in lowering them.

At first sight epistemic adjustments may seem to be very sensible. We could for instance adjust the requirements of evidence in toxicology so that they coincide with the requirements for the practical decisions that we intend to make to protect ourselves against toxic substances. After such an adjustment has been performed, things will, presumably, be much simpler since we no longer need to distinguish between the criteria for practical and intrascientific decisions.

However, due to the variability of our practical uses of science, there is no single, well-determined way to adjust the standards of evidence to all practical uses of a particular piece of information. We may for instance ask questions about the safety of a vaccine when it is considered for use under normal conditions or when it is asked for under the conditions of an extreme emergency. Our willingness to act upon weak evidence of a side effect will be different in these two contexts. Therefore, we cannot adjust the corpus to suit all practical applications. The closest that we can come would be to adjust the evidence criteria for each statement to *one* of the levels that are suitable in practical applications of that statement.

Epistemic adjustments differ from decisional adjustments in propagating to all contexts where the statement may be referred to. In the case of the aluminium bar, suppose that the experts make an epistemic adjustment, agreeing that they do not really have knowledge about the strength of the bar. Since knowledge (and the concomitant corpus membership) is context independent, this adjustment will also extend to the transport cage context where it may be unsuitable. This is a quite general mechanism. It is impossible for a universal corpus to provide the criteria of evidence that we need in the variety of practical contexts where we have to make our decisions. In the case of the aluminium bar, an upward epistemic adjustment would possibly have to be followed by a downward decisional adjustment. ("We do not know for sure that it satisfies the criteria, but it is highly probable that it does. Therefore we can use it for this purpose.")

Changes in the two directions differ substantially in how detrimental they are to the corpus and to the system of scientific knowledge. A general-purpose corpus can fulfil its intended role in the knowledge system only if it has a high degree of reliability. Therefore, substantial lowerings of the entry requirements can be damaging by making the corpus unreliable. Raising the entry requirements does not have this effect. It leads to issues being kept open unnecessarily, rather than being settled the wrong way. Such raisings can make the corpus somewhat less useful, but they do not threaten its integrity. Furthermore, as already mentioned we have a strong tendency to assume that what we call knowledge is reliable enough for all practical purposes. This tendency provides an impetus to raise the entry requirements of the corpus when this is needed to avoid the discordant combination of accepting a statement as knowledge and rejecting it as unreliable for practical purposes.

8.4 A Multi-purpose Corpus

In Sect. 8.2 we outlined a simple model in which science is assumed always to be performed to achieve knowledge for its own sake. In Sect. 8.3 we discussed how such a system has to be adjusted when it encounters practical applications with evidential requirements that differ from those suitable for knowledge per se. But actual science did not start as a system of "pure" knowledge that was later exposed to contexts of application. Instead it developed, from its very beginnings, under the combined and sometimes conflicting requirements of knowledge per se and knowledge *ad applicandum*. In many areas of science, including the medical, veterinary, agricultural, and technological sciences, practical usefulness is the ultimate aim of most investigations. In this section we will treat science as a praxis that develops over time under the combined pressures of intra- and extrascientific requirements.

Based on what we saw in Sect. 8.3 we should not be surprised to find irregularities in the entry requirements of the corpus. Consider the following two statements about a new pharmaceutical drug:

(a) "This drug has no serious side-effects."
(b) "This drug causes blindness in some of those who take it."

Before (a) becomes accepted in clinical practice, extensive evidence from each of the phases of drug testing must be available, and in most cases this evidence has to include several large, independent clinical trials. Only if such evidence is available will the medical community consider (a) to be known. In contrast, much less evidence is required before (b) is considered to be known. Usually one well-conducted epidemiological study is sufficient for the conclusion that a new pharmaceutical drug has a specific side-effect. This difference in evidence requirements depends, of course, on the practical consequences of a mistaken belief in (a) respectively (b).

Hence, the demands of evidence for considering something as a scientific fact (an element of the corpus) may depend on its foreseen areas of application. But there are limits to how much the criteria of evidence can be adjusted to suit practical requirements. The downward limit is the most decisive one; we cannot allow a statement into the corpus unless we have quite strong evidence for it. There are of course also restrictions in the other direction. If the entry requirements are too high then the corpus will be too small to give action-guidance reasonably often (Godfrey-Smith 1991). But the scientific corpus is our joint repository of reliable information, and in the construction of such a repository the avoidance of error has higher priority than the avoidance of unsettledness.

In general, the evidence requirements for including a particular statement in the corpus are based on the requirements for accepting it as knowledge per se, unless there are practical applications in which higher requirements are needed for that particular statement. In such cases, the requirements for corpus inclusion are adjusted to coincide with the highest evidence requirements in any such application. In short, the entry requirements are calibrated to the most demanding application.

These considerations give rise to a model of the scientific knowledge process that can be summarized in the following five theses:

1. Science is a human activity and therefore subject to the limitations of human cognition. In order to make our account of the world cognitively manageable we "fix" highly plausible statements, i.e. we treat them as true rather than assigning a high but non-unit probability to them. This fixation is only provisional, and it will be revoked if new information gives us reason to question one of the fixed beliefs.
2. These provisional knowledge claims comprise together the scientific corpus, or mass of scientific knowledge. It consists of those statements about scientific subject matter that are taken as given by the collective of researchers in their continued research, unless new data give reason to question them. Due to the interconnections between the sciences there is only one corpus of science, common to the different sciences.
3. The scientific corpus is our common repository of reliable knowledge, developed not only for the purposes of knowledge per se but also for a wide variety of applications. It is constructed to be reliable enough to be acted upon in all contexts.
4. In order to make the corpus reliable, its entry requirements are strict. In most cases, they are based on the requirements for knowledge per se, and will then also be sufficient for all other applications. But if there are practical applications that demand a higher degree of reliability than what is needed for knowledge per se, then the entry requirements are calibrated upwards to the most demanding such application (epistemic adjustment).
5. Downward adjustments of the entry requirements are avoided in order not to make the corpus unreliable. When decisions have to be based on information that is not reliable enough for inclusion into the corpus, then this is achieved by letting non-corpus information influence the decision (decisional adjustment).

8.5 Conclusion

In the final model as presented in Sect. 8.4, what is counted as scientific knowledge can be influenced by practical considerations, but not in ways that threaten the reliability of science. Furthermore, scientific knowledge is context dependent in the sense that it matters for the acceptance or non-acceptance of a knowledge claim in which contexts it is expected to be applied. However, at the same time scientific knowledge is context *in*dependent in the sense that once the status of a knowledge claim has been determined, this status is constant across contexts of application. I hope to have shown that a model along these lines provides a more realistic account of the ideal that science should strive for than models requiring that the context of application have no influence at all on the acceptance or rejection of scientific knowledge claims.

Appendix: Formal Representation of the Corpus Model

Since the corpus model operates with a set of sentences held provisionally to be true, it can be formally expressed in the style of belief revision theory. In that tradition, a belief state is represented by a set of sentences held to be true, and changes are represented by operations that add sentences to that set and/or remove sentences from it (Levi 1980; Alchourrón et al. 1985; Hansson 1999).

In one important respect this mode of formal representation is in fact better suited for scientific knowledge claims than it is for individual beliefs: Beliefs held by individuals are often non-sentential. When you "believe what you see", your beliefs are not primarily sentential, but in standard belief revision models they have to be represented by sentences. In contrast, sentential representation is much more realistic for scientific knowledge claims. Science is a collective process that relies on verbal communication. Therefore, scientific knowledge claims have to be expressed in sentences in order to be taken seriously.

However, the operations of change that have been developed to represent changes in individual beliefs are not in all respects suited to represent the scientific knowledge process. In Hansson (2010) a model corresponding to the approach of Sect. 8.2 was outlined.

In such a model, it is necessary to distinguish between data and theory. The incorporation of new data into the scientific corpus is largely an accumulative process, in the sense that data are added but seldom retracted. However, this accumulativity does not apply to theoretical statements since the acquisition of new data can induce us to give up previous theoretical beliefs.

The formal model contains a set B of sentences that represents the corpus. To avoid unnecessary complications we will assume that B contains both the data and the accepted theoretical statements. Two types of operations on B are needed: Expansion by data and theoretical consolidation.

Expansion by data can be represented by the standard expansion operator $+$ of belief change, such that $B + p$ is the smallest corpus that includes both B and p (and consequently $p \in B + p$).

The standard operations of (individual) belief revision cannot be used to represent theoretical consolidation. They are aimed at inconsistency management whereas theoretical consolidation addresses the broader issue of explanation management, i.e. search for the best explanation of the available data. As a first approximation we can use an operator © such that B© is the outcome of deliberation on B aimed at finding the best theoretical account of the data in B. In a fully developed account, consolidation operators affecting only a part of the corpus would have to be introduced. (Cf. Hansson and Wassermann 2002.) Furthermore, the indeterminateness of theoretical consolidation would have to be accounted for. However, as a first approximation we can use a single, deterministic operator © acting on the whole corpus. (On the properties of ©, see Hansson (2010).)

Data expansion and theoretical consolidation are two independent operations that are initiated independently of each other. In particular, theoretical consolidation is not performed automatically after each acquisition of new data. In order to economize with the resources for theoretical work, the outcomes of previous inferences are retained, and they can influence later consolidations. Therefore, $B + p_1 + p_2©$ need not coincide with $B + p_1© + p_2©$.

In order to account for the influence of practical applications on corpus entry (as explained in Sects. 3 and 4 above) we need an additional operator, to be denoted $\ominus$ and called an operator of dubitation. We interpret $\ominus_x\alpha$ as saying that in the context x, a decision has been made to act as if α is not true. Note that α represents a theoretical statement, not an item of data. The context index (x in $\ominus_x\alpha$) can be omitted, and $\ominus\alpha$ then means that in some context, a decision has been made to act as if α is not true.

The following are two plausible properties of $\ominus$:

$\alpha \notin B \ominus \alpha$
If $\alpha \notin B$ then $B \ominus \alpha = B$

In the more interesting case when $\alpha \in B$, $B \ominus \alpha$ will be the outcome of removing α from B. In the terminology of belief revision theory, $\ominus$ is a contraction operator. We can expect it to satisfy:

$\alpha \notin B \ominus \alpha©$,

i.e., an operation of dubitation is not revoked by an operation of consolidation performed immediately afterwards. However, $\alpha \notin B \ominus \alpha + p©$ should not be satisfied in general, since p may carry information that provides new reasons to believe in α.

References

Alchourrón, C. E., Gärdenfors, P., & Makinson, D. (1985). On the logic of theory change: Partial meet contraction and revision functions. *Journal of Symbolic Logic, 50*, 510–530.

Brown, J. (2008). Subject-sensitive invariantism and the knowledge norm for practical reasoning. *Noûs, 42*(2), 167–189.

Fantl, J., & McGrath, M. (2007). On pragmatic encroachment in epistemology. *Philosophy and Phenomenological Research, 75*(3), 558–589.

Feleppa, R. (1981). Epistemic utility and theory acceptance: Comments on Hempel. *Synthese, 46*, 413–420.

Godfrey-Smith, P. (1991). Signal, decision, action. *Journal of Philosophy, 88*, 709–722.

Hansson, S. O. (1996). What is philosophy of risk? *Theoria, 62*, 169–186.

Hansson, S. O. (1999). *A textbook of belief dynamics: Theory change and database updating*. Dordrecht: Kluwer.

Hansson, S. O. (2008). Regulating BFRs—from science to policy. *Chemosphere, 73*, 144–147.

Hansson, S. O. (2010). Changing the scientific corpus. In E. J. Olsson & S. Enqvist (Eds.), *Belief revision meets philosophy of science* (pp. 43–58). Dordrecht: Springer.

Hansson, S. O., & Wassermann, R. (2002). Local change. *Studia Logica, 70*, 49–76.

Hempel, C. G. (1960). Inductive inconsistencies. *Synthese, 12*, 439–469.

Jeffrey, R. C. (1956). Valuation and acceptance of scientific hypotheses. *Philosophy of Science, 23*, 237–249.

Levi, I. (1980). *The enterprise of knowledge*. Cambridge: MIT Press.
Levi, I. (1991). *The fixation of belief and its undoing*. Cambridge: Cambridge University Press.
McLaughlin, A. (1970). Science, reason and value. *Theory and Decision, 1*, 121–137.
Mooney, C. (2005). *The republican war on science*. New York: Basic Books.
Peirce, C. S. (1934). The fixation of belief. In C. Hartshorne & P. Weiss (Eds.), *Collected papers of Charles Sanders Peirce* (Vol. 5, pp. 223–247). Cambridge: Harvard University Press.
Ziman, J. (1996). Postacademic science: Constructing knowledge with networks and norms. *Science Studies, 9*, 67–80.

Chapter 9
Action, Failure and Free Will Choice in Epistemic *stit* Logic

Jan Broersen and John-Jules Charles Meyer

9.1 Introduction

The central axiom of *stit* theory is independence of agency. This axiom states that simultaneous choices of different agents are independent in the sense that a choice of one agent cannot impair the choice making capacity of other agents. The axiom of independence can then be said to express freedom of choice.[1] But freedom of choice is different from freedom of will or freedom of action.

In this paper we will suggest how to formally study the differences between freedom of choice, freedom of will and freedom of action. To do so, we will extend stit theory with agent specific epistemic operators thereby introducing the subjective viewpoint into logics for agency. We argue that only by introducing this subjective viewpoint we can formalize free will choice and the distinctions between choosing, acting and failing.

But before explaining what the paper is about, let us first try to roughly establish the ontology and terminology that we will use throughout the text. An *action type* is a state transition of a certain type ("closing the door" = going from a state where the door is open to a state where the door is closed). Having our background in computer science, throughout the paper we will systematically neglect the difference between action types and actions. So, from now on, if we refer to an action of the "closing the

[1]Freedom of choice does not mean that agents cannot be strongly compelled to choose in a certain way.

J. Broersen (✉) • J.-J.C. Meyer
Department of Information and Computing Sciences, Utrecht University, PO Box 80.089, 3508 TB Utrecht, The Netherlands
e-mail: J.M.Broersen@uu.nl; J.J.C.Meyer@uu.nl

F. Lihoreau and M. Rebuschi (eds.), *Epistemology, Context, and Formalism*, Synthese Library 369, DOI 10.1007/978-3-319-02943-6_9,

door" type, we will simply talk about the *action* of "closing the door".[2] There can be one agent responsible for an action (John closes the door), there can be several agents responsible for one action (John and Mary together close the heavy door) and there can be one agent responsible for several simultaneous actions (John closes the door and turns his head). Even though in many formalisms in computer science it is customary to name actions (Dynamic Logic (Harel et al. 2000), Situations Calculus (McCarthy 1979)), in stit theory action names are not in the object language. In our stit formalism we express that the group A collectively chooses as to see to it that next φ as $[A \ \mathsf{xstit}]\varphi$ ('x' stands for 'next' and 'stit' stands for 'Seeing To It That'). We will also often read $[A \ \mathsf{xstit}]\varphi$ as A 'does' φ thereby identifying an action with the condition it brings about. This is not too far removed from the name giving in natural language, where the action name "closing the door" emphasizes the effect of the action (the door being closed) and not so much the fact that the action only makes sense in a transition from a state where the door is open. A *choice* in our stit setting is an effort or attempt of an agent to see to it that a certain condition holds. As said, choices are independent. But, actions are not. Agents are generally thought of as free to choose but not necessarily as free to act. The difference is due to the fact that choice application can be unsuccessful. Consider two agents, each on one side of a closed door. One can choose to open it while at the same time the other can choose to keep it closed. Which action will occur in this situation depends on whose choice will be successful. Note that in this ontology and terminology actions are not independent: the agents cannot concurrently perform the actions of opening the door and keeping it closed.

Although we will suggest a formal definition of free will choice, what we will *not* be concerned with in this paper is the freedom of the will. Freedom of the will concerns the issue that agents are free to deliberate and free to form any intention they think appropriate. However, our operator for free will choice is only about the absence of coercion. And we are not inclined to assume that an action that is not coerced is therefore willed. In our view, willed action is connected to an agent's intentions and deliberations. But when we say that an agent acts 'out of free will' we only say that it was not forced to do what it did, that is, it could have done otherwise, or, it was not coerced. This is the kind of free will choice we will formalize in this paper. The possible connection of free will choice with intention (and we believe this is very much connected with Robert Kane's contribution to the free will discussion Kane (2003)), we plan to discuss and formalize elsewhere.

Another motivation for this work is that we think that failure of choices and having the reasoning capabilities to cope with it is a central element of (artificial) intelligence. One of the things we will emphasize is that failure is always relative to an intention and/or an epistemic attitude. This makes failure of choices subjective. Nature never fails, only agents can think they do, or agents can think other agents do. Since we do not consider intention in this paper, our notion of failure will be

[2]Computer scientist are used to think of actions as some kind of instructions defined by a programming environment, which explains why they do not distinguish between actions and action types.

with respect to an agent's epistemic attitude towards action. We will model failure as the agent believing to exercise a choice, while the action actually occurring is one that is at odds with this belief.

9.2 Objective Action: XSTIT^p

In this section we define the base logic, which is a variant of XSTIT. XSTIT was first presented in Broersen (2008, 2009a), and corrected in Broersen (2011). The version we consider here is a variant that we call XSTIT^p. In the axiomatization, the difference with XSTIT is exactly one axiom schema concerning modality-free propositions p, which explains the name. Another difference with XSTIT is that we do not define the semantics directly in terms of *relations* over a two dimensional state-history structure, but in terms of functions. In particular we will introduce the notion of an h-relative effectivity function, which is a specialization of the notion of effectivity function from Coalition Logic (Pauly 2002) where choices are relative to histories. We think the semantics in terms of functions is more insightful than the earlier semantics in terms of relations, for which the main motivation was that it enables to give a straightforward completeness proof.

The modal language of XSTIT^p is given by the following definition:

Definition 9.2.1. Given a countable set of propositions P and $p \in P$, and given a finite set Ags of agent names, and $A \subseteq Ags$, the formal language $\mathcal{L}_{\mathsf{XSTIT}^p}$ is:

$$\varphi := p \mid \neg\varphi \mid \varphi \wedge \varphi \mid \Box\varphi \mid [A\ \mathsf{xstit}]\varphi \mid X\varphi$$

Besides the usual propositional connectives, the syntax of XSTIT^p comprises three modal operators. The operator $\Box\varphi$ expresses 'historical necessity', and plays the same role as the well-known path quantifiers in logics such as CTL and CTL* (Emerson 1990). Another way of talking about this operator is to say that it expresses that φ is 'settled'. However, settledness does *not* necessarily mean that a property is *always* true in the future (as often thought). Settledness may, in general, apply to the condition that φ occurs 'some' time in the future, or to some other temporal property. This is reflected by the fact that settledness is interpreted as a universal quantification over the *branching* dimension of time, and *not* over the dimension of duration. The operator $[A\ \mathsf{xstit}]\varphi$ stands for 'agents A jointly see to it that φ in the next state'. The third modality is the next operator $X\varphi$. It has a standard interpretation as the transition to a next state.

Definition 9.2.2. A function-based XSTIT^p-frame is a tuple $\langle S, H, E\rangle$ such that:

1. S is a non-empty set of static states. Elements of S are denoted s, s', etc.[3]

[3]In the meta-language we use these symbols both as constant names and as variable names. The same holds for the symbols $h, h', \ldots$ used to refer to histories.

2. H is a non-empty set of possible system histories of the form $\ldots s_{-2}, s_{-1}, s_0, s_1, s_2, \ldots$ with $s_x \in S$ for $x \in \mathbb{Z}$. Elements of H are denoted h, h', etc. We denote that s' succeeds s on the history h by $s' = succ(s, h)$ and by $s = prec(s', h)$. Furthermore (we assume universal quantification of unbound meta-variables):

a. if $s \in h$ and $s' \in h'$ and $s = s'$ then $prec(s, h) = prec(s', h')$

3. $E : S \times H \times 2^{Ags} \mapsto 2^S$ is an h-effectivity function yielding for a group of agents A the set of next static states allowed by the joint actions taken by the agents in the group A relative to a history.[4] For h-effectivity functions we define the following constraints:

a. if $s \notin h$ then $E(s, h, A) = \emptyset$
b. if $s' \in E(s, h, A)$ then $\exists h' : s' = succ(s, h')$
c. $succ(s, h) \in E(s, h, A)$
d. $\exists h' : s' = succ(s, h')$ if and only if $\forall h$: if $s \in h$ then $s' \in E(s, h, \emptyset)$
e. if $s \in h$ then $E(s, h, Ags) = \{succ(s, h)\}$
f. if $A \supset B$ then $E(s, h, A) \subseteq E(s, h, B)$
g. if $A \cap B = \emptyset$ and $s \in h$ and $s \in h'$ then $E(s, h, A) \cap E(s, h', B) \neq \emptyset$

In Definition 9.2.2 above, we refer to the states s as 'static states'. This is to distinguish them from what we call 'dynamic states', which are combinations $\langle s, h \rangle$ of static states and histories. Dynamic states will function as the elementary units of evaluation of the logic. This means that the basic notion of 'truth' in the semantics of this logic is about dynamic conditions concerning choice applications. This distinguishes *stit* from logics like Dynamic Logic and Coalition Logic whose central notion of truth concerns static conditions holding for static states.

The name 'h-effectivity functions' for the functions defined in item 3. above is short for 'h-relative effectivity functions'. This name is inspired by similar terminology in Coalition Logic whose semantics is in terms of 'effectivity functions'. An effectivity function in Coalition Logic is a function $E : S \times 2^{Ags} \mapsto 2^{2^S}$ mapping static states to sets of sets of static states. Each set in 2^{2^S} then represents a choice. In our h-effectivity functions, choices are always relative to a history (the history that is part of the dynamic state we evaluate against), which is why h-effectivity functions map to sets instead of to sets of sets.

Condition 3.a. above states that h-effectivity is empty for history-state combinations that do not form a dynamic state.

Condition 3.b. ensures that next state effectivity as seen from a current state s does not contain states s' that are not reachable from the current state through some history.

Condition 3.c. states that the static state next of some other static state on a history is always in the effectivity set relative to that history state pair for any group of agents.

[4] We could also define this as a function: $E : S \times H \times 2^{Ags} \mapsto 2^{S \times H} \setminus \emptyset$ to emphasize the relation with similar formalisms based on a single state (Herzig and Schwarzentruber 2008).

Condition 3.d. above states that any next state is in the effectivity set of the empty set and vice versa. This underlines the special role of the empty set of agents in this formalism. On the one hand, the empty set is powerless, since it does not have genuine alternatives for choices, like agents generally do. On the other hand, it is almighty, since whatever is determined by the effectivity of the empty set *must* occur in next states. This is why we will associate the empty set of agents with 'nature' and its effectivity with 'causation'.

Condition 3.e. above implies that a simultaneous choice application of all agents in the system uniquely determines a next static state. A similar condition holds for related formalisms like ATL (Alur et al. 2002) and Coalition logic (CL for short). However, we want to point here to an important difference with these formalisms. Although 3.d uniquely determines the next state relative to a simultaneous choice for all agents in the system, it does not determine the unique next 'dynamic state'. This is important, because dynamic states are the units of evaluation. In ATL and CL, static states are the units of evaluation. As a consequence, CL will not be definable in this logic.

Conditions 3.f. expresses coalition (anti-)monotony. The second subset relation in this property is not strict, because we can always add a dummy agent with the same properties as the empty set of agents: it does not have real choices and always 'goes with the flow'. This increases the number of agents while leaving the choices of all agents as they are.

Condition 3.g. above states that simultaneous choices of different agents never have an empty intersection. This is the central condition of 'independence of agency'. It reflects that a choice application of one agent can never have as a consequence that some other agent is limited in the choices it can exercise simultaneously. Note that this emphasizes that we need to refer to the sets in the outcome of effectivity functions as 'choices' and not as 'actions'. As explained in the introduction, for action we do not have independence.

The conditions on the frames are not as tight as the conditions in the classical *stit* formalisms of Belnap et al. (2001). Appart from the crucial difference concerning the effect of actions (as said, in XSTIT^p actions take effect in next states), the classical *stit* formalisms assume conditions that in our meta-language can be represented as:

h. $E(s, h, A) \neq E(s, h', A)$ implies $E(s, h, A) \cap E(s, h', A) = \emptyset$
i. $E(s, h, A \cup B) = E(s, h, A) \cap E(s, h, B)$

Condition h. says that the choices of a group A are mutually disjoint. Condition i. says that the choices of a group are exactly the intersections of the choices of its sub-groups. Condition i. is strictly stronger than the coalition (anti-)monotony property 3.f., which only says that the choices of a group are *contained* in the choices of its sub-groups. Since they result in much tidier pictures, in the visualizations of the frames we will consider below, we will actually assume both these conditions. However, we do not include them in the formal definition of the frames, because

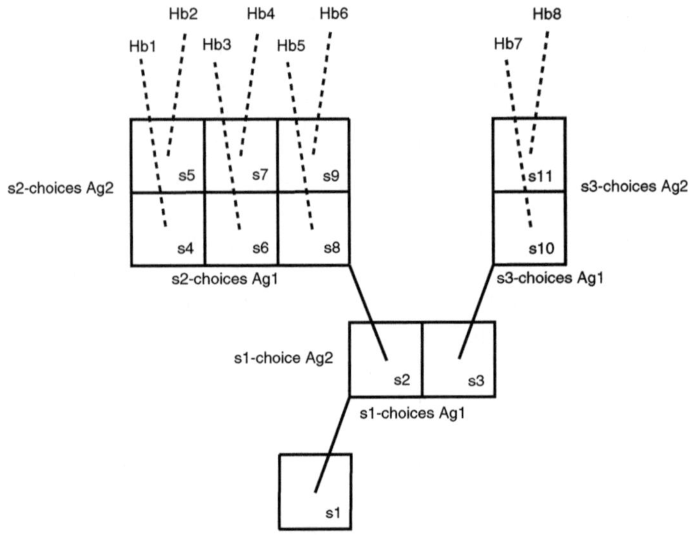

Fig. 9.1 Visualization of a partial two agent XSTIT^p frame

both conditions are not modally expressible (e.g., in modal logic we can give axioms characterizing that an intersection is non-empty, but we cannot characterize that an intersection is empty). This means that they will not have an effect on our modal logic of agency whose semantics we will define in terms of the above frames.

Figure 9.1 visualizes a frame of the type defined by Definition 9.2.2. The small squares are static states in the effectivity sets of $E(s, h, Ags)$. Combinations of static states and histories running through them form dynamic states. The big, outmost squares forming the boundaries of the game forms, collect the static (and implicitly also the dynamic) states in the effectivity sets of $E(s, h, \emptyset)$. Independence of choices is reflected by the fact that the game forms contain no 'holes' in them. We hope that the figure makes it clear that the semantics is a so called 'bundled' semantics. In this bundled semantics choice application is always thought of as the separation of two bundles of histories: one bundle ensured by the choice exercised and one bundle excluded by that choice.

We now define models by adding a valuation of propositional atoms to the frames of Definition 9.2.2. Here we deviate from the XSTIT defined in Broersen (2011) which allows for different valuations of dynamic states based on the same static state. Here we will not allow this, and impose that all dynamic state relative to a static state evaluate atomic propositions to the same value. This corresponds to the intuition that atomic propositions, and modality-free formulas in general do not represent dynamic information. Their truth value should thus not depend on a history but only on the static state. This choice does however make the situation non-standard. It is a constraint on the models, and not on the frames. This implies that we cannot directly use standard correspondence theory (van Benthem 1984) or Sahlqvist theory (Blackburn et al. 2001) to obtain completeness.

Definition 9.2.3. A frame $\mathcal{F} = \langle S, H, E \rangle$ is extended to a model $\mathcal{M} = \langle S, H, E, \pi \rangle$ by adding a valuation π of atomic propositions:

- π is a valuation function $\pi : P \longrightarrow 2^S$ assigning to each atomic proposition the set of static states relative to which they are true.

The truth conditions for the semantics of the operators are fairly standard. The non-standard aspect is the two-dimensionality of the semantics, meaning that we evaluate truth with respect to dynamic states built from a dimension of histories and a dimension of static states.

Definition 9.2.4. Relative to a model $\mathcal{M} = \langle S, H, E, \pi \rangle$, truth $\mathcal{M}, \langle s, h \rangle \models \varphi$ of a formula φ in a dynamic state $\langle s, h \rangle$, with $s \in h$, is defined as:

$$
\begin{array}{ll}
\mathcal{M}, \langle s,h \rangle \models p & \Leftrightarrow s \in \pi(p) \\
\mathcal{M}, \langle s,h \rangle \models \neg\varphi & \Leftrightarrow \text{not } \mathcal{M}, \langle s,h \rangle \models \varphi \\
\mathcal{M}, \langle s,h \rangle \models \varphi \wedge \psi & \Leftrightarrow \mathcal{M}, \langle s,h \rangle \models \varphi \text{ and } \mathcal{M}, \langle s,h \rangle \models \psi \\
\mathcal{M}, \langle s,h \rangle \models \Box\varphi & \Leftrightarrow \forall h' : \text{ if } s \in h' \text{ then } \mathcal{M}, \langle s,h' \rangle \models \varphi \\
\mathcal{M}, \langle s,h \rangle \models X\varphi & \Leftrightarrow \text{if } s' = succ(s,h) \text{ then } \mathcal{M}, \langle s',h \rangle \models \varphi \\
\mathcal{M}, \langle s,h \rangle \models [A \text{ xstit}]\varphi & \Leftrightarrow \forall s', h' : \text{if } s' \in E(s,h,A) \text{ and } s' \in h' \text{ then} \\
& \quad \mathcal{M}, \langle s',h' \rangle \models \varphi
\end{array}
$$

Satisfiability, validity on a frame and general validity are defined as usual.

Note that the historical necessity operator quantifies over one dimension, and the next operator over the other. The *stit* modality combines both dimensions. Now we proceed with the axiomatization of the base logic.

Definition 9.2.5. The following axiom schemas, in combination with a standard axiomatization for propositional logic, and the standard rules (like necessitation) for the normal modal operators, define a Hilbert system for XSTIT^p:

(p)	$p \rightarrow \Box p$ for p any modality free proposition
	S5 for $\Box$
	KD for each $[A \text{ xstit}]$
(Det)	$\neg X \neg\varphi \rightarrow X\varphi$
($\emptyset$ = SettX)	$[\emptyset \text{ xstit}]\varphi \leftrightarrow \Box X\varphi$
(Ags = XSett)	$[Ags \text{ xstit}]\varphi \leftrightarrow X\Box\varphi$
(C-Mon)	$[A \text{ xstit}]\varphi \rightarrow [A \cup B \text{ xstit}]\varphi$
(Indep-G)	$\Diamond[A \text{ xstit}]\varphi \wedge \Diamond[B \text{ xstit}]\psi \rightarrow \Diamond([A \text{ xstit}]\varphi \wedge [B \text{ xstit}]\psi)$ for $A \cap B = \emptyset$

Theorem 9.2.1. *The Hilbert system of Definition 9.2.5 is complete with respect to the semantics of Definition 9.2.4.*

The proof strategy is as follows. First we establish completeness of the system *without* the axiom $p \rightarrow \Box p$, relative to the frames of Definition 9.2.2. All remaining axioms are in the Sahlqvist class. This means that all the axioms are expressible as first-order conditions on frames and that together they are complete with respect to the frame classes thus defined, cf. Blackburn et al. (2001, Theorem 2.42). It is easy to find the first-order conditions corresponding to the axioms, for instance, by using the on-line SQEMA system (Conradie et al. 2006). So, now we know that every formula consistent in the slightly reduced Hilbert system has a model based on an abstract frame. Left to show is that we can associate such an abstract model to a concrete model based on an XSTIT^p frame as given in Definition 9.2.2. This takes some effort, since we have to associate worlds in the abstract model to dynamic states in the frames of Definition 9.2.2 and check all the conditions of Definition 9.2.2 against the conditions in the abstract model (3.c. corresponds with the D axiom, 3.d. corresponds to ($\emptyset =$ SettX), 3.e. to ($Ags =$ XSett), 3.f. to (C-Mon), 3.g. to (Indep-G)). Once we have done this, we have established completeness of the axioms relative to the conditions on the frames. Now the second step is to add the axiom $p \rightarrow \Box p$. This axiom does not have a corresponding frame condition. Indeed, the axiom expresses a condition on the models. But then, to show completeness, we only have to show that we can always find a model obtained by the construction just described that satisfies the axiom $p \rightarrow \Box p$. But this is straightforward. From all the possible models resulting from the first step, we select the ones where propositional atoms in dynamic states based on the same static state have identical valuations. Since consistent formulas also have to be consistent with the axiom $p \rightarrow \Box p$ for any non-modal formula p, we can always do that. This means that a satisfying model for a consistent formula is always obtainable in this way and that completeness is preserved.

In the rest of the paper we discuss logical properties not in terms of the multi-agent frames of the type pictured in Fig. 9.1, but in terms of single agent 'views' on such frames. To demonstrate this, in Fig. 9.2 we give agent 1's view on the frame of Fig. 9.1. In this visualization, the choices for agent 1, as given by the relation $R_{\{1\}}$, appear as ellipses grouping different possible sets of next states. We see the set of static states S pictured as little circles. Strictly speaking elements from the set H of histories are not pictured. The lines through the static states in the picture represent 'history bundles' (which explains the names 'Hb' in the picture). In this figure (but also in Fig. 9.1) branching of time is then represented as branching of bundles of histories. Since this is only a partial frame, from the viewpoint of any static state there may still be infinitely many choices ahead, which means that the number of histories in a bundle through any pictured static state can also be infinite.

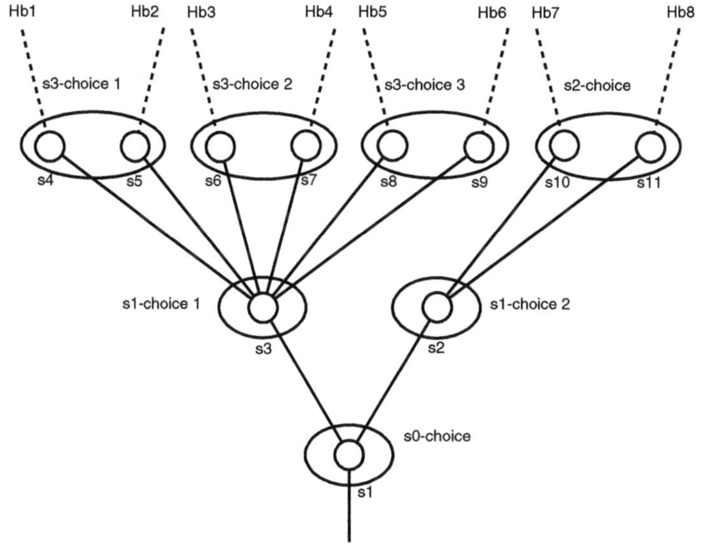

Fig. 9.2 Visualization of the partial XSTIT frame of Fig. 9.1, from the perspective of agent 1

9.3 Indeterminism and Causation

In Sect. 9.2 in the brief explanation of condition 3.d. we already pointed to the special role of the empty set of agents. Here we will come back to this role in a discussion on how we might model causation and determinism within this indeterminist framework.

Figure 9.2 shows how in *stit* theory agency is about exercising control over non-determinism. All the choices of agent 1 in the picture represent different possibilities for the agent's potential to control non-determinism. For instance, in static state s_1 it has a choice between two deterministic alternatives. In static state s_2 it has nothing to choose from since there is only one non-deterministic alternative; what state results depends on the choice of the other agent. In s_3 the agent has a choice between three alternatives that are in themselves non-deterministic. Note that we talk about the choices as concerning 'the potential' for controlling non-determinism. This is because the choices in the picture only represent an agent's *objective* possibilities to control non-determinism. In Sect. 9.4 we will add an agent's epistemic attitude towards these objective choices. This will enable us to express to what extent an agent *knows* about its abilities to control non-determinism.

What researchers not familiar with the semantics of *stit* formalisms often wonder about is what the role is of the 'actual history' that *stit* formulas are evaluated against. What is the conceptual explanation for this technical construction?

Sometimes it is even suggested that the presence of this actual history points to the circumstance that *stit* is not an indeterminist theory at all.[5] The reasoning behind this is roughly as follows. The presence of an actual history reflects what is 'actually' going on. Of course one can argue (as these people would say) that agents, by selecting choices, can force the actual history to be another one (a choice can then be seen as forcing a jump to another history). However, if the agent switches history, then, these critics would argue, we could just as well say that the agent was already on that history in the past. So, agents actually have no power to switch: what they do is determined.

However, we believe this view is grounded in at least two confusions. First of all, with exactly the same reasoning we would have to conclude, independent of any formalism, that our world is deterministic, because when looking back in time we only see one history, which, in hindsight, in the past we could have truthfully claimed to be the initial part of the deterministic future. However, the fact that the world evolved in a certain direction does not imply that it could not have evolved in a different direction. The second confusion really goes back to a mistaken view on what modal logical semantics is. The models give meaning to the formulas of the logic. But, there is not a one-to-one correspondence between formulas and models. Formulas are satisfied by many different models. So the formal meaning of a formula $[A\ \textsf{xstit}]p$ is reflected by the *set* of models that satisfy it. Different models for this formula will in general have different 'actual' histories relative to the same choice. Now, the logic is about which formulas follow from which other formulas. This quantifies over models. In particular, deductive logical consequence is commonly defined as all the models satisfying the premise also satisfying the conclusion. So logical reasoning is defined in terms of *all* the models satisfying a formula, which then accounts for the non deterministic nature of the framework.

Given these observations, and given the discussions on free will and determinism that will follow later on, we want to explain how to define causal relationships in our framework. Our view on causation here is that it is a relation between conditions. The sun shining forcefully causes my skin to turn dark. The wind shaking the tree causes the apples to fall to the ground. We assume that two conditions that are causally related are disjoint in time and that causation cannot work backwards in time. So, if a certain condition p is a cause for some other condition q, the condition p precedes q in time. In our setting a causal relation is then a relation between conditions of subsequent states. But it is not a relation any agent or group of agents can influence. Our view here is that as soon as a condition for the next state depends on what an agent or group of agents choses, it therefore does not causally depend on the conditions of the current state. So we impose a clear separation between conditions that occur irrespective of the choices of agents and conditions that are due to the choices of agents; conditions of the first kind we say are 'caused', while conditions of the second kind are brought about by agents. Under this view, a causal

[5]See also the discussion in Belnap et al. (2001) concerning the 'thin red line'.

relation over subsequent points in time is an event that no agent can influence, which may be because no agent has the ability or the opportunity to do so.[6] And in our framework, what cannot be influenced by any agent is determined by the empty set of agents. Our view is that the empty set of agents represents nature, and that its effectivity reflects what is causally determined by the laws of nature. Then for a causal relationship between two conditions holding for subsequent points in time, we come to the following definition.[7]

Definition 9.3.1. "φ causes ψ" is defined as: $\varphi \rightarrow [\emptyset\ \mathsf{xstit}]\psi$

Now if causal determinism were true, next states could in principle be completely and uniquely described by formulas of the form just defined. But then it would follow that the set of concrete existing agents with genuine choices (choices with alternatives) must be empty. This emphasizes that our *stit* theory is a non-deterministic theory of agency.

9.4 A Theory of Necessarily Successful Choice Application

In this section we aim to formalize the concept of successful action within our framework. As explained, we will measure success of an action against an agent's epistemic attitude towards the choice it exercises. If this epistemic attitude obeys the truth axiom, that is, if what an agent thinks to be doing is necessarily also what it actually does, we have a theory of successful action. We will now study this idea formally by extending XSTIT^p with an epistemic operator $K_a\varphi$ for knowledge of individual agents a.

Herzig and Troquard were the first to consider the addition of knowledge operators to a *stit*-logic (Herzig and Troquard 2006). Later on the framework was adapted and extended by Broersen et al. (2006, 2007). The epistemic fragment of the present logic extends our earlier work on epistemic *stit* in several ways. In particular, new properties for the interaction of knowledge and action are proposed. Also the semantics, being two-dimensional, is different from the one in Broersen et al. (2007). Finally, the modeled concept is 'knowingly doing', whereas in e.g. Herzig and Troquard (2006) the aim is to model 'knowing how'.

Definition 9.4.1. We extend the syntax of Definition 9.2.1 with an operator for knowledge, resulting in:

$$\varphi \ldots := p \mid \neg\varphi \mid \varphi \wedge \varphi \mid \Box\varphi \mid [A\ \mathsf{xstit}]\varphi \mid X\varphi \mid K_a\varphi$$

[6] A possible weakness of our view here is that it suggests that as soon as some agent has the opportunity and ability to prevent the apple from falling from the tree as the result of the wind shaking the tree, without actually seeing to it that the apple does not fall, the falling is not caused by the shaking, but due to the choice of the agent not to prevent it from falling.

[7] In view of the criticism expressed in the previous footnote, we can say that Definition 9.3.1 rather gives a minimum criterion for causal relations than a complete definition.

Note that the stit-operators concern groups of agents, while the knowledge operator concerns individual agents. We extend XSTIT's semantic basis by the following definitions.

Definition 9.4.2. The class of K-extended XSTIT^p frames consists of frames $\mathcal{F} = \langle S, H, E, \{\sim_a \mid a \in Ags\}\rangle$ such that:

- $\langle S, H, E\rangle$ is a function-based XSTIT^p-frame
- The $\sim_a$ are epistemic equivalence relations over dynamic states $\langle s, h\rangle$ (corresponding to the modal frame class S5).

We can now extend Definition 9.2.4 with the clause for the truth condition for the knowledge operator.

Definition 9.4.3. The truth condition for the knowledge operator K_a is defined as:

$$\mathcal{M}, \langle s, h\rangle \models K_a\varphi \Leftrightarrow \langle s, h\rangle \sim_a \langle s', h'\rangle \text{ implies that } \mathcal{M}, \langle s', h'\rangle \models \varphi$$

With the above definitions we can express that agent *a knowingly* sees to it that φ as $K_a[a\ \mathsf{xstit}]\varphi$ (Broersen 2008). Semantically: an agent knowingly does something if it exercises a choice for that something in all the dynamic states in the epistemic equivalence set containing the *actual* dynamic state. In Broersen et al. (2007) we also called this 'conformantly' doing, in analogy with the notion of conformant planning (Goldman and Boddy 1996), which looks at plans that are successful under incomplete knowledge of the current state.

We will briefly go through some notions that are expressible. As said above, 'knowingly doing' is modeled by $K_a[a\ \mathsf{xstit}]\varphi$. Then, 'having the ability to do something', where we assume that ability involves that the agent knows what it is doing when it 'exercises' the ability, is expressed as $\Diamond K_a[a\ \mathsf{xstit}]\varphi$. With a 'strategic'[8] notion of *stit*, as in Broersen et al. (2006) or Broersen (2009b) the strategic notion of 'knowing how' can be expressed as $\Diamond K_a[a\ \mathsf{sstit}]\varphi$. However, we will not consider the strategic setting, and thus the 'knowing how' setting here. The notion of 'knowing to have the capacity to ensure a certain effect, without knowing what to do to ensure that effect', is expressed as $K_a \Diamond [a\ \mathsf{xstit}]\varphi$. An agent seeing to it that it knows something, or, learns, is expressed by $[a\ \mathsf{xstit}]K_a\varphi$. Other variations speak for themselves.

Let us now consider the concept of knowingly doing in terms of the frames and models based on these. Figure 9.3 visualizes a possible way to add agent 1's epistemic indistinguishability relation to the frame of Fig. 9.2. We need some background knowledge to interpret this visualization in the right way. We know that the epistemic indistinguishability (or, equivalence) relation $\sim_a$ partitions the dynamic states of a frame. Equivalence classes of dynamic states based on some

[8]What is meant by 'strategic' here is that an action possibly involves several subsequent choices. In game theory one refers to such settings as 'extensive games'.

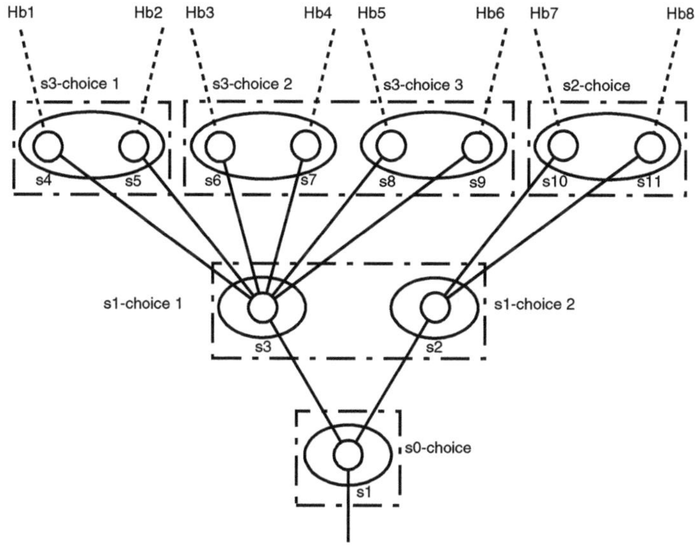

Fig. 9.3 Knowingly doing in a K-extended XSTIT frame

static state s are hard to visualize directly as partitions of s. Therefore, in Fig. 9.3, such equivalence classes are visualized indirectly as dotted rectangles grouping all possible states next of s. For any specific dynamic state, by application of the combined operator $K_a[a \text{ xstit}]\varphi$ (that is, by following elements of the concatenated relations $\sim_a \circ R_{\{a\}}$) we reach all the dynamic states within a specific dotted rectangle. In the picture, these dynamic states are always a subset of all possible next states.

In Fig. 9.3 we see that from static state s_3, there are three objective alternatives for the agent (s3-choice 1, s3-choice 2 and s3-choice 3), while there are two choices the agent can knowingly perform (the two dotted rectangles grouping choices together). The dotted rectangles represent the two sets of states reachable through $\sim_a \circ R_{\{a\}}$ from different dynamic states based on static state s_3. In this particular frame, in s_3 the agent cannot distinguish between s3-choice 2 and s3-choice 3; as far as it knows, these choices are identical, which is visualized by the dotted rectangle surrounding them.

That knowledge has an entirely different character here than in most systems with epistemic operators, is maybe best explained through the notion of 'moment determinacy' (Horty 2001). Semantically, moment determinacy of an operator M is defined by the condition that the truth value of M is independent of the history h in dynamic states $\langle s, h \rangle$. Syntactically, moment determinacy can be defined as follows: M is moment determinate if $M\varphi \rightarrow \Box M\varphi$ is valid. An example of a moment determinate modality is 'unconditional obligation' (however, see Wansing

(2001) for a different opinion on the moment determinacy of obligation). In general it is assumed that what one is unconditionally obliged to do does not depend on what one does. Of course the exception is when one considers obligations that are explicitly conditional on what an agent does (if you drive a car, you need to carry your license; if you kill, you have to kill gently (Forrester 1984)).

Now, in the present framework, knowledge is not moment determinate. We cannot conclude to $K_a\varphi \rightarrow \Box K_a\varphi$, because that does not hold for the substitution $[[a \text{ xstit}]\psi/\varphi]$. And this seems right: an agent's knowledge should not only depend on the moment of consideration. If we can assume that an agent knows what it does when it chooses something, what it knows depends on what it chooses to do, and not only on the state.

9.4.1 *Properties of Necessarily Successful Choice*

We now discuss possible properties for the interaction between knowledge and action. These properties are all expressible as Sahlqvist formulas, which means that they correspond and are complete with respect to proper first-order definable subclasses of the frames given in Definition 9.4.2

9.4.1.1 Ignorance About Choices of Others

It is a fundamental property of agency that an agent cannot know what other agent's choose simultaneously. Agents can have an opinion about what other agents choose, they can also believe that some other agent exercises a certain choice, but they cannot *know* it. This is not the same as the independence of agency property, that only says that an agent's objective possibilities for choosing are independent of another agent's objective possibilities for choosing.

Definition 9.4.4. The property of ignorance about concurrent choices of others is defined as the axiom:

$$(IgnCC) \quad K_a[b \text{ xstit}]\varphi \rightarrow K_a\Box[b \text{ xstit}]\varphi \text{ for } a \neq b$$

The property (IgnCC) expresses that if an agent knows that something results from the choice of another agent, it can only be that the agent knows it is settled that something results from a choice of the other agent. In other words: the agent knows it only because it knows the choice of the other agent does not make a difference in bringing about the condition at hand. This expresses that agents cannot know about *genuine* choices of other agents: an agent cannot know what another agent sees to *deliberatively* (see Sect. 9.6).

9.4.1.2 Knowledge About the Next State

Definition 9.4.5. The property of knowledge about the next state is defined as the axiom:

$$\textit{(XK)} \quad K_a X\varphi \rightarrow K_a[a \ \textsf{xstit}]\varphi$$

The (XK) property expresses that the only things an agent can know about the next state are the things it sees to itself. In terms of the K-extended frame of Fig. 9.3 the axiom says that the ellipses visualizing the objective alternatives are always contained inside the dotted rectangles, that is, knowingly doing is closed under objective alternatives. This also implies that agents can only know about a separation of histories if that is due to their own choice.

9.4.1.3 Recollection of Effect

Definition 9.4.6. The property of effect recollection is defined as the axiom:

$$\textit{(Rec-Eff)} \quad K_a[a \ \textsf{xstit}]\varphi \rightarrow [a \ \textsf{xstit}]K_a\varphi$$

(Rec-Eff) expresses that if agents knowingly see to something, then they know that something is the case in the resulting state.

9.4.1.4 Commutativity of Possibility and Knowledge

The following two axioms characterize commutativity between historical possibility and knowledge. These axioms relate directly to the problem of free will choice that we will discuss later on.

Definition 9.4.7. Commutativity between historical necessity (settledness) and knowledge is embodied by the following two axioms:

$$\textit{(R-KS-comm)} \quad K_a\Box\varphi \rightarrow \Box K_a\varphi$$
$$\textit{(L-KS-comm)} \quad \Box K_a\varphi \rightarrow K_a\Box\varphi$$

(R-KS-comm) says that knowledge of settledness implies settledness of knowledge.

(L-KS-comm) says that agents cannot be uncertain about the static state they are in; they can only be uncertain about the choices of other agents and their own objective alternatives. So if we also want to reason about uncertainty of the static states agents are in, this property is too strong.

9.4.2 Derivable Properties

For the derivable properties we give in this sub-section, we will not give the derivation in the Hilbert style deductive system. Proofs in such systems are cumbersome, and do not help in understanding the property. Instead we will rely on correspondence theory and observations in terms of the semantics. However, due to the completeness we know that Hilbert style derivations exist.

The first derivable property we consider is already in the base system extended with S5 knowledge and the axiom (XK). The property is an independence property for subjective choice. If objective alternatives of agents are independent (the *Indep-G* axiom of Sect. 9.2) then also knowingly performed choices are independent.

Proposition 9.4.1. *Given the axioms of* XSTIT^p, *the S5 axioms for* K_a *and the axiom (XK) for knowingly doing we can derive* independence of subjective choice, *which is defined as:*

$$\text{(Indep-K)}\quad \Diamond K_a[a\ \mathsf{xstit}]\varphi \wedge \Diamond K_b[b\ \mathsf{xstit}]\psi \rightarrow \Diamond(K_a[a\ \mathsf{xstit}]\varphi \wedge K_b[b\ \mathsf{xstit}]\psi)$$

Using correspondence theory we conclude the property follows. The independence of agency property from XSTIT says that intersections of choices of different agents are never empty. Now since a knowingly performed (i.e., subjective) choice always contains at least one objective action (the axiom (XK)), intersections of subjective choices of different agents are also never empty.

Properties that are derivable from the other axioms we discussed above are the following.

Proposition 9.4.2. *The following properties are derivable in the system extended with the discussed additional axioms:*

$$\text{(HK-confl)}\quad \Diamond K_a\varphi \rightarrow K_a \Diamond \varphi$$
$$\text{(Unif-Str)}\quad \Diamond K_a[a\ \mathsf{xstit}]\varphi \rightarrow K_a \Diamond [a\ \mathsf{xstit}]\varphi$$

The axiom (HK-confl) for confluency follows from the fact that $\Box$ and K_a are both S5 and the commutativity of their interaction (this is easy through correspondence theory: we only need, for instance, either symmetry for $\Box$ and (R-KS-comm) or symmetry for K_a and (L-KS-comm)). The axiom (Unif-Str) follows from (HK-confl) by uniform substitution.

(Unif-Str) expresses that if an agent can knowingly see to something, it knows seeing to that something is one of its causal capacities. For instance: the fact that I can knowingly break the cup by throwing it on the floor implies that I know to have the causal power to break the cup. For an example concerning the absence of the implication in the opposite direction, consider the case of a blind person in a room with a light switch (see Broersen et al. 2007): the blind person knows it has the causal power to ensure the room is sufficiently lighted, but it has no means to knowingly see to it.

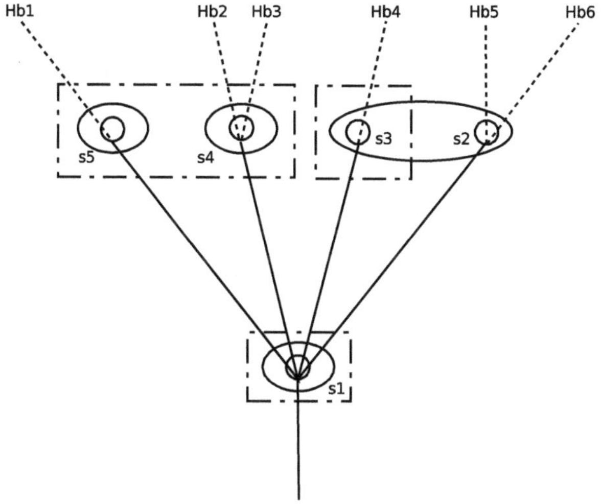

Fig. 9.4 Unsuccessful action in a B-extended XSTIT frame

9.5 A Theory of Possibly Failing Choice Application

Knowingly performed actions are successful actions in the sense that the actual dynamic state (history-state pair) is among the dynamic states in the epistemic equivalence class (game theorists would say: 'the information set'). From the veridicality of knowledge (the S5 truth axiom) we derive that knowingly doing is successful: what an agent knows to be doing is also what objectively happens.

The distinction between objective action (as represented by $[a\ \mathsf{xstit}]\varphi$) and subjective choice (as represented by $K_a[a\ \mathsf{xstit}]\varphi$) is enough to account for the difference between, for instance, an agent knowingly and therefore successfully sending an email and (by the same choice application) unknowingly but objectively crashing a server. But, clearly, what this distinction does not account for is the fact that choices can be unsuccessful. In general, what we think to be doing, is not necessarily what happens. It can even be the case that we think to perform a certain action and achieve the opposite. For instance, we perform the action of securing a precious vase that is too close to the edge of a table, and by doing so, we cause it to fall to the ground.

The system built so far can be adapted to allow for the fact that choice application is not necessarily successful, in an elegant way. What we need to do is to allow for a possible discrepancy between what one thinks one does and what actually happens. So, what we need to do, is to weaken the notion of knowingly doing to its *belief* analog. We do not have a good word for the notion thus resulting; maybe 'believing to do' is the phrase that comes closest.

Let us explain the concept of believing to do and the way it allows action to be non-successful in terms of an example frame. In Fig. 9.4 we see a situation where in s_1 the agent has three objective alternatives. Assume that the actual dynamic state is one based on s_1 and one of the histories of the bundles $Hb5$ or $Hb6$. Now, also assume that the agent believes to do the action visualized as the dotted rectangle around s_3. Now this agent is in for a surprise. The action it believes to do is not the action it really performs. The agent believes to end up in s_3, but due to an action of some other agent, not pictured in this frame, it ends up in s_2. So, its choice is unsuccessful because of some other agent unexpectedly interfering.

The general semantic picture is thus that we want to allow for the situation where the actual dynamic state is not among the dynamic states that are epistemically accessible. Let us now very briefly discuss the logic this leads to. We change the knowledge operator in a belief operator, resulting in the following syntax.

Definition 9.5.1. We extend the syntax of Definition 9.2.1 with an operator for belief and intentional action, resulting in:

$$\varphi \ldots := p \mid \neg\varphi \mid \varphi \wedge \varphi \mid \Box\varphi \mid [A \ \mathsf{xstit}]\varphi \mid X\varphi \mid B_a\varphi$$

Definition 9.5.2. The class of B-extended XSTIT^p frames consists of frames $\mathcal{F} = \langle S, H, E, \{B_a \mid a \in Ags\}\rangle$ such that:

- $\langle S, H, E\rangle$ is a function-based XSTIT^p-frame
- The B_a are epistemic accessibility relations over dynamic states $\langle s, h\rangle$ obeying seriality and positive and negative introspection (corresponding to the modal frame class KD45).

Definition 9.5.3. The clause for the truth condition of belief is:

$$\mathcal{M}, \langle s, h\rangle \models B_a\varphi \Leftrightarrow \langle s, h\rangle B_a \langle s', h'\rangle \text{ implies that } \mathcal{M}, \langle s', h'\rangle \models \varphi$$

9.5.1 Properties of Possibly Failing Choice

For the axioms, we cannot simply turn all the axioms for knowingly doing in Sect. 9.4 into belief equivalents. First of all, of course, we now take KD45 instead of S5 for the individual epistemic operators.

For knowingly doing in terms of knowledge, in Definition 9.4.5 we had the (XK) property. We explained in Sect. 9.4 that in terms of the frames of Fig. 9.3 this says that the ellipses visualizing the objective alternatives are always contained inside the dotted rectangles, that is, knowingly doing is closed under objective actions. But that is exactly the property we do not want here, to allow for a discrepancy between what an agent believes to be doing and actually is doing. So here, what one believes to be doing is not closed under the objective causal capabilities one has. In Fig. 9.4

this is visualized by the third ellipse around s_2 and s_3 not being contained in the dotted rectangle around s_3. So, in the example pictured by the frame, in s_1 the agent believes it has the power to ensure the conditions of the dynamic states based on s_3, but, in reality, it might end up in s_2, satisfying the possibly different conditions in this state. Another way to put this is in terms of the satifisfiability of the negation of axiom (XK), that is, we believe that a sensible requirement for possibly failing choice is that the formula $B_a X\varphi \wedge \neg B_a[a \text{ xstit}]\varphi$ is satisfiable for at least some substitutions of φ. This reflects that it must be possible for an agent to *believe* that a certain condition holds in the next state without the agent believing that it is itself responsible for this effect through its current choice.

Now, since the (XK) property has no belief equivalent, we also cannot use it to derive an independence axiom as the one of Proposition 9.4.1. That independence of possibly failing choice is not derivable we can also conclude using correspondence theory: since subjective choice is no longer closed under objective action (the axiom (XK)), we can easily come up with a counterexample for the axiom where the intersection of two subjective and possibly failing actions is empty. Yet, we believe this property should hold for possibly failing choice. If objective actions and subjective choices of different agents are independent, certainly possibly failing subjective choices of different agents should be independent. But since we do not derive that in the system obtained so far, we have to explicitly add the axiom.

Definition 9.5.4. *Independence of possibly failing choice* is defined as the axiom:

$$\textit{(Indep-B)}\quad \Diamond B_a[a \text{ xstit}]\varphi \wedge \Diamond B_b[b \text{ xstit}]\psi \rightarrow \Diamond(B_a[a \text{ xstit}]\varphi \wedge B_b[b \text{ xstit}]\psi)$$

For reasons similar to those for the failing of the property (XK), the belief version of the property (IgnCC) of Definition 9.4.4 fails. In particular, we think it should be possible for an agent to believe some other agent exercises a certain choice resulting in a condition that the agent believes is not settled for the next state. That is, the formula $B_a[b \text{ xstit}]\varphi \wedge \neg B_a\Box[b \text{ xstit}]\varphi$ for $a \neq b$ should be satisfiable for at least some substitutions for φ.

Finally, for the axioms the axioms (Rec-eff) of Definition 9.4.6 and the commutativity axioms of Definition 9.4.7 we believe any argument to accept these properties for successful choice also applies as an argument to accept them for possibly failing choice.

Definition 9.5.5. The 'B-recollection of effects' (B-Rec-Eff) property, and commutativity of belief and historical necessity are defined as the axioms:

$$\begin{array}{ll}\textit{(B-Rec-Eff)} & B_a[a \text{ xstit}]\varphi \rightarrow [a \text{ xstit}]B_a\varphi \\ \textit{(R-BS-comm)} & B_a\Box\varphi \rightarrow \Box B_a\varphi \\ \textit{(L-BS-comm)} & \Box B_a\varphi \rightarrow B_a\Box\varphi\end{array}$$

9.5.2 Ways in Which to Go Wrong

We think it is an interesting question to ask whether or not there are (logical) limits to the way in which exercising a choice can go wrong. These limits would then possibly point to additional axioms to be considered. We briefly discuss two possible positions and an axiom possibly distinguishing between them.

The first view is that there is always some sense in which a choice cannot go wrong. This connects to Anscombe's position in her famous book "Intention" (Anscombe 1963) where she says, after Aquinas, that *practical knowledge* is "the cause of what it understands". And as Vanderveken (2005) explains in his paper on *attempt*, "No agent can fail to make the attempt that he or she is trying to make at a moment. For in trying to make an attempt the agent eo ipso makes that very attempt". In the formal models of our semantics we can try to account for this by formulating a constraint saying that although agents can be wrong about the choices exercised by others, they can never be wrong about the choice they exercise themselves. An agent then sees to something 'modulo' its beliefs about simultaneous choices of other agents and 'modulo' its beliefs about the causal effectivity of nature. If these beliefs turn out to be wrong, the agent may fail.

Now if we would want to express in our logic that agents have a different epistemic attitude towards their own choices than with respect to choices of others, we have to face a technical limitation of our formalism. The epistemic indistinguishability relations we use for the interpretation of the epistemic modalities are not fit to represent the difference between uncertainty being between choices of the agent itself or between choices of the other agents in the system. In our setting indistinguishability is neutral in this respect, since it is over anonymous dynamic states, and not directly between choices of agents. So, we cannot, for instance, express that an agent has an S5 epistemic attitude with respect to its own choices and a KD45 epistemic attitude towards the choices of others. However, we can give an axiom that distinguishes between the two positions that an agent either can or cannot be mistaken about its own choice. If an agent is never mistaken about its own choice, in our semantic setting, a resulting unexpected state can only be due to mistaken beliefs about simultaneous choice applications of other agents. But, we can argue, that if an agent cannot be mistaken about its own choice, the states it believes to be obtaining are always a subset of its objective action. And then we might argue that this subset cannot be empty, since otherwise the agent would not be believing to do what it does. This would then be expressible as the following axiom

Definition 9.5.6. The axiom for 'never being mistaken about one's own choice' is:

$$\textit{(NoMistake)}\quad B_a[a\ \mathsf{xstit}]\varphi \rightarrow \langle a\ \mathsf{xstit}\rangle\varphi$$

Absence of the axiom would allow for the logical possibility that agents can even be mistaken about the choice they objectively exercise. Agents then may be believing to exercise a choice that is completely disjoint from the choice they objectively perform. Note that like the truth axiom for S5 knowledge this axiom concerns an implication from an agent's subjective truth to an objective truth.[9] And as such the axiom embodies a limit to the degree in which a belief concerning choice application can be mistaken. Although we think the discussion raised by this axiom is worth mentioning here, we do not have a strong opinion on its truthfulness or appropriateness

9.5.3 Derivable Properties

Like for successful choice, for possibly failing choice confluency and uniformity of strategy are derivable.

Proposition 9.5.1. *The following properties are derivable in the system extended with the discussed additional axioms:*

$$\begin{array}{ll}(\text{HB-confl}) & \Diamond B_a\varphi \to B_a \Diamond \varphi \\ (\text{B-Unif-Str}) & \Diamond B_a[a\ \mathsf{xstit}]\varphi \to B_a \Diamond [a\ \mathsf{xstit}]\varphi\end{array}$$

There are (at least) two possible ways to derive the axiom (HB-confl). The first is from symmetry of $\Box$ and (R-BS-comm). The second uses D, 4 and 5 for B_a (in KD45 we do not have symmetry) and (L-BS-comm). Again, the axiom (B-Unif-Str) follows from (HB-confl) by uniform substitution.

9.6 Free Will Choice

In this section we propose a definition for free will choice. As explained in the introduction, the main ingredients will be (1) freedom of coercion, (2) subjectivity and (3) the possibility of failure. But we begin by defining what we call, after Horty and Belnap (1995), a 'deliberative' version of the xstit operator.

9.6.1 Deliberative xstit

Horty and Belnap's (1995) deliberative stit involves a side condition stating that an agent could have chosen otherwise. In our xstit formalism we can give an analogous definition, resulting in the following.

[9] And, if we replace the diamond version of the modality by the box version, we would actually get the truth axiom for knowingly doing. And than, again, we are back in the situation where choice cannot be unsuccessful.

Definition 9.6.1. $[A \text{ dxstit}]\varphi \equiv_{def} [A \text{ xstit}]\varphi \wedge \Diamond\neg[A \text{ xstit}]\varphi$

This definition is different from the one by Horty and Belnap in two respects. First, the side condition $\Diamond\neg[A \text{ xstit}]\varphi$ talks about next states. But this is because in our present setting effectivity concerns next states, while Horty's and Belnap's focus is on immediate effects. Second, the side condition talks directly about the possibility for the agent to refrain. In Horty and Belnap's definition the side condition merely talks about the possibility for some alternative result. If we would have coppied that idea, the above side condition would get the form $\Diamond X\neg\varphi$. However, for objective alternatives this difference is logically irrelevant, witness the following proposition.

Proposition 9.6.1. *The following is a theorem of the logic* XSTIT^p*:*
$([A \text{ xstit}]\varphi \wedge \Diamond\neg[A \text{ xstit}]\varphi) \leftrightarrow ([A \text{ xstit}]\varphi \wedge \Diamond X\neg\varphi)$

Now we think that Definition 9.6.1 falls short of defining deliberateness for two reasons. First of all, deliberateness of a choice obviously alludes to the deliberation process giving reason to an agent's choice. But this then refers to an agent's desires, goals, intentions, will. And as we said in the introduction, from the fact that there is an alternative for a choice, which is the main idea behind the definition of deliberateness as given by Horty and Belnap, we do not want to conclude that therefore a choice must be willed.

Our second concern with Definition 9.6.1 as a possible characterization of deliberateness is that it only refers to an agent's objective actions. In a setting where we distinguish between objective action and knowingly performed choice, as the one we have put forward in the previous sections, that cannot be right. In our view, a choice is only *deliberate* if the agent knows or believes it to be. The existence of an objective alternative for a choice that the agent however could *not* have knowingly taken cannot be a reason for calling a choice deliberate. So, what is missing is the subjectivity of deliberateness.

9.6.2 Free Will Choice That Is Objectively Not Coerced

By adding subjectivity of choices to the picture, in this section we arrive at a definition of free will choice. We will no longer be concerned with the concept of deliberateness. As explained in the previous section, we identify deliberate action with willed choice. But willed choice is stronger than free will choice. Willed choice originates in or is initiated by an agent's desires, needs, feelings, etc. We will define free will choice to be weaker than that; it is a choice or alternative that according to the agent is not forced upon it, that is, choice without constraint, choice that is not coerced.

Our first definition of free will choice, the one in this sub-section, is cast in terms of operators for knowingly doing.

Definition 9.6.2. $[a \text{ freew}']\varphi \equiv_{def} K_a[a \text{ xstit}]\varphi \wedge \Diamond K_a\neg[a \text{ xstit}]\varphi$

There are several things to notice about the notion of free will choice defined here. First we want to draw attention to the subtlety in the side condition. It says that there is an alternative to the agent's choice the agent could have knowingly taken. Now, we believe it would not have been right to have defined the side condition as $K_a \diamond \neg[a \text{ xstit}]\varphi$. This would not be strong enough for a definition of free will. We would have that a free will choice is a knowingly performed choice (the $K_a[a \text{ xstit}]\varphi$-part) for which the agent knows it has the objective possibility to do otherwise, however, without knowing what to choose to do otherwise. But this seems too weak. Our definition is stronger. This also follows in the logic: a side condition of the form $K_a \diamond \neg[a \text{ xstit}]\varphi$ is implied by our side condition $\diamond K_a \neg[a \text{ xstit}]\varphi$ through the (Unif-Str) axiom.

The second observation is that due to the veridicality of knowledge, the notion of free will choice defined above is one where it is an *objective* truth that an agent is not coerced. This is because the side condition says it was possible for the agent to have knowingly refrained from the choice it currently knows to be exercising. Then, because knowledge is veridical and obeys the truth axiom, the alternative must have been an objectively existing alternative. However, if we switch from necessarily successful choice to possibly failing choice, this might no longer be true.

9.6.3 Free Will Choice That Is Subjectively Not Coerced

In this section we give our central definition for free will choice. The notion of free will choice we defined in the previous section is insufficient because it assumes conscious choices are necessarily successful. However choice might fail, and we have to incorporate that into the definition of free will choice. So here we will characterize free will choice as choice that is subjectively free from coercion, and where the agent can thus be mistaken about this.

Definition 9.6.3. $[a \text{ freew}]\varphi \equiv_{def} B_a[a \text{ xstit}]\varphi \wedge \diamond B_a \neg[a \text{ xstit}]\varphi$

Figure 9.5 gives a situation where an agent executes a free will choice even though the alternative it could have 'consciously' (we use this word in the absence of a word that is the belief analog of 'knowingly') taken is one that, objectively does not exist. Let us assume that the actual history in the actual dynamic sate is one from the bundle $Hb6$. Then, objectively, the agent exercises the choice we call "s2-choice" in the picture. And let us assume that as the result of this choice p will be true. Note that this means that objectively, the agent could not have refrained from p and that p is caused by nature (the empty set of agents). So, we have that $\neg \diamond \neg[\{agt\} \text{ xstit}]p$ or $\Box[\{agt\} \text{ xstit}]p$. But subjectively, the picture can be different. Relative to the actual dynamic state, the agent might be mistaken about the static state it is in. Let us assume that even though the agent objectively exercises the choice "s2-choice", it is mistaken about the static state it is in, and that it believes to exercise the choice "s1-choice 2" that also ensures the condition p. Now, relative to this choice "s1-choice 2" that the agent believes to be exercising, the agent had the alternative

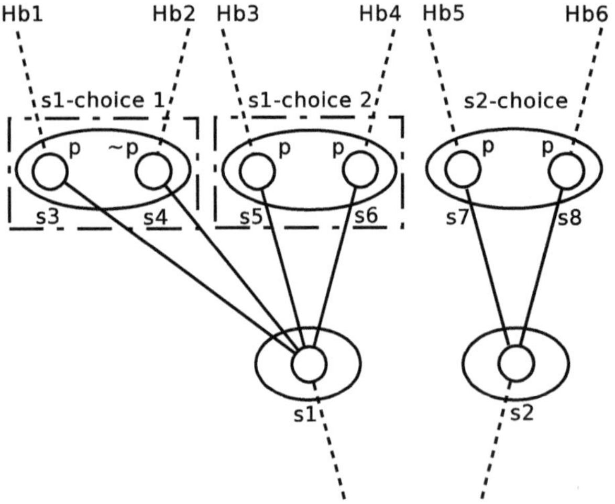

Fig. 9.5 A subjectively free will choice can be objectively coerced

choice "s1-choice 1" which, we assume does not ensure p. That is, although the agent $B_{agt}[\{agt\}\ \mathsf{xstit}]p$ we have that $\Diamond B_{agt}\neg[\{agt\}\ \mathsf{xstit}]p$. That is, it believes it could have refrained from p, that is, in a certain sense, given by our definitions, the agent performs a free will choice, even though objectively it is coerced. These considerations lead to the following propositions.

Proposition 9.6.2. *Free will choice for φ is consistent with causal determinedness of φ. That is, the set $\{[a\ \mathsf{freew}]\varphi, [\emptyset\ \mathsf{xstit}]\varphi\}$ is consistent in XSTIT^p extended with axioms of Sect. 9.5.1.*

Note that the proposition does not hold for free will choice defined in terms of knowingly doing. That is, the set $\{[a\ \mathsf{freew}']\varphi, [\emptyset\ \mathsf{xstit}]\varphi\}$ is *not* consistent.

Proposition 9.6.3. *Agent a's free will choice for φ is consistent with agent b's free will choice for φ and with agent b's free will choice for $\neg\varphi$. That is, the sets $\{[a\ \mathsf{freew}]\varphi, [b\ \mathsf{freew}]\varphi\}$ and $\{[a\ \mathsf{freew}]\varphi, [b\ \mathsf{freew}]\neg\varphi\}$ are consistent in XSTIT^p extended with axioms of Sect. 9.5.1.*

Now note that our central message is not simply that free will relative to the bringing about of a condition φ goes together with φ being causally determined only because an agent can believe to have alternatives for φ while in fact it has not. Our definitions are more subtle than that. The definition of free will choice only says that there is the possibility of consciously executing an alternative. It does not say explicitly that the agent believes this to be a possibility. To be precise, in the logic we do not have that $[a\ \mathsf{freew}]\varphi \rightarrow B_a \Diamond B_a\neg[a\ \mathsf{xstit}]\varphi$. This is a rather subtle point relating directly to the interactions we allow between the $\Box$ modality and the

B_a modality. In Definition 9.5.5 we mentioned right and left commutativity, and we already saw how these played a role in the correct formulation of the side condition through the uniformity of strategy axiom (the discussion below Definition 9.6.2). At this point we do not have a complete overview of the possible interactions and their consequences. We leave this for future research.

Note that there is an obvious connection here with the question we posed in Sect. 9.5.2 about whether or not there are limits to the degree to which a choice can go wrong. If we assume such limits, then this has consequences for the connection between subjective and objective coercion.

9.6.4 The Connection with Frankfurt's Argument

In (1969) Harry Frankfurt famously argued that the concept of 'moral responsibility' does not imply the existence of alternative possibilities for actions. Frankfurt and many others suggested that this argument not only applies to the concept of moral responsibility but also to that of free will. Then, since the connection with what we have put forward in the previous sections seems so obvious, we will explain here how Frankfurt's argument relates to our theory.

Let us first roughly define the concepts Frankfurt's argument is concerned with. Let us refer to 'the Existence of Alternative Possibilities' with the acronym 'EAP'. Now, before Frankfurt, many philosophers have contended the truth of the so called 'principle of alternative possibilities' (often abbreviated as 'PAP') saying that an agent is morally responsible for an action only if it could have done otherwise. Schematically: PAP = "Moral Responsibility for an action $\Rightarrow$ EAP for an action". Now Frankfurt's argument concerns the satisfiability of the negation of this inference, that is, Frankfurt claims the following schema can be satisfied: "Moral Responsibility for an action & not EAP for an action". Here is what Frankfurt says in his original paper Frankfurt (1969) on the issue:

> Now if someone had no alternative to performing a certain action but did not perform it because he was unable to do otherwise, then he would have performed exactly the same action even if he could have done otherwise. The circumstances that made it impossible for him to do otherwise could have been subtracted from the situation without affecting what happened or why it happened in any way. Whatever it was that actually led the person to do what he did, or that made him do it, would have led him to do it or made him do it even if it had been possible for him to do something else instead.
>
> Thus it would have made no difference, so far as concerns his action or how he came to perform it, if the circumstances that made it impossible for him to avoid performing it had not prevailed. The fact that he could not have done otherwise clearly provides no basis for supposing that he might have done otherwise if he had been able to do so. When a fact is in this way irrelevant to the problem of accounting for a person's action it seems quite gratuitous to assign it any weight in the assessment of his moral responsibility.
>
> The principle of alternate possibilities should thus be replaced, in my opinion, by the following principle: a person is not morally responsible for what he has done if he did it *only* because he could not have done otherwise.

Now, morally responsible action and free will choice to us seem to be different concepts (even though in the literature many seem to identify them). In particular, the concept of moral responsibility, as opposed to that of free will, cannot be seen as independent from a theory of norms. However, Frankfurt's line of reasoning has also been used directly in the debate on free will. In particular, it has been suggested that it provides an argument in defense of compatibilism. And this is where it comes very close to the theory we put forward in this paper.

Compatibilism is the claim that causal determinism is consistent with free will. Schematically: "compatibilism = consistent (determinism, free will choice)". Now many philosophers contend that determinism implies that there are no alternatives for actions: (1) "determinism $\Rightarrow$ not EAP for an action". Furthermore, many subscribe to the position that free will implies that alternatives must exist: (2) "free will choice $\Rightarrow$ EAP for an action". Combining (1) and (2) we would have to conclude that compatibilism is not true. However, several authors have claimed that Frankfurt's position can be used to attack inference (2), thereby defending compatibilism.[10] And this position seems to be very close to the propositions we presented in the previous section. For instance, Proposition 9.6.2 says that in our logic, a free will choice for φ is consistent with causal determinedness of φ. Nevertheless, we do not agree with the Frankfurt style argument against compatibilism.

Our point is that even if we agree the reasoning put forward by Frankfurt concludes that moral responsibility does not imply EAP, it does not follow by that same reasoning that also free will does not imply EAP. Frankfurt's original argument concerns moral responsibility. And indeed, for *moral* responsibility, EAP is not required because morality cannot be considered independent of an agent's will and norm related attitudes. So, even if there are no alternatives, the agent is still morally responsible, since if an alternative *would* have been there, the grounding of an agent's choice in an agent's will and moral convictions would have led it to do the same action. For free will choice this is different. If we define free will choice only as absence of coercion, as we think is appropriate and as we did in this paper, clearly we cannot conclude that a choice is free on the basis of the reasoning that if an alternative would have been there, the agent would have acted the same. If free will only concerns the possibility of a free choice between existing alternatives, then in case an alternative would have been there the agent might have chosen differently.

Then it might seem that our theory provides an alternative way to defend a position that is close to compatibilism. But it is remarkable that this is accomplished within an *indeterministic* framework like *stit*. Compatibilism is most often advocated by determinists who want to argue that although our world is deterministic, agents can still have free choice. Here we have an indeterministic framework where we point to the possibility as formulated in Proposition 9.6.2 that free will with respect to a result can be consistent with determinedness of that result. And the

[10]Note that this does not say Frankfurt's claim is an argument *for* compatibilism: strictly speaking it only attacks an argument against compatibilism, which is not necessarily the same.

basis for this is not, like in Frankfurt's argument, that free choice is grounded in our will, but in the special way choice can be subjective and possibly mistaken.

9.7 Conclusion

This paper explored the possibility to logically represent action failure as having a mistaken belief about the choice one exercises. This has consequences for the definition of free will choice in terms of choices for which there are alternatives with an alternative result. We showed that it is possible to perform a free will choice that obtains a result that objectively is determined by nature. We discussed how this relates to Frankfurt's argument about coerced choice for which an agent can nevertheless be morally responsible. The logic and its possible extensions we put forward are normal modal logics with a fairly standard (though two-dimensional) semantics. The advantage of this is that we can apply Sahlqvist theory to overcome the main hurdle in the completeness proofs.

At this point, not all the intricacies and consequences of the possible interactions between the historical necessity modality and the epistemic knowledge and belief modalities are yet investigated and understood. This paper should be seen as a first significant step in the logical study of the properties of free will choice.

References

Alur, R., Henzinger, T. A., & Kupferman, O. (2002). Alternating-time temporal logic. *Journal of the ACM, 49*(5), 672–713.

Anscombe, G. E. M. (1963). *Intention* (2nd ed.). Ithaca: Cornell University Press.

Belnap, N., Perloff, M., & Xu, M. (2001). *Facing the future: Agents and choices in our indeterminist world.* Oxford/New York: Oxford University Press.

Blackburn, P., de Rijke, M., & Venema, Y. (2001). *Modal logic: Volume 53 of Cambridge tracts in theoretical computer science*. Cambridge: Cambridge University Press.

Broersen, J. M. (2008). A logical analysis of the interaction between 'obligation-to-do' and 'knowingly doing'. In L. W. N. van der Torre & R. van der Meyden (Eds.), *Proceedings 9th international workshop on deontic logic in computer science (DEON'08): Volume 5076 of lecture notes in computer science*, Luxembourg (pp. 140–154). Springer.

Broersen, J. M. (2009a) A complete stit logic for knowledge and action, and some of its applications. In M. Baldoni, T. Cao Son, M. B. van Riemsdijk, & M. Winikoff (Eds.), *Declarative agent languages and technologies VI (DALT 2008): Volume 5397 of lecture notes in computer science*, Estoril (pp. 47–59).

Broersen, J. M. (2009b). A stit-logic for extensive form group strategies. In *WI-IAT '09: Proceedings of the 2009 IEEE/WIC/ACM international joint conference on web intelligence and intelligent agent technology*, Milano (pp. 484–487). Washington, DC: IEEE Computer Society.

Broersen, J. M. (2011). Deontic epistemic *stit* logic distinguishing modes of mens rea. *Journal of Applied Logic, 9*(2), 127–152.

Broersen, J. M., Herzig, A., & Troquard, N. (2006). A STIT-extension of ATL. In M. Fisher (Ed.), *Proceedings tenth European conference on logics in artificial intelligence (JELIA'06): Volume 4160 of lecture notes in artificial intelligence*, Liverpool (pp. 69–81). Springer.

Broersen, J. M., Herzig, A., & Troquard, N. (2007). A normal simulation of coalition logic and an epistemic extension. In D. Samet (Ed.), *Proceedings theoretical aspects rationality and knowledge (TARK XI)*, Brussels (pp. 92–101). ACM Digital Library.

Conradie, W., Goranko, V., & Vakarelov, D. (2006). Algorithmic correspondence and completeness in modal logic I: The core algorithm SQEMA. *Logical Methods in Computer Science, 2*(1), 1–26.

Emerson, E. A. (1990). Temporal and modal logic (chap. 14). In J. van Leeuwen (Ed.), *Handbook of theoretical computer science, volume B: Formal models and semantics* (pp. 996–1072). Amsterdam: Elsevier Science.

Forrester, J. W. (1984). Gentle murder, or the adverbial Samaritan. *Journal of Philosophy, 81*(4), 193–197.

Frankfurt, H. G. (1969). Alternate possibilities and moral responsibility. *The Journal of Philosophy, 66*(23), 829–839.

Goldman, R. P., & Boddy, M. S. (1996). Expressive planning and explicit knowledge. In *Proceedings of the 3rd international conference on artificial intelligence planning systems (AIPS-96)*, Edinburgh (pp. 110–117). AAAI.

Harel, D., Kozen, D., Tiuryn, J. (2000). *Dynamic logic*. Cambridge: MIT.

Herzig, A., & Schwarzentruber, F. (2008). Properties of logics of individual and group agency. In C. Areces & R. Goldblatt (Eds.), *Advances in modal logic* (Vol. 7, pp. 133–149). London: College Publications.

Herzig, A., & Troquard, N. (2006). Knowing how to play: Uniform choices in logics of agency. In G. Weiss & P. Stone (Eds.), *5th international joint conference on autonomous agents & multi agent systems (AAMAS-06)*, Hakodate (pp. 209–216). ACM.

Horty, J. F. (2001). *Agency and deontic logic*. Oxford/New York: Oxford University Press.

Horty, J. F., & Belnap, N. D. (1995). The deliberative stit: A study of action, omission, and obligation. *Journal of Philosophical Logic, 24*(6), 583–644.

Kane, R. H. (2003). Free will: New directions for an ancient problem. In R. H. Kane (Ed.), *Free will*. Malden: Blackwell.

McCarthy, J. (1979). Ascribing mental qualities to machines. In M. Ringle (Ed.), *Philosophical perspectives in artificial intelligence* (pp. 222–270). Atlantic Highlands: Humanities Press.

Pauly, M. (2002). A modal logic for coalitional power in games. *Journal of Logic and Computation, 12*(1), 149–166.

van Benthem, J. (1984). Correspondence theory. In D. M. Gabbay & F. Guenthner (Eds.), *Handbook of philosophical logic* (Vol. II). Dordrecht/Boston: Reidel.

Vanderveken, D. (2005). Attempt, success and action generation: A logical study of intentional action. In D. Vanderveken (Ed.), *Logic, thought and action* (pp. 316–342). Dordrecht: Springer.

Wansing, H. (2001). Obligations, authorities, and history dependence. In H. Wansing (Ed.), *Essays on non-classical logic* (pp. 247–258). River Edge: World Scientific.

Chapter 10
Belief, Intention, and Practicality: Loosening Up Agents and Their Propositional Attitudes

Richmond H. Thomason

10.1 Introduction: Framing the Problem

A lot has been written about the modularity of mind, but although I will be arguing for a modular account of the attitudes, I want to set aside what has been said about this topic in cognitive science and philosophy. In particular, I am not going to try to develop an account that could be fitted to the body of results obtained by cognitive psychologists. Nor do I want to articulate a formal theory of special-purpose reasoning and ground it in psychology by speculating about how it may correspond to a mental processing module.

Instead, I'm interested in general-purpose problem solving and its practical employment. This includes game-playing, planning, and calculation, as well as explicit, articulated reasoning about language, objects in space, and events in time. In fact, it includes just about anything that Allen Newell would put in the "intendedly rational band,"[1] or at what he calls "the knowledge level."[2] I believe that logic is the right tool for theorizing about the sort of reasoning that takes place at this level. As a first approximation, I take an analysis involving a first-order or even higher-order modal logic to be appropriate. Innovations from logical Artificial Intelligence, such as nonmonotonic consequence relations, may be useful additions to the logical framework.

For the purposes of this paper, I'm interested in practical reasoning: deliberation about what goals to pursue, how to pursue them, and the relation of goals and plans

[1] See (Newell 1992, Chap. 7). Newell's division of psychological theory into various levels is very helpful for methodological purposes.

[2] See Newell (1982).

R.H. Thomason (✉)
Department of Philosophy, University of Michigan, Ann Arbor, MI 48109-1003, USA
e-mail: rthomaso@umich.edu

F. Lihoreau and M. Rebuschi (eds.), *Epistemology, Context, and Formalism*, Synthese Library 369, DOI 10.1007/978-3-319-02943-6_10,

to what to do on a given occasion. I want a theoretical model that will engage this sort of reasoning—that, in particular, will provide a useful theoretical framework for practical reasoning, viewed at a fairly high level of abstraction.

The theory of programming languages and of program verification provides a good model for what I mean by "a fairly high level of abstraction." A programming language is a formalized medium for articulating complex imperatives for specialized agents. A semantics for the language makes it possible to prove that the instructions are correct, showing that under certain conditions if the program is executed properly then the goals of the program will be satisfied. Often a failed attempt at such a proof will draw attention to a specific flaw in the program.[3]

This approach depends heavily on logical theory; but at the same time it engages the reasoning of an agent in significant and useful ways. At the same time, it abstracts away from many properties of the agent. It doesn't matter what operating system the computer uses, or how many processors the computer has, or (except for efficiency) to what extent parallelism is exploited in the program execution. It is irrelevant how the lower-level reasoning is implemented at the circuit level, after the program has been compiled.

In this work, we have a successful combination of logical sophistication,[4] a formal model of the reasoner, and an abstraction from many low-level details that still is able to engage significant and useful features of the reasoning, and that can deliver useful results such as correctness proofs.

It is a bit of a stretch to extend this approach to cases that include human agents. With computers, we have specifications of correct behavior at the circuit level, and of the compiler that transforms a program into lower-level instructions. Despite the intense interest in recent years in neuropsychology, we have no such thing for human beings and (almost) no such thing for animals. Even so, I don't think that the extension is overly painful. Knowledge-level theories are appropriate and useful in robotics, and in this domain—even though we might have a specification of the agent as a computer running a particular operating system, the environments with which the agent has to deal are so rich and full of uncertainty that the importance of a specification at this level diminishes to little or nothing.[5]

When knowledge-level accounts of practical reasoning are used in robotics, they are usually incorporated in a "Belief-Intention-Desire" (or "BDI") model.[6] In the simplest case, we imagine that the agent has goals, in the form of a set of desired world-states.[7] The agent also has beliefs about the current world-state, as well as beliefs about the preconditions and immediate effects of actions in the agent's

[3]See, for instance, Clarke et al. (1999).

[4]Temporal logics are used in this area.

[5]The literature in this area is extensive. See, however, Doherty (2004), Nebel (2002), Reiter (2001), and Shanahan and Rundell (2004).

[6]The original idea was proposed in Bratman et al. (1988). See Wooldridge (2000) for a more extensive treatment of the topic, together with a formal language for reasoning about BDI agents.

[7]This account of desires is in fact much too simple, but it will do for our purposes here.

repertoire. Means-end reasoning then produces plans—sequences of actions that the agent believes will achieve the goal. One of these plans is selected and turned into an intention.[8] Intentions are then scheduled for execution, and normally the agent will then act on them.

Now, we can often reliably infer a (humanlike) agent's intentions, and can observe an agent's actions. The BDI model connects beliefs to intentions and actions. Even though there is some slippage in scheduling and execution, some uncertainty about desires, and alternative hypotheses about beliefs may be available to explain the observations, we do have evidential connections that can be pretty reliable. Developing a BDI-like architecture by filling in the details and elaborating the components could improve these connections.

In common sense BDI behavioral prediction one infers an intention (and hence, under the right circumstances, an action) from a belief in the presence of a supposed desire. For instance, if my wife is looking for the car keys and I tell her I left them on the kitchen counter, I'll expect her to look there. Conversely, in common sense behavioral explanation one infers a belief from an action, in the presence of a supposed intention. If I see my wife looking on the kitchen counter before going out to get in the car, I may infer that she believes that she doesn't have the car keys.

10.2 Methodological Considerations

10.2.1 Applications and Examples

Like other areas of contemporary philosophy, epistemology is too disengaged from challenging applications, and too driven by armchair examples, which often are far-fetched and unrealistic. This tendency is harmful in many ways. (1) Typically, realistic examples are more interesting and fruitful for philosophical purposes than contrived, unrealistic examples. (2) It is usually easier to produce systematic variations in realistic examples, providing evidence that can be connected with some confidence to generalizations, and eventually, to theories. (3) There is no reliable philosophical methodology for constructing purely imaginary examples, so philosophical inquiry that is driven by these examples tends to be capricious and unsystematic. (4) It is not as if we understand all the simple examples that are relevant to any area of philosophy, and so are forced to construct more complex cases in order to test our theories. It is easy to construct simple examples that challenge any area of philosophy. (5) Just as hard cases tend to make bad law, far-fetched examples tend to make bad philosophy, because we simply are not likely to have robust, reliable intuitions about bizarre examples.

[8]Further desires, in the form of preferences for some plans over others, may play a role in the selection.

The examples I use in this paper will, I hope, be realistic; in one instance (Sect. 10.4), I contrast a realistic example with a product of philosophical imagination.

10.2.2 Decision Theory

Although I will be proposing an alternative to accounts of decision-making that use expected utility, what I will say is meant to be compatible with decision-theoretic approaches, as long as these are not applied generally, to all decisions whatsoever.

The model of decision-making developed in Savage (1972) requires an agent to bring a probability measure and a utility function to bear on every situation calling for a decision. The simplest way to achieve this would be to insist that the agent is equipped with an all-purpose probability measure and decision function, defined over a huge space including every hypothetical outcome with which the agent may have to deal.

This is clearly unworkable in many realistic deliberative situations. Even if we only require that in any decision situation the agent must be able to construct a probability measure and utility function that is appropriate for the situation, the probabilities and utilities are not always available. In fact, the ingredients we need for a decision-theoretic calculation can't be had except in cases with relatively few variables, with limited interactions between these variables, and with a relatively large amount of time for reflection. The use of computers has enlarged the cases where we can hope for such solutions, but even so such cases are relatively rare in practice.

That is why we need an alternative model of decision-making that appeals to reasons and reasoning, even if is not rational in the decision-theoretic sense. Such a model is also more faithful to the patterns we find in human decision-making.[9]

10.2.3 Intentions Require Beliefs

I will assume the following principle: ***intentions presuppose the appropriate beliefs***. That is, there can be no intention without the appropriate beliefs. Suppose, for instance, that I approach a door that I closed an hour ago, leaving it unlocked, with the intention to open it by simply turning the handle and pulling. Then I must

[9]I am not saying that we should discard decision theory. It is fine in the cases where the deliberative situation can be modeled with global probabilities and utilities. But most deliberative situations simply can't be modeled this way. Perhaps some day we will learn how to combine decision theory with more flexible and qualitative forms of reasoning. That too, would be fine. But at the moment, we have to use many models of deliberation, if we want to be appropriately general.

believe that the door is unlocked, even if I don't have this belief explicitly in mind. If I didn't believe that the door was unlocked, I might well *try* to open it by turning the handle and pulling, hoping that it's unlocked. But under these circumstances, I can't intend to open it this way.

The idea that an action aiming at a desired outcome cannot take place without the belief that the outcome will be achieved is close to the principle that I just stated. But I do not accept this idea.

The difference between the two is best clarified using a decision that could be managed in two different ways by a deliberating agent: a probability-based style and a belief-based style. Suppose that I'm playing a game of five-card stud poker. The last card has been dealt. My four visible cards show a pair of jacks, and nothing better. In fact, all I have is a pair of jacks. One opponent is left in the game. The pot amounts to $500. Her hand shows a king, but no pairs. It is her turn to bet; she bets $250. Let's suppose that my choices are either to call her bet or to fold. If her down card is a king, she will win if I call her bet; otherwise, I win if I call her bet.

Case 1. I use decision theory. The utility is given by the amount of my stake in the outcome situation. Assuming I have a stake of $1,000, the utility of folding is 1,000. The utility of calling the bet if she doesn't have a pair of kings is 1,750. The utility of calling the bet if she has a pair of kings is 750. Having counted the cards, I take the probability that she has a pair of kings to be 0.0571. The expected utility of folding, then, is 1,000. The expected utility of calling the bet is $(0.0571 \times 750) + (0.9429 \times 1{,}750)$, or about 1,693. I maximize expected utility and call the bet.

Case 2. I have observed my opponent bluffing before. I know that the likelihood of her having a pair or kings is very low. Taking these to be reasons, I form the belief that she doesn't have a pair of kings. I call the bet, because according to my belief this will net me $750.

In Case 1, it would be wrong to say that I intend to win $750. I call the bet, hoping to win $750, and of course I'm trying to win $750, but I don't intend to win because the losing outcome is not ruled out by what I believe.

In Case 2, I do intend to win $750. I have the intention because I have formed the appropriate belief about what cards my opponent holds.

It is the same if we contrapose. Suppose that in Case 2 you take me aside and persuade me that my opponent might have a pair of kings. Having given up the belief that she doesn't have a pair of kings, I have to give up my intention to win by calling the bet. But the discarded intention may not prevent me from calling the bet. I can perfectly well say "Yes, she might have that pair; but I still intend to call her," elaborating by saying she probably is bluffing. In effect, I fall back on a qualitative version of Case 1. What I *can't* coherently say is "Yes, she might have that pair; but I still intend to win the pot." Again, we see that the intention requires the appropriate belief.

There may be cases where an agent acts on both sorts of deliberations, and cases where it is hard to tell whether an intention on a hope is in play. But there are also clear cases of both sorts of deliberate action. The distinction between acting with the intention to achieve a goal and acting in the hope that a desired outcome will be achieved is well grounded in common sense, and intuitions about the clear cases are very robust. In fact, the principle that intentions presuppose beliefs is, I think, entirely plausible.

This means, among other things, that situations that call for us to form intentions can act as inducements to provide the requirements for the intentions by acquiring appropriate beliefs. Suppose, for instance, that I have a standing goal not to overspend, and that my immediate problem is to decide whether to buy a new computer that I want. I need to effect this decision by forming an intention to buy the computer while not overspending or an intention to refrain from buying it.

In this situation, I need an appropriate belief. Suppose that there is just one pivotal issue: whether I can afford to buy the computer. Then somehow, I have to either form a belief that I can afford it or form a belief that I can't afford it. In resolving the issue, of course, I might gather information about my finances. But if this information doesn't suffice to produce a belief as to whether the computer is affordable, I can also adjust what counts as affordable in one direction or another. Otherwise, like an epistemic Buridan's Ass, I will be stuck.

An agent that must, in some cases, form intentions in order to make decisions, may find itself in situations in which a decision must be made, but the available information does not suffice to precipitate a belief. The need for mechanisms to deal with such quandaries has consequences for how beliefs must function in the overall cognitive architecture, motivating a modular picture of an agent's beliefs. In Sect. 10.5, we will see how this plays out.

10.3 A Proposal About Belief

Later in this paper I'll present some logical theories. At the moment, I just want to present the general idea.

First, stipulate that we are concentrating on belief as a practical attitude: the "B" attitude of a BDI agent.

On a monolithic picture of practical belief, there is a single, ideally consistent general-purpose pro-attitude, "belief," that applies generally across the various practical situations that an agent faces in life. An agent has a single "belief base" that is applied to whatever decisions may come its way. Of course, the beliefs are updated—perhaps nonmonotonically—in light of experience. But on any single occasion when an agent is bringing beliefs to bear on several independent decisions, it will be drawing on the same, general-purpose attitude. And monolithic belief is dynamically inflexible: it can only be updated by rational revision in the light of new evidence. On some idealizations this update may be nonmonotonic, so beliefs could be lost as the result of observations. But the beliefs cannot change without new information.

On this view, an agent's beliefs are like the goods in a ready-made clothing store. There is a procedure for updating the inventory. Independently, a customer can go to the store and find clothing. The supplies of clothing are unrelated to the needs of the customer; they depend only on the state of the inventory.

I propose to think of the belief shop as more like a gentleman's tailor. The tailor keeps materials and tools for making clothing. A customer goes to the tailor, is measured, and orders custom-made clothing.

I want to say that appropriate beliefs for a particular practical purpose are manufactured for the occasion, and that the manufacturing process may involve reasoning. Instead of a single belief attitude, we have an open-ended and loosely organized family of belief-like attitudes. The family is open-ended because there are mechanisms for constructing these attitudes. And a new belief-like attitude may be constructed for a particular occasion.[10]

A constraint on the belief-producing reasoning that enforces joint consistency—in effect, requiring that all the beliefs that the reasoning produces should be part of a single consistent theory—would make the modular account of belief equivalent to the monolithic one. But (for reasons I'll get to) we do not want to impose such a constraint. The beliefs that are appropriate for one practical occasion may be inconsistent with those that are appropriate for another.

Let's assume the view of beliefs as modalities, characterized semantically by relations over possible worlds. Although it makes many idealizations,[11] this picture of epistemic attitudes has been successfully used in many applications having to do with reasoning about knowledge and belief.[12] This makes belief a modality. Belief is realized syntactically as an operator $\Box$ taking formulas into formulas, Where ϕ is a formula and a denotes an agent, $[\, a \,]\phi$ is a formula, expressing the proposition that the agent denoted by a believes the proposition expressed by ϕ. The usual interpretation of $[\, a \,]$ associates it with modal frames that are euclidean and serial; this corresponds to the axiomatization called **KD45** in Fagin et al. (1995).

The logical model that I'm recommending is not a great departure from this approach—but instead of equipping each agent a with a single belief operator $[\, a \,]$, I give an agent a family of belief operators $[\, a, i \,]$. As before, these operators take formulas into formulas. Where ϕ is a formula, $[\, a, i \,]\phi$ is a formula representing the proposition that epistemic module i of agent a believes the proposition that ϕ. As before, each operator is interpreted using a euclidean, serial relation. The resulting logic looks at first like a multiagent modal logic of the familiar sort, but in fact intra-agent modality is different in some important ways from inter-agent modality. In the inter-agent case, agents reason about one another's attitudes in much the same way that they reason about any other feature of their worlds. In the intra-agent case, modules of the same agent access one another in transactions that transmit information directly. We might expect such an important difference to affect the logic.[13]

[10]Of course, there is such a thing as habit, and often the reasoning is minimal and routine.

[11]Logical omniscience is the hardest to swallow of these idealizations.

[12]See Fagin et al. (1995).

[13]In unpublished work, I explore the use of a non-normal modal logic for distributed belief. That is because $[\, a, i \,]\, [\, a, j \,]\phi$ is peculiar if the contents of j are not accessible to i. The options are to

The indices representing epistemic modules needn't be unstructured. In fact, it is convenient to think of them as bundles of features representing the provenance and status of the information contained by the associated module. In fact, the main thing I want to do in the rest of this paper is to consider some features that could be used to organize these information modules, and to suggest how they might be used in reasoning.

I will begin with a problem from the philosophical literature.

10.4 Kripke's Pierre Puzzle

The Pierre puzzle is stated in Kripke (1979). Briefly, Pierre grew up in France, where he learned about "Londre," always hearing charming things about Londre. "Londre est jolie," he says to himself, and continues to believe accordingly. Later he moves to an unpleasant part of London, learns English by immersion, and believes that London is not at all pleasant. He never realizes that Londre and London are the same city.

Although it doesn't constitute an entire solution, a modular account of belief seems to be a necessary condition for resolving this problem. (I am assuming it is out of the question to suppose that some beliefs are in English and some in French.) You can't begin to say anything very helpful about the puzzle unless you associate two belief modules with Pierre: one associated with his life in France and the other with his life in England. Certainly, there may be a lot of overlap between the two, but the overlap needn't be complete—in unusual cases, there may even be unresolved contradictions—and cases where Pierre's second language learning is imperfect may induce such discrepancies. When Pierre hears French, or speaks French, or even thinks to himself in French,[14] the life-in-France module is activated. When Pierre hears English, or speaks English, or even thinks to himself in English, the life-in-England module is activated.

As I said in Sect. 10.2.1, I believe that artificial examples tend to make for artificial philosophy. Whether or not you agree with me about this, I would also like to suggest that realistic, and if possible naturally occurring examples are more likely to be instructive than ones that are fantastic and contrived. Let me illustrate this point by contrasting the case of Drew McDermott's sink with the Pierre example.

I was told this as a true story, but haven't verified it. What makes it especially funny is the fact that McDermott is a computer scientist who at one time worked on planning.

---

treat it as false or as truthvalueless in this case; I choose the former option, which produces a logic like **S3**. But these details are not important for present purposes.

[14]I only assume that some thinking is accompanied by subvocalization. I certainly do not assume that all thinking is associated with a language.

> Once, McDermott's sink was so badly blocked that he had to remove the U-joint. He put a bucket under the sink, loosened the joint with a wrench, and the water in the sink ran into the bucket. Several minutes later he had to get the bucket out of the way, so he took it out and emptied it into the sink.

It seems plausible to me to say that, when he emptied the bucket, McDermott believed that the water would go on the floor, though perhaps the belief wasn't activated at the time.[15] But also, in a way, he must have believed at the same time that the water would go down the drain. According to the model of practical reasoning I subscribed to in Sect. 10.1, we can't explain his action of pouring the water into the sink without ascribing to him the belief that the water would go down the drain. Drew's probable reaction to this mishap is instructive; most likely he was startled. but not at all surprised. He was startled because he expected the water to go down the drain. He wasn't surprised because he knew it wouldn't.

As with Pierre, we can come to grips with this example by supposing that belief is modular. To me, the realistic story is much more compelling, and I think it is likely to be more instructive. But more important for my present purposes—because it is more closely connected to reasoning than lapses of attention—is the interaction between belief and the appreciation of risk.

10.5 Risk

Consider a case where a probability measure and a utility function are not available in a situation calling for reasoned action. An agent that fell back on BDI reasoning in these cases would either be reckless or paralyzed if the beliefs weren't tailored to the occasion. If the standards for belief are overly relaxed for the decision situation, then hearsay evidence, as well as long chains of defeasible inference, could justify a belief. Then the monolithic agent would be reckless: eating a mushroom just because an inexpert friend has declared it to be safe, or passing on a hill because there was no oncoming traffic on the last several hills. Suppose, on the other hand, that the standards are stringent. Then the agent would be paralyzed: unable to eat a spinach salad because it might be contaminated, or unable to back up a car because someone might have just crawled behind it.

In fact, however, human beliefs are influenced by a sense of risk.[16] Without any change in the available evidence, a belief can disappear in the presence of risk, and can appear in the absence of risk.[17] Contrast the following two cases.

---

[15]I even think it's plausible even if emptying the bucket was automatic. Even automatic, habitual actions are intentional, and so have to be based on beliefs.

[16]For related work, see Armendt (2010). Armendt is working in the framework of subjective probability, but the ideas are very similar.

[17]I described cases like this in Thomason (1987).

(5.1) Normally, when I park my car, I turn off the lights. I park my car downtown, near a service station, and leave it to do some errands. Ten min away from the car, it occurs to me that I don't remember turning off the minutes.

(5.2) Normally, when I park my car, I turn off the lights. I park my car at a remote trailhead, 12 miles from the nearest highway, and set off on day hike. Ten min away from the car, it occurs to me that I don't remember turning off the minutes.

The only significant difference between Examples 10.5.1 and 10.5.2 is risk. In the first case, I can easily produce the belief that I turned the lights off, based on the (defeasible) reason that I usually turn them off. In the second case, I can't produce it. If I'm a worrying type, I may even be able to produce the belief that I didn't turn them off.

This mechanism of adjusting beliefs to risk would not be possible with monolithic belief—in the absence of new information, there would be no adjustment to be made. But if beliefs are ad hoc, and if one criterion for choosing the beliefs that are appropriate for a reasoning situation is a qualitative measure of the expected utility of acting on them, we can begin to explain how such adjustments can occur. In this example, we can assume that the only relevant proposition is whether the lights are off, so—if we simplify and think of a modality as a set of propositions—the issue is whether to believe a unit set of propositions, and the credibility of the set is equal to the credibility of the proposition that the lights are off. In both cases, this credibility is significant, but lower than the highest level. Say it is 0.8 on a scale of 0 to 1. In Example 10.5.2, the badness of the outcome of acting on the belief is high. Say it is -7 on a scale of -10 to $+10$. This attaches a risk factor of $0.8 \times -7 = -5.6$ to acting on the belief. This high risk may prevent the supposition that the lights are on from being used as a belief in this practical situation.

In many deliberative situations, and especially when the risk is high, or there is emotional involvement, or there is social pressure to have reasons for decisions, we seem to be condemned to form intentions backed up by reasons. And these reasons will have to function as beliefs in the deliberative situation.

I am supposing that most hikers in the situation that I describe would have to deliberate in belief-based mode. Suppose that the rational thing to do in this case, according to the decision-theoretic model, were to flip a coin and then proceed with the hike or turn back to check the car lights, depending on the outcome of the coin toss. I would expect that few hikers could muster the detachment required to adopt this protocol and proceed with the hike, supposing this to be the recommended action. Without a belief that the lights are off, worry would prevent the hiker from following through.

We have seen that an intention to hike and then drive home requires a belief that the lights are off. On the monolithic model of beliefs, there would be no mechanism for forming the appropriate belief. There is no way to get new information about the car lights without walking back to the car. So an intention to hike and then drive home would be impossible on this model. But in fact some hikers in this situation, condemned to belief-based deliberation, will decide to continue with the hike.

In this case, and in many similar cases that will occur to you, an agent can't act without the appropriate beliefs. An agent in this predicament, who is inclined to adopt a risky course of action, is in a state of *belief hunger*; to continue with the hike, the agent needs the appropriate belief. In this case, and in fact typically, reasons for adopting the belief are easy to find. The hiker has a habit of turning off the car lights; this is the norm. It is most likely that in fact the lights are off. These are the resources that we usually appeal to in forming defeasible beliefs, and they apply in this case. Of course, belief hunger and its satisfaction has its pathologies, including beliefs formed in the face of compelling evidence to the contrary, and self-deceptive beliefs. But I'm not interested in the pathology here; I do not want to say that the hiker who adopts a belief that the lights are off and proceeds with the hike is epistemologically defective, or that the process of forming the belief is particularly unreasonable, even if it is somewhat risky.[18]

I hope it's clear that I have nothing against deliberation that appeals to calculated expected utility. I certainly don't want to do away with this method of deciding what to do. Often, tradeoffs between the desirability of outcomes and the likelihood of achieving them need to be reconciled in practical decision-making, and these tradeoffs call for such calculations. How, then, does the picture I'm painting differ from, say, Leonard Savage's?[19]

Well, I don't take expected utility to be the whole story about how even an ideally rational agent reasons in practical situations; in fact, I think it doesn't fit the reasoning in most cases. I differ from Savage in not wanting to postulate global, all-purpose utility and probability functions, and in denying that probability functions make beliefs unnecessary in practical reasoning. I think that sometimes people act on intentions, and sometimes they act on hopeful expectations. Intentions require beliefs, and these beliefs can be manufactured ad hoc for the decision-making situation at hand. Furthermore, I am willing to allow qualitative and approximate methods for calculating utility.[20]

---

[18]One way to solve the problem of repeated decisions that according to game theory would best be solved by randomizing, but that require a reasoned decision, is to enhance a randomizing method with social or even religious approval. The ancient Greeks and Romans used the flight of birds and the entrails of animal sacrifices to make decisions, some at least of which match this description. Plains indians apparently used the motions of insects to decide where they would hunt.

[19]See Savage (1972).

[20]Many such methods are discussed in the Artificial Intelligence literature. In fact, there is an extensive literature on qualitative preferences, on calculating qualitative preferences over plans, and on integrating these preferences with planning algorithms. See Baier and McIlraith (2008) for a recent survey. Most of this work does not yet consider cases where uncertainty, risk, and the consequent need for expected utility is present; but see Fargier and Sabbadin (2005).

10.6 An Application to Cooperative Reasoning

A great deal has been written since the publication of Stalnaker (1972) about the dynamics of the common ground in a conversation.[21,22] Far less has been said about how the common ground is initialized. Almost nothing is said about how it can be initialized so as to promote modal mutuality.[23] The requirement of mutuality for the common ground is strongly motivated by theoretical considerations. It is also supported by linguistic evidence; see Clark and Marshall (1981, 415–420).

But this requirement raises a problem: how can we account for the reasoning that gives rise to a sense of mutuality? How, for instance, when we begin a conversation with someone on an airplane, can we find a common ground?

Clark and Marshall, as well as many other authors, speak of the attitude associated with the common ground of a conversation as if it were a matter of the mutual beliefs or even the mutual knowledge of the participants. But neither alternative works. The attitude can't be knowledge, because conversations can easily presuppose what is false. It can't be belief, because the rules of conversation don't require the participants to go away from the talk exchange believing whatever they have assumed for the sake of their conversation. Situations can arise in which you don't entirely trust what someone is saying, but don't want to be rude or to disrupt the conversation with objections.[24] In these cases you simply suspend disbelief. In effect, this means that you create an ad hoc attitude of acceptance-for-the-sake-of-the conversation.[25] Some of the things accepted in this way might serve as beliefs for certain purposes. We might be quite confident that other such things are false. Notice that much the same thing can happen in reading a work of fiction. You can learn a lot about the Napoleonic Wars by reading Dostoyevsky, but of course you shouldn't believe that all the people, places, and events in *War and Peace* are historical.

This idea of an ad hoc conversational modality goes a long way towards explaining the mutuality of the common ground. We initialize this modality by tailoring it to our interlocutors—by putting things in it that we have good reason to suppose they will put in the modality they are constructing for us. We can provide a mechanism for constructing the modality by supposing that learning a proposition is more complicated than simply adding the information it contains to a basket full

---

[21] There is some overlap between what I say in this section and the motivating parts of Thomason (2000, 2002).

[22] Stalnaker uses the term 'presuppositions'. Here, I use Herbert Clark's term. See Clark and Marshall (1981).

[23] Many others use the term 'common', referring, for instance, to 'common knowledge'. I prefer 'mutual', because it is less likely to be confused with other group attitudes. For details about the logic of mutuality, see Fagin et al. (1995, Chap. 6).

[24] This could be a matter of genuine distrust, as in a conversation with an overeager salesman. But it can also happen in story-telling. When we hear an entertaining story that is presented as recalled history, we may not be sure which parts of it are fact, which are enhanced, and which are entirely fictional. Usually, it isn't important to sort this out.

[25] Stalnaker makes this suggestion in Stalnaker (1975).

of beliefs. We need to tag what we have learned with background information. How did we learn it? Did we learn it under circumstances that we would expect to apply to other people? What sort of people would these be? If what we have learned is enriched in this way, constructing an ad hoc attitude might just be a matter of selecting propositions with certain features.

You can find an informal version of this proposal in Clark and Schober (1989). The authors put the idea in terms of speech communities.

> The common ground between two people—here, Alan and Barbara—can be divided conceptually into two parts. Their *communal common ground* represents all the knowledge, beliefs, and assumptions they take to be universally held in the communities to which they mutually believe they both belong. Their *personal common ground* represents all the mutual knowledge, beliefs, and assumptions they have inferred from personal experience with each other.
>
> Alan and Barbara belong to many of the same cultural communities ...
>
> 1. *Language*: American English, Dutch, Japanese
> 2. *Nationality*: American, German, Australian
> 3. *Education*: University, high school, grade school
> 4. *Place of Residence*: San Francisco, Edinburgh, Amsterdam ...

There is more about the problem of mutuality in Thomason (2000, 2002), and in fact a full solution to the problem has other ingredients. But treating the belief-like attitudes associated with conversations as flexible, ad hoc modalities is an important component.

10.7 Time and Social Pressure

In situations calling for a reasoned decision, time pressure can enhance belief hunger. Social pressure can have a similar effect.[26]

Philosophers of practical reasoning have paid attention to many sorts of practical pathologies, some of them invented. But little attention has been paid to dithering.

Consider a nervous driver at a stop sign at a busy intersection on a dark night. He needs to drive across the intersection. He looks left. A car zooms by from that direction. He looks right. It's clear. He looks left, it's clear. But wait—he can't see what's going on to the right, and doesn't believe it's clear anymore. So he looks right. He repeats the process until he realizes that he'll never get across this way. Time is pressing. But he can't move unless the road is clear. So he lowers his standards, saying to himself "If it was clear to the right a second ago it's clear now." And he hits the gas. Sometimes, of course, there may be no intention to cross the intersection, and no belief—just a sort of desperate hope. But I think that in this sort of case the need to act will sometimes induce a belief.

[26]There is some overlap here with Thomason (2007).

Jury duty can produce an enhanced and extreme case of pressure to believe. For responsible jurors, anyway, the duties call for a reasoned decision, and require certain beliefs about the facts of the case. In many cases, the risk factor (at least, the moral risk factor) can be high. But a holdout member of a jury can be under severe time pressure, as well as social pressure, to reach a decision. Most often, I suspect, this pressure induces a belief that might not otherwise have come into being.

10.8 The Hypothetical Dimension

Supposing blends into entertaining, entertaining blends into positing, positing blends into occasional belief, and occasional belief blends into entrenched, global belief. On the model that I'm advocating, there is no real need to draw a line at a particular place in order to separate genuine from pseudo beliefs. But the practicalizing mechanism that assembles an attitude for a decision-making situation would need to take these distinctions into account. To take two extremes, we would not want something supposed purely for the sake of argument to ever be practicalized. On the other hand, a supposition about what my name is should be generally and freely available in just about any reasoning situation.

In fact, if we don't draw a sharp line at any point in the continuum between supposing and believing, there is still no difficulty in preventing imagination and fiction from contaminating serious deliberation. The same mechanisms that apply when we gather information from external sources can and do apply when we assemble information from our own attitudes in order to construct an ad hoc, practical belief attitude. In Sect. 10.5, I included estimated credibility, adjusted for risk, among these factors. If things assumed for the sake of argument or for the sake or a conversation, or for following a work of fiction, were assigned credibility 0, this should suffice to keep them at bay in practical situations.

But in fact I don't think that low credibility is the only disbelief-inducing mechanism. Temporary suppositions—assumptions for the sake of argument, or for contingency planning—can be forgotten once they have served their purpose. There is no point in maintaining a supposition that is of no future use. And it's implausible that we don't practicalize whatever we have understood in a conversation or read in a work of fiction simply because these things have low credibility. Perhaps assumptions can be labeled as impractical or hypothetical in various ways.

10.9 Activated Belief and Interactions Between Modules

Thinking of pro-attitudes as modular, as resources that can be marshaled and brought to bear on a particular problem, would allow agents to follow a more relaxed approach to storing and maintaining declarative information. This information could be stored in modules devoted to specific topics; these modules could be organized along taxonomic lines. Although consistency is always desirable, it would not be vital to check ensure global consistency across modules, as long as consistency is monitored when information is gathered from different modules for some specific purpose.[27]

This way of organizing things has turned out to be important in managing large-scale knowledge bases. If the task is actually more a matter of constructing a knowledge base than of acquiring large amounts discrete, unrelated information—that is, if the task is to decide how to formalize a topic and provide axioms and a reasoning mechanism—then it is very difficult to make progress on large scale repositories without modularizing the task. For a description of how this works out in the context of a specific knowledge representation project, see Guha (1991).

This approach, of course, will not work without procedures for collecting and organizing information from different modules. The architecture that suggested by this idea would involve more or less independent loci for representing, storing, and managing information, with general mechanisms for transferring the information. Some attention (but not enough) has been given to providing a logic for this sort of architecture.[28]

10.10 Minsky, the Society of Mind and the Emotions

Although I think that something like the sort of epistemology I advocate here is pretty inevitable if you take seriously the idea that epistemology should have something to do with the sort of reasoning that is used in problem solving, I suspect that it will seem pretty radical to traditional epistemologists. I would like to mention briefly what Marvin Minsky has to say about the architecture of human thought, if only to differentiate what I am doing from his views, and to point out that modular epistemology can be far more radical.

Minsky's published work on this topic goes back to Minsky (1985), but the most recent and comprehensive statement of the ideas is Minsky (2006).

If societies can be said to reason, the reasoning would have to be distributed, involving separate modules that may communicate seldom or never. And societies can be anarchic, and to the extent that anyone can be said to be in charge, the leadership can change frequently, and change in ways that are disorderly. Minsky wants to transfer these features of societies to the mind.

Minsky has surprisingly little (surprisingly, because Minsky's background, after all, is in Artificial Intelligence) to say about how this idea would play out in

---

[27]This purpose could be to produce the active beliefs to be directed at a specific problem. But modules may need from time to time to acquire information from one another for internal maintenance purposes.

[28]For many years, John McCarthy has stressed the need for a "logic of context" and made suggestions about what such a logic should look like. As far as I know, McCarthy and Buvač (1998) is the latest of his papers on the topic. Also see Thomason (2005).

terms of reasoning, and especially in relation to problem solving. Although Minsky (2006) contains many suggestive comments that could be applied to reasoning, and especially to the interactions between emotions and reasoning, there is no systematic or detailed account of the reasoning mechanisms. However, it is clear that he imagines that humans can invoke a variety of reasoning styles, that these styles are related to cognitive resources that can be activated to a greater or lesser extent, that the emotions play a role in the activation, and that this process is more or less unruly.

The account of belief that I have proposed is committed to none of these things. In fact, it is confined to rational or at least reasonable epistemology. On the model that I have proposed, beliefs are in fact resources that can be activated and deactivated. But I think of this process as rule-governed, driven by the needs of a problem situation, and reasonable, even if not rational in a strictly decision-theoretic sense.

I don't doubt that there are interactions—in both directions—between human emotions and human beliefs and other truth-directed attitudes, and that here Minsky has many insights to offer, even if he seems to be unwilling to develop these insights. In fact, a weakness of BDI models is that they have little or nothing to say about the origin or maintenance of desires, and any account of this would have to take the emotions into consideration. But I don't think that such an account would need to be as unruly as Minsky seems to think.

10.11 Conclusions

Agents who reason in the way I have suggested we in fact reason will have a way to abuse the process of deliberation. But human beings seem to be such agents. Others have noticed this; some have taken a perverse sort of pride in it.[29] But we can admit that the mechanism is available to us, without suggesting that its abuse is a good thing. In fact, mature, thoughtful people will tend to avoid such abuse; this is part of what it is to be a mature, thoughtful person.

I don't doubt that for some combinations of deliberating agents and deliberative problems, belief-based intentions are not the best way of reasoning.[30] But belief-based planning and intention formation may well be a good general-purpose method for agents with human cognitive capacities. In any case, we seem to be stuck with this method—condemned to it, as I said, in many of the deliberative situations we have to deal with.

---

[29]Ralph W. Emerson, with his "A foolish consistency is the hobgoblin of little minds, adored by little statesmen and philosophers and divines," is an example. Emerson apparently is thinking of consistency in beliefs from one occasion to another, and feels that self-reliant men are above such things.

[30]Special-purpose computers and chess playing may be such a combination, for instance.

In this paper, I have tried to suggest what belief would need to be like for agents in this position. It turns out, if I'm right, that belief would have to be different from what many philosophers and decision scientists have imagined it to be.

Acknowledgements Thanks for comments to Sarah Buss, Jason Konek, David Manley, Daniel Singer, Peter Railton.

References

Armendt, B. (2010). Stakes and beliefs. *Philosophical Studies, 147*(1), 71–87.
Baier, J.A., & McIlraith, S.A. (2008). Planning with preferences. *The AI Magazine, 29*(4), 25–36.
Bratman, M.E., Israel, D., Pollack, M. (1988). Plans and resource-bounded practical reasoning. *Computational Intelligence, 4*, 349–355.
Clark, H.H., & Marshall, C.R. (1981). Definite reference and mutual knowledge. In A. Joshi, B. Webber, & I. Sag (Eds.), *Elements of discourse understanding* (pp. 10–63). Cambridge: Cambridge University Press.
Clark, H.H., & Schober, M. (1989). Understanding by addressees and overhearers. *Cognitive Psychology, 21*, 211–232.
Clarke, E.M., Grumberg, O., Peled, D.A. (1999). *Model checking*. Cambridge: MIT.
Doherty, P. (2004). Advanced research with autonomous unmanned aerial vehicles. In D. Dubois, C.A. Welty, & M.-A. Williams (Eds.), *KR2004: Principles of knowledge representation and reasoning*, Whistler (pp. 731–732). Menlo Park: AAAI.
Fagin, R., Halpern, J.Y., Moses, Y., Vardi, M.Y. (1995). *Reasoning about knowledge*. Cambridge: MIT.
Fargier, H., & Sabbadin, R. (2005). Qualitative decision under uncertainty: Back to expected utility. *Artificial Intelligence, 164*(1–2), 245–280.
Guha, R.V. (1991). Contexts: A formalization and some applications. Technical report STAN-CS-91-1399, Stanford Computer Science Department, Stanford.
Kripke, S.A. (1979). A puzzle about belief. In A. Margalit (Ed.), *Meaning and use: Papers presented at the second Jerusalem philosophy encounter* (pp. 239–288). Dordrecht: Reidel.
McCarthy, J., & Buvač, S. (1998). Formalizing context (expanded notes). In A. Aliseda, R. van Glabbeek, & D. Westerståhl (Eds.), *Computing natural language* (pp. 13–50). Stanford: CSLI.
Minsky, M. (1985). *The society of mind*. New York: Simon and Schuster.
Minsky, M. (2006). *The emotion machine*. New York: Simon & Schuster.
Nebel, B. (2002). The philosophical soccer player. In D. Fensel, F. Giunchiglia, D.L. McGuinness, & M.-A. Williams (Eds.), *KR2002: Principles of knowledge representation and reasoning*, Toulouse (p. 631). San Francisco: Kaufmann.
Newell, A. (1982). The knowledge level. *Artificial Intelligence, 18*(1), 82–127.
Newell, A. (1992). *Unified theories of cognition*. Cambridge: Harvard University Press.
Reiter, R. (2001). *Knowledge in action: Logical foundations for specifying and implementing dynamical systems*. Cambridge: MIT.
Savage, L. (1972). *The foundations of statistics*, 2nd edn. Dover: New York.
Shanahan, M., & Rundell, D. (2004). A logic-based formulation of active visual perception. In D. Dubois, C.A. Welty, & M.-A. Williams (Eds.), *KR2004: Principles of knowledge representation and reasoning*, Whistler (pp. 64–72). Menlo Park: AAAI.
Stalnaker, R.C. (1972). Pragmatics. In D. Davidson & G.H. Harman (Eds.), *Semantics of natural language* (pp. 380–397). Dordrecht: Reidel.
Stalnaker, R.C. (1975). Pragmatic presuppositions. In M.K. Munitz & P. Unger (Eds.), *Semantics and philosophy* (pp. 197–213). New York: Academic.

Thomason, R.H. (1987). The multiplicity of belief and desire. In M.P. Georgeff & A. Lansky (Eds.), *Reasoning about actions and plans* (pp. 341–360). Los Altos: Kaufmann.
Thomason, R.H. (2000). Modeling the beliefs of other agents. In J. Minker (Ed.), *Logic-based artificial intelligence* (pp. 375–473). Dordrecht: Kluwer.
Thomason, R.H. (2002). The beliefs of other agents. http://www.eecs.umich.edu/~rthomaso/documents/nmk/index.html.
Thomason, R.H. (2005). Making contextual intensional logic nonmonotonic. In A. Dey, B. Kokinov, D. Leake, & R. Turner (Eds.), *Modeling and using context: 5th international and interdisciplinary conference*, Pairs (pp. 502–514). Berlin: Springer.
Thomason, R.H. (2007). Three interactions between context and epistemic locutions. In B. Kokinov, D.C. Richardson, T.R. Roth-Berghofer, & L. View (Eds.), *Modeling and using context: Sixth international and interdisciplinary conference, context 2007*, Roskilde (pp. 467–481). Berlin: Springer.
Wooldridge, M.J. (2000). *Reasoning about rational agents*. Cambridge: Cambridge University Press.

Chapter 11
Character Matching and the Locke Pocket of Belief

Gregory Wheeler

11.1 Introduction

The Lockean thesis maintains that an individual fully believes a proposition φ just when he has a high level of confidence in φ. The trouble with the Lockean thesis, according to probabilists like Richard Jeffrey, is that it licenses throwing away perfectly good information. Any numerically determinate degree of belief that happens to fall above the Lockean's threshold for full acceptance is abandoned in favor of a qualitative label, 'full belief'. What orthodox probabilists want to know is whether there is anything gained in the exchange.

To be sure, some probabilists take the case against full belief too far: the idea that full belief can be entirely replaced by credal probability, for example, is a non-starter. Probability presupposes possibility, and judgments of possibility—even if only to pick *this* algebra rather than *that* one for your probability structure—are categorical. Further still, there are alternatives to probabilism. Henry Kyburg's lottery paradox (Kyburg 1961) was a campaign button for his ϵ-acceptance theory of evidential probability, which is deeply at odds with probabilism. David Makinson's puzzle about prefaces (Makinson 1965) preceded his important work on systems that facilitate genuine inductive expansion (Makinson 2005), yet inductive expansion is notoriously difficult to square with probabilism, cf. Levi (1980), and Paris and Simmonds (2009).

Nevertheless, Kyburg's lottery paradox and Makinson's paradox of the preface have developed a life of their own as Rorschach tests for the metaphysics of rational belief. In what sense, if any, is belief categorical? It what sense, if any, is it gradable? How weird does the logic have to be to have it both ways? The orthodox probabilist answers *none*, *completely*, and *too weird*. The conventional Lockean says that

G. Wheeler (✉)
Munich Center for Mathematical Philosophy, LMU Munich
e-mail: gregory.wheeler@lrz.uni-muenchen.de

F. Lihoreau and M. Rebuschi (eds.), *Epistemology, Context, and Formalism*, Synthese Library 369, DOI 10.1007/978-3-319-02943-6_11,

rational full belief summarizes information conveyed by a high degree of credal probability and the logic for full belief is classical except that it will not be closed under conjunction. Here then is a threshold acceptance view that is purported to be in harmony with the spirit of probabilism: 'Full belief' is simply code for 'has high credal probability'. But then the harmonious Lockean faces the question that started us off: why bother?

11.2 Character Matching

In the course of defending a mission for harmonious Lockeanism, Scott Sturgeon introduces a normative principle called *character matching* which maintains that the character of a belief should match the character of the evidence upon which it is based.

> When evidence is essentially sharp, it warrants a sharp or exact attitude; when evidence is essentially fuzzy ...it warrants at best a fuzzy attitude. In a phrase: evidential precision begets attitudinal precision; and evidential imprecision begets attitudinal imprecision (Sturgeon 2008, p. 159).

Sturgeon's idea is that everyday evidence is often imprecise in character; so, by the principle of character matching, everyday evidence will seldom rationalize numerically determinate credences but instead will typically rationalize only regions of credal space. Yet, when imprecise evidence for a claim occupies the range $[\theta, 1]$, for a suitably high threshold value θ between $1/2$ and 1, Sturgeon claims that 'lending that confidence to [the] claim functions exactly like believing it in a threshold-based way' (Sturgeon 2008, p. 160). Harmonious Lockeanism is thus conceived to be an extension of probabilism to cover the majority of cases in which everyday evidence is strong but imprecise. So, the harmonious Lockean is not throwing away information when he fully believes: he is making the best of the information he's got.

That commonplace evidence is more often precise than imprecise is surely right. I may observe that A is more frequent than B either by rough observation of the occurrence of A's versus the occurrence of B's or by more careful methods of statistical estimation. Neither case yields numerically determinate frequencies, however, unless of course my estimation is gotten directly from a complete description of the occurrence of A's and the occurrence of B's in the population. If I know the proportion of red balls in an urn is exactly 0.85 because I loaded the balls into the urn myself, say, then I know that a sample set of 100 balls from the urn should contain roughly 85 red balls. I can leverage my knowledge of the population, i.e., the urn, to calibrate my sampling mechanism. If instead I do not know the proportion of red balls in the urn but I draw several 100-ball sample sets randomly, never observe less than 80 red balls in a sample and likewise never observe more than 90 balls in a sample, then I may estimate (conservatively) that the proportion of red balls in the urn is between 0.8 and 0.9. In this manner I learn about the proportion of red balls in the population by observing samples from that population. Why? Because it is extremely unlikely to go through an exercise like this one, observe the same proportions of red balls from a set of 100-ball samples, yet have it be the case that I am drawing from an urn whose proportion of red balls is in fact outside of the interval [0.8, 0.9]. We may fully believe that the actual proportion of red balls is between 0.8 and 0.9 because, by manipulating the number of samples drawn, we may control the risk faced from adopting this attitude in error. We may judge that the proportion of red balls in the urn is within [0.8, 0.9], or that the proportion of red balls is roughly [0.8, 0.9]. If we happen to know that error in our samples is distributed normally, we may judge that the proportion of red balls is roughly 0.85. Analogously, we may judge that the length of a table leg is 71 ± 0.03 cm, or that it is roughly 71 cm, or roughly between 70.97 and 71.03 units centimeter in length—depending on what is known about the instrument, the measurement procedure, and the conditions under which the measurements are taken.

But while it is clear that much of our evidence is imprecise, it is far less clear what bearing this should have on rational full belief. Sturgeon maintains that high imprecise credence is identical to full belief, and the linchpin to his argument is the normative principle that 'epistemic perfection demands character match between evidence and attitude' (Sturgeon 2008, p. 160).

One might probe whether the character matching principle is true by considering cases where precise evidence appears to at best warrant only imprecise belief. Imagine that Fen the fence is trying to sell You[1] a rigged lottery ball machine. Fen tells You that the machine is calibrated to dispense a red ball 70 % of the time and to dispense an even numbered ball 60 % of the time, and that is all that You are told about the machine. A ball is dispensed. Arguably, before observing the ball, Your credence that it is red is 0.7 and Your credence that the ball is even is 0.6. However, Your credence that the ball is both red *and* even is indeterminate, taking any value between 0.3 and 0.7.[2] Here the character of Your evidence is precise but incomplete: knowing the probability that a dispensed ball is red and the probability that a dispensed ball is even warrants at best an imprecise attitude about the ball being both red and even.

The example is not a problem for Sturgeon, however. The reason that Your disposition toward the proposition [*the ball is both red and even*] is a credal *state* bound by the closed interval $[0.3, 0.7]$ rather than a numerically precise credal *probability* is due directly to Your evidence, which is that the probability of the ball being both red and even is between 0.3 and 0.7. Thus, rather than being an objection to the character matching principle, the example instead appears to be a

[1]Following a long tradition that includes Walley, de Finetti, and Good, I sometimes use 'You' to denote an intentional system and invite you, the reader, to play along in the role.

[2]In general, for arbitrary propositions A and B, if $P(A)$ and $P(B)$ are defined with respect to a probability structure M, then with respect to M we have, cf. Wheeler (2006):

- $P(A \wedge B) \in [\max(0, P(A) + P(B) - 1), \min(P(A), P(B))]$, and
- $P(A \vee B) \in [\max(P(A), P(B)), \min(P(A) + P(B), 1)]$.

sterling example: Your imprecise belief that the ball is both even and red matches the imprecise character of Your available evidence.

Although the character of evidence and attitude appear to match in this example they do not match as a rule. To illustrate why, imagine that it is the middle of the night and Claudius cannot sleep because of a recurring cough. Groggy, he makes his way in the dark to the medicine cabinet for cough syrup, finds a bottle, unscrews the top, and swallows a liquid that burns rather than soothes his throat. Panicked, he gropes for the light to see what he has ingested, knocking to the floor and shattering two bottles, A and B. Claudius determines that he drank from one of the two, neither of which contains cough syrup. Although unable to determine for certain which bottle he drank from, he fully believes that D [*it is more likely that Claudius drank from A than from B*].

At hospital the attending physician, Ridgeon, tells Claudius that A-poisoning is best treated by rest, whereas the recommended treatment for B-poisoning is to have ones stomach pumped. Pumping is inadvisable for A-poisoning, however, and while sleeping off B-poisoning won't kill him, it entails a much longer recovery period than stomach pumping. To make the example concrete, suppose Ridgeon's utilities for these intervention options are given by the following table.

Now suppose that Claudius has told Ridgeon the entire story so far except that he has withheld reporting to the doctor that D, that it is more likely that he ingested A than B. Based on the partial information that Ridgeon has about Claudius's case, Ridgeon's preference about which intervention is best for Claudius is highly indeterminate, ranging from 0.1 to 1 for rest and from 0 to 0.9 for the pump. The doctor's dilemma is so because, at this stage, Ridgeon has no evidence whatsoever about whether it was A or B that Claudius ingested: for Ridgeon, the probability that Claudius drank A is within $[0, 1]$ and the probability that Claudius drank B is within $[0, 1]$.

Now suppose that Claudius offers up to Ridgeon the missing piece of information. With the addition of D, Ridgeon's evidence is that the probability that Claudius has A-poisoning is within $(0.5, 1]$ and the probability that Claudius has B-poisoning is within $[0, 0.5]$. The new item of evidence is very imprecise, offering only slight evidence for A-poisoning over B-poisoning. Indeed, the evidence for A-poisoning is well outside the 'bel-region' that Sturgeon imagines is the top 'five to fifteen percent of the scale' for credal probability that is supposed to sustain threshold-based belief, cf. Sturgeon (2008, pp. 160–161). Yet, although imprecise, notice that this evidence suffices to resolve the doctor's dilemma decisively in favor of rest.[3]

[3]To simplify matters, one may calculate expected utility (eu) on the closed interval $[0.5, 1]$ instead of the clopen interval $(0.5, 1)$ without loss of generality. (See note 4.) There are four expected utilities to calculate: (1) eu(Rest) = 1, when the probability that A is maximal and B is minimal; (2) eu(Rest) = 0.44, when the probability of A is minimal and B is maximal; (3) eu(Pump) = 0.45, when B is maximal, and (4) eu(Pump) = 0. Because (pump, A) = 0 in Table 11.1, we may ignore those probability values in the last pair of calculations for Pump.

Table 11.1 Ridgeon's payoff table

	A	B
Rest	1	0.1
Pump	0	0.9

Ridgeon's attitude toward the proposition R [*Rest is the best treatment for Claudius*] should change from an uncommitted attitude to full rational belief upon receiving the highly imprecise evidence about which bottle Claudius drank from.[4]

Curiously, the doctor's full belief that R is in a sense made stronger rather than weaker by the imprecise character of D. Were Ridgeon an orthodox probabilist and insist upon extracting a numerically precise credence from Claudius about his belief that he drank from A, his request would add nothing to support Ridgeon's full belief that rest is best, and we might fairly question the doctor's good judgment for bothering to ask.

In short, Ridgeon's full belief that R rests on evidence about A-poisoning whose imprecision extends beyond the bel-region to correspond to a high-threshold full belief. What's more, and mentioned as an aside in Footnote 4, there is decisive evidence in this case in favor of rest even when the lower-bound for A poisoning is strictly below $1/2$. The upshot is that if Claudius either (1) reported that he more likely drank from bottle A than from B, (2) reported that it is no more than slightly more likely that he ingested B than A, or (3) reported any numerically precise credence strictly greater than $0.44\overline{4}$ that he drank A rather than B, then Ridgeon would have formed the same categorical belief that rest is the best treatment for Claudius. None of these three options describes evidence in the bel-region, nor is the region of credal probability associated with R necessarily in the bel-region.

11.3 Pocket of Belief

Full belief and credence do not necessarily match in character nor should they. Credal probability (degrees of belief) encodes a disposition to make a collection of bets on the truth of φ. (That's Ramsey.) Credal states are a set of admissible credal probability functions, where the conditions for admissibility are a subtle affair. (That's Levi.) The disposition to fully believe φ, on the other hand, is the

[4]Notice that a decisive resolution in favor of R does not even depend on the evidence pointing in favor of Claudius having consumed A rather than B. The same result holds for all probability functions P such that $P(A)$ is strictly greater than $0.44\overline{4}$.

disposition to act as if φ were true relative to some specified range of actions. This is not the same thing as a disposition to accept bets on φ.[5]

We imagine that Ridgeon, once he has the last piece of evidence (D) about Claudius's case, acts as if it is true that rest is the best treatment for him. It is in this respect that full belief is contextually dependent, since an agent's disposition to act as if φ is true may vary across contexts even when both the possible set of actions and the evidence for φ are held constant.

Some think that this observation about full belief means that the disposition to fully believe depends on the magnitude of the stake. 'The more you care the less you know', as Jason Stanley has put it.[6] And there are plenty of examples that appear to support this view. A farmer might act as if a vaccine for flu is non-toxic to his pigs, but refuse to act as if the same vaccine is non-toxic to his children. In short, he may fully believe that the injection is safe for his pigs but not for his kids. This may be so even if the vaccine's fatality rate for children is less than the fatality rate for pigs. The farmer simply values his children much more than he values his pigs, viewing the risk of error acceptable for his pigs but not for his kids.

But focusing on the magnitude of the risk of being wrong is only half of the story; we must also focus on the potential payoff from being right. Return again to our farmer, and suppose the question before him now is whether to inoculate his pigs and his kids against a relatively new strain of *Escherichia coli* which affects 1/3 of each population. The new antibiotic poses identical risk to swine and humans, killing 1 out of 15 in each treated group. However, whereas pigs almost always recover from this strain of *E. Coili* on their own, children rarely survive it. Faced with this situation, the farmer would give the antibiotic to his children but not to his pigs. That is, in this case the farmer would fully believe that the treatment is non-toxic to his children but toxic to his pigs. Although the farmer values his children much more than he values his pigs, it is still the case that he values his pigs.

What this last example illustrates is that although full believe is context dependent, it does not depend upon the total magnitude of the stake put at risk, as stakes-relative views imagine, but instead depends on the ratio of the amount put at risk (r) by acting as if φ were true when φ is false, to the amount gained (w) by acting as if φ were true when φ is true.[7] Adopting a model of Kyburg's,[8] we say that an agent fully ($r : w$) believes that φ with respect to a context C of available actions iff: for any act $A \in C$, if

---

[5]The probability of a sequence of 50 flips of a fair coin all landing heads is 8.882×10^{-16} and ordinarily we act as if this outcome will not occur. But, no one is willing to *offer* odds of \$1 to \$1.126 quadrillion against seeing 50 straight heads; Wall Street traders are a cautionary exception. Furthermore, few would bother to take those odds even if offered.

[6]But the idea goes back at least to R. B. Braithwaite (1946).

[7]We assume that an agent has a cardinal utility function over states of the world such that his utilities are linear and satisfy the von Neumann-Morgenstern axioms.

[8]An earlier version of the following risk-reward theory of full belief appears in Kyburg (1990, pp. 244–255)

1. The agent judges A to cost r^* if φ is false,
2. The agent judges A to payout w^* if φ is true,
3. $^{r^*}/_{w^*} < {}^{r}/_{w}$, then

the agent acts as if φ is true.

If an agent fully $(r : w)$ believes that φ (with respect to some C), then it follows that he fully $(w : r)$ disbelieves $\neg\varphi$ in C. Since to risk r is to potentially gain $-r$, to gain w is to have risked $-w$, $^{-r}/_{-w} = {}^{w}/_{r}$, and $\neg\varphi$ is false if and only if φ is true, it follows that full $(w : r)$ disbelief that $\neg\varphi$ (in C) holds just in case, for any act $A \in C$, if (1) the agent judges to cost w^* if $\neg\varphi$ is false, (2) to payout r^* if $\neg\varphi$ is true, (3) $^{w^*}/_{r^*} > {}^{w}/_{r}$ (equivalently, $^{-r^*}/_{-w^*} < {}^{r}/_{w}$), then the agent acts as if $\neg\varphi$ is false. An agent $(r : w)$ suspends judgment with respect to φ in C if the agent neither fully $(r : w)$ believes φ in C, nor fully disbelieves φ in C. From the conjugacy relation between belief and disbelief, i.e., fully $(r : w)$ belief that φ in C if and only if full $(w : r)$ disbelief that $\neg\varphi$ in C, we say that $^{r}/_{w}$ forms a *pocket of belief*.

To illustrate, suppose that the ratio $^{1}/_{20}$ represents the pocket of belief for ordinary contexts, i.e., for an ordinary set of actions from which the agent must choose. This means that an agent who fully $(1 : 20)$ believes the proposition T [*lottery ticket #591* losses] would judge his loss—assume the ticket is his—to be r^* if T is false, the payout to be w^* if T is true, and the risk-reward ratio $r^* : w^*$ associated with his acting 'as if T is true' would be strictly less than $^{1}/_{20}$. Suppose now that 1,000 lottery tickets are sold for \$1.00 each and the house takes a penny from each ticket sale, leaving \$990 as the payoff to a single, fairly drawn ticket. And let's suppose a context where the most consequential action the agent considers is whether to discard the ticket before the drawing. Then, the agent 'loses' $r^* = -\$989$ acting as if T when T is false, and is 'rewarded' $w^* = -\$1$ if T is true. Yet, $^{1}/_{989} \not> {}^{20}/_{1}$, so the agent *does not* act as if $\neg T$ is false, and he does not act as if T is true, either. Rather, he will, like most of us would under ordinary circumstances, suspend judgment about T, perhaps waiting until the outcome of the lottery is announced to decide what to do with the ticket. Here the character of the evidence for T is in the bel region, but the agent neither fully believes T nor fully disbelieve it: he has a good reason to suspend judgment.

Given the same evidence about T, an agent's attitude may change from suspended judgment to full belief either by adjusting the pocket of full belief with respect to T, say to $1 : 990$, or by creating a genuine risk for acting as if T when T is false. However, it might be difficult to reconcile a $^{1}/_{990}$ pocket of belief with the ordinary terms for a lottery drawing, and adjusting the risk-reward ratio to drag T inside the pocket of full belief may be to change the example altogether. No matter. The reluctance to fully believe T in this context provides no sound basis for generalization: there are plenty of so-called 'lottery propositions', cf. Hawthorne (2004) that are consonant with the pocket of ordinary full belief. For example, return to the length of the table leg mentioned earlier. For the sake of argument, suppose that there is likewise a 1 in 1,000 chance that the true length of table leg #591 is not within the interval estimate 71 ± 0.03 cm that is warranted by the measurement. Unlike lottery tickets, suspending judgment until the announcement of the table leg's true length is not an option. What's more, there are appreciable rewards to fully believing L [*Table leg #591 is* 71 ± 0.03 cm] when L is true: someone's acting as if L were true figured in the table's construction, for instance. So, while there is a non-negative risk to acting as if L is true when it is not—a wobbly table, an unhappy customer—the reward in most contexts makes this a risk worth taking. Or course, here too an agent's attitude may change from 'full belief' to 'suspended judgment' by altering the parameters in the model to place the proposition L outside of the pocket of ordinary full belief, and this likewise may occur without altering the character of the evidence.

So far we've seen that the character of evidence and belief need not match. Imprecise and weak evidence can warrant full belief (Ridgeon), whereas high-thresholded evidence sometimes warrants full belief (table legs) and sometimes does not (lottery tickets). But there is one last point. On Sturgeon's telling, Lockean belief is a form of 'attitudinal imprecision'. So, while the principle of character matching fails to explain the relationship between evidence and Lockean belief, one might think that Sturgeon is at least right in claiming that Lockean belief is imprecise in character. But, alas even this isn't necessarily so, for we may normalize the ratio of risk-to-reward by defining $\beta = {}^{w}\!/_{r+w}$ along with a classical probability function for some agent Y, P_Y, over a propositional language. Then, if Y fully $(r : w)$ believes φ, there is a $\beta \in [0, 1]$ such that the agent fully ${}^{\beta}\!/_{1-\beta}$ believes φ and $P_Y(\varphi) > \beta$, cf. Kyburg (1990). So, to illustrate, if Y fully $(1 : 20)$ believes φ, then $P_Y(\varphi) > {}^{20}\!/_{21} \approx 0.95$.

Here then is Character Matching turned inside out. For implicit in the Lockean model for full acceptance is a conjugacy relation that defines full rejection in terms of full acceptance: given some threshold parameter ${}^{1}\!/_{2} < \theta < 1$, a Lockean agent fully accepts φ when his credence that φ is above θ just in case the agent fully rejects $\neg\varphi$ when his credence for $\neg\varphi$ is below $1 - \theta$. Thus, full Lockean belief and full Lockean disbelief occur in the tails of the 0, 1 interval. The pocket of belief, in normalized form, yields a numerically precise credal probability—if it yields one at all—that is within the Lockean pockets of full belief and full disbelief, and it will not yield a numerically precise measurement outside of them. So, for a $(1 : 20)$ pocket of full belief, full belief can occur only when credences are *between* 0.95 and 1, and full disbelief occurs only when credences are between 0 and 0.05. It is not necessary that there be numerically precise credences: a qualitative, comparative judgment might be enough to classify all acts in a context as inside the pocket. But, if there are sharp credal probabilities worth considering, you'll find them in Locke's pocket.

Acknowledgements This work was supported by award LogiCCC/0001/2007 from the European Science Foundation. A version of this paper was presented at the 2010 APA Pacific Division Meeting in San Francisco. Thanks to Franck Lihoreau, Jonathan Weisberg and Sarah Wright for their comments.

References

Braithwaite, R.B. (1946). Belief and action. *Proceedings of the Aristotelian Society, 20*, 1–19.

Hawthorne, J.P. (2004) *Knowledge and lotteries*. Oxford: Clarendon.

Kyburg, H.E., Jr. (1961). *Probability and the logic of rational belief.* Middletown: Wesleyan University Press.

Kyburg, H.E., Jr. (1990). *Science and reason*. New York: Oxford University Press.

Levi, I. (1980). *The enterprise of knowledge*. Cambridge: MIT.

Makinson, D.C. (1965). The paradox of the preface. *Analysis, 25*, 205–207.

Makinson, D.C. (2005). *Bridges from classical to nonmonotonic logic*. London: King's College Publications.

Paris, J., & Simmonds, R. (2009). O is not enough. *The Review of Symbolic Logic, 2*, 298–309.

Sturgeon, S. (2008). Reason and the grain of belief. *Noûs, 42*(1), 139–165.

Wheeler, G. (2006). Rational acceptance and conjunctive/disjunctive absorption. *Journal of Logic, Language and Information, 15*(1–2), 49–63.

Chapter 12
A Modal Logic of Perceptual Belief

Andreas Herzig and Emiliano Lorini

12.1 Introduction

We present a simple logic called L-PB (*Logic of Perceptual Belief*) which allows to represent the relationships between an agent's beliefs and the information that the agent obtains by his senses.

From the conceptual point of view, the interesting aspect of the logic L-PB is that it provides a clear account of the way doxastic mental states are determined by perception. Different from traditional approaches based on Kripke semantics proposed in computer science (Fagin et al. 1995), economics (Aumann 1999) and philosophy (Hintikka 1962), in which the concept of *possible world* is taken as the basic object in the semantics for interpreting belief modal operators, in L-PB the primitive objects are agents' perceptions (i.e. agents' *perceptual data*) and the modal operators of belief are interpreted on the basis of them. We might say that in L-PB agents' beliefs are *grounded* on perceptions.

From the technical point of view, the logic L-PB provides a semantics that is simpler and more compact than the traditional Kripke-style semantics: L-PB models are basically valuations of atomic formulas. Our logic is related to the logic DL-PA that we proposed in order to reconstruct Coalition Logic and Coalition Logic of Propositional Control (Herzig et al. 2011a,b).

The rest of the paper is organized as follows. In Sect. 12.2 we present the syntax and the semantics of our basic logic L-PB in which it is assumed that an agent cannot have inconsistent perceptual data nor inconsistent beliefs. The modal operator of L-PB obeying the principles of the modal logic KD, in Sect. 12.3 we present two variants: first, a stronger version where it obeys principles of positive and negative

A. Herzig (✉) • E. Lorini
University of Toulouse, CNRS, IRIT-LILaC, 118 Route de Narbonne,
31062 Toulouse Cedex 9, France
e-mail: andreas.herzig@irit.fr; emiliano.lorini@irit.fr

F. Lihoreau and M. Rebuschi (eds.), *Epistemology, Context, and Formalism*,
Synthese Library 369, DOI 10.1007/978-3-319-02943-6_12,

introspection, i.e. modal logic KD45; second, an even stronger version where the modal operator of belief models an S5-notion of perceptual knowledge. Both these logics being static, we present in Sect. 12.4 an extension by events in the style of dynamic epistemic logics. Finally, Sect. 12.5 discusses related work.

12.2 A Logic of Perceptual Belief

We present the syntax and the semantics of the logic L-PB. Different from Hintikka's standard account in terms of possible worlds and accessibility relations, our semantics of belief is in terms of primitives denoting that an agent receives from his senses the datum that some propositional variable is true or false. We give a complete axiomatization and a decidability result.

12.2.1 Syntax

Assume a countable set of basic facts $Prop^0 = \{p^0, q^0, \ldots\}$ and a finite set of agents $Agt = \{i_1, \ldots, i_{|Agt|}\}$. The language $\mathcal{L}$ of the logic L-PB is the set of formulas defined by the following grammar in Backus-Naur Form (BNF):

$$Atm : p ::= p^0 \mid \mathsf{datum}^{\top}(i,p) \mid \mathsf{datum}^{\perp}(i,p)$$

$$Fml : \phi ::= p \mid \neg\phi \mid \phi \wedge \phi \mid \mathsf{B}_i\phi$$

where p^0 ranges over the set of basic facts $Prop^0$, p ranges over the set of atomic formulas Atm, and i ranges over the set of agents Agt.

Atm includes basic facts and special constructions $\mathsf{datum}^{\top}(i,p)$ and $\mathsf{datum}^{\perp}(i,p)$ which are used to describe what a given agent has perceived. $\mathsf{datum}^{\top}(i,p)$ is read "the agent i has perceived p to be true" or "the agent i has received (from his senses) the datum that p is true", whereas $\mathsf{datum}^{\perp}(i,p)$ is read "the agent i has perceived p to be false" or "the agent i receives (from his senses) the datum that p is false". Similar constructions are used in Lorini and Castelfranchi (2007). They are supposed to capture what Dretske calls *perceptual recognition* or *meaningful perception* (Dretske 1981, 1995). According to Dretske, the latter is an epistemic form of perception which occurs at later stages in the extraction and use of sensory information, and which should be distinguished from a non-epistemic form called *sense perception*, occurring at an earlier stage. In sense perception an agent perceives an *object* O (or event) without necessarily identifying or recognizing it in a particular way. For example, one can see a cat on the sofa and mistake it for a rumpled sweater. On the contrary, meaningful perception requires the recognition that a given *fact* φ is true (i.e., the perceptual judgement that the *fact* φ is true). An agent's meaningful perception that φ is true directly determines the agent's belief that φ is true. For example, one can see that there is a cat on the sofa thereby coming to believe that there is a cat on the sofa. Let p^0 denote the fact "the cat is on the sofa". Then $\mathsf{datum}^{\top}(i,p^0)$ expresses that agent i perceives that the cat is on the sofa. Note that our language allows for higher-order perception: $\mathsf{datum}^{\top}(j,\mathsf{datum}^{\top}(i,p^0))$ expresses that j perceives that i perceives that the cat is on the sofa. In the sequel we sometimes write $\mathsf{datum}^{\tau}(i,p)$ as a placeholder for $\mathsf{datum}^{\top}(i,p)$ or $\mathsf{datum}^{\perp}(i,p)$. We read the disjunction $\mathsf{datum}^{\top}(i,p) \vee \mathsf{datum}^{\perp}(i,p)$ as "i has perceived *whether* p", or "i has learned *whether* p".

The formula $\mathsf{B}_i\phi$ is read "the agent i believes that φ is true". As we will show later, this concept of belief obeys the principles for a modal operator of belief as introduced by Hintikka in terms of modal logic KD (Hintikka 1962). In Sect. 12.3 we will show how the logic L-PB can be easily adapted in order to model a fully introspective notion of perceptual belief obeying the principles of modal logic KD45 (Sect. 12.3.1) and also a fully introspective and truthful notion of perceptual knowledge obeying the principles of modal logic S5 (Sect. 12.3.2).

The other Boolean operators $\top$, $\perp$, $\vee$, $\rightarrow$ and $\leftrightarrow$ are defined from $\neg$ and $\wedge$ in the standard way.

Let Atm_{ϕ} be the set of atoms from Atm occurring in ϕ. For example $Atm_{\mathsf{datum}^{\top}(i,p)} = \{p, \mathsf{datum}^{\top}(i,p)\}$.

12.2.2 Semantics

The model-theoretic semantics of the logic L-PB is much simpler than those of common doxastic and epistemic logics: an L-PB model is simply a valuation of atomic formulas having consistent data.

Definition 12.2.1 (L-PB model). An L-PB model is a valuation $V \subseteq Atm$ such that for all $p \in Atm$ and for all $i \in Agt$:

(C1) If $\mathsf{datum}^{\top}(i,p) \in V$ then $\mathsf{datum}^{\perp}(i,p) \notin V$.

Constraint (C1) means that an agent cannot get inconsistent information from his senses, that is, an agent cannot have inconsistent perceptual data.

Definition 12.2.2 (Doxastic alternatives). For every agent $i \in Agt$ we define a relation $\mathcal{B}_i$ on the set of L-PB models as follows: $V\mathcal{B}_iV'$ if and only if for every $p \in Atm$,

1. If $\mathsf{datum}^{\top}(i,p) \in V$ then $p \in V'$;
2. If $\mathsf{datum}^{\perp}(i,p) \in V$ then $p \notin V'$.

In words, $V\mathcal{B}_iV'$ means that V' is a model that agent i considers possible at V, or V' is a doxastic alternative of agent i at V. That is, V' only differs from V in the atomic formulas that agent i did not perceive (i.e. that are not part of agent i's set of perceptual data). The relation $\mathcal{B}_i$ is therefore such that agent i considers possible at V every valuation that is compatible with his perceptions at V, i.e. every valuation V' such that $V' \models \mathsf{datum}^{\top}(i,p) \rightarrow p$ and $V' \models \mathsf{datum}^{\perp}(i,p) \rightarrow \neg p$. The relation $\models$ is the standard satisfaction relation between models and formulas that is defined as follows.

Definition 12.2.3 (Truth conditions). Let V be a L-PB model satisfying constraint (C1). The truth conditions are as follows:

$$V \models p \quad \text{iff } p \in V, \; for \;\; p \in \text{Atm};$$
$$V \models \neg\phi \quad \text{iff } V \not\models \phi;$$
$$V \models \phi \wedge \psi \text{ iff } V \models \phi \text{ and } V \models \psi;$$
$$V \models \mathsf{B}_i\phi \quad \text{iff } V' \models \phi \text{ for all } V' \text{such that } V\mathcal{B}_i V'.$$

When $V \models \phi$ holds we say that ϕ is true in V.

Validity and satisfiability are defined in the standard way. An example of a L-PB validity is the formula

$$\mathsf{B}_i\phi \rightarrow \neg\mathsf{B}_i\neg\phi$$

That formula schema is actually nothing but the standard modal axiom D.

One might criticize the fact that the logic L-PB captures only one aspect of the relationship between perception and beliefs. Indeed, it is not simply the case that an agent's beliefs are determined by what the agent perceives (as it is assumed in L-PB); an agent's perception also involves some sort of inferential process and is therefore affected by the agent's beliefs. In other words, the relationship between perception and beliefs is bidirectional. For example, in order to perceive that the cat is on the sofa, the agent has to interpret the raw input data obtained through his sensors by means of some abductive process. This abductive process is based on the agent's pre-existent beliefs about the concepts of *cat, sofa*, etc. (e.g. the belief that "a cat has four legs", or the belief that "the sofa is brown", etc.) We are aware that this is a limitation of the logic L-PB. However, building a logical model of perception based on abduction (or some other kind of inferential process) goes beyond the objective of the present work. We refer to Shanahan (2002) for a recent paper on this topic. We envisage to explore that research avenue based on our work in Herzig et al. (2011b).

12.2.3 Axiomatization and Decidability

We give results concerning axiomatizability and decidability of our logic. We proceed in a somewhat uncommon order: we first prove soundness, then decidability, and finally completeness.

(PC)	All tautologies of propositional calculus
$(\wedge_{\mathsf{B}_i})$	$\mathsf{B}_i(\varphi \wedge \psi) \leftrightarrow (\mathsf{B}_i\phi \wedge \mathsf{B}_i\psi)$
(DataCons)	$\mathsf{datum}^{\top}(i,p) \rightarrow \neg\mathsf{datum}^{\perp}(i,p)$
(BelData$_1$)	$\mathsf{datum}^{\top}(i,p) \rightarrow \mathsf{B}_i p$
(BelData$_2$)	$\mathsf{datum}^{\perp}(i,p) \rightarrow \mathsf{B}_i \neg p$
(BelData$_3$)	$\mathsf{B}_i(p \vee \phi) \rightarrow (\mathsf{datum}^{\top}(i,p) \vee \mathsf{B}_i\phi)$
(BelData$_4$)	$\mathsf{B}_i(\neg p \vee \phi) \rightarrow (\mathsf{datum}^{\perp}(i,p) \vee \mathsf{B}_i\phi)$
(MP)	$\dfrac{\varphi, \varphi \rightarrow \psi}{\psi}$
(Nec$_{\mathsf{B}_i}$)	$\dfrac{\varphi}{\mathsf{B}_i\varphi}$

Fig. 12.1 Axiomatization of L-PB

Our axiomatization is given in Fig. 12.1. A formula is a *L-PB theorem* if is derivable from instances of the axiom schemas by means of the inference rules. Examples of L-PB theorems are $\mathsf{B}_i\, p \leftrightarrow \mathsf{datum}^{\top}(i,p)$ and $\mathsf{B}_i \neg p \leftrightarrow \mathsf{datum}^{\perp}(i,p)$: they are instances of **(BelData)** that are respectively obtained by setting P^+ to $\{p\}$ and P^+ to $\emptyset$ and by setting P^+ to $\emptyset$ and P^+ to $\{p\}$.

Theorem 12.2.1. *For every L-PB formula ϕ, if ϕ is a L-PB theorem then ϕ is L-PB valid.*

Proof. It suffices to prove that every instance of our axiom schemas in Fig. 12.1 is valid in L-PB models, and that the two inference rules preserve validity in L-PB models. □

The following provable equivalence will be useful in the sequel.

Proposition 12.2.2. *Let P^+ and P^- be two finite, disjoint subsets of Atm. Then the equivalence*

$$\textit{(BelData)}\ \mathsf{B}_i\left((\bigvee_{p \in P^+} p) \vee (\bigvee_{p \in P^-} \neg p) \right)$$

$$\leftrightarrow \left((\bigvee_{p \in P^+} \mathsf{datum}^{\top}(i,p)) \vee (\bigvee_{p \in P^-} \mathsf{datum}^{\perp}(i,p)) \right)$$

is valid.

We now give a mechanical procedure that allows us to decide the problem whether a given formula ϕ is valid in the class of L-PB models. Basically there are two steps: first, transform ϕ into an equivalent formula without modal operators; second, we check whether $\Gamma_{\phi}^{\mathsf{L\text{-}PB}} \rightarrow \psi$ is valid in classical propositional logic,

1 **input:** a formula ϕ.
2 **output:** a formula $red(\phi)$ without modal operators.
3 **begin**
4   **while** there is a modal operator in ϕ **do**
5   choose a subformula $\mathsf{B}_i\psi$ of ϕ such that ψ is without modal operators;
6   put ψ in conjunctive normal form:
7   replace ψ by $\chi_1 \wedge \cdots \wedge \chi_n$ such that every χ_k is a clause;
8   distribute B_i over conjunctions:
9   replace $\mathsf{B}_i(\chi_1 \wedge \cdots \wedge \chi_n)$ by $\mathsf{B}_i\chi_1 \wedge \cdots \wedge \mathsf{B}_i\chi_n$;
10   replace every $\mathsf{B}_i\chi_k = \mathsf{B}_i\big((\bigvee_{p\in P^+} p) \vee (\bigvee_{p\in P^-} \neg p)\big)$ by
11                 $(\bigvee_{p\in P^+} \mathsf{datum}^\top(i,p)) \vee (\bigvee_{p\in P^-} \mathsf{datum}^\perp(i,p))$
12   **endwhile**;
13     $red(\phi) := \phi$
14 **end**

Fig. 12.2 Reduction procedure for L-PB

where $\Gamma_\phi^{\text{L-PB}}$ contains those instances of the axiom schema **(DataCons)** that are relevant for ϕ. The algorithm for the first step is given in Fig. 12.2. Remember that a *literal* is either an atom from *Atm* or the negation of an atom from *Atm*, and that a *clause* is a disjunction of literals.

Proposition 12.2.3. *Let ϕ be any L-PB formula. Then the algorithm of Fig. 12.2 terminates, $red(\phi)$ contains no modal operators, and $\phi \leftrightarrow red(\phi)$ is a theorem of L-PB.*

Proof. Lines 6–7 apply equivalences that are valid in classical propositional logic. Lines 8–9 apply axiom ($\wedge_{\mathsf{B}_i}$). Lines 10–11 apply axiom **(BelData)**. Therefore when the algorithm returns a formula $red(\phi)$ then this formula is equivalent to the input formula ϕ.

Finally, there is only a finite number of modal operators in ϕ, and every passage of the while-loop in lines 4–12 eliminates one modal operator. The algorithm therefore terminates, and the output $red(\phi)$ contains no more modal operators. □

Proposition 12.2.4. *Let ϕ be a L-PB formula without modal operators. Then ϕ is L-PB valid if and only if $\left(\bigwedge \Gamma_\phi^{\text{L-PB}}\right) \to \phi$ is valid in classical propositional logic, where*

$$\Gamma_\phi^{\text{L-PB}} = \{\neg(\mathsf{datum}^\top(i,p) \wedge \mathsf{datum}^\perp(i,p)) : p \in Atm_\phi\}$$

Proof. Note first that the set $\Gamma_\phi^{\text{L-PB}}$ is finite; its conjunction $\bigwedge \Gamma_\phi^{\text{L-PB}}$ is therefore well-defined. Then in order to prove the proposition we prove that $\Gamma_\phi^{\text{L-PB}}$ contains all the instances of the axiom schema **(DataCons)** that are relevant for ϕ. □

Theorem 12.2.5. *The validity problem of L-PB is decidable.*

Proof. Let ϕ be a L-PB formula. By Proposition 12.2.3 there is a L-PB formula without modal operators $red(\phi)$ such that $red(\phi) \leftrightarrow \phi$ is L-PB valid. While

$red(\phi)$ contains no modal operators, it is not a formula of classical propositional logic yet because it may contain the special atoms $\mathsf{datum}^{\top}(i,p)$ and $\mathsf{datum}^{\perp}(i,p)$. However, by the above Proposition 12.2.4, ϕ is L-PB valid if and only if $\left(\bigwedge \Gamma_{\phi}^{\text{L-PB}}\right) \to \phi$ is valid in classical propositional logic. □

We finally use that our decision procedure is correct in order to prove completeness.

Theorem 12.2.6. *For every L-PB formula ϕ, if ϕ is L-PB valid then ϕ is a L-PB theorem.*

Proof. Suppose ϕ is L-PB valid. Then $red(\phi)$ is L-PB valid because of Proposition 12.2.3 (and because of soundness of the axiomatics of L-PB, i.e. Theorem 12.2.1). Then

$$\left(\bigwedge \Gamma_{\phi}^{\text{L-PB}}\right) \to red(\phi)$$

is valid in classical propositional logic by Proposition 12.2.4. Due to the completeness of the latter that implication is also provable in classical propositional logic. It follows that $red(\phi)$ is provable in L-PB. Finally, ϕ is provable in L-PB by Proposition 12.2.3. □

Remark. We have seen that the 'D' axiom schema $\mathsf{B}_i\phi \to \neg\mathsf{B}_i\neg\phi$ is L-PB-valid. The logic L-PB being complete, each instance of it can be proved from our axiomatics. It is therefore not necessary to add it to the axiomatization. However, note that it seems that the schema itself cannot be proved. This is not surprising because the uniform substitution rule is not admissible (as it often happens in dynamic epistemic logics).

12.3 Varying the Properties of Belief

Our basic logic L-PB lacks principles of introspection as advocated in Fagin et al. (1995), and we now show that such principles can be validated in a straightforward way. We also show that the move from belief to S5-like knowledge is easy to perform.

12.3.1 Adding Positive and Negative Introspection

L-PB^{Intr} (*Logic of Perceptual Belief with Introspection*) is the first variant of the logic L-PB that we study. In L-PB^{Intr} it is assumed that agents' beliefs are positively and negatively introspective. In order to formalize this assumption, we need to add two constraints to the definition of a model.

(PIntrPerc)	$\mathsf{datum}^{\tau}(i,p) \rightarrow \mathsf{datum}^{\top}(i,\mathsf{datum}^{\tau}(i,p))$
(NIntrPerc)	$\neg\mathsf{datum}^{\tau}(i,p) \rightarrow \mathsf{datum}^{\perp}(i,\mathsf{datum}^{\tau}(i,p))$

Fig. 12.3 Further axioms for $\mathsf{L\text{-}PB}^{Intr}$

Definition 12.3.1 ($\mathsf{L\text{-}PB}^{Intr}$ **model).** A $\mathsf{L\text{-}PB}^{Intr}$ model is a $\mathsf{L\text{-}PB}$ model V satisfying the following additional constraints. For all $p \in Atm$ and $\tau \in \{\top, \perp\}$:

(C2) If $\mathsf{datum}^{\tau}(i,p) \in V$ then $\mathsf{datum}^{\top}(i,\mathsf{datum}^{\tau}(i,p)) \in V$;
(C3) If $\mathsf{datum}^{\tau}(i,p) \notin V$ then $\mathsf{datum}^{\perp}(i,\mathsf{datum}^{\tau}(i,p)) \in V$.

Constraint (C2) captures positive introspection for perception: if an agent perceives whether p then the agent perceives that he perceives whether p. Constraint (C3) is the corresponding principle of negative introspection: if it is not the case that i perceives whether p then 'i is aware of that', i.e. i perceives that he does not perceive whether p.

Theorem 12.3.1. *$\mathsf{L\text{-}PB}^{Intr}$ validity is decidable, and the set of $\mathsf{L\text{-}PB}^{Intr}$ validities is completely axiomatized by the axiom schemas and rules of inference of Fig. 12.1 plus the axiom schemas of Fig. 12.3.*

Proof. The proof is the same as before; the only difference is that in Proposition 12.2.4 we have to augment the set of formulas $\Gamma_{\phi}^{\mathsf{L\text{-}PB}^{Intr}}$ by the relevant constraints coming with (C2) and (C3):

$$\begin{aligned}\Gamma_{\phi}^{\mathsf{L\text{-}PB}^{Intr}} &= \{\neg(\mathsf{datum}^{\top}(i,p) \wedge \mathsf{datum}^{\perp}(i,p)) : p \in Atm_{\phi}\} \cup \\ &\quad \{\mathsf{datum}^{\top}(i,p) \rightarrow \mathsf{datum}^{\top}(i,\mathsf{datum}^{\top}(i,p)) : p \in Atm_{\phi}\} \cup \\ &\quad \{\mathsf{datum}^{\perp}(i,p) \rightarrow \mathsf{datum}^{\top}(i,\mathsf{datum}^{\perp}(i,p)) : p \in Atm_{\phi}\}\end{aligned}$$

Note that the set $\Gamma_{\phi}^{\mathsf{L\text{-}PB}^{Intr}}$ is still finite. □

Remark. Just as it was the case for the axiom schema of seriality D, the introspection axiom schemas 4 and 5 need not be part of the axiomatization. Indeed, the formula schemas $\mathsf{B}_i\phi \rightarrow \mathsf{B}_i\mathsf{B}_i\phi$ and $\neg\mathsf{B}_i\phi \rightarrow \mathsf{B}_i\neg\mathsf{B}_i\phi$ are both $\mathsf{L\text{-}PB}^{Intr}$-valid. Due to the completeness of the logic $\mathsf{L\text{-}PB}^{Intr}$, each of their instances is $\mathsf{L\text{-}PB}^{Intr}$ derivable.

12.3.2 From Perceptual Belief to Perceptual Knowledge

We call $\mathsf{L\text{-}PK}$ (*Logic of Perceptual Knowledge*) the second variant of $\mathsf{L\text{-}PB}$. $\mathsf{L\text{-}PK}$ formalizes the notion of fully introspective and truthful knowledge as commonly assumed in artificial intelligence (Fagin et al. 1995).

(CorrectPerc$_\top$)	$\mathsf{datum}^{\top}(i,p) \rightarrow p$
(CorrectPerc$_\bot$)	$\mathsf{datum}^{\bot}(i,p) \rightarrow \neg p$

Fig. 12.4 Further axioms for L-PK

We start by adding two constraints to the definition of a model.

Definition 12.3.2 (L-PK model). A L-PK model is a L-PB^{Intr} model V satisfying the following additional constraints, for all $p \in Atm$ and $\tau \in \{\top, \bot\}$:

(C4) If $\mathsf{datum}^{\top}(i,p) \in V$ then $p \in V$;
(C5) If $\mathsf{datum}^{\bot}(i,p) \in V$ then $p \notin V$.

These constraints capture the fact that an agent's perception is correct: if an agent perceives that p is true (resp. false) then p is indeed true (resp. false).

Theorem 12.3.2. *The validities of* L-PK *are completely axiomatized by the axiom schemas and inference rules of Fig. 12.1 plus the axiom schemas of Fig. 12.3 and in Fig. 12.4.*

Proof. The proof is again the same as before; the only difference is that we again have to augment the set of formulas $\Gamma_{\phi}^{\mathsf{L\text{-}PK}}$ of Proposition 12.2.4 by the relevant constraints coming with (C4) and (C5):

$$\begin{aligned}
\Gamma_{\phi}^{\mathsf{L\text{-}PK}} &= \{\neg(\mathsf{datum}^{\top}(i,p) \wedge \mathsf{datum}^{\bot}(i,p)) : p \in Atm_{\phi}\} \cup \\
&\{\mathsf{datum}^{\top}(i,p) \rightarrow \mathsf{datum}^{\top}(i,\mathsf{datum}^{\top}(i,p)) : p \in Atm_{\phi}\} \cup \\
&\{\mathsf{datum}^{\bot}(i,p) \rightarrow \mathsf{datum}^{\top}(i,\mathsf{datum}^{\bot}(i,p)) : p \in Atm_{\phi}\} \cup \\
&\{\mathsf{datum}^{\top}(i,p) \rightarrow p : p \in Atm_{\phi}\} \cup \\
&\{\mathsf{datum}^{\bot}(i,p) \rightarrow \neg p : p \in Atm_{\phi}\}
\end{aligned}$$

Note that $\Gamma_{\phi}^{\mathsf{L\text{-}PK}}$ is again finite. □

Remark. Just as for axioms D, 4 and 5 it is not necessary to add axiom T to the axiomatization. Indeed, the following formula schema is L-PK-valid:

$$\mathsf{B}_i\phi \rightarrow \phi.$$

Due to the completeness of L-PK, each instance of these schemas is provable.

12.4 A Dynamic Logic of Perceptual Belief

In this section we present a dynamic extension of the logic L-PB called DL-PB (*Dynamic Logic of Perceptual Belief*). To that end we introduce *mental actions* $\mathsf{perc}^{\top}(i,p)$ and $\mathsf{perc}^{\bot}(i,p)$ of i learning that p is true or false. We also consider the symmetric mental actions of forgetting that p is true or false, respectively written $\mathsf{forg}^{\top}(i,p)$ and $\mathsf{forg}^{\bot}(i,p)$.

These actions will be the arguments of dynamic operators $[\alpha]$, similar to Propositional Dynamic Logic (Harel et al. 2000) and to Dynamic Epistemic Logics (van Ditmarsch et al. 2007).

The language of the logic DL-PB is in terms of atomic formulas, actions, and complex formulas. It is defined by the following grammar in Backus-Naur Form (BNF):

$$Atm : p ::= p^0 \mid \mathsf{datum}^{\top}(i,p) \mid \mathsf{datum}^{\bot}(i,p)$$

$$Act \ : \alpha ::= \mathsf{perc}^{\top}(i,p) \mid \mathsf{perc}^{\bot}(i,p) \mid \mathsf{forg}^{\top}(i,p) \mid \mathsf{forg}^{\bot}(i,p)$$

$$Fml : \phi ::= p \mid \neg\phi \mid \phi \wedge \phi \mid \mathsf{B}_i\phi \mid [\alpha]\phi$$

where p^0 ranges over the set of basic facts $Prop^0$ and i ranges over the set of agents Agt.

Formulas of the form $[\alpha]\phi$ are read "after the occurrence of the action/event α, ϕ will be true". We distinguish four types of actions (or events) in the set Act:

- $\mathsf{perc}^{\top}(i,p)$ is the action of perceiving that p is true (i.e. of adding the information that p is true to the set of perceptual data);
- $\mathsf{perc}^{\bot}(i,p)$ is the action of perceiving that p is false (i.e. of adding the information that p is false to the set of perceptual data);
- $\mathsf{forg}^{\top}(i,p)$ is the action of forgetting that p is true (i.e. of removing the information that p is true from the set of perceptual data);
- $\mathsf{forg}^{\bot}(i,p)$ is the action of forgetting that p is false (i.e. of removing the information that p is false from the set of perceptual data).

These actions are supposed to be *private*: when i perceives that p is true then the other agents do not learn that i perceives that; actually we shall even suppose that i himself does not learn that he perceives that p is true. We made that choice because our basic logic L-PB does not obey any introspection principle. Our updates allow that another agent j perceives that i perceives p: he then updates his beliefs about i's beliefs, but does not change his own opinion about the status of p. Note that an agent's perception may be incorrect: i may perceive that p is true while p is actually false.

Definition 12.4.1 (Truth conditions). Let V be a L-PB model satisfying constraint (C1). The truth conditions for the dynamic operators $[\alpha]$ are:

$$V \models [\mathsf{perc}^{\top}(i,p)]\phi \text{ iff } (V \cup \{\mathsf{datum}^{\top}(i,p)\}) \setminus \{\mathsf{datum}^{\bot}(i,p)\} \models \phi$$

(Red$_\neg$)	$[\alpha]\neg\phi$	$\leftrightarrow \neg[\alpha]\phi$
(Red$_\wedge$)	$[\alpha](\phi \wedge \psi)$	$\leftrightarrow [\alpha]\phi \wedge [\alpha]\psi$
(Red$_{\mathsf{perc}^\top(i,p)}$)	$[\mathsf{perc}^\top(i,p)]q$	$\leftrightarrow \begin{cases} \top & \text{if } q = \mathsf{datum}^\top(i,p) \\ \bot & \text{if } q = \mathsf{datum}^\bot(i,p) \\ q & \text{else} \end{cases}$
(Red$_{\mathsf{perc}^\bot(i,p)}$)	$[\mathsf{perc}^\bot(i,p)]q$	$\leftrightarrow \begin{cases} \top & \text{if } q = \mathsf{datum}^\bot(i,p) \\ \bot & \text{if } q = \mathsf{datum}^\top(i,p) \\ q & \text{else} \end{cases}$
(Red$_{\mathsf{forg}^\tau(i,p)}$)	$[\mathsf{forg}^\tau(i,p)]q$	$\leftrightarrow \begin{cases} \bot & \text{if } q = \mathsf{datum}^\tau(i,p) \\ q & \text{else} \end{cases}$

Fig. 12.5 Reduction axioms for DL-PB

$$V \models [\mathsf{perc}^\bot(i,p)]\phi \text{ iff } (V \cup \{\mathsf{datum}^\bot(i,p)\}) \setminus \{\mathsf{datum}^\top(i,p)\} \models \phi$$
$$V \models [\mathsf{forg}^\top(i,p)]\phi \text{ iff } V \setminus \{\mathsf{datum}^\top(i,p)\} \models \phi$$
$$V \models [\mathsf{forg}^\bot(i,p)]\phi \text{ iff } V \setminus \{\mathsf{datum}^\bot(i,p)\} \models \phi$$

Observe that all the updated models on the right hand side of the truth conditions[1] satisfy constraint (C1).

For example the formulas $[\mathsf{perc}^\bot(i,p)]\mathsf{B}_i\neg p$ and $\mathsf{B}_j\mathsf{B}_i p \to [\mathsf{perc}^\bot(i,p)]\mathsf{B}_j\mathsf{B}_i p$ are valid for every i and j.

The set of equivalences of Fig. 12.5 are all valid. Together with axiom schema **(BelData)** these equivalences work as reduction axioms: they allow to eliminate all the modal operators from formulas. Consider for example the formula $[\mathsf{perc}^\bot(i,p)]\mathsf{B}_i\neg p$. It can be rewritten to $\top$ in two steps.

$$\begin{aligned} [\mathsf{perc}^\bot(i,p)]\mathsf{B}_i\neg p &\leftrightarrow [\mathsf{perc}^\bot(i,p)]\mathsf{datum}^\bot(i,p) && \text{(by } \mathbf{(BelData)}\text{)} \\ &\leftrightarrow \top && \text{(by } (\mathbf{Red}_{\mathsf{perc}^\bot(i,p)})\text{)} \end{aligned}$$

Consider now the formula $[\mathsf{forg}^\top(i,p)](\neg\mathsf{B}_i p \wedge \neg\mathsf{B}_i\neg p)$. It can be rewritten to $\top$ in three steps.

$$\begin{aligned} [\mathsf{forg}^\top(i,p)]\neg\mathsf{B}_i p &\leftrightarrow [\mathsf{forg}^\top(i,p)]\neg\mathsf{datum}^\top(i,p) && \text{(by } \mathbf{(BelData)}\text{)} \\ &\leftrightarrow \neg[\mathsf{forg}^\top(i,p)]\mathsf{datum}^\top(i,p) && \text{(by } (\mathbf{Red}_\neg)\text{)} \\ &\leftrightarrow \neg\bot && \text{(by } (\mathbf{Red}_{\mathsf{forg}^\tau(i,p)})\text{)} \\ &\leftrightarrow \top \end{aligned}$$

[1]These are the L-PB models $V \cup \{p^0\}$, $V \setminus \{p^0\}$, $(V \cup \{\mathsf{datum}^\top(i,p)\}) \setminus \{\mathsf{datum}^\bot(i,p)\}$, $(V \cup \{\mathsf{datum}^\bot(i,p)\}) \setminus \{\mathsf{datum}^\top(i,p)\}$, $V \setminus \{\mathsf{datum}^\top(i,p)\}$, and $V \setminus \{\mathsf{datum}^\bot(i,p)\}$.

Note that the action of "forgetting about p" can be defined as the action of forgetting that p is true followed by the action of forgetting that p is false. As the following validity highlights, the result of this action is that the agent does not believe anymore whether p is true[2]:

$$[\mathsf{forg}^{\top}(i,p)][\mathsf{forg}^{\perp}(i,p)](\neg\mathsf{B}_i p \wedge \neg\mathsf{B}_i\neg p).$$

12.5 Related Works

Van der Hoek et al. have recently proposed a logic of knowledge that is based on the concept of partial observability (van der Hoek et al. 2011). They assume that each agent i is able to 'see' a subset of the overall set of Boolean variables; that is, i is able to correctly perceive the value of these variables. Therefore i cannot distinguish two valuations V and V' if and only if V and V' assign the same truth values to the Boolean variables that i can see. They then propose the following definition of knowledge: at a given valuation V, the agent i knows that φ is true if and only if φ is true at all valuations that i cannot distinguish from the actual valuation V.

We share with van der Hoek et al. the idea of providing a semantics for knowledge that is more compact and simpler than the traditional Kripke-style semantics: just as they do, we assume that epistemic models are valuations of atomic formulas. However, our logic differs from theirs in several respects. First, while they only consider S5-knowledge, we here start from the weaker notion of KD-belief. As we have shown in Sect. 12.3.2, our approach is very flexible as it allows to define S5-knowledge by imposing the corresponding constraints on L-PB models. We conjecture that van der Hoek et al.'s logic of knowledge can be embedded into the logic L-PK we have presented in Sect. 12.3.2.

A second difference is that van der Hoek et al.'s logic does not have constructions describing what a given agent perceives. The interesting aspect of our logic is that it allows to represent first-order perceptions of the form "agent i perceives that p_0 is true" and higher-order perceptions of the form "agent i perceives that agent j perceives that p is true", "agent i perceives that agent j perceives that the agent i perceives that p is true", etc. These constructions can be used to represent what in the cognitive science literature is called *mutual perception* or *joint attentional state* (Tommasello 1995; Clark and Marshall 1981). In particular, we can say that the agents in a set of agents C *mutually perceive that p is true up to level n* if and only if, every agent in C perceives that p is true, every agent in C perceives that every agent in C perceives that p is true, and so on up to level n. The formal definition is as follows. We use $\mathsf{datum}^{\top}(i,p_1 \wedge \ldots \wedge p_n)$ as an abbreviation of $\mathsf{datum}^{\top}(i,p_1) \wedge \ldots \wedge \mathsf{datum}^{\top}(i,p_n)$ and $\mathsf{EPerc}_C\, p$ as an abbreviation of $\bigwedge_{i \in C} \mathsf{datum}^{\top}(i,p)$ (i.e.

[2]See van Ditmarsch et al. (2009) for a similar notion of *forgetting*.

every agent in C perceives that p is true). We can then inductively define $\mathsf{EPerc}^k_C\, p$ for every natural number $k \in \mathbb{N}$:

$$\mathsf{EPerc}^0_C\, p \stackrel{\text{def}}{=} p$$
$$\mathsf{EPerc}^k_C\, p \stackrel{\text{def}}{=} \mathsf{EPerc}_C \mathsf{EPerc}^{k-1}_C\, p, \text{ for } k > 0$$

We define $\mathsf{MPerc}^n_C\, p$ as an abbreviation of $\bigwedge_{1\leq k\leq n} \mathsf{EPerc}^k_C\, p$, for all natural numbers $k \in \mathbb{N}$. The formula $\mathsf{MPerc}^n_C\, p$ denotes C's mutual perception that p is true up to level n. It is easy to verify that mutual perception implies mutual belief. That is, for every $n \in \mathbb{N}$ the following formula is L-PB valid:

$$\mathsf{MPerc}^n_C\, p \rightarrow \mathsf{MBel}^n_C\, p$$

where $\mathsf{MBel}^k_C\, p$ denotes the standard notion of C's mutual belief that p up to level n.[3]

A third difference between van der Hoek et al.'s approach and ours is that they only consider the static aspects of their logic of knowledge. In Sect. 12.4 we have also considered the dynamic aspects of our logic of perceptual belief.

12.6 Conclusion

We have proposed a modal logic of perceptual belief L-PB which allows to represent the basic relationships between an agent's beliefs and the information that the agent obtains by his senses. We have studied both the static and the dynamic aspects of this logic. We have modeled perception as a private action; actually even when i perceives that p is true then i himself does not learn that he perceives that p is true. We opted for that choice because our basic logic L-PB does not obey any introspection principle. The integration of such principles can be done, but requires a more elaborate account.

It is worth pointing out that our basic logic L-PB satisfies the principle D of consistency of beliefs, while other extensions of doxastic logic with events such as e.g. Kooi's (2003) have to abandon that principle.

It can be claimed that our logic pushes further the program of dynamic epistemic logics: semantically, the latter abandon the accessibility relation for the dynamic operator and replace it by model updates, while keeping the accessibility relation

[3]Precisely, $\mathsf{MBel}^k_C\, p$ can be defined in the three steps as follows. First, we define $\mathsf{EBel}_C\, p$ as an abbreviation of $\bigwedge_{i\in C} \mathsf{B}_i$. Then, we inductively define $\mathsf{EBel}^k_C\, p$ for every $k \in \mathbb{N}$: $\mathsf{EBel}^0_C\, p \stackrel{\text{def}}{=} p$ and $\mathsf{EBel}^k_C\, p \stackrel{\text{def}}{=} \mathsf{EBel}_C \mathsf{EPerc}^{k-1}_C\, p$ for $k > 0$. Finally, we define $\mathsf{MBel}^n_C\, p$ as an abbreviation of $\bigwedge_{1\leq k\leq n} \mathsf{EBel}^k_C\, p$.

for the belief operator. In contrast, we also abandon the belief relation and replace it by information about data, ending up with valuations of classical propositional logic that have to obey a consistency constraint between data.

Directions of future work are manifold. An interesting extension of our logic is the integration of operators of (perceptual) common belief and (perceptual) distributed belief. This will allow to study the collective aspect of the notion of perceptual belief introduced in this paper. We also think that the logic L-PB might offer an interesting framework for studying the origin of common belief: how common belief can arise in a situation of *co-presence* in the sense of Clark and Marshall (1981), that is, when the agents mutually perceive a given fact p.[4] For example, we may mutually believe that there is a table between us *because* I can see that there is a table between us, you can see that there is a table between us, I can see that you can see that there is a table between us, you can see that I can see that there is a table between us, and so on. Finally, a more technical perspective is to investigate in more depth the differences between L-PB and standard modal logic KD. We have shown that all the KD principles are valid in our logic; however, the converse is not true: the formula $\mathsf{B}_i(p \vee q) \rightarrow (\mathsf{B}_i p \vee \mathsf{B}_i q)$ is L-PB valid for every $p \in Atm$, while this is not the case in KD. While the logics therefore differ at the level of formula instances, we conjecture that there is no *formula schema* distinguishing L-PB and KD. This is related to the fact that the uniform substitution rule is not admissible in L-PB that we have already noticed (see the remark in the end of Sect. 12.2).

References

Aumann, R. (1999). Interactive epistemology I: Knowledge. *International Journal of Game Theory, 28*(3), 263–300.

Clark, H. H., & Marshall, C. R. (1981). Definite reference and mutual knowledge. In A. K. Joshi, B. Webber, & I. A. Sag (Eds.), *Elements of discourse understanding* (pp. 10–63). Cambridge/New York: Cambridge University Press.

Dretske, F. (1981). *Knowledge and the flow of information*. Cambridge: MIT.

Dretske, F. (1995). Meaningful perception. In D. N. Osherson & S. M. Kosslyn (Eds.), *An invitation to cognitive science (Vol. 2): Visual cognition*. Cambridge: MIT.

Fagin, R., Halpern, J., Moses, Y., & Vardi, M. (1995). *Reasoning about knowledge*. Cambridge: MIT.

Harel, D., Kozen, D., & Tiuryn, J. (2000). *Dynamic logic*. Cambridge: MIT.

Herzig, A., Lorini, E., Moisan, F., & Troquard, N. (2011a). A dynamic logic of normative systems. In T. Walsh (Ed.), *International joint conference on artificial intelligence (IJCAI)*, Barcelona (pp. 228–233). Morgan Kaufmann.

Herzig, A., Lorini, E., & Troquard, N. (2011b). A dynamic logic of institutional actions. In *Computational logic in multi-agent systems (CLIMA): Vol. 6814. Lecture notes in computer science* (pp. 295–311). Berlin: Springer.

[4]See Lorini et al. (2005) and Pfeiffer-Leßmann and Wachsmuth (2009) for some recent works on this topic.

Hintikka, J. (1962). *Knowledge and belief.* New York: Cornell University Press.
Kooi, B. P. (2003). Probabilistic dynamic epistemic logic. *Journal of Logic, Language and Information, 12*, 381–408.
Lorini, E., & Castelfranchi, C. (2007). The cognitive structure of surprise: Looking for basic principles. *Topoi, 26*(1), 133–149.
Lorini, E., Tummolini, L., & Herzig, A. (2005). Establishing mutual beliefs by joint attention: Towards a formal model of public events. In *Proceedings of the 27th annual conference of the cognitive science society (CogSci 2005)*, Stresa, (pp. 1325–1330). Lawrence Erlbaum.
Pfeiffer-Leßmann, N., Wachsmuth, I. (2009). Formalizing joint attention in cooperative interaction with a virtual human. In *Proceedings of KI 2009: Advances in artificial intelligence, 32nd annual german conference on AI*, Paderborn (pp. 540–547).
Shanahan, M. (2002). A logical account of perception incorporating feedback and expectation. In *Proceedings of the 8th international conference on principles of knowledge representation and reasoning (KR 2002)*, Toulouse (pp. 3–13). Morgan Kaufmann.
Tommasello, M. (1995). Joint attention as social cognition. In C. Moore & P. Dunham (Eds.), *Joint attention: Its origins and role in development* (pp. 103–130). Hillsdale: Lawrence Erlbaum.
van der Hoek, W., Troquard, N., & Wooldridge, M. (2011). Knowledge and control. In *Proceedings of the 10th international joint conference on autonomous agents and multiagent systems (AAMAS'11)*, Taipei (pp. 719–726). ACM.
van Ditmarsch, H. P., van der Hoek, W., & Kooi, B. (2007). *Dynamic epistemic logic. Synthese Library, 337*, Springer.
van Ditmarsch, H., Herzig, A., Lang, J., & Marquis, P. (2009). Introspective forgetting. *Synthese, 169*(2), 405–423.

Chapter 13
Hyperintensionality and *De Re* Beliefs

Paul Égré

The aim of this essay is to deal with the problem of hyperintensionality of belief sentences—basically, the failure of substitutivity of synonymous expressions under the scope of *believe*—using the apparatus of quantified modal logic and the machinery of counterpart semantics. Consider the following sentence, taken from Muskens (1991), in which we assume the conditional is a material conditional (use another paraphrase if appropriate):

(1) Peter believes that if door A is locked, then door B is not locked, but he does not believe that if door B is locked, then door A is not locked.

In standard epistemic logic (Hintikka 1969) and in intensional logic (Montague 1970), an ascription of belief like this one, which involves two logically equivalent sentences, is predicted to be inconsistent. In Montague grammar, in particular, the proposition expressed by each embedded sentence is the same, and since beliefs are conceived as relations between individuals and propositions, the beliefs of an agent are predicted to be closed under logical equivalence. In epistemic logic, the situation is even more problematic, since beliefs are predicted to be closed under logical consequence.[1] Both frameworks predict agents to be 'logically omniscient' in that sense.[2]

[1]This is not automatically so in Montague grammar, though closure under logical consequence is predicted there too, given closure under logical equivalence, if belief is assumed to be closed under conjunction.

[2]Logical omniscience and hyperintensionality are intertwined problems often conflated, although hyperintensionality is arguably a semantic problem concerning our *ascriptions* of belief; the

P. Égré (✉)
Institut Jean-Nicod (CNRS, ENS, EHESS), École Normale Supérieure, Département d'Études Cognitives, 29, rue d'Ulm, 75005 Paris, France

NYU, Department of Philosophy, 5, Washington Place, 10003 New York, NY, USA
e-mail: paulegre@gmail.com

F. Lihoreau and M. Rebuschi (eds.), *Epistemology, Context, and Formalism*, Synthese Library 369, DOI 10.1007/978-3-319-02943-6_13,

There clearly are, however, contexts in which a sentence like (1) above can be uttered consistently. On the other hand, there is also a sense in which the same content is ascribed (or denied) to Peter in either conjunct of (1). The aim of the present proposal is to reconcile these two intuitions, by offering an account of hyperintensionality in terms of context-dependence: the basic idea I try to articulate in this paper is that Peter's belief, even though opaque, can be analyzed as a *de re* belief about one and the same proposition (or about the same objects and relation each time), but under different counterpart relations, playing the role of modes of presentation, and acting as a pragmatic component in the evaluation of sentences.

The prime inspiration for this essay comes from a specific paper by J. Gerbrandy (2000) on counterpart semantics for *de re* beliefs, itself following a longer and wider tradition of dealing with modes of presentation and perspectival reference in terms of counterpart relations.[3] In this paper, I offer to generalize Gerbrandy's semantics to a second-order modal logic, in order to account for cases of hyperintensionality involving expressions of distinct syntactic categories (coreferential proper names, cointensional predicates, logically equivalent sentences). Thus the idea is that cases of hyperintensionality should be analyzed on a par with other classic instances of opacity for belief sentences, and the aim is to get a uniform treatment of all those cases. My proposal, which comes out very close in this respect to the treatment of hyperintensionality proposed by Cresswell and von Stechow (1982), rests on the idea that belief sentences can be given a *de re* logical form, even in situations which would standardly be analyzed as *de dicto*. This idea raises problems of its own, which will be discussed along the way, but it also contains some potential benefits (like avoiding the resort to impossible worlds beyond standard belief worlds).

The paper is structured as follows. In Sect. 13.1, I briefly review the *de dicto* treatment of opacity given in Hintikka's modal framework. In Sect. 13.2, I give some arguments in favor of a *de re* analysis of opacity, and review the treatment of Gerbrandy in Sect. 13.3. Section 13.4 presents an intuitive generalization of Gerbrandy's analysis to cases of hyperintensionality involving predicates and full sentences. I give an evaluation of the merits and limits of this proposal in Sect. 13.5. The details of the logic and semantics are deferred to the appendix of this paper.

---

problem of logical omniscience can be construed more broadly as an epistemological problem about the modeling of belief proper, and only secondarily as a problem for ascriptions in natural language. In what follows, I am mostly concerned with the semantics of belief ascriptions, and primarily talk of hyperintensionality for that matter.

[3]Much of the inspiration of Gerbrandy's semantics stems from Kaplan (1969) on quantifying in, as well as from Hintikka (1969), Kraut (1983), and several members of the Amsterdam school of semantics, including Zeevat, Dekker, van Rooij and Aloni. Counterpart relations originally appear in Lewis (1968). Edelberg (1992), Zeevat (1996a,b), van Rooij (2006), and Dekker and van Rooij (1998) have used counterpart relations to deal with opacity phenomena and in particular to handle 'Hob-Nob' sentences. See in particular van Rooij (2006, Appendix A) and Aloni (2001, 2005) for distinct but closely related counterpart semantics for first-order modal logic of belief. See also Percus and Sauerland (2003), who use the idea to account for *de se* attitudes.

13.1 Opacity in Epistemic Logic

Contexts of propositional attitudes are notoriously opaque. Under the scope of a verb like *believe*, two expressions which are intuitively synonymous are not always substitutable to each other *salva veritate*. Much of the original motivation for developing systems of modal epistemic logic has been to provide an adequate semantic analysis of those opacity phenomena. According to Hintikka's influential treatment, cases of opacity should be analyzed as cases of *referential multiplicity* (Hintikka 1969). Using the apparatus of first-order modal logic, Hintikka showed, for instance, how to analyze the consistency of a sentence like:

(2) Peter believes that Cicero is a philosopher, but he does not believe that Tully is a philosopher.

In Hintikka's analysis, the proper names "Tully" and "Cicero", although coreferential at the actual world, can simply refer to distinct individuals in the belief worlds of Peter. In the relevant context, Peter misrepresents to himself one and the same individual as two potentially distinct individuals. The most straightforward way to paraphrase the sentence is by giving it a *de dicto* analysis, in which the belief operator takes the largest possible scope ("$\Box$" stands for the belief operator, "c" and "t" for "Cicero" and "Tully", and "P" for "philosopher"):

(3) $\Box P(c) \wedge \neg\Box P(t)$.

Given the standard semantics for the belief operator ($\Box\phi$ is true at a world if ϕ is true at all epistemically accessible worlds), this sentence is satisfiable in a model in which c and t denote two distinct individuals in at least one belief world, such that the individual denoted by t falls out of the extension of the predicate P at that world (but where the individual denoted by c belongs to that extension at every world).

The same analysis can be extended to analyze the failure of substitutivity of two predicates with the same intuitive meaning, as in:

(4) Peter believes that John is an eye-doctor, but he does not believe that John is an ophthalmologist.

Again, Peter can simply be wrong about the meaning of "ophthalmologist", despite the coextensionality of "eye-doctor" and "ophthalmologist" at the actual world. If Peter believes that ophthalmologist are eye-doctors with special skills, but happens not to believe that all eye-doctors have such skills, then the sentence is perfectly consistent. The sentence can be paraphrased *de dicto* in quantified modal logic ("O" stands for "ophthalmologist". The other translation conventions are left implicit in the rest of the paper):

(5) $\Box E(j) \wedge \neg\Box O(j)$.

The sentence is satisfiable in a model in which the extension of E and O differ in at least one belief world, such that the individual denoted by j falls out of the extension of O at that world (but falls in the extension of E at all worlds).

A problem for this analysis arises with the case of logically equivalent sentences. Consider again Muskens' example, where the conditional is assumed to be a material conditional each time:

(6) Peter believes that if door A is locked, then door B is not locked, but does not believe that if door B is locked, then door A is not locked.

Again, the standard logical form for this sentence in quantified modal logic is the following *de dicto* representation:

(7) $\Box(L(a) \to \neg L(b)) \wedge \neg\Box(L(b) \to \neg L(a))$.

By the compositional rules of evaluation of the sentences, the two embedded sentences receive the same truth-value at all worlds, including the belief worlds of the agent, contradicting the intuitive consistency of (6). The problem comes from the fact that the semantics gives the logical connectives a uniform behavior throughout the models. This problem is known, since the work of Cresswell (1973), as the problem of the hyperintensionality of belief contexts: in standard epistemic logic and in Montague Grammar, expressions with the same intension are inadequately predicted to be substitutable to each other in every context *salva veritate*, including in the scope of belief operators. The problem is to some extent aggravated in epistemic logic proper, since beliefs are predicted to be closed even under logical consequence more generally, due to the upward monotonicity of the $\Box$ operator, making the agents "logically omniscient". In classic intensional logic, conversely, the status of sentences like (2) and (4) is to a large extent analogous to that of (6), as soon as two coreferential proper names like "Cicero" and "Tully" are assumed to denote the same individual at all worlds, or if two predicates like "eye-doctor" and "ophthalmologist" are taken to express the same concept, and so to have the same intension.[4]

To handle the hyperintensionality of belief operators, one possibility (entertained successively by Montague, Cresswell, Rantala, and advocated by Hintikka (1975)) is to add a second layer of belief worlds, so-called *logically impossible worlds*, namely non-standard worlds where the embedded sentences can receive arbitrary truth-values in a non-compositional way. Thus one can account for the consistency of (7) if there is a logically impossible world among Peter's epistemic alternatives

[4]As an ESSLLI reviewer pointed out, one should strictly speaking distinguish two levels of hyperintensionality, depending on how fine-grained one takes the notion of intensional equivalence to be. Strictly speaking, an operator $\circ$ is *hyperintensional* if there are two formulas ϕ and ψ, a model M and a world w such that $\models (\phi \leftrightarrow \psi)$ (that is ϕ and ψ are logically equivalent), $M, w \models \circ\psi$ and $M, w \not\models \circ\psi$. And following the reviewer's suggestion, one may call an operator *superintensional* if there are two formulas ϕ and ψ, a model M and a world w such that $M \models (\phi \leftrightarrow \psi)$ (that is ϕ and ψ are model-equivalent), $M, w \models \circ\psi$ and $M, w \not\models \circ\psi$. Hyperintensionality is stronger than superintensionality, since logical equivalence entails model-equivalence. What example (4) suggests is that belief operators are at least superintensional (the predicates E ("eye-doctor") and O ("ophthalmologist") need not be equivalent at every world of *every* model—they are model-equivalent only in virtue of a meaning postulate). Example (6), on the other hand, suggests that belief operators are hyperintensional in the strict sense.

such that $(L(b) \rightarrow \neg L(a))$ is false at that world, while $(L(a) \rightarrow \neg L(b))$ is true at all his belief worlds.[5] This move, it is important to note, is exactly in the spirit of the analysis of the previous two examples, since this amounts to saying that Peter fails to see the equivalence between the two sentences "if door A is locked, then door B is not locked" and "if door B is locked, then door A is not locked". In a way, made explicit by Muskens (1991) and anticipated by Thomason (1980), this solution can be seen as treating logical constants as part of the non-logical vocabulary, and as allowing some variation in the denotation of the logical connectives at the belief worlds, in the same way in which singular terms and predicates are allowed to change their denotation at the belief worlds of the agent. In that manner, a compositional semantics can be given for beliefs, which accounts for opacity at all the relevant syntactic levels.

13.2 *De Re* Beliefs and Opacity

Despite the coherence of Hintikka's treatment of opacity, there remain several reasons to look for a different solution. A first point of criticism, which has been recurrent on the side of the supporters of Kripke's theory of proper names, concerns the leeway that allows proper names, in particular, to take distinct denotations at the belief worlds of the agent. For a strict Kripkean, proper names are rigid, which means that two names that are coreferential at the actual world should have the same denotation at all the worlds, including the epistemic worlds.[6] A strict supporter of Kripke's theory may allow the predicate "eye-doctor" and "ophthalmologist" to take different values at the belief worlds of Peter, if he grants that those two predicates have a descriptive content, on which Peter can make a mistake. But he will probably disagree with the case of proper names, on the ground that proper names have no descriptive content.

This piece of criticism is not entirely compelling, however. For it is one thing to say that proper names are rigid and do not behave like hidden definite descriptions in

[5]Impossible worlds semantics is compositional on standard worlds. It is non-compositional on non-standard worlds in that the truth value of a sentence there is assigned holistically, and does not functionally depend on the truth-value of its constituents in that world or in other worlds. See Fagin et al. (1995, Chap. 9) for a concise exposition of impossible worlds semantics.

[6]Such a view is expressed, in particular, by Récanati (2000a, p. 395) in his defense of the principle of semantic innocence, originally put forward by Davidson (1968), according to which the semantic value of referential expressions in attitude contexts should remain constant. Thus Récanati writes: "According to Hintikka (1962, pp. 138–141), failures of substitutivity in belief contexts show that two co-referential singular terms, though they pick out the same individual in the actual world, may refer to different objects in the ascribee's belief world. That option is ruled out in the present framework; for we want the ontology to be that of the ascriber all along: we want the singular terms to refer to the same objects, whether we are talking of the actual world, or about the ascribee's belief world. That is the price to pay for semantic innocence." A more detailed criticism of this view is presented in Égré (2007).

general, and another thing to say that, as a matter of plain fact, one can fail to realize that two coreferential proper names are indeed coreferential.[7] For who endorses the view of rigidity, on the other hand, the argument that proper names should take the same value at all worlds, including the belief worlds of the agent, should be applied a fortiori to the case of logical constants: from a semantic as well as from a cognitive point of view, logical expressions are arguably better candidates for rigidity than even proper names. Indeed, whereas the reference of a noun like "Cicero" may vary, logical expressions like "or" or "not" are referential only in a derived sense, and one does not clearly see what meaning they could have other than their actual meaning.

This objection threatens the compositional analyses of substitution failures put forward by Thomason or Muskens, in which logical connectives are put on a par with non-logical expressions. One reason to defend their analysis, however, is that there is no doubt that one can get confused about the meaning of complex sentences composed out of logical expressions with an unambiguous meaning. In what follows, nevertheless, I offer to concede as much as possible to the Kripkean requirement of rigidity, for proper names as well as for logical constants, but with an aim to preserving as much as possible from Hintikka's own conception of opacity as referential multiplicity. More precisely, I shall attempt to find a compromise between the broadly Davidsonian view, according to which the expressions occurring in a belief report should keep their semantic value fixed in the model, and the broadly Fregean view, according to which modes of presentation play a crucial role, at the level of belief, in the way propositions are apprehended.

This brings us to a second objection against the classic Hintikkean treatment of opacity, which concerns the representation of *de re* beliefs. In the previous section we gave each of the sentences (2)–(6) a *de dicto* logical form, giving the belief operator the largest possible scope (over singular terms, in particular). Several authors, however, starting with Kaplan (1969), have defended the idea that a belief report can be opaque, and nevertheless be relational or *de re* at the same time (see Kraut 1983; Heim 1992; Richard 1990; Récanati 2000a,b). Récanati, for instance, quoting (Loar 1972), insists that "*even on the opaque reading of a belief sentence in which a singular term occurs, reference is made to some particular individual*" (Récanati 2000a, italics his), namely the individual that the singular term is actually referring to.[8] This claim reflects the following intuition: when one makes a belief ascription like (2), one does not simply mean, according to Récanati, that Peter makes a metalinguistic mistake concerning the meaning of the proper names "Cicero" and "Tully". In Récanati's theory, the use of two distinct, although coreferential proper names, is just a way of pragmatically indicating that Peter represents to himself one and the same individual under two distinct modes of presentation. When I say in different contexts:

(8) Peter believes that Cicero is an orator

[7] On this, see Gerbrandy (2000, p. 151) and Aloni (2001, pp. 44–45).

[8] By singular term, Récanati means a proper name in the passage under discussion.

(9) Peter does not believe that Tully is an orator.

I am each time talking about Cicero-Tully, namely about one and the same individual. When I utter the conjunction of the two sentences, I'm still making reference to Cicero-Tully, but the names, being contrasted, pragmatically point to distinct modes of presentation. This intuition is cashed out, in Récanati's theory, in the form of a principle of "semantic innocence", taken up from Davidson (1968) (see Footnote 6), according to which the semantic value of the proper names "Tully" and "Cicero" ought to remain constant, irrespective of the context in which they occur.[9]

Taking this intuition seriously, and considering that a belief can be opaque and nevertheless *de re*, the paraphrase of (2) in modal epistemic logic might therefore be:

(10) $\exists x(x = c \wedge \Box O(x)) \wedge \exists y(y = t \wedge \neg\Box O(y))$.

The problem here is that, if c and t denote the same individual d in the actual world (the world of evaluation), the standard semantics for first-order modal logic constrains the variables x and y to denote d across the belief worlds of Peter. Given a first-order model $\langle W, R, D, I\rangle$, an assignment g and a world w, $M, w, g \models \exists x\Box\phi$ if and only if there is a d in D_w such that for every w' such that wRw', $M, w', g[d/x] \models \phi$.

This, however, is very problematic. First, it makes the ascription a plain contradiction, since the statement then is equivalent to $\exists x(x = c \wedge \Box O(x)) \wedge \exists x(x = c \wedge \neg\Box O(x))$. However, it seems that a sentence like (2) can be uttered without contradiction. Moreover, it makes a *de re* belief ascription incompatible with situations of mistaken identity, which seems too strong. There are cases where a belief is clearly *de re*, and yet does involve a failure to make a correct identification on the part of the ascribee. The paradigm case is Quine's example of Ralph, who believes of Ortcutt, thought of as "the man seen at the beach", that he is not a spy, and who also believes of Ortcutt, thought of as "the man in the brown hat", that he is a spy. In this scenario, it seems one can make the following belief ascription:

(11) Ralph believes of Ortcutt that he is a spy and Ralph also believes of Ortcutt that he is not a spy.

The conjunction of Ralph's *de re* beliefs can be represented in modal logic by the following sentence, in which the proper names take wide scope over the belief operator:

(12) $\exists x(x = o \wedge \Box S(x)) \wedge \exists x(x = o \wedge \Box\neg S(x))$.

---

[9]See Récanati (2000b, Chap. 1) for a defense of the notion of semantic innocence. According to the theory of direct reference, which Récanati endorses, a proper name is a rigid designator, which picks out the same individual in all the possible worlds. Because rigidity, strictly speaking, is lost in the standard *de dicto* analysis of belief reports in epistemic logic, it seems also that semantic innocence is lost: the semantic contribution of a proper name in a belief report is not exclusively its actual reference, so if the ordinary meaning or semantic value of a proper name is taken to be its reference, then belief operators are seen as shifting the semantic value of proper names

This paraphrase, however, is a problem for the standard semantics of first-order modal logic, since it should then follow that Ralph believes of Ortcutt that he is and is not a spy (see Quine 1971; Aloni 2001), namely:

(13) $\exists x(x = o \wedge \Box(S(x) \wedge \neg S(x)))$.

Quine's example, as argued by Gerbrandy and Aloni, provides a good indication that the standard semantics of first-order modal logic ought to be amended in order to account for *de re* beliefs with mistaken identity. My suggestion here is that roughly the same semantic account which Gerbrandy gives to analyze Quine's example can be extended to parse a sentence like (2) as *de re* instead of *de dicto*. I will first review his account, then I will attempt to show how to extend this analysis to cases of hyperintensionality involving predicates and full sentences.

13.3 Counterpart Semantics

The two sentences "Ralph believes of Ortcutt that he is a spy", and "Ralph believes of Ortcutt that he is not a spy" are intuitively compatible because the truth of each of them depends on a distinct *mode of presentation*. This mode of presentation need not be explicitly expressed in the sentence, but can be salient to both the speaker and hearer in the discourse situation, so that the two sentences will be seen as mutually compatible. In Gerbrandy's analysis, a mode of presentation is seen as a *method of cross-identification*, namely as a way of identifying an individual across epistemic alternatives.[10] Thus one and the same actual individual can have distinct counterparts in the epistemic alternatives of an agent, corresponding to several identification methods. In Quine's scenario, for example, there is one method of identification which "connects objects in Ralph's epistemic alternatives just in case they are the man that Ralph saw…at the beach" (Gerbrandy 2000, p. 155), and another method which connects objects in Ralph's belief worlds just in case they are the man Ralph saw in the brown hat. Both methods connect objects in Ralph's epistemic alternatives to Ortcutt at the actual world.

In Gerbrandy's semantics, epistemic sentences are evaluated relative to such identity relations, which play the role of a pragmatic parameter. Let us define an epistemic structure as a quadruple $\langle W, R, D, I\rangle$, where W is a set of worlds, R is an epistemic accessibility relation between the worlds, D is a function which associates to each world w a domain of individuals D_w, and I is an interpretation function for the non-logical vocabulary. Formally, a method of identification can be defined as a relation C between ordered pairs (w, d) of worlds and individuals such that $d \in D_w$. If $(w, d)C(w', d')$, d' will be called a counterpart to d in w'. Methods of identification are defined by Gerbrandy as equivalence relations.

[10]The notion of method of cross-identification originates from Hintikka (1969), and is elaborated upon in Kraut (1983).

A further constraint, which is argued for also in Aloni (2001), is to require those relations to be functional, namely such that one individual at a world has at most one counterpart at another world by the identification method, and also to be total, in the sense that if an individual has an epistemic counterpart at a belief world, it has a counterpart at every belief world.[11] Intuitively, if one individual is represented as two distinct individuals by an agent, it is because there are two distinct underlying modes of presentation there. In other words, there should not be more counterparts of an actual individual at a belief world than there are modes of presentation of that individual. But moreover, once a counterpart of an actual individual "inhabits" a belief world, it should also persist at all the belief worlds.

Gerbrandy's semantics for first-order modal logic is standard, except for the epistemic operators and the assignment of variables, which both need to be made sensitive to the identification relations. Thus, given a method of identification C and a pair of worlds w, w', two assignment functions g and h for the variables are in the counterpart relation induced by C if and only if h assigns to x in w' the counterpart of the individual which g assigns to x in w:

- $g \mapsto_C^{w,w'} h$ iff for every variable x, $(w, g(x))C(w', h(x))$.

The specific satisfaction clauses are the following:

- $M, w, g \models_C \exists x\phi$ iff there is a $d \in D_w$ such that $M, w, g[d/x] \models_C \phi$
- $M, w, g \models_C \Box\phi$ iff for every w' such that wRw', for every h such that $g \mapsto_C^{w,w'} h : M, w', h \models_C \phi$.

Given these definitions, Gerbrandy can account for the Ortcutt case. Take a model M with three worlds, where w is the actual world, in which o denotes d, namely Ortcutt, and w' and w'' are the two epistemic alternatives of Ralph. Let us call C_b the identification relation for the beach encounter, and C_h the identification relation for the hat encounter. In w' and w'', d_b is Ortcutt as seen as the beach, namely the counterpart of d under C_b, and in w' and w'', d_h is Ortcutt as seen with the hat, namely the counterpart of d under C_h. Supposing d_b is outside and d_h is within the denotation of S at both w' and w'', one then has:

(14) $M, w \models_{C_b} \exists x(x = o \wedge \Box\neg S(x))$ & $M, w \models_{C_h} \exists x(x = o \wedge \Box S(x))$.

Using Gerbrandy's counterpart semantics, it is therefore possible to account for Ralph's beliefs, without ascribing a logical contradiction to Ralph.

Now, I would like to suggest that this machinery can be used to give a *de re* analysis of the Tully-Cicero example we started with. Recall sentence (2), here repeated as (15):

(15) Peter believes that Cicero is an orator, but he does not believe that Tully is an orator.

[11]In what follows, I thus write $C(w, d)(w')$ to denote the counterpart of d in w', relative to w, or $C(d)(w')$ when the world in which d lives is clear.

First, we can note that here, unlike in the Ortcutt case, the negation takes wide scope over the belief verb. Formally, this is not a problem, since in the model described for the Ortcutt case, it also holds that:

(16) $M, w \models_{C_b} \exists x(x = o \wedge \neg\Box S(x))$.

that is, Ralph does not believe that Ortcutt is a spy under the beach identification relation. In the Tully-Cicero example, we can imagine in the same way that Peter's modes of presentations are the names "Tully" and "Cicero": Peter is simply not sure whether those two English names denote the same individual or not. What this means is that there is at least one epistemic alternative where Cicero-thought-of-as-"Cicero" and Cicero-thought-of-as-"Tully" are distinct individuals. In that situation, the names play the role of methods of identification. It is therefore easy to define two identification relations, namely C_c and C_t, such that, in a three world model analogous to the previous one, it holds that:

(17) $M, w \models_{C_c} \exists x(x = c \wedge \Box O(x))$ & $M, w \models_{C_t} \exists x(x = t \wedge \neg\Box O(x))$.

Using counterpart relations, the standard *de dicto* analysis of a sentence like (15) can therefore be cast into a *de re* analysis, in the spirit of Récanati's suggestions concerning the relational character of opaque belief reports involving proper names.

The kind of reinterpretation we suggest here must nevertheless face some problems. More specifically, the analysis, unless sufficiently constrained, might generate readings that are not desirable. For instance, since t and c are coreferential terms in the actual world w, it also holds in the model that:

(18) $M, w \models_{C_t} \exists x(x = c \wedge \neg\Box O(x))$.

This suggests that, in the situation under discussion, one could say something like:

(19) Peter believes that Cicero is an orator, and Peter does not believe that Cicero is an orator.

But are there situations of discourse where we would utter what seems like a more direct contradiction than an ascription like (15)? My view is that an utterance of this kind is not inconceivable, already in the Ortcutt case (in which the negation is under the scope of "believe"). But it makes a difference, from a pragmatic point of view, to utter (19) rather than to utter "Peter believes that Cicero is an orator, but he does not believe that Tully is an orator", as the former, unlike the latter, suggests a logical inconsistency on Peter's part. Thus Récanati considers that the use of two distinct proper names, in the appropriate context, can help the hearer toward the assumption that distinct modes of presentation are involved (Récanati 2000b, Chap. 11). In that case one could imagine that the counterpart relations C_t and C_c functionally depend on the expressions used, namely upon the names c and t. But if an utterance like (19) is even conceivable, then we don't need to make this assumption.

This question, incidentally, is reminiscent of Kripke's puzzle about belief (Kripke 1979). In the situation described by Kripke, there are good grounds to say: "Pierre believes that London is pretty", and equally plausible grounds to say "Pierre does not believe that London is pretty". Kripke asks which of these two ascriptions one should endorse. In this sense, the situation is more dramatic than in Quine's formulation of the Ortcutt case, where the negation takes narrow scope over the attitude verb. Although Kripke insists that we make up our mind whether or not Pierre believes that London is pretty, the answer appears to be that we might say each of them in different contexts. To be sure, we can imagine a conversation in which we say: "In a sense, Peter believes that London is pretty, but in another sense he does not believe that London is pretty". Gerbrandy uses his semantics to give an account of Kripke's puzzle in terms of *de re* belief along exactly those lines. If C_l is the identification relation mapping London to Pierre's representation of the city called "London", and $C_{l'}$ is the identification relation mapping London to Pierre's representation of the city called "Londres", then one can consistently have (letting P stand for "pretty", and l for "London"):

(20) $M, w \models_{C_{l'}} \exists x(x = l \wedge \Box P(x))$ & $M, w \models_{C_l} \exists x(x = l \wedge \neg\Box P(x))$.

Summarizing what we said so far, Gerbrandy's analysis of *de re* belief is useful for several reasons. First, as we have seen, it provides a pragmatic account of cases of mistaken identity. Second, as I have just shown, it helps to flesh out the intuition that a belief can be relational, and nevertheless be opaque at the same time.

It has actually been suggested that proper names might systematically outscope attitude verbs. This was suggested even for definite descriptions, for totally different reasons, in Heim's analysis of the presupposition projection of attitude verbs (Heim 1992).[12] Other authors, like (Kraut 1983), have been even more radical, by defending the idea that there are no *de dicto* attitudes. In what follows, I shall use in a systematic way the idea that at least some *de dicto* belief reports can be restated as *de re* belief reports involving specific acquaintance relations or modes of presentation on the part of the believer, by extending to expressions of other syntactic categories the treatment given here of proper names. While doing so, it is important to bear in mind that I do not mean to reject the well-foundedness of the *de re-de dicto* distinction in general, and more precisely that the generalization of *de re* belief presented in the next section preserves the usual semantic function of scope distinctions for quantified expressions.[13]

[12]See Heim (1992, pp. 210–211): "Another way of summarizing the suggestion I just made is this: there is not really just one *de re* reading (for a given constituent), but there are many - one for each acquaintance relation that the context might supply. And some of those many, namely those where the acquaintance relation happens to include the subject's awareness that the *res* fits the same description used by the speaker, are very similar to the *de dicto* reading: more precisely, they entail it. In a way, I am blurring the distinction between *de re* and *de dicto* readings. But that may not be such a bad thing. More often than not, the two are impossible to tell apart."

[13]Unlike Kraut (1983), therefore, I do not consider that "John believes that someone is a spy" can systematically be analyzed as: $\exists x \Box S(x)$. See Aloni (2001, p. 134 sqq.) for a detailed criticism of Kraut's position, based in particular on Kaplan's "tallest spy" example. The epistemic semantics presented in the Appendix is an enrichment of the standard semantics: as such, it is able to make the same scope distinctions that can be made in standard first-order modal epistemic logic, in particular for the treatment of indefinites.

13.4 Generalization

In the previous section, we have seen that a certain *de dicto* analysis of substitution failures of proper names can be expressed in terms of a *de re* analysis, using the additional machinery of counterpart semantics. In this section my aim is to show that this analysis can be extended to handle cases of substitution failures involving predicates instead of proper names, and even full sentences, as in the examples by which we started, by allowing higher-order quantification over properties. This generalization presupposes that it does make sense to talk about *de re* belief about higher-order entities.

13.4.1 Higher-Order De Re *Beliefs*

The idea of generalizing the notion of *de re* belief was originally put forward by Cresswell and von Stechow (1982) and used to account for cases of hyperintensionality of belief involving, in particular, mathematical sentences. A sentence like "Poirot believes that $2 + 2 = 4$" can be given several *de re* logical forms in their account. For instance, the sentence can mean that Poirot believes of 2 and 2 and of the property of summing up to 4 that this property applies to these numbers; or it can mean that Poirot believes of the numbers 2, 2 and 4 and of the property for two numbers to sum to a third that this property applies to these numbers. In our framework, these two logical forms would correspond to:

(21) $\exists x \exists y \exists X (x = 2 \wedge y = 2 \wedge X = \lambda xy.(x + y = 4) \wedge \Box X(xy))$

(22) $\exists x \exists y \exists z \exists X (x = 2 \wedge y = 2 \wedge z = 4 \wedge X = \lambda xyz.(x + y = z) \wedge \Box X(xyz))$.

The important point, in Cresswell and von Stechow's account, concerns the fact that the object of the ascribed belief will presumably be different each time.

A second reason to introduce higher-order quantification is that it is needed in order to account for the so-called *non-specific de re* readings of indefinite descriptions in attitude contexts, as in the sentence "Peter believes that some soccer player has a dog", where "some soccer player" is taken *de re* by the speaker, but does not refer to any particular soccer player relative to the believer (see Bonomi 1995). This would happen in a context in which Peter sees a certain dog outside a restaurant, which he thinks belongs to one of the people he saw inside the restaurant, but such that only I, the speaker, know that these people are soccer players.[14] In that case, both the first-order *de dicto* analysis, $\Box \exists x (S(x) \wedge D(x))$, and the first-order *de re* analysis, $\exists x (S(x) \wedge \Box D(x))$ are false, and the correct analysis seems to

[14]I am indebted to M. Aloni for pointing out Bonomi's example to me. *Non-specific de re* readings have been discussed independently by J.D. Fodor (1970) and R. Baüerle (1983). See von Fintel and Heim (2002).

be: $\exists X(X = S \wedge \Box \exists x(X(x) \wedge D(x)))$, namely "there are soccer players such that Peter believes that one of them has a dog".

A third argument in favour of the genereralization of the notion of *de re* belief, finally, concerns the fact that one can devise scenarios analogous to Quine's Ortcutt case of mistaken identity with properties. Imagine, for instance, a situation in which Peter has two friends, Jack and Jill, having exactly the same profession, namely eye-doctor, but suppose that Peter is under the misconception that Jack's job is scary (by coincidence, whenever he visits Jack, he sees him perform delicate eye-surgery) while he thinks Jill's job is not (by coincidence, whenever he visits her, he sees her just testing people's eyesight). Unbeknownst to Peter, Jack and Jill perform exactly the same tasks, but at different times. Peter thinks moreover that whoever does the same job as Jack does a scary job, and likewise whoever does the same job as Jill does not do a scary job. As in Quine's example, it seems correct to say:

(23) Peter believes that being an eye-doctor is scary and Peter believes that being an eye-doctor is not scary.

The example invites us to treat "being an eye-doctor" as a property about which Peter has two opposite *de re* beliefs. The two conjuncts of (23) may then be analyzed as $\exists X(X = E \wedge \Box Scary(X))$ and $\exists X(X = E \wedge \Box \neg Scary(X))$ respectively. If we let C_{Jack} be the identification relation that connects the actual property of being an eye-doctor to the way Peter conceptualizes it when he sees Jack, and C_{Jill} be the identification relation that connects the property of being an eye-doctor to the way Peter conceptualizes it when he sees Jill, the sentence (23) can be represented as:

(24) $M, w \models_{C_{Jack}} \exists X(X = E \wedge \Box Scary(X))$
$\& \; M, w \models_{C_{Jill}} \exists X(X = E \wedge \Box \neg Scary(X))$.

13.4.2 Counterparts of Properties

Granting the legitimacy of higher-order *de re* beliefs, one can apply the same strategy of reinterpreting certain *de dicto* beliefs in terms of *de re* beliefs involving special acquaintance relations. Let us consider again sentence (4), here repeated as (25):

(25) Peter believes that John is an eye-doctor, but he does not believe that John is an ophthalmologist.

We suppose that "eye-doctor" and "ophthalmologist" do have the same meaning, namely that they express the same concept or property. In Montague Grammar, as mentioned earlier, the translation of a statement like (25) would be inconsistent, for then this would mean that "eye-doctor" and "ophthalmologist" denote the same function from possible worlds to sets of individuals, and therefore that "John is an eye-doctor" and "John is an ophthalmologist" express the same proposition, namely the same object of belief, contrary to our intuition.

However, although the content of Peter's belief is different each time in the context where (25) is uttered appropriately, there is a sense in which Peter's belief involves the same objective property of being an eye-doctor (or ophthalmologist). Suppose a different situation in which I know nothing special about Peter, and Jack says to me: "Peter believes that John is an eye-doctor!", while it is known to both me and Jack that John's actual profession is dentist. I might repeat this information about Peter's misconception to someone else, say Luke, by saying: "guess what, Peter believes that John is an ophthalmologist!". All it takes is for me and Luke and presumably Jack to share the same linguistic conventions. According to Récanati, a situation like this is the default situation: it is the ascriber who "endorses" the words used in the ascription, and not the ascribee. For Récanati, contexts where substitution fails are contexts where the ascriber points to an additional mode of presentation, which is relevant psychologically.

This intuition can be expressed more formally in terms of *de re* attitudes. By allowing properties also to have epistemic counterparts, one might say that Peter believes of John, and of the property of being an eye-doctor, under one counterpart relation that this property applies to John, and under a different counterpart relation that it fails to apply to John. Suppose that C_O is the method of identification which connects sets of individuals in Peter's epistemic alternatives just in case they correspond to the meaning of "ophthalmologist" for Peter, and C_E is the method of identification which connects sets of individuals in Peter's epistemic alternatives just in case they correspond to the meaning of "eye-doctor" for John. Both of them connect those sets to the set of eye-doctors at the real world. It is easy to define a model in which, at w, O and E are coextensional, and such that:

(26) $M, w \models_{C_O} \exists x \exists X(x = j \wedge X = O \wedge \neg \Box X(x))$
$\& \; M, w \models_{C_E} \exists x \exists X(x = j \wedge X = E \wedge \Box X(x))$.

The case of logically equivalent sentences can be dealt with in the same way, provided one makes room for complex predicates. Let us consider again sentence (6), here repeated as (27):

(27) Peter believes that if door A is locked, then door B is not locked, but does not believe that if door B is locked, then door A is not locked.

The standard *de re* reading of "Peter believes that if door A is locked, then door B is not locked" in first-order modal logic is:

(28) $\exists x \exists y(x = a \wedge y = b \wedge \Box(L(x) \rightarrow \neg L(y)))$.

From this logical form, there is just one step to a generalized *de re* analysis of (27), namely:

(29) $\exists x \exists y \exists X(x = a \wedge y = b \wedge X = \lambda xy.(L(x) \rightarrow \neg L(y)) \wedge \Box X(xy))$.

This means that Peter believes of door A, of door B, and of the relation such that if one object is locked, then another is not locked, that this relation applies to those individuals. This generalized *de re* analysis allows one to use the machinery of counterpart semantics in order to handle the substitution failure of logically equivalent sentences. All it takes is to suppose that the complex relation $\lambda xy.(L(x) \rightarrow \neg L(y))$ has different counterparts in the belief worlds of Peter, depending on the situation in which he is. Thus there might be two methods of identification (for relations), such that:

(30) $M, w \models_{C_1} \exists x \exists y \exists X(x = a \wedge y = b \wedge X = \lambda xy.(L(x) \rightarrow \neg L(y)) \wedge \Box X(xy))$
& $M, w \models_{C_2} \exists x \exists y \exists X(x = a \wedge y = b \wedge X = \lambda xy.(L(y) \rightarrow \neg L(x)) \wedge \neg\Box X(xy))$.

Again, one should suppose that these methods of identification are made salient to the hearer by the use of distinct syntactic expressions in each utterance (thus C_1 and C_2 are distinct, in a way that is correlated to the syntactic difference between $\lambda xy.(L(x) \rightarrow \neg L(y))$ and $\lambda xy.(L(y) \rightarrow \neg L(x))$). This reflects the intuition that Peter misperceives the identity of a logical relation between two objects and properties. At the same time, this allows us to preserve the idea that Peter's belief, although confused, can very well be a *de re* belief about the objects a and b (for instance in a situation in which he perceives the two doors A and B).

One may wonder, finally, how to account for an example like the following, under the same assumption that the conditional is a material conditional each time:

(31) Peter believes that if it's raining, it's cold, but does not believe that if it's not cold, it's not raining.

The standard analysis of the embedded sentences in this example is to see them as predicates of arity 0, namely as propositional symbols. The treatment of hyperintensionality we have just sketched can be extended in the same manner, provided talk of *de re* beliefs is allowed for predicates of arity 0. All it takes is to be able to name such predicates. Suppose A is a predicate of arity 0 which represents the statement "it is raining", and B a predicate of arity 0 which represents the statement "it is cold". Then $\lambda.A$ will represent the proposition expressed by A, and $\lambda.(A \rightarrow B)$ will represent the proposition expressed by $A \rightarrow B$. A *de re* analysis of:

(32) Peter believes that if it's raining, it's cold.

is then possible, provided one allows for the use of variables and lambda-abstracts of arity 0:

(33) $\exists X(X = \lambda.(A \rightarrow B) \wedge \Box X)$.

By using counterpart relations again, it is possible to account for an example like (31). Intuitively, this means that Peter believes of one and the same proposition, under one mode of presentation that it holds, and under a different mode of presentation that it does not hold. The notion of proposition in question is defined extensionally in the system, since a predicate of arity 0 denotes a truth-value, like the corresponding lambda-abstract. Just as the counterpart relation for first-order variables pairs up individuals, the counterpart relation for a second-order variable of arity 0 pairs up truth-values. I refer to the Appendix for a step by step presentation of the language and of its semantics.

13.5 Assessment

In the previous section I have suggested that opaque belief sentences can be analyzed *de re* instead of *de dicto* in a systematic way, granting the possibility of evaluating all sentences under specific cross-identification relations, playing the role of modes of presentation. In this section, I offer to assess both the merits and the limits of this account. Several aspects of the present account are examined in greater detail, in particular the extension of the treatment of hyperintensionality to the case of closure under strict logical consequence more generally.

13.5.1 Pragmatic Enrichment

The first feature of this analysis is the fact that it treats the phenomenon of hyperintensionality as essentially context-sensitive. If ϕ and ψ are intensionally equivalent sentences, then in some contexts, when uttered after "Peter believes", the clauses "that ϕ" and "that ψ" do express the same information, whereas in other contexts they don't. By giving belief sentences a generalized *de re* logical form, one accounts for the intuition that the belief is about certain entities whose value is determined first relative to speaker. When I say : "Peter believes that John is an eye-doctor", there is a sense in which I say exactly the same thing as in: "Peter believes that John is an ophthalmologist". Each time, the same literal content is used to make the ascription. As Récanati argues, situations in which it is appropriate to utter "Peter believes that John is an eye-doctor but does not believe that John is an ophthalmologist" are situations where this content is pragmatically enriched by reference to specific modes of presentation.

In order to introduce modes of presentation in the interpretation of sentences, we need a way to make them pragmatically available, however. Otherwise, one faces the objection that by calling on any appropriate counterpart relation, the meaning of any sentence or constituent can be freely enriched without constraint. For the cases of hyperintensionality we discussed, the pragmatic mechanism we postulate is the following: by uttering "X believes ϕ but does not believe ψ" to a hearer with whom she shares the knowledge that ϕ and ψ have the same meaning (in the case of logically equivalent sentences), or meanings that are closely related (in the case of a sentence that is an accessible logical consequence of another—see below), the speaker directs the hearer toward salient modes of presentation. Appeal to modes of presentation is typically needed to preserve the consistency of what is said, in accordance with Grice's maxim of Quality, when it is clear that the speaker does not intend to ascribe a plain inconsistency to the believer (see Aloni (2001, p. 148) on the articulation of the maxim with other maxims in the interpretation of *de re* beliefs).

For Récanati, the mechanism of pragmatic enrichment does not imply a modification of the basic semantic value of the predicates "ophthalmologist" and "eye-doctor", which should remain constant in the model. The relevant feature of Gerbrandy's semantics in this respect is that this pragmatic enrichment is materialized by the additional parameter of cross-identification relations, so that when a lexical expression takes wide scope over the belief verb, only its actual denotation matters. One can always assume, moreover, that the default parameter, in the case where belief sentences are given a generalized *de re* logical form, is the relation of plain identity. When I utter: "Peter believes that Cicero was poor", without saying more about Peter, the hearer should assume that Peter's belief is about Cicero as commonly identified.

13.5.2 Comparisons

A second distinctive feature of this analysis is that it provides a uniform treatment of cases of opacity. More precisely, it allows us to treat in the same way cases of opacity involving proper names, predicates, and full sentences. In principle, the present framework affords the same kind of fine-grainedness that is found in other approaches to hyperintensionality, as in Thomason's treatment in terms of primitive propositions (Thomason 1980), and Muskens' related treatment using impossible worlds (Muskens 1991). The reason is that counterpart relations can be determined by any syntactic component in the embedded sentence.[15] For instance, a sentence like "John believes that if door A is locked then door B is not locked" can be given several *de re* logical forms, as we have seen, including one form in which all the embedded material is scoped out by means of a propositional variable (a variable of arity 0):

(34) $\exists X(X = \lambda.(L(a) \rightarrow \neg L(b)) \wedge \Box X)$.

This means that of the proposition that if door A is locked then door B is not locked, Peter believes that it holds. Using appropriate counterpart relations, it is possible to say that Peter believes of that proposition, under one counterpart relation that it holds, and under a different counterpart relation that it does not hold. In Thomason's framework, this corresponds to the fact that the sentences "if door A is locked then door B is not locked" and its contrapositive can very well express different primitive propositions within a model, or equivalently, be true and false at different non-standard worlds, in the case of the impossible worlds approach.[16]

[15]The second-order language we use in the appendix is less expressive than Thomason's or Muskens's respective type theories, but this is not substantial to our argument, since the machinery of counterpart relations can in principle be superimposed on any appropriate higher-order language.

[16]Thomason's system of Intentional Logic is a type theory based on the types e, t and p, where e and t are the usual types of truth values and individuals, and p is a type for propositions. Sentences, which express propositions, are of type p and are interpreted over a separate domain D_p of primitive propositions. In Thomason's system, for instance, a sentence like "if door A is locked, then door B is locked" would be translated by $L(a) \sqsupset \sim L(b)$, where the negation symbol $\sim$ is of type pp, the conditional symbol $\sqsupset$ is of type $p(pp)$, a and b are of type e—or

However, unlike the approach of Thomason or Muskens, our approach of hyperintensionality in terms of counterpart relations does not commit us to a domain of primitive propositions, or of impossible worlds. Ontologically, this is a gain, since all we need are the standard belief worlds of the agent, without having to treat logical constants as non-logical constants. I take it that this is psychologically more plausible too: standard belief worlds, in Hintikka's original analysis, are worlds which are already "impossible" in one sense, since in those worlds "Tully" and "Cicero" can denote distinct individuals. Of course, such worlds are not logically impossible, but only metaphysically impossible. Here, however, all these impossibilities are treated at the same level. Belief worlds are worlds in which the identity of an individual, or property, or proposition, can split, depending on the underlying mode of presentation.

The closest antecedent to the present approach is Cresswell and von Stechow's (1982) generalization of the notion of *de re* belief to higher-order entities, as we saw above. Our approach is very close to theirs in that depending on the material that is scoped out from the embedded sentences, the beliefs ascribed to the agents have different possible structures, as seen in examples (21) and (22) above. Similarly, where our account, following Gerbrandy's, uses counterpart relations to model the perspectival nature of *de re* belief, Cresswell and von Stechow's account involves acquaintance relations, in terms of which Quine's puzzle is dealt with in a parallel fashion (see Cresswell and von Stechow (1982, p. 509), who call these relations 'suitable relations', after Lewis (1979)). In Cresswell and von Stechow's theory, moreover, each constituent that is taken *de re* comes with a suitable relation, meaning that different relations are associated with first-order and higher-order constituents. Cresswell and von Stechow's framework is more expressive than ours, since they do not put a restriction on higher-order types. In principle, our account could easily be generalized even further, to make room for variables of all finite types, with corresponding counterpart relations. If on the other hand we consider the restriction of Cresswell and von Stechow's account to types of order at most 2, then our approach can be seen essentially as an internalization of theirs within a Hintikkean semantics, with counterpart relations playing the role of suitable relations.[17]

---

possibly $(ep)p$—and L is of type ep. In a model of Intentional Logic, it is therefore possible to have $[\![L(a) \sqsupset \sim L(b)]\!] = p_1$ and $[\![L(b) \sqsupset \sim L(a)]\!] = p_2$, where $p_1 \neq p_2$. Muskens's intensional theory uses the types t and e and the world type s, but for the same purpose. The complex type st is used everywhere where Thomason would use p: thus propositions are not primitive, but correspond to sets of possible worlds. As in Thomason's framework, however, $L(a) \sqsupset \sim L(b)$ and $L(b) \sqsupset \sim L(a)$ can a priori denote distinct sets of possible worlds (which are logically impossible in this respect). Some axioms are given on the logical vocabulary to ensure that the two sentences are Boolean equivalent over a restricted set of logically standard worlds. In particular, where i is a constant of type s denoting the actual world, it follows that $[\![(L(a) \sqsupset \sim L(b))(i)]\!] = [\![(L(b) \sqsupset \sim L(a))(i)]\!]$. Thomason has similar axioms for a constant $c^{\cup}$ of type pt to ensure that $[\![c^{\cup}(L(a) \sqsupset \sim L(b))]\!] = [\![c^{\cup}(L(b) \sqsupset \sim L(a))]\!]$.

[17]Further differences remain, as Cresswell and von Stechow outline a treatment of *de se* attitudes, which lies beyond the scope of the present paper, and they allow for belief to be partial.

A point worth noting is that on their account, "believe" denotes a relation of ascription of an n-place property to n terms, under as many relations of acquaintance (Cresswell and von Stechow 1982, p. 514). Prima facie, this suggests that the objects of "believe" are special objects, namely structured propositions. Importantly, however, Cresswell and von Stechow warn that they do not view structured meanings as special entities (see Cresswell and von Stechow 1982, p. 515). On their account, a proposition remains a possible world proposition, except that the corresponding function may take more arguments as input than just possible worlds, depending on the number and type of variables that are quantified over. The situation is the same in our framework: "believe" remains a relation between an agent and the proposition corresponding to the objective meaning of the embedded sentence, with the proviso that the objects or properties about which the belief is are apprehended under subjective modes of presentation. This makes another difference with the approaches of Thomason and Muskens: Thomason, for instance, does not clearly take a stand on whether primitive propositions expressed by embedded sentences should correspond to the objective meanings of structured sentences, or whether they rather encode a subjective notion of mode of presentation. In the present approach, by contrast, the objective meaning of expressions is supposed to be fixed relative to the speaker. Modes of presentation are seen as subjective (although possibly correlated to syntactic structures), as implemented in terms of counterpart relations.

13.5.3 Conjunction and Identity

Along with the benefits that we claim for this treatment of hyperintensionality, two imperfections may be pointed out. The first concerns the treatment we made of conjunction in all the examples we presented so far, and the second the treatment of identity. Both limitations are already present in Gerbrandy's approach, and are inherited in the other examples we discussed.[18] Thus, in order to get a consistent paraphrase of a sentence like (11) above, namely "Ralph believes of Ortcutt that he is a spy, and Ralph believes of Ortcutt that he is not a spy", we have used a metalinguistic conjunction in the form:

(35) $M, w \models_{C_b} \exists x(x = o \wedge \Box S(x))$ & $M, w \models_{C_h} \exists x(x = o \wedge \Box\neg S(x))$.

There is no way, in that system, to get a consistent reading of the conjunctive sentence $\exists x(x = o \wedge \Box S(x)) \wedge \exists x(x = o \wedge \Box\neg S(x))$, since sentences are evaluated with respect to only one contextually given counterpart relation, which we assumed to be functional. Likewise, the system is not be adequate to handle identity statements, like "Peter does not believe that Cicero is Tully", if one analyzes the latter *de re* as $\exists x \exists y(x = c \wedge y = t \wedge \neg\Box(x = y))$, since by functionality in each belief world x and y have to be mapped to the same individual.

[18] See Gerbrandy (2000, p. 153) for a discussion of these problems. The constraint of functionality is called *non-overlap* by Gerbrandy.

A first possible way out would be to relax the constraint of functionality assumed on counterpart relations (namely that if $(w, d)C(w', d')$, and $(w, d)C(w', d'')$, then $d' = d''$), but this would undermine the intuitive one-to-one correspondence between identification methods and modes of presentation. Another more promising possibility would be to allow reference to modes of presentation directly at the sentential level, by indexing variables, as done in Aloni (2001, 2005).[19] In Aloni's system, a sentence like (11), that is "Peter believes that Ortcutt is a spy, and he believes that Ortcutt is not a spy", is represented as: $\exists x_n(x_n = o \wedge \Box S(x_n)) \wedge \exists y_m(y_m = o \wedge \Box\neg S(y_m))$. Likewise, "Peter does not believe that Cicero is Tully" can be paraphrased as "$\exists x_n \exists y_m(x_n = c \wedge y_m = t \wedge \neg\Box(x_n = y_m))$. In her system, the indices are indices of different conceptual covers.[20] Alternatively, we could let the indices denote different counterpart relations supposed to be salient in the discourse context, and evaluate sentences with respect to a family of counterpart relations. Given a *family* C of identification methods, let C_i denote the identification method indexed by i. We write $g \mapsto_C^{w,w'} h$ iff for every index i and every variables x_i and X_i, $(w, g(x_i))C_i(w', h(x_i))$ and $(w, g(X_i))C_i(w', h(X_i))$. Using this mechanism, we could account for the consistency of mistaken beliefs about identity, and still maintain that the belief is about one and the same actual entity, seen under different modes of presentation.[21]

13.5.4 Logical Consequence

So far we have talked only of the problem of closure of belief under logical equivalence. The standard modal semantics for belief makes a stronger prediction, however, namely that beliefs are closed under logical consequence. This is due, as we have seen, to the fact that $\Box$ is an upward monotone operator. The same strategy we used to block closure under logical equivalence can be used to block closure under logical consequence, however. To illustrate it, let us consider an extreme and

---

[19] I am indebted to M. Aloni for these suggestions.

[20] See Aloni (2001, pp. 130–133). A conceptual cover is a set of individual concepts such that for every world and individual of the domain, there is one and only one concept selecting that individual at that world. Aloni shows that there is a systematic correspondence between conceptual covers and methods of cross-identification which she calls *proper*, namely equivalence relations such that each individual has one and only one counterpart in each world.

[21] Another way of dealing with the conjunction problem would be to assume that "believe" is an operator that introduces existential quantification over counterpart relations. However, that would not automatically solve the problem of identity sentences. See for instance van Rooij (2006, Appendix A) for a system in which counterpart relations are existentially quantified over, but in which the law of necessary identity is preserved, including for belief operators. Cresswell and von Stechow (1982, pp. 509, 511–512) also assume that "believe" introduces existential quantification over suitable relations. It is not fully clear to me whether their account formulates adequate truth-conditions for sentences of the form: "x does not believe of Cicero and of Tully that they are identical".

artificial example first. The example, incidentally, becomes more plausible if the verb "believe" is replaced by "see":[22]

(36) Peter believes that John is wearing a red tie, but he does not believe that John is wearing a tie.

Let us suppose that this is a *de re* belief about John, whose standard logical form in first-order modal logic would be:

(37) $\exists x(x = j \wedge \Box \exists y(T(y) \wedge R(y) \wedge W(xy)) \wedge \neg \Box \exists y(T(y) \wedge W(xy))$.

This statement is contradictory in the standard semantics, since it implies that in all of Peter's belief worlds, John has a red tie, and also that, in one of his belief worlds, John does not have a tie. If we use instead a richer representation by scoping out expressions denoting properties, then another way to analyze sentence (36) is the following:

(38) $$\exists x \exists X \exists Y[x = j \wedge X = \lambda x.\exists y(T(y) \wedge R(y) \wedge W(xy)) \\ \wedge Y = \lambda x.\exists y(T(y) \wedge W(xy)) \wedge \Box X(x) \wedge \neg \Box Y(x)].$$

Fix a model $M = \langle W, R, D, I \rangle$, with C a generalized counterpart relation (see appendix). If C coincides with the usual identity relation for individuals and properties, then (38), evaluated relative to M, w and C, will also be inconsistent. Let us note $G = \lambda x.\exists y(T(y) \wedge R(y) \wedge W(xy))$ (*wearing a red tie*), and $G' = \lambda x.\exists y(T(y) \wedge W(xy))$ (*wearing a tie*). In that case, the denotation of G in w in included in the denotation of G' in w: $\langle G \rangle_{M,w,C} \subseteq \langle G' \rangle_{M,w,C}$. However, if C is such that, in at least one of Peter's belief worlds, say w', the counterpart of (the denotation) of G is not included in the counterpart of (the denotation) of G', ie $C(w, \langle G \rangle_{M,w,C})(w') \nsubseteq C(w, \langle G' \rangle_{M,w,C})(w')$, then (38) is satisfiable in w. This means that of two properties, such that the first entails the second, their counterparts in Peter's belief worlds are not necessarily in the same inclusion relation.

The idea that counterpart relations needn't preserve actual inclusion relations can easily be extended to more realistic examples. The following is a more plausible ascription using "believe":[23]

---

[22]Indeed, there is a way to say: "Peter sees that John is wearing a red tie, but he does not see that John is wearing a tie!", for instance by stressing "tie" in the second conjunct—suggesting that Peter fails to *realize* that John is wearing a tie, although he sees John and one can report that he sees that John has a red tie. If it is plausible, the example suggests that Peter conceptualizes the visual information "red tie" as a whole, in a way that does not give him the information "tie". The fact that the example is harder to accept with "believe" indicates that the lexical semantics of attitude verbs is relevant to these issues of hyperintensionality. One generally admits that "believe that" distributes over conjunction. The case is less clear with "see that".

[23]I am indebted to B. Spector for this example. The report is facilitated if the constituent "Mary or John" is stressed. Otherwise the report sounds more natural if the sentence is: "Peter was informed that exactly two of Mary, John and Susan will go to the party, but does not realize that Mary or John will go to the party". I use "believe" everywhere for the sake of uniformity, assuming that "being informed that" entails "believe that" in this context, and that failing to realize entails failure to believe (that assumption is more controversial).

(39) Peter believes that exactly two of Mary, John and Susan will go to the party, but does not believe that Mary or John will go to the party.

The report is more easily acceptable than the previous one because although the ascriptions together suggest lack of logicality on the part of Peter, the discrepancy between the embedded sentences is not as obvious as in the former case. The idea remains the same, however: a natural interpretation of this sentence is that John does not extract the correct logical information expressed by "x or y" from the logical information expressed by the quantified expression "exactly two of x, y and z". Using the second-order apparatus presented in the Appendix, the sentence can be paraphrased as:

(40) $$\begin{aligned}&\exists x\exists y\exists z[(x = m \wedge y = j \wedge z = s)\\ &\wedge\exists X(X = \lambda xy.(G(x) \vee G(y))\\ &\wedge\exists Y(Y = \lambda xyz.((G(x) \wedge G(y) \wedge \neg G(z)) \vee (G(x) \wedge \neg G(y) \wedge G(z)) \vee\\ &(\neg G(x) \wedge G(y) \wedge G(z)))\\ &\wedge\Box Y(xyz) \wedge \neg\Box X(xy)]\end{aligned}$$

The sentence is consistent relative to an interpretation and a method of identification C mapping all variables x, y, z and Y to their actual denotation at the belief worlds of Peter, but such that X (namely $\lambda xy.(G(x) \vee G(y))$) is mapped to an epistemic counterpart relation that does not stand in the expected entailment relation to the denotation of Y. More generally, the sentence is consistent if one supposes that the actual property denoted by Y (*for exactly two of three individuals to go to the party*) gets mapped to an epistemic counterpart that does not stand in the correct entailment relation to the counterpart of the property denoted by X (*for either one of two individuals to go to the party*). Since logical expressions like "or" or "exactly two of" are handled syncategorematically in our language, we cannot associate epistemic counterparts to logical expressions directly: but it should be clear that this is what the semantics achieves here, and that the extension to a categorematic treatment with generalized quantifiers would not raise special difficulties.

One aspect in which the treatment of logical consequence differs from that of logical equivalence is that conjunction needn't be handled metalinguistically in the case of proper logical consequence: this is due to the fact that if P and Q denote distinct properties in the actual world, they can be mapped to distinct epistemic counterparts under one and the same method of identification. By contrast, in the case of logically equivalent sentences, the functionality constraint on identification methods imposes that there be two distinct methods in order to get distinct counterparts.

Despite this, the extension of our treatment of hyperintensionality to the case of logical consequence (as opposed to logical equivalence) should not induce the thought that all cases of substitution failures involving logical consequence can be accounted for by reference to psychological modes of presentation. There is an important distinction to make, in this respect, between the *partial* character of our beliefs, and the *perspectival* character of our beliefs. Let us consider, for instance, the following knowledge report:

(41) Peter knows that $2+2=4$, but he does not know that every integer can be written as a product of primes.

The report is true in a situation in which Peter is a child who has never heard of prime numbers. A blunt way to treat the report in our framework would be to suppose that, in at least one of Peter's belief worlds, an epistemic counterpart of the proposition expressed by "every integer can be written as the product of prime numbers" receives the value false. Such a treatment would be inadequate, however: what the sentence expresses is not that Peter is mistaken about the propositions expressed, but rather that he simply does not have any kind of acquaintance with the proposition expressed by "every integer can be written as the product of prime numbers". The proper way to treat this example would be to have a partial logic, using a third truth value for sentences that are neither true nor false at the worlds of the believer.[24]

The problem of belief partiality is orthogonal to our main concern in this paper, however. This is an important caveat, for our account is directed first and foremost at the perspectival character of beliefs. In what precedes, we have been careful to take examples for which it is clear from the context that the believer does not lack acquaintance with any of the semantic components of the sentences used in the reports, but rather fails from what she believes to make identifications or connections that are available to the speaker. For instance, in the context of "Peter believes that exactly two of Mary, John and Susan will go to the party", the sentence "Peter does not believe that John or Mary will go to the party" excludes the possibility that Peter is not acquainted with John or Mary.

13.5.5 Iterated Belief Reports

An interesting perspective for the present account, finally, concerns multiple belief reports, namely sentences with embedded modalities, like:

(42) Mary believes that Peter believes that Cicero is a philosopher.

In the Appendix, we consider a simple epistemic language with only one belief operator. As such, the language is not expressive enough to handle a sentence like (42), but it can easily be enriched with as many belief operators as there are agents to consider. A test case for our approach concerns the analysis of hyperintensionality with sentences of that kind. Adapting a classic example from Mates (1950), let us consider a sentence like:

(43) Mary is confident that Peter believes that Cicero is a philosopher, but she doubts that Peter believes that Tully is a philosopher.

Interestingly, the interpretation of the sentence will tend to vary depending on what is assumed in the context about Mary. The most salient interpretation for such a

[24]See for instance van Rooij (2006, p. 242), whose semantics of first-order modal logic for belief is partial. Van Rooij uses partiality to block the inference from "Mary believes that John walks" to "Mary believes that John walks and Bill talks or doesn't talk", in a situation in which Mary has no belief about Bill. See also Cresswell and von Stechow (1982), whose semantics for belief is partial too.

sentence is one in which Mary knows that Cicero and Tully are the same person, but wonders whether Peter is aware of the fact. Another possibility, however, is that Mary is the one confused: for instance, she may know that Cicero is a philosopher, but think that Tully is a dog, and moreover be inclined to think that Peter shares exactly her beliefs. Either way, however, the sentence can be analyzed uniformly by giving wide scope to both proper names over the belief operators:[25]

(44) $\exists x(x = c \wedge \Box_m \Box_p P(x)) \,\&\exists x(x = t \wedge \neg\Box_m \Box_p P(x))$.

The sentence will be consistent if each conjunct is referred to a distinct epistemic counterpart relation, as in the earlier examples.[26] What kind of epistemic counterpart relation are we talking about here? As before, we are talking of a counterpart relation that connects individuals from the actual world to individuals *in Peter's belief worlds*; the only difference, here, is that Peter's belief worlds are now seen *from Mary's perspective*. In the first kind of context, in which Mary does not make any incorrect identification, Mary considers that Peter might be mistaken; in the second kind of context, Mary is mistaken herself, and simply projects her own ontology onto Peter's worlds. In terms of cross-identification methods, this means that the cross-identification methods that connect individuals in the actual world to individuals in Peter's belief worlds will have different structures, depending on Mary's intermediary conceptualization. The kind of ambiguity induced by a sentence like (43) is typically of a pragmatic nature therefore; from a semantic point of view, we see that the nesting of attitude operators can be handled in essentially the same way in which we handled the case of non-nested modalities.

13.6 Conclusion

In this paper I have argued that from the perspective of ordinary belief attributions, the problems of hyperintensionality of belief reports can be treated on a par with classic double vision puzzles concerning first-order *de re* belief attributions, in agreement with the analysis of belief reports originally proposed by Cresswell and von Stechow (1982). The main benefit of this approach is that it affords a unified treatment of substitution failures for expressions of distinct syntactic categories, and that hyperintensionality is handled in terms of the pragmatic relativity of belief attributions to contextually given modes of presentation.

[25]"Be confident" is analyzed as "believe" here, and "doubt" as "not believe". $\Box_m$ represents "Mary believes that" and $\Box_p$ "Peter believes that".

[26]Note that the present treatment does not exclude logical forms with intermediate scope, like $\Box_p \exists x(x = c \wedge \Box_m P(x))$. One can expect scope ambiguities when c is a definite description. In the case where c is a proper name, however, I endorse Récanati's arguments (Récanati 2000b, pp. 125–129) in assuming that they don't give rise to scope ambiguities ("genuine singular terms give rise to no such scope ambiguities, they are, as Geach once put it, 'essentially scopeless'", Récanati (2000b, p. 125)). Like Récanati, I set aside the issue of fictitious proper names here.

From the point of view of epistemic logic, which we used as our framework, the present account can be seen as a natural extension of Hintikka's original account of substitution failures in belief contexts, since the logic we presented allows us to give a *de re* representation of sentences that would standardly be analyzed as *de dicto*. In Hintikka's favorite account of hyperintensionality, however, the failure of substitution of logically equivalent expressions involves the addition of a special layer of logically impossible worlds. In the present approach, impossible worlds do not have to be introduced on top of standard belief worlds, since at all levels counterpart relations explain how the objective meaning of an expression gets to be apprehended as two different subjective meanings, or how two distinct objective meanings get to be collapsed to one subjective meaning. The inspiration behind these alternative treatments of hyperintensionality remains fundamentally the same, however, since expressions that are synonymous for the attributor are allowed to take arbitrary denotations at the believer's worlds, depending on the mode of presentation that is relevant.

Besides the technical and expressive limitations of the particular framework we used here, there remains a more fundamental issue, which is whether the pragmatic component of our approach does not do too much work in the explanation of those substitution failures. Likewise, we left open the nature of the constraints on how much material can be scoped out and read *de re* in belief sentences. On this issue, the best reason one may have to hold on to a standard *de dicto* analysis of the examples by which we started is the fact that in all relevant situations, belief reports generally have a quotational component, without which the ascription simply could not be made. Our approach, however, is not incompatible with a quotational analysis of such substitution failures, for arguably this quotational component is not eliminated, it is simply deferred to the level of counterpart relations.

Acknowledgements A preliminary version of this paper originally appeared in the Proceedings of the ESSLLI 2006 Workshop on *Logics for Resource-Bounded Agents*, T. Agotnes & N. Aleshina eds, under the title "Logical Omniscience and Counterpart Semantics". The present, more extended version, was originally submitted to *Linguistics and Philosophy* end of 2006, and got two valuable referees reports asking for revisions, which I kept postponing until today, leaving the paper on the backburner. Despite the years and what I now see as some inherent limitations to the approach presented, several people suggested that it would be useful still to publish this more extended version. I am grateful to F. Lihoreau and M. Rebuschi for giving me this opportunity to do so and to incorporate those revisions, and I thank two anonymous L&P reviewers for their helpful comments. I also thank, for the helpful feedback and comments they gave me then, M. Aloni, J. van Benthem, D. Bonnay, J. Dubucs, B. Geurts, N. Klinedinst, E. Maier, R. Muskens, F. Récanati, P. Schlenker, B. Spector and T. Williamson, as well as audiences at the First PALMYR workshop 2005 held in Amsterdam, at the *Journées de Sémantique et de Modélisation* held in Bordeaux 2006, and participants at the seminars PhilForm and Propriétés in Paris.

This chapter is a revised and expanded version of my paper "Logical Omniscience and Counterpart Semantics", originally presented in T. Agotnes and N. Aleshina eds., *Proceedings of the ESSLLI 2006 Workshop on Logics for Resource-Bounded Agents.*

Appendix: A Second-Order Epistemic Logic

This appendix gives the details of the generalization of Gerbrandy's semantics to a second-order modal language. The language, which I call $L_2(\Box)$, is a second-order logic enriched with a unary modal operator (intended as an epistemic operator), in which it is possible to name complex predicates by the usual mechanisms of lambda-abstraction. The present treatment is inspired in part by the presentation of higher-order logic given in the first chapter of Fitting (2002). I only state the semantics here and do not investigate how it could be axiomatized.

Another central issue concerns the treatment of quantifiers, and in particular whether we should work with fixed or variable domains (see Fitting and Mendelsohn 1998). The use of counterpart relations makes it natural to let the domains vary, if we think of quantifiers as ranging over objects actually existing at a world, and of counterpart relations as establishing links between distinct ontologies (in particular that of the speaker, and that of the agent whose belief is reported). In what follows we thus place no restriction on the domains (except indirectly, by means of the conditions on counterpart relations), and likewise we give an actualist interpretation to the non-logical vocabulary, that is constants and predicates are world-bound.[27]

The Language $L_2(\Box)$

The definition of $L_2(\Box)$ is in two steps: first I introduce the language L_1 of first-order logic with predicates of arity 0 (propositional symbols), then the notion of a lambda-abstract, which is needed for the definition of the second-order part. The construction is in two steps in order to exclude lambda-abstracts of the form $\lambda x.\Box P(x)$, essentially for reasons of simplicity, so that only non-modal properties can be named. The language is built on an alphabet which includes:

(i) A denumerable set Var of individual variables: $x, y, z, \ldots$

(ii) For all $n \geq 0$, a denumerable set VAR_n of predicate variables of arity n: $X^n, Y^n, Z^n, \ldots$. By definition, $VAR = \bigcup_n VAR_n$

(iii) A denumerable set $Cons$ of individual constants: $c, c', c'', \ldots$

(iv) For all $n \geq 0$, a denumerable set $CONS_n$ of predicate constants of arity n: $P^n, Q^n, R^n, \ldots$. By definition, $CONS = \bigcup_n CONS_n$.

[27]Following the treatment of Kripke (1963), the interpretation of *variables* is possibilist, however, namely assignments are defined over the union of all the domains. The semantics thus corresponds to a variant of Kripke's, considered by Kripke (1963, n. 11). One motivation to be actualist on the non-logical vocabulary is that the semantics validates the exportation principle $\exists x\Box\phi \rightarrow \Box\exists x\phi$ for atomic formulae ϕ, like $P(x)$, which is plausible from an epistemic point of view, although it does not validate it in full generality (for instance it fails for $\phi := \forall y(y \neq x)$). A possibilist treatment of the non-logical vocabulary does not validate the exportation principle even for atomic formulae, however, but would have the advantage of maintaining a principle of uniform substitution.

(v) Logical connectives: $\neg, \wedge, \exists$
(vi) Additional symbols: λ, .,), (
(vii) Modality: $\Box$
(viii) Equality symbol: $=$

Individual Terms

Every element of $Cons$ or Var is an individual term.

L_1-Formulas

If t and t' are individual terms, $t = t'$ is a L_1-formula
A predicate constant of arity 0 is a L_1-formula
If $t_1, \ldots, t_n$ are individual terms, and P is a predicate constant from $CONS_n$, then $P(t_1, \ldots, t_n)$ is an L_1-formula.
If ϕ and ψ are L_1-formulae, then so are $\neg\phi$ and $(\phi \wedge \psi)$.
If ϕ is an L_1-formula, then $\exists x\phi$ is a L_1-formula
Nothing else is an L_1-formula.

Lambda-Abstracts

If ϕ is an L_1-formula, and $x_1, \ldots, x_n$ are distinct variables from Var, $\lambda x_1, \ldots, x_n.\phi$ is a lambda-abstract of arity n. We denote by ABS_n the set of lambda-abstracts of arity n, and ABS the set of lambda-abstracts.
If ϕ is an L_1-formula, then $\lambda.\phi$ is a lambda-abstract of arity 0.

$L_2(\Box)$-Formulae

Every L_1-formula is a $L_2(\Box)$-formula, and if $X \in VAR_0$, X is an $L_2(\Box)$-formula.
If T and T' are respectively a variable in VAR_n, a constant in $CONS_n$, or a lambda-abstract in ABS_n, then $T = T'$ is an $L_2(\Box)$-formula.
If T is a variable in VAR_n, a constant in $CONS_n$, or a lambda-abstract of ABS_n, and $t_1, \ldots, t_n$ are individual terms, then $T(t_1, \ldots, t_n)$ is an $L_2(\Box)$-formula.
If ϕ is an $L_2(\Box)$-formula, and X is variable of $VAR_n (n \geq 0)$, then $\exists X\phi$ is an $L_2(\Box)$-formula
If ϕ and ψ are $L_2(\Box)$-formulae, then so are $\neg\phi$ and $(\phi \wedge \psi)$.
If ϕ is an $L_2(\Box)$-formula, then $\Box\phi$ is an $L_2(\Box)$-formula.
Nothing else is an $L_2(\Box)$-formula.

Semantics for $L_2(\Box)$

Model

An $L_2(\Box)$-model M is a quadruple $\langle W, R, D, I\rangle$ where W is a non-empty set; R is a relation on W; D is a function which to each world w associates a domain of individuals D_w; I is an interpretation function with domain $W \times (Cons \cup CONS)$, such that: $I_w(c) \in D_w$ if c is an individual constant and $I_w(P) \subseteq (D_w)^n$ for P a predicate constant of arity n.
If P is a predicate symbol of arity 0 (a propositional symbol), then one notes: $I_w(P) = 0$ instead of $I_w(P) = \emptyset$ and $I_w(P) = 1$ instead of $I_w(P) = \{\emptyset\}$. More generally, if D is a set, one notes $D^0 = 1$.

Assignment Functions

An assignment function g assigns to a variable x an element in $\bigcup_{w\in W} D_w$, and to a variable X in VAR_n an n-ary relation over $\bigcup_{w\in W} D_w$ (if X has arity 0, again one writes $g(X) = 0$ or $g(X) = 1$).
An assignment g' is an $x_1, \ldots, x_n$-variant of an assignment g if g and g' give the same values to all variables except at most $x_1, \ldots, x_n$.

Method of Identification

A method of identification C is an equivalence relation between couples (w, d) such that $w \in W$ and $d \in D_w$, and between couples (w, R) such that $w \in W$ and R is an n-ary relation over D_w. Thus the counterpart of an n-ary relation is an n-ary relation. One supposes moreover that C is functional, that is, given (w, d) and w', there is at most one $d' \in D_{w'}$ such that $(w, d)C(w', d')$, and similarly in the case of relations. A further natural constraint is to suppose that C is total in the following sense : if d has a counterpart at one world under C, then it has a counterpart at every other world under C. Thus one can designate by $C(w, d)(w')$ and $C(w, R)(w')$ the respective counterparts in w' of individual d and relation R of w.

Definition

$g \mapsto_C^{w,w'} h$ iff for every variable $x \in Var$ and $X \in VAR$, $(w, g(x))C(w', h(x))$ and $(w, g(X))C(w', h(X))$.

Satisfaction of the Formulae

In what follows, I note $T^{(n)}$ to mean that T is a predicate constant, a predicate variable, or a lambda-abstract of arity n. Similarly, $P^{(n)}$ means that P is a predicate constant of arity n, and $X^{(n)}$ means that X is a predicate variable of arity n.
If t is an individual term: one notes $\langle t\rangle_{M,w,g,C} = I_w(t)$ if t is a constant, and $\langle t\rangle_{M,w,g,C} = g(t)$ if t is a variable.
Likewise, one writes $\langle T\rangle_{M,w,g,C} = I_w(T)$ if T is a predicate constant, and $\langle T\rangle_{M,w,g,C} = g(T)$ if T predicate variable.
Finally, if $T = \lambda x_1 \ldots x_n.\phi$, then $\langle T\rangle_{M,w,g,C} = \{(g'(x_1),\ldots,g'(x_n)); g'$ is an $x_1,\ldots,x_n$-variant of g and $g'(x_i) \in D_w$ $(1 \leq i \leq n)$, and $M,w,g' \models_C \phi\}$
If $T = \lambda.\phi$, then $\langle T\rangle_{M,w,g,C} = 1$ if $M,w,g \models_C \phi$ and $\langle T\rangle_{M,w,g,C} = 0$ if $M,w,g \not\models_C \phi$.
$M,w,g \models_C t = t'$ iff $\langle t\rangle_{M,w,g,C} = \langle t'\rangle_{M,w,g,C}$
$M,w,g \models_C T = T'$ iff $\langle T\rangle_{M,w,g,C} = \langle T'\rangle_{M,w,g,C}$
$M,w,g \models_C T^{(0)}$ iff $\langle T\rangle_{M,w,g,C} = 1$, for $T \in VAR_0 \cup CONS_0$.
$M,w,g \models_C T^{(n)}(t_1,\ldots,t_n)$ iff $(\langle t_1\rangle_{M,w,g,C},\ldots,\langle t_n\rangle_{M,w,g,C}) \in \langle T\rangle_{M,w,g,C}$.
$M,w,g \models_C \neg\phi$ iff $M,w,g \not\models_C \phi$
$M,w,g \models_C (\phi \wedge \psi)$ iff $M,w,g \models_C \phi$ and $M,w,g \models_C \psi$
$M,w,g \models_C \exists x\phi$ iff there exists $d \in D_w$ such that $M,w,g[d/x] \models_C \phi$
$M,w,g \models_C \exists X^{(n)}\phi$ if there exists an n-ary relation $R \subseteq (D_w)^n$ such that $M,w,g\,[R/X] \models_C \phi$
$M,w,g \models_C \Box\phi$ iff for all w' such that wRw', and for all h such that $g \mapsto_C^{w,w'} h$: $M,w',h \models_C \phi$

References

Aloni, M. (2001). *Quantification under conceptual covers*. ILLC dissertations series. Amsterdam: ILLC.

Aloni, M. (2005). Individual concepts in modal predicate logic. *Journal of Philosophical Logic, 34*(1), 1–64.

Baüerle, R. (1983). Pragmatisch-semantische Aspekte der NP-interpretation. In M. Faust et al. (Eds.), *Allgemeine Sprachwissenschaft, Sprachtypologie und Textlinguistik* (pp. 121–131). Tübingen: Narr.

Bonomi, A. (1995). Transparency and specificity in intensional contexts. In P. Leonardi & M. Santambrogio (Eds.), *On Quine, new essays* (pp. 164–185). Cambridge: Cambridge University Press.

Cresswell, M. J. (1973). Hyperintensional logic. *Studia Logica, 34*, 25–38.

Cresswell, M. J., & von Stechow, A. (1982). *De Re* belief generalized. *Linguistics and Philosophy, 5*, 503–535.

Davidson, D. (1968). On saying that. *Synthese, 19*, 130–146.

Dekker, P., & van Rooij, R. (1998). Intentional identity and information exchange. In R. Cooper & T. Gamkrelidze (Eds.), *Proceedings of the second Tbilisi symposium on language, logic and computation*. Tbilisi State University, Tbilisi.

Edelberg, W. (1992). Intentional identity and the attitudes. *Linguistics and Philosophy, 15*, 561–596.

Égré, P. (2007). Semantic innocence and substitutivity. In M. J. Frápoli (Ed.), *Saying, meaning and referring, essays on François Récanati's philosophy of language* (pp. 221–238). New York: Palgrave Macmillan.

Fagin, R., Halpern, J., Moses, Y., & Vardi, M. (1995). *Reasoning about knowledge*. Cambridge: MIT.

Fitting, M. (2002). *Types, tableaus, and Gödel's god: Vol. 13. Trends in logic, Studia Logica library*. Boston: Kluwer Academic.

Fitting, M., & Mendelsohn, R. L. (1998). *First-order modal logic*. Boston: Kluwer Academic.

Fodor, J. D. (1970). *The linguistic description of opaque contexts*. PhD thesis, MIT.

Gerbrandy, J. (2000). Identity in epistemic semantics. In L. Cavendon, P. Blackburn, N. Braisby, & A. Shimojima (Eds.), *Logic, language and computation: Vol. 3. Lecture notes* (pp. 147–159). Stanford: CSLI.

Heim, I. (1992). Presupposition projection and the semantics of attitude verbs. *Journal of Semantics, 9*, 183–221.

Hintikka, J. (1962). *Knowledge and belief: An introduction to the logic of the two notions*. Cornell: Cornell University Press.

Hintikka, J. (1969). Semantics for propositional attitudes. In L. Linsky (Ed.), *Reference and modality: vol. Readings in philosophy* (pp. 145–167). London: Oxford University Press. (Reprint, 1971)

Hintikka, J. (1975). Impossible possible worlds vindicated. *Journal of Philosophical Logic, 4*, 475–484.

Kaplan, D. (1969). Quantifying in. In L. Linsky (Ed.), *Reference and modality: Vol. Readings in philosophy* (pp. 112–144). London: Oxford University Press. (Reprint, 1971)

Kraut, R. (1983). There are no *de dicto* attitudes. *Synthese, 54*, 275–294.

Kripke, S. (1963). Semantical considerations on modal logic. *Acta Philosophica Fennica, 16*, 83–94.

Kripke, S. (1979). A puzzle about belief. In A. Margalit (Ed.), *Meaning and use* (pp. 239–283). Dordrecht/Boston: Reidel

Lewis, D. (1968). Counterpart theory and quantified modal logic. In M. J. Loux (Ed.), *The possible and the actual* (pp. 11–128). Ithaca: Cornell University Press. (Reprint)

Lewis, D. (1979). Attitudes *de dicto* and *de se*. In *Philosophical papers* (Vol. 1, pp. 133–159). New York: Oxford University Press.

Loar, B. (1972). Reference and propositional attitudes. *Philosophical Review, 81*, 43–62.

Mates, B. (1950). Synonymity. In L. Linsky (Ed.), *Semantics and the philosophy of language*, (pp. 111–136). Urbana: University of Illinois Press. (Reprint, 1950)

Montague, R. (1970). Pragmatics and intensional logic. In R. H. Thomason (Ed.), *Formal philosophy: Selected papers of Richard Montague* (pp. 119–147). New Haven: Yale University Press.

Muskens, R. (1991). Hyperfine-grained meanings in classical logic. *Logique et Analyse, 34*(133–134), 159–176

Percus, O., & Sauerland, U. (2003). On the LFs of attitude reports. In M. Weisgerber (Ed.), *Proceedings of the conference SuB7 – Sinn und Bedeutung* (pp. 228–242). Constance: Konstanz University.

Quine, W. V. O. (1956). Quantifiers and propositional attitudes. In L. Linsky (Ed.), *Reference and modality* (Readings in philosophy, pp. 101–111). London: Oxford University Press. (Reprint, 1971)

Récanati, F. (2000a.) Opacity and the attitudes. In A. Orenstein & P. Kotatko (Eds.), *Knowledge, language and logic* (pp. 367–406). Dordrecht/Boston: Kluwer Academic.

Récanati, F. (2000b.) *Oratio Obliqua, Oratio Recta, an essay on metarepresentation*. Cambridge: MIT.

Richard, M. (1990). *Propositional attitudes. An essay on thoughts and how we ascribe them*. New York: Cambridge University Press.

Thomason, R. H. (1980). A model theory for propositional attitudes. *Linguistics and Philosophy, 4*, 47–70.
van Rooij, R. (2006). *Attitudes and changing contexts: Vol. 132. Synthese library*. Dordrecht: Springer.
von Fintel, K., & Heim, I. (2002). Lecture notes on intensional semantics. Manuscript, MIT.
Zeevat, H. (1996a). Le mécanisme des relations de réplique. *Languages, 30*, 99–123. (Translation in French. Original title: "The Mechanics of the Counterpart Relation", 1994)
Zeevat, H. (1996b). A neoclassical analysis of belief sentences. In *Proceedings of the 10th Amsterdam colloquium* (Number part III, pp. 723–742). ILLC, University of Amsterdam.

Chapter 14
Knowledge Is Justifiable True Information

Jaakko Hintikka

What is knowledge? Plato devoted his entire dialogue *Theaetetus* to this question, but it is still very much with us, for the better or for the worse. One of the definitions Theaetetus essays (in the so-called dialogue at187b) is true belief, and many of our contemporaries take this to be at least a partial answer, a part of the definiens of knowledge. It has also been argued more recently that it cannot be a full definition. Most philosophers have accepted these criticisms of the "true belief" characterization. If so an epistemologist's problem is to find out how to turn this necessary epistemic requirement into a sufficient condition. This question already asked in *Theaetutus* is essentially the question that is asked and answered in this paper. Nevertheless, it is not completely accurate, in that the word "belief" carries implications that unnecessarily complicate the problem. Plato's word is *doxa*, and several translators render it as "judgment" rather than "belief". In any case, the kind of belief considered here is the one ostensively used for instance in contemporary decision theory. Such belief cannot be mere opinion. No rational being makes bets or acts otherwise on the basis of opinions *qua* opinions. Belief, too, and not only knowledge, requires reasons, typically perhaps in the form of evidence. An epistemologically perceptive detective like Inspector Maigret does not entertain any beliefs about a crime he is investigating before collecting enough evidence and pondering on it. "The time for belief has not come yet" he might say *à la* Maigret.

Saying this may sound merely like the voice of common sense and perhaps it is little more than that. But the "true belief" formula tends to confuse the issues when it comes to the definition of knowledge independently of the precise kind of belief that is involved here. This is because the reasons for a rational belief are of the same kind as the reasons for a knowledge claim, and hence do not help to define knowledge.

J. Hintikka (✉)
Department of Philosophy, Boston University, 745 Commonwealth Avenue,
Room 516, Boston, MA 02215, USA
e-mail: hintikka@bu.edu

F. Lihoreau and M. Rebuschi (eds.), *Epistemology, Context, and Formalism*,
Synthese Library 369, DOI 10.1007/978-3-319-02943-6_14,

A neutral term that is preferred here is "information". Information does not come with reasons; it is given to you so to speak for informational purposes only. It may enable the recipient to make a decision, but it does not justify a decision. Even misinformation is a kind of information in a way in which disbelief is not a species of belief.

Arguably, the notion of information is more basic than the notion of knowledge. It has the same defects and virtues as Austin claimed for his term "performative". It is a foreign word and an ugly word, and perhaps it does not mean very much. But it has one good thing about it: it is not a deep word. Being informed that S is merely being made aware that S. This is as familiar a situation in life as anything one can imagine, and it does not involve any deep conceptual complications. Its logical behavior is clear. Indeed, what is known as epistemic logic becomes much clearer and more obvious if we think of it as the logic of true information rather than as the logic of the deep concept of knowledge.

For these reasons, the term information will in any case be used in this paper. This may be partly a merely terminological matter. The substantial question is what more there is to knowledge than true information. The candidate for this role that is most often discussed by philosophers is justification. Rightly or wrongly, it is thought that the "classical" or "received" attempted definition is "justified true belief" which is here replaced by "justified true information". This will be called the "received" formula.

This attempted definition may not be entirely wrong. However, the role of the notion of justification is often misunderstood in recent discussions. It is thought that justification means in the received formula justification for making a knowledge claim. If so, the justification might take the form of evidence, perhaps in the form of high probability. The famous criticism by Gettier of the received formula is predicated on construing justification in this way.

This way of interpreting the role of the justification requirement is nevertheless an abject misunderstanding of the function of justification in epistemology in general and in the meaning of knowledge in particular. We do not have the concept of knowledge in our conceptual repertoire because it enables us to put forward more or less justified knowledge claims. The role of the notion of knowledge does not concern the justification of certain language acts, but acts *simpliciter*. Subject to sundry qualifications, the idea is that we are justified in acting on the item of information to the effect that S if we *know* that S. The purpose is to justify, not claiming to know something, but acting on that knowledge.

But if so, the received interpretation of the received formula is mistaken. For what justifies you to act on the belief (information) that S is the fact that S is true. And this truth is a fact that is not logically implied by whatever evidence one happens to have for or against the proposition in question. In the received formula it is guaranteed by the truth clause ("*true* belief"), not by the justification clause.

One can see what has happened in the earlier discussion. The focus has been on the justification of making a knowledge claim. Such justification must naturally be subjective, in the sense of referring to the agent's cognitive and evidential state. But such subjective justification cannot be an objective reason for acting on one's knowledge of a proposition. Such justification can only be based on the truth of the known statement. This truth is an objective fact about the world, and likewise whatever the truth makers are to which its being true is due, must likewise be objective features of the world. Hence the relevant justification for acting on what one knows must be independent of the agent, including the agent's evidential status. It has to be an objective fact about the world.

Thus the justification clause in the received formula cannot refer to anything like evidential justification. And yet something else has to be required of knowledge alias true belief in order for it to serve its justification-indicating function. Already in the *Theaetetus*, the "received" definition of knowledge was considered by Socrates and *Theaetetus*, with the discussion ending in a rejection. Some additional requirement is required to back up somehow the truth of a belief in a way that does not merely amount to its epistemic plausibility.

In the *Theatetus*, the eponymous speaker suggests as a definition of knowledge true belief accompanied by *logos*. But what does that mean? If you interpret it as "reason", we have a restatement of the problem rather than a proposed solution, for the next question is naturally: What counts as such a reason?

Of course, *logos* could mean "verbal expression" or "account". But account of what? It has been seen that it cannot be an account of the plausibility of the true belief, but must be an account of its truth. The discussion in the *Theaetetus* suggests strongly that what is meant there by the term *logos* is an analysis of its target, maybe a definitional account.

This suggestion will be pursued here. But what does a definitory account of the truth of a sentence S in a first-order (quantificational) language consist in?

In this essay, a line of thought is formulated by reference to such languages. The argument presented is nevertheless not restricted to quantificational languages. It can be seen to apply to all languages for which a game-theoretical semantics can be given. Such applicability is not hindered if the language in question is made richer, unlike the applicability of Tarski-type truth definitions as they are often thought of as being. Hence there are no reasons to think that it is not mutatis mutandis applicable to the strongest relevant language at all, namely to our actual working language.

Now what would a definitory account of truth look like in a first-order language? A naïve but suggestive answer is that S is shown to be true by the existence of suitable "witness individuals". For a simple existential sentence $(\exists x)F[x]$ a witness individual b is one that satisfies $F[x]$. For dependent existential quantifiers the witness individuals depend on other individuals. For instance, for $(\forall x)(\exists y)F[x, y]$ to be true there must exist a witness individual b satisfying $F[a, b]$ for each individual a. Here b of course depends on a. These dependencies are codified in what is known as the Skolem function of S. The truth of S then means, in a sense that is as natural as it is simple, the existence of a full set of Skolem functions for S. This characterization of truth says little more than that there are "witness entities" showing by their existence the truth of S, now including "witness functions" a.k.a. Skolem functions.

By means of certain basic game-theoretical ideas, referred to as "game-theoretical semantics", the idea of truth can be articulated further. Skolem functions formulate collectively a winning strategy for one of the players in certain two-person, constant sum games called semantical games. The game with a sentence S is called $G(S)$. Such games can be thought of as games of verification on the part of the player called the Verifier, against the challenges of another player called the Falsifier. The verifier tries to produce (choose) only true sentences, the Falsifier at least one false sentence. A winning strategy for the verifier is one that leads to a win against any strategy of one's opponent. Skolem functions codify such winning strategies in the verification-games which can be thought of as our basic verification "games".

The crucial fact here is that the truth of S amounts to the existence of a full ensemble of Skolem functions codifying a winning strategy. Hence to know that S means knowing that there exists (in a mathematical sense) a winning strategy for the Verifier in $G(S)$. It does not mean that the verifier knows what that strategy is. $A fortiori$, an agent who asserts that he or she (or it, if the knower is a computer with a database) knows S does not have to know what the winning verificatory strategies in $G(S)$ are in order to make a true knowledge claim. The agent is only making a purely existential statement.

But now it is obvious that such purely existential information is not what we call knowing that S. It is not enough to be aware that S can somehow be verified. One must be aware how it can be verified, so that one can in principle ascertain its truth oneself. And clearly it is this kind of potential backing that in a perfectly good sense justifies acting on the information that S.

This then is the right definition of knowledge. It is not knowledge that S can be verified, but *how* it can be verified. More formally, we can think of a proposition S as a propositional function $S(f)$ of its ensembles of Skolem functions f. Then the truth of S is expressed by $(\exists f)S(f)$. Knowing that S is not just being aware that it is true, which is expressed by $K(\exists f)S(f)$. It must be expressed by

(*) $$K(\exists f/K)S[f].$$

Here the slash / is the independence indicator studied in independence-friendly (IF) logic. In a (less apt) notation (*) could be written as $(\exists f)KS[f]$.

That this is the right analysis of knowledge can be seen in different ways by studying its features and its consequences more closely. Here only a few explanations are given.

The first question that arises here pertains to the logical correctness of (*). How can (*) possibly serve as a definition of knowledge since the notion of knowledge is already used there in the form of the knowledge operator K? Are we not formulating a blatantly circular definition?

An answer was in effect already given earlier in this essay. The notion that K expresses in (*) should be thought of as information rather than knowledge in the ("deep") sense of knowledge that philosophers are inquiring into. It expresses merely an agent's awareness of certain facts. It is all what is needed for the epistemic logic that is being presupposed in (*). We are dealing with a definition of knowledge in terms of information. Information merely takes over the role of belief used in the received formula.

Admittedly the definition (*) does not take the form of an extra clause added to the "true belief" definition formula. But it can be seen as implementing a kind of justification requirement. I am justified in acting on the assumption that S, if I know how to verify it, in other words, if I so to speak, have a recipe for verifying it as well. I do not have to have the strategy in mind when I am making a knowledge claim any more than I have to have the multiplication table in mind when I use it. But I must be in the position to appeal to it whenever I am uncertain or challenged.

Thus the analysis (*) does justice to the justification requirement. For what would justify a knowledge claim more conclusively than being in a position to verify it in the teeth of maximal obstacles? Moreover, being in such a position is an objective feature of the information in one's possession. A computer could truly be said to be in such a position, depending on its database.

This objectivity of knowledge is worth emphasizing. The existence of an ensemble of Skolem functions is a combinational fact about the world. It is not a fact about what a human agent, even an idealized human agent can actually do. It is about the existence of functions of a certain kind, not as higher-order entities but as functions-in-extension in a set-theoretical or more accurately combinational sense.

The objectivity of information in the relevant sense is guaranteed by taking information in this sense to be the mirror image (dual) of the kind of probability in which the probability $P(S)$ of S is a measure of how disorderly the distribution of objects is that is allowed by the truth of S. This measure is a generalization of the thermodynamical notion of entropy. It was proposed by John von Neumann and is defined in a forthcoming paper. This probability measure is neither pragmatist nor subjective, and it does not involve a believer's epistemic state. Accordingly, it can be used in the otherwise objective definition of information.

Since the existence of a full set of Skolem functions for S implies the truth of S, we can drop the truth clause from our definition of knowledge. (Justifiability in the sense relied on in (*) implies truth.)

The definition (*) is connected with a way of trying to characterize knowledge that has not yet been mentioned here. It is the idea of knowledge as nondefeasible true belief. This idea receives a near-literal vindication here. For the semantical game $G(S)$ played with S is from the perspective of the falsifier an attempt to defeat a claim that S is true. Then (*) says that there is a strategy of refuting all such attempts. This is little more than to say that a claim that S is true is nondefeasible.

This might seem to suggest that what is needed for knowledge is less some relation of the known proposition to reality than its compatibility with all possible true prima facie objections. This is what encourages coherence "theories" of truth. Such theories are mistaken but the mistake is subtle, too subtle for many philosophers. It is not so much a mistake about truth as a mistake about logic. A proof of the logical truth of S is at bottom not an argument from assumptions as a thought experiment, a frustrated attempt to construct a counter-example, a model in which S is false, ergo it must be logically true.

In this thought-experiment, a logician must consider in the most literal sense all possible ways of constructing at least in imagination a counter example. In this sense, S must be compatible with all possibilities. But this does not mean that logical truth means universal compossibility. It does not imply a coherence theory of truth or of knowledge. Yet in this way we can see a small kernel of truth in coherentist theories.

This is made manifest by the fact that IF logic gives us a way of formulating and even proving consistency. Incidentally, it then gives a way to carry out Hilbert's project of proving consistency of sundry formal theories. Indeed, Hintikka and Karakadilar have proved in this way the consistency of elementary arithmetic.

The sense of consistency needed here can be expressed by $\neg \sim S$, which says that S is not false. But $K\neg \sim S$ means something distinctly different from KS. This is in effect as close to a fatal objection of coherentism as one can hope to reach.

It can also be seen now that the idea that the extra requirement (over and above true belief) means asking for an account (if that is what *logos* is) is quite apt. What is required is a specification of the kind of state or situation one has to be in order for us to say truly that one knows something, say that S.

Since this state or situation is objective, an agent can be in it without being aware of it. This is of course right. An agent may be in the position to verify conclusively that S without actively thinking of it. Hence the requirement of belief must be handled with caution. A knower need not be aware of the account more than (say) the alphabet must be present in the mind of a reader. In general, it is advisable to speak of justifiable information rather than of justified belief.

The analysis (*) of knowledge also throws light on the question of the relation of knowledge, information and belief to awareness. Purely logically, $(\exists f)KS(f)$ does not imply $K(\exists f)S(f)$. Hence one can know that S in the sense defined here without knowing that S is true. But this should not be surprising. It is in a sense a corollary to the objectivity of knowledge. As has been emphasized on the analysis presented here, to know that S is to be in a position to verify that S. But a person can objectively speaking be in such a position without knowing that he or she is. In this sense, one can know that S without being aware of it. One is tempted to express this by saying that one can know without knowing that one knows. (Justice Holmes once averred that he did not like people who know that they know.) However, expressing oneself in this way is not quite literal use of words in the sense defined here.

Likewise, it is by the same token tempting to say that one can know something without believing it. Such expressions are tricky, however. The reason is that knowledge is a matter of information. And the information that a person has in his or her "database" must be accessible. This accessibility need not mean actual presence in consciousness, but it does require potential awareness. A person who can solve an equation need not have in mind a recipe or an algorithm for doing so, but he or she must be able to actualize them in his or her mind. The same holds generally of knowledge.

What is the moral of this story? Maybe an analogue with a Wittgensteinian dictum: One can distill a great deal of epistemology into a drop of logic.